By Hester W. Chapman

Fiction

Biography

THE TRAGEDY OF CHARLES II

in the years

1630–1660

Thus saith the Lord God: Remove the diadem and take off the crown; this shall not be the same; exalt him that is low, and abase him that is high. I will overturn, overturn, overturn it: and it shall be no more until he come whose right it is ... EZEKIEL, *Chapter xxi*

CHARLES II AS A YOUNG MAN

HESTER W. CHAPMAN

The Tragedy of
CHARLES II
in the years
1630-1660

WITH ILLUSTRATIONS

LITTLE, BROWN AND COMPANY
Boston   Toronto

PRINTED IN THE UNITED STATES OF AMERICA

To Noël Coward

CONTENTS

PART ONE

The Prince of Wales

PART TWO

The Outcast

PART THREE

The Wanderer

CONTENTS

PART FOUR
The Black Boy

ILLUSTRATIONS

BOURBON LINE

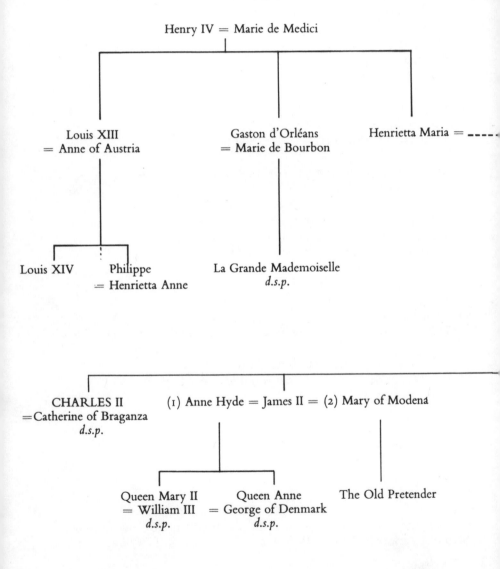

Henry IV = Marie de Medici

Louis XIII
= Anne of Austria

Gaston d'Orléans
= Marie de Bourbon

Henrietta Maria = - - - -

Louis XIV

Philippe
= Henrietta Anne

La Grande Mademoiselle
d.s.p.

CHARLES II
=Catherine of Braganza
d.s.p.

(1) Anne Hyde = James II = (2) Mary of Modena

Queen Mary II
= William III
d.s.p.

Queen Anne
= George of Denmark
d.s.p.

The Old Pretender

STUART LINE

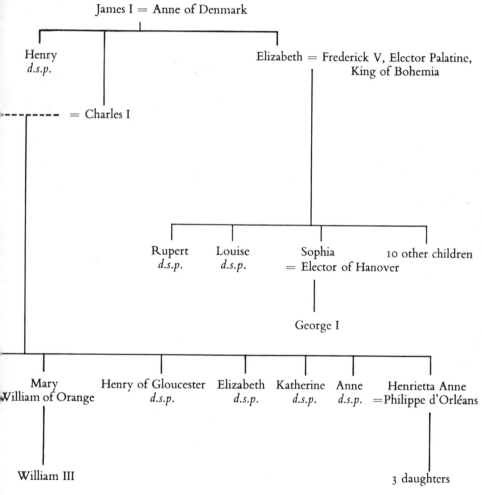

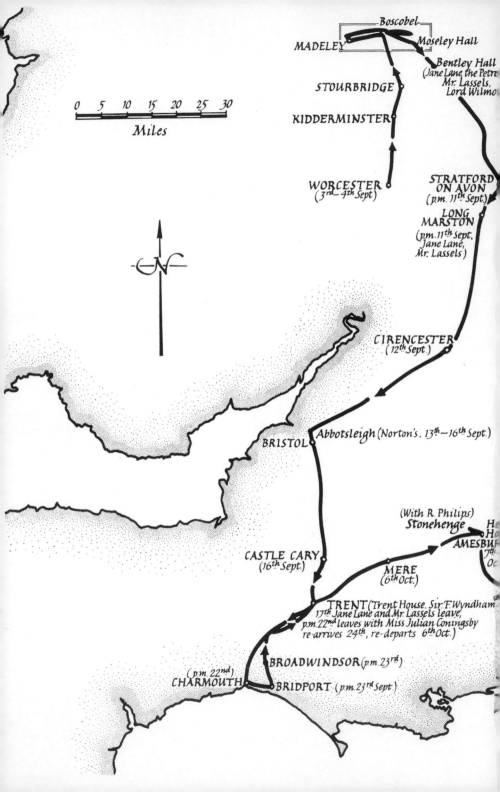

Detail of the area outlined opposite

Hobbal Grange
(5 p.m. 4th, 9 p.m.
leaves with Penderel)

(6th–7th sleeps in priest's
hole, leaves p.m. 7th, re-arrives
and re-departs 8th)

Boscobel

4th–5th Sept.
Madeley House
(leaves 11th 5th)

'Whiteladies'
(a.m. 4th Sept.)

'The Oak'
(a.m. 6th)

Spring Coppice
(a.m. 4th)

8th

7th sleeps at
cottage

Escort of
Penderels and Yates

Moseley Hall
(9th–10th)

MADELEY

from STOURBRIDGE

Colonel Lane conducts
Charles to Bentley Hall

The Flight of Charles
after the Battle of Worcester
from September 3 to October 15
anno domini 1651

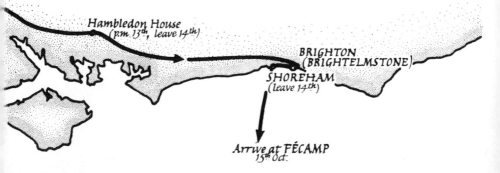

Hambledon House
(p.m. 13th, leave 14th)

BRIGHTON
(BRIGHTELMSTONE)

SHOREHAM
(leave 14th)

Arrive at FÉCAMP
15th Oct.

ACKNOWLEDGMENTS

THE author has pleasure in acknowledging the meticulous and sensitive criticisms of Miss Rosamond Lehmann in matters of treatment and style. The skilled and learned advice of Mr B. S. Quintrell and the kind encouragement of Dr C. V. Wedgwood and Mr George Rylands have been of enormous value and received with the deepest appreciation; none is responsible for the form of, or the views expressed in, this study.

Van Dyck's 'Children of Charles I', the Woutier of the Duke of York and Cooper's miniature of the Duke of Monmouth are reproduced by gracious permission of Her Majesty Queen Elizabeth II. Grateful thanks are also due to His Grace the Duke of Grafton for permission to reproduce the Van Dyck portraits of Charles I and Henrietta Maria, and the portrait of Charles II by Philippe de Champaigne; to the Most Honourable the Marquess of Anglesey, F.S.A., for the Mignard of the Duchess of Orléans; to the National Portrait Gallery for the print of the Duke of Gloucester after Luttichuys and the portrait after Hannemann of the Earl of Clarendon; to the Scottish National Portrait Gallery for the Dobson of Charles II as Prince of Wales and the Scougal of the first Marquess of Argyll; to the Rijksmuseum, Amsterdam, for the Van der Helst of Princess Mary of Orange; and to the Musée de Versailles for the Bourguignon of La Grande Mademoiselle. To Mr Michael Gibbs the author is indebted for his research into the question of likenesses of Lucy Walter and for the portrait here reproduced.

FOREWORD

————◆•◆•◆————

SEVERAL hundred books have been written about Charles II. The earliest of these were produced when he was a young man; thenceforward personal memoirs, panegyrics, diatribes, collections of speeches and letters, and biographies of every type have appeared, and will no doubt continue to do so. Although all but half a dozen of these volumes are now out of print, it is clear that he is still one of the most popular figures in European history. He has been the subject of innumerable novels, plays and films, with the result that certain aspects of his temperament and career are as well known as if he were a millionaire, a leading actor or a successful politician. Yet no detailed record of his childhood and adolescence exists. Nor is there any account of his spiritual and intellectual progress from his seventeenth to his thirty-first year – that is, from his first departure out of English territory in the summer of 1646 to his return in the spring of 1660 – in spite of the fact that a number of biographers have confined themselves to that period alone. It is as if his adventures and his legend had combined rather to obscure than to illuminate the development of his character; and this may be because although the adventures were sordid, the legend at once became romantic, and has remained so until the present day.

Historians have intensified this confusion by their disagreements. For some time after Charles's death his political abilities were admired and his private life mildly criticized. In the nineteenth century his reputation both as a ruler and a personality sank very low; he was harshly censured by all but a few. Then, some years after the first World War, it rose again: he was not only praised for his statesmanship, but presented as the perfect combination of patriot, wit, lover, scientist and sportsman.

These variations of judgment have made him interesting but enigmatic. To attempt a study of his life from infancy to manhood is not therefore supererogatory; for the apparently triumphant climax of his Restoration does not in fact provide the happy ending such a limitation suggests. The story of his youth is one of moral defeat: the holocaust of

13

a soul. As a boy, he acquired many virtues and most of the graces. By the time he was thirty those graces were greatly enhanced. Of virtue there remained nothing but the façade: a spectral reminder of qualities corrupted and destroyed by disillusion, bitterness, misery and despair.

PART ONE

The Prince of Wales

(MAY 1630–MARCH 1646)

Fair was the dawn; and but e'en now the skies
Showed like to cream, inspired with strawberries:
But on a sudden, all was changed and gone
That smiled in that first sweet complexion.
Then thunder-claps and lightning did conspire
To tear the world, or set it all on fire.
                                        Hesperides

CHAPTER ONE

HENRIETTA MARIA AND CHARLES I

I

ON the morning of March 27th, 1625, James I died at his palace of Theobalds, and his only surviving son Charles, then in his twenty-fifth year and still unmarried, became King of England.

Although Charles I had been carefully trained for his position and was considered by those who knew him intimately to be better qualified for it than his father, he suffered from two serious disabilities. His elder brother Henry who outshone him during their boyhood had died of smallpox in 1612, leaving him miserably conscious of his own inadequacy; for Charles was undersized, weak-legged – he could not walk or stand upright till his seventh year[1] – and stammered atrociously. Everything that could be done for him was done. Eventually resolution combined with pride to overcome his muscular feebleness. By the time he became Prince of Wales he was a superb horseman, a tireless walker and an exquisite dancer; but he never conquered that fatal impediment. Sometimes the sentences came out with a rush; sometimes he could not utter a syllable.[2] He now partially concealed this defect with a self-imposed reserve and coldness of manner which struck most people as majestic, even formidable, but which in fact hid an uncertain and hesitating attitude of mind. It was as if Charles had driven his stammer inwards and masked it. This was the result rather of instinct than of thought; for he was not clever, although, emulating his father's and brother's standards, he had to appear so. He was well read, a good linguist and expressed himself fluently on paper. The discernment in and care for the visual arts for which he became famous did not develop – perhaps they were not encouraged – till just before his accession.

Such a temperament requires undeviating support and approval. Charles, failing to find them in his shrewd, conceited, eccentric old father (James, like most of his family, aged early and looked and behaved as if he were seventy long before he reached his fifties), fell back on the magnificent and egregious Duke of Buckingham, then the most powerful and the most hated man in England. Described by the Commons as 'the cause of all our miseries, the grievance of grievances', George Villiers was, although unwittingly – for the young men were devoted friends – the new King's first evil genius. The second was Henrietta Maria, younger sister of Louis XIII, whom Charles married three months after his accession.

He used that time to reform, outwardly at least, his father's Court, and this without Buckingham's help or advice; for the Duke, although intolerably arrogant, was inclined to be easy-going over matters of protocol, precedence and etiquette. Not so Charles. After years of chafing against the ramshackle methods, unkempt luxury, dirty splendours and general slip-sloppery of the nineteen palaces from which the late King had ruled the most turbulent people in Europe, he now rapidly enforced system, cleanliness and order sustained by lists of instructions. At Whitehall, Windsor and Hampton Court His Majesty's rules were pinned up in all the principal rooms; [3] and very soon those noblemen who had been used to meet their late master ambling unsteadily through ante-chambers and passages, his arm round the neck of some handsome young man, now found themselves constrained, according to their rank and office, to wait in one superbly decorated, exquisitely formal setting before obtaining admittance to another. Old Jemmy, as his subjects called him,[4] had left a trail of mud, blood, dogs' excreta and the smell of drink and sweaty clothing behind him; his thick, lecturing, hectoring voice had poured out streams of talk on religion, sport, books, politics and personalities to anyone he came across. He was full of his jokes, as we say now; scriptural analogies, puns, tropes, quotations and bawdiness made up his conversation. He would slobber, boast, become enraged and hysterical, then suddenly profound, acute and rather amusing. His moods had been incalculable, his aspect repulsive and ludicrous.

Now both the scene and the principal actor transported the audience to another world. A neat, tiny, graceful figure, perfectly apparelled, noble, dignified and serene, paced the long galleries, stood surrounded by his awestruck gentlemen, or emerged from the private to the state apartments as if in a coranto or a masque. His quiet attention, his polite denials – 'By your favour, I think otherwise' – 'Sir, I am not of your opinion'[5] – discouraged the 'bold address' of an older and more casual generation; weighted by his stammer, such reproofs reduced them to uneasy silence. His remote correctness, his calm, gentle tone remained unbroken – until one of those meticulously worked out rules was infringed. Then the 'sweet, grave melancholy' expression changed to one of icy displeasure; and the 'imperious and lofty' demeanour that his contemporaries never forgot sometimes yielded to what they described as sharp reprehensions, or even violence.[6]

This contrast so alarmed the offenders that they were apt to lose their heads and thus get into worse trouble. It was said that Sir Henry Vane the younger, entering a room reserved for Privy Councillors and hearing the King approach, concealed himself behind a hanging. His Majesty, glancing round to see that all was as it should be, noticed the bulge and poked at it with his cane. 'When he saw Sir Henry he was very angry, held his cane over him and struck him.' Charles was equally enraged and surprised when, some years later, he realized that the insulted gentleman had taken the Parliamentary side against him.[7]

For seventeen years – from his accession to the summer of 1642 – Charles's Court was to maintain the solemn elegance and semi-institutional propriety which he may have admired when he and Buckingham visited that of Philip IV in the last months of his father's reign. That expedition, in which the old King saw 'my Dog Steenie' and Baby Charles as two 'dear, adventurous knights worthy to be put in a *romanso*',[8] had ended in humiliation; one that Charles now wiped out by creating a new and glorious existence against a background of variegated beauty co-ordinated by himself and produced by the greatest artists in Europe – Van Dyck, Rubens, Bernini, Inigo Jones.

The new King did not attempt to alter the outward structure of Whitehall, the most notable of his palaces. His father had intended Inigo Jones to rebuild it entirely, but lack of funds prevented this, with the result that by 1625 the main, low-lying portion, erected a century earlier for Cardinal Wolsey, was rather incongruously dominated by the Great Hall, the Banqueting House and Henry VIII's Holbein Gateway. The effect, although wildly unsymmetrical, was one of negligent splendour. During the first years of his reign Charles emphasized this sprawling tendency with additions which spread past York House to Charing Cross. He employed Inigo Jones to turn the Cockpit into a theatre and commissioned Rubens to paint the ceiling of Jones's Banqueting House. This, the memorial to two kings and two men of genius, all that now remains of Charles's golden days, was never finished. Van Dyck was to have covered the walls with frescoes recording the history of the Garter; again, the money ran out, and the King had more room for his collection of pictures. By the time he left Whitehall in 1642 that palace alone contained four hundred and sixty masterpieces including those of Titian, Raphael, Holbein, Correggio, Rubens and Van Dyck.[9]

Charles's private apartments were on the first floor, overlooked the Privy Garden and comprised a Withdrawing-Room, Breakfast-Room, Bed-Chamber and Lesser Withdrawing-Room. They were approached by the Adam and Eve staircase (the picture of our first parents did not survive the Civil War), and led into the smaller Council Chamber; from its windows the King could listen to the sermons preached from Edward VI's open-air pulpit below.[10]

The interior decoration of the rooms was immensely elaborate and provided an exuberant mixture of pseudo-classic, Gothic and Renaissance styles. Gilded panelling, newel-posts supporting life-size, highly coloured deities or heraldic beasts, carved screens, Flemish tapestries, Elizabethan armour, satin, damask and velvet hangings – all these were successfully combined, or so it would seem from contemporary drawings. Selective richness eliminated confusion; the King's instinct for order and design found its most perfect expression in a display that might dazzle but never displeased the eye. In this, the choicest of his settings, he installed his fifteen-year-old Queen on the evening of June 23rd, 1625.

Negotiations for the marriage had begun in the previous summer, under Buckingham's aegis. When the Commons vetoed it the King and the Duke caused it to be celebrated by proxy before Parliament could meet again. On the French side too, there had been many difficulties, for Pope Urban VIII, Henrietta Maria's godfather, held up the dispensation till his conditions were agreed upon; the most important of these were that Henrietta and her attendants should be allowed the free exercise of their religion, and that her children should be brought up under her sole care till they reached their teens.[11] The Queen and her advisers understood – or later, said they had understood – this to mean that her sons and daughters were to be educated in the Roman Catholic faith until the age of thirteen. In the contract this was not so stated; nor would Charles have consented to such a clause. The marriage therefore took place on a basis of misapprehension, and for three years was highly unsatisfactory. Charmed at first sight by his pretty and graceful bride, Charles soon found her recalcitrant, peevish and unsympathetic, a spoilt, silly child. He and Buckingham combined to relegate her, and the Duke made it clear that she was to receive neither power nor consideration. Henrietta retaliated by refusing to be crowned according to heretical rites, or even to look on at her husband's coronation. She was rude to his courtiers, and isolated herself in her imported household of fifty persons, among whom were some twenty priests. Charles continued to complain of her to Buckingham, who finally took it upon himself to tell her that 'Queens of England have had their heads cut off before now', with the result that she declared war on the King's entourage. The over-sensitive Charles became completely estranged, and her resentment hardened into furious resistance.

Scenes of violence ensued. Shaking all over with rage at their insolence, Charles turned his wife's attendants out of Whitehall, 'like so many wild beasts', as he told Buckingham. When she rushed to the window to call after them, he held her back; in the struggle she smashed the window and relapsed into screaming hysterics. Finally the King resolved the situation by sending back all but twenty of her suite to France. This strong-man behaviour was weakened by his reliance on Buckingham. Henrietta Maria could not respect a husband ruled by another, and that the jumped-up favourite – some said the degraded catamite – of his father.

So the relationship went from bad to worse until, on August 24th, 1628, an obscure, half-pay officer put an end to Henrietta Maria's difficulties with 'a poor tenpenny knife' in an inn at Portsmouth. The great Duke, stabbed to the heart, died on the dining-room table, and all England rejoiced. In his agonizing grief Charles turned to his beautiful young wife. She at once responded and proceeded to subjugate him completely.[12]

Those courtiers who had hated and feared the Duke commented joyously on this happy ending. 'The King,' wrote one, 'has now so wholly made over all his affection to his wife that I dare say they are out of the danger of any other favourites. She has also returned such a fondness and liking for him and his person as it is of much comfort to themselves as of joy to their good servants.' So no one was surprised when a few weeks after Buckingham's death Her Majesty became pregnant. In May 1629 she was prematurely confined of a boy who died in a few hours. 'God,' wrote Dr Mayerne to the Secretary of State, 'hath shown us a Prince of Wales, but the flower hath been cut down the same instant that it saw the light.' He added that the Queen was 'full of strength and courage'.[13]

The doctor's optimism was justified. In August 1629 Henrietta was once more pregnant, and in April of the following year she retired to St James's Palace, where her labour began at four in the morning of May 29th, 1630. Just before midday she gave birth to a large, swarthy, lusty son, whose appearance was celebrated by bonfires, bells and wild rejoicing. Only the Puritans refused to share in these gaieties. They shut their doors, fasted and 'showed their sorrow' by openly announcing that they had prayed for a barren Queen and the ultimate succession of the King's sister, Queen Elizabeth of Bohemia, now dispossessed and exiled with her children in Holland. These trivial demonstrations were mocked at or ignored, and the King proceeded in state to St Paul's to give thanks. Congratulations poured in, and all over Europe secretaries hurried to compose messages of goodwill. It was announced that the christening of Prince Charles would take place on June 27th.

II

He was a very ugly, very solemn baby. He slept a great deal, seldom cried and looked like a changeling. Indeed, it was difficult to believe that such small, delicately made parents could have produced this solid creature, who within a few days of his birth was inspected by a number of foreign envoys. Among these Soranzo, the Venetian ambassador, was particularly impressed by the Prince's strength and vigour. 'The nurses told me,' he reported, 'that after his birth he never clenched his fists but always kept his hands open. From this they augur that he will be a prince of great liberality.'[14] Charles's horoscope was more specific, and untrue in all but two particulars. He would be handsome, with 'hair and eyes somewhat tending to black, thin beard, shrill voice, a mincing gait and will live either to a hundred and eight or sixty-six years, be very fortunate ... attain wealth by marriage and war and be particularly fond of mathematicians, sailors, merchants, learned men, painters and sculptors.'[15]

The astral omens accompanying his birth – a total eclipse of the sun and a new star in a clear sky, 'as if it prognosticated what a blessing he was going to be' – having cancelled one another out, the King could give all his attention to his plans for the christening. The choice of godparents caused some alarm, for two of them – Prince Charles's maternal grandmother Marie de Medici and his uncle, Louis XIII – represented Catholicism in its most virulent form. Further annoyance was created by the appointment of the Countess of Roxburgh – a Catholic who had converted his other grandmother, Anne of Denmark – as Governess of his household. 'I can see no cause of joy,' said a Puritan minister when he heard of this, and he added gloomily, 'It is uncertain what religion the King's children will follow, when brought up under so devoted a mother to the Church of Rome.'

The national hatred of Roman Catholicism, not yet at its height, reached a penultimate climax with the Prince's birth. It had been violently expressed and foolishly defied from the moment that his mother arrived in England. If she had observed the conditions of her marriage contract and exercised her religion privately, she might have become popular with all but the extreme Puritans, for she was vivacious, talented and – as long as she got her own way – able to please. When it became known that thousands of pounds were being spent on the decoration of her chapel, that one of her Jesuits had attempted to baptize her first child and that her confessor was accustomed to wrangle with the King's chaplain as to which of them should say grace when Their Majesties dined in public, the High

Church party objected as strongly as, if more courteously than, the dissenting section. Meanwhile, Henrietta Maria's entourage poisoned Anglo-French relations by their tittering mockery of the older and less fashionable courtiers, who began to complain of favours and places being given to foreigners. The King's stiff formality and ungracious manners (his cold granting of a request was almost as displeasing to the recipient as a refusal would have been), although disregarded by the French contingent, were bitterly wounding to those who remembered his father's 'light, familiar way'. When Charles I tried to be impartial he merely appeared uncivil; and once freed from Buckingham's spell, he became so uxorious that his deep and sincere devotion to his Church seemed to be yielding to his wife's caprices. She could have put an end to both social and religious ill feeling by the exercise of tact and discretion. That she scorned to do so was partly the cause of her husband's tragedy and of her eldest son's misfortunes. So it was that although Laud was summoned to baptize the Prince, the Anglican Duchess of Richmond stood sponsor and Lady Dorset, another impeccable Anglican, soon replaced the Countess of Roxburgh as Governess, suspicion of popery, or crypto-popery, surrounded the ceremony.

This was magnificently celebrated in the private chapel, of St James's. All the rooms through which the Prince was carried were hung with new tapestries. The font stood on a stage in the middle of the aisle, so that everyone could see and hear what rites were used. (The Duchesse de la Trémouille, who asked to hold the baby, as sponsor for Marie de Medici, was not allowed to do so, and left England in a huff.) The English Duchess gave her godson a diamond ring, and the City fathers presented him with a gold cup, 'a yard in length', valued at £1,200. As soon as he was christened as Prince of Great Britain, France and Ireland (the title of Prince of Wales was bestowed later) he was taken back to the state apartments for his parents' blessing, while the Tower cannon thundered a welcome and the bonfires blazed all night.

NOTES

1 H. Cary, *Memoirs*, p. 644.
2 W. Lilly, *Several Observations upon the Life and Death of Charles I*, p. 9.
3 T. Carte, *A History of the Life of James, Duke of Ormonde*, vol. I, pp. 355–7.
4 Lilly, p. 64.
5 Sir Richard Bulstrode, *Memoirs and Reflections*, pp. 184–5.
6 J. Welwood, *Memoirs*, p. 80; Lilly, p. 9.
7 Carte, ibid.
8 G. M. Trevelyan, *England under the Stuarts*, p. 105.
9 J. E. N. Hearsey, *Bridge, Church and Palace*, pp. 209–12.
10 Ibid.
11 A. Strickland, *Lives of the Queens of England*, vol. IV, p. 149.
12 Bishop G. Goodman, *The Court of King James the First*, vol. II, p. 228.
13 *Calendar of Domestic State Papers*, Dec. 21st, 1628; May 13th, 1629.
14 *Calendar of State Papers Venetian*, vol. XXII, p. 350.
15 *Cal. D. S. P.*, June 27th, 1630.

—————◆◆◆◆————

CHAPTER TWO

NURSERY DAYS

I

I F it is true that security, affection and an ordered but varied routine
create a happy infancy which eventually results in a well balanced
development, then Prince Charles was extremely fortunate. Although
the secrets of royal as of other nurseries generally remain inviolate, the
background of his earliest years seems to have approached the ideal,
judged by the standards of any age. First of all, his parents' quarrelling
period was over, and apart from occasional disagreements about his
mother's too much advertised Catholicism, they were in accord and increasingly devoted. Henrietta Maria, young, beautiful, healthy, sure of her
husband's love and rejoicing in her children (Charles's birth was followed
by those of two brothers and five sisters during the next sixteen years),
afterwards realized how lucky she was. She often told Madame de Motteville, her friend in exile, that she was the happiest woman in the world at
that time – 'as mother, wife and queen', she added.[1]

The King appeared equally contented, perhaps because he was inwardly
more self-confident, and surer than ever that everything he did contributed
to the well-being of his subjects. He knew himself, and was described by
his few intimates, to be a good father and husband, a devout Christian and
a conscientious ruler. He could not have looked below the surface of his
situation because it appeared to him, as to the most acute of his contemporaries, solid and perdurable. Edward Hyde – afterwards Lord Clarendon, then an unknown young lawyer – was to recall the years of the
second Charles's infancy as the first Charles himself would have described
them. 'It was no wonder,' he says, 'if England was thought secure ... ; the
Court in great plenty, or rather ... excess and luxury; the country rich
and ... fully enjoying the pleasure of its own wealth ... All these blessings
... were enjoyed by ... a King of the most harmless disposition, the most
exemplary piety, the greatest sobriety, chastity and mercy, that any prince
hath been endowed with ... '[2]

In such an atmosphere it followed that all the reports of the little Prince
were favourable. 'His ... likelihood, strength, mirth and night's rest

increase daily,' wrote Dr Chambers; and when he was three months old this physician described him as thriving and serene. 'He neither sucked nor wakened but once all this night and is yet asleep,' he announced, adding hopefully, if not quite truthfully, 'His favour and complexion amend daily.'[3]

In fact, the Prince's swarthiness was his mother's only worry. 'He is so dark,' she wrote to one of her French ladies, 'that I am ashamed of him.' In all other respects he was, of course, quite remarkable. 'If my son knew how to talk,' she went on, 'I think he would send you his compliments; he is so fat and so tall, he is taken for a year old, and he is only four months; his teeth are already beginning to come. I will send you his portrait as soon as he is a little fairer ... ' As the weeks went by and the baby's colouring still recalled that of his Medici ancestors, Henrietta Maria adopted a semi-deprecating, semi-amused attitude. 'He is so ugly that I am ashamed of him,' she repeated, 'but his size and fatness supply the want of beauty. I wish you could see the gentleman, for he has no ordinary mien; he is so serious in all that he does that I cannot help fancying him far wiser than myself.'[4]

The Queen's joking description was to acquire an ironic significance. Her eldest son really did show himself a good deal wiser than she was, long before he grew up; and this was partly because from his earliest years he became accustomed to her moods, disregarding her fits of temper as he did her commands, her laughter and her tears. Henrietta Maria never acquired self-control; indeed she despised it. Her letters and her confidences to her women friends make it clear that she saw herself as a fascinating spitfire. Her husband, who may sometimes have found his own reserve an encumbrance, encouraged her in this behaviour, although he did not always like it. When he gave her a brooch and inadvertently scratched her as he pinned it on, he was very much upset by her throwing it on the ground in a fury;[5] but her liveliness continued to entrance him, and he could never resist either her petulant cajolery or her dictatorial tone. So Henrietta Maria, proudly aware of her power over the King, was led to believe that she could dominate his ministers, his children, and even foreign statesmen, simply by expressing her wishes. She brushed aside all criticism and encouraged her husband to do the same. Critics were not merely inconvenient adversaries; they were wicked rebels. When it was no longer possible to ignore them, they must be crushed.

This attitude of mind affected her relationship with Prince Charles as soon as he was of an age to trouble her; meanwhile, the custom of establishing the Heir-Apparent in a household of his own detached him from her in another sense. He remained at St James's Palace in charge of Lady Dorset and a vast entourage. This included a Welsh wet-nurse, two chamberlains, two physicians, an apothecary, a lawyer, eight rockers and a number of needlewomen, cooks, pages and ushers. All these officials had their own attendants; and this upper staff was waited on and catered for by another and still larger contingent. Thus the Prince's establishment, for which £5,000 a year was allowed, comprised between two and three hundred persons.[6] His parents, who preferred the palaces of Greenwich, Woodstock and Theobalds to Whitehall, visited him regularly; but from the moment of his birth he was made to feel that his existence was completely independent of theirs. It was therefore to be expected that he very soon developed that detachment of spirit which his mother, not quite seriously, described when he was a few months old. This was enhanced by his strength and intelligence; her hope that he might be physically and mentally in advance of his age was soon realized.

The Queen's account gives the impression that Charles was beginning to take notice. Again, he was fortunate in his surroundings; for the interior decoration of St James's Palace provided an almost perfect example of sixteenth-century elegance. Here Tudor iconoclasm was shown at its richest and most irreligious. Neither in the four Great Courts nor in the Chapel Royal was there any trace of scriptural inspiration. Painted and gilded fleur-de-lys, sunbursts, white harts, daggers, portcullises, and the famous thornbush from which Henry VII had plucked his crown on Bosworth Field – these were the first objects that a child, lying in his nurse's arms, would have taken in: and interlacing them the initials of the six queens whom that other Henry had briefly honoured.[7]

In this intricate splendour the Prince already held court. When he was seven months old 'our young master' was reported as 'continuing in a blessed prosperity of health', and this rapid growth entailed further expenditure. Soon after his first birthday his bill for 'mercers' wares' came to £310 4s. 7d., and already words were being put into his mouth by those seeking favours of the King. In a poem addressed to his father 'little C,' begged 'a boon of Charles the Great', asking leave for a Welsh bishop to translate his works into English.[8]

As soon as he was out of his swaddling clothes Prince Charles was dressed in long white satin or cambric frocks and tight caps tied under the chin; he wore these till he could walk without help; then grown-up suits were made for him: there was no transitional stage. His toys were not specifically masculine; he had many dolls, some dressed as horsemen, and others made of a composition of gum and sugar, so that when he put them in his mouth he could enjoy the taste; later these were supplemented by lead soldiers, figures in painted alabaster, wood, silver and gold, cannon, hobby-horses on wheels and animals covered with real skin. It was at about this time, when he was beginning to walk, that Charles took what was afterwards described as 'a strange and unaccountable fondness for a wooden billet, without which in his arms he would never go abroad or lie down in his bed'. His attendants at once fell into prophecy. 'When he comes to years of maturity,' was their conclusion, 'either oppressors or blockheads will be his greatest favourites; or else, when he comes to reign, he will either be like Jupiter's log ... or he will rather choose to command his people with a club than rule by the sword.'9 The wooden billet remained with Charles throughout his infancy. No one dared replace it by a more suitable plaything.

When he was eighteen months old the Princess Mary was born, christened the same day and installed at St James's. Two years later James Duke of York appeared; a beautiful, fair, blue-eyed baby, he became his mother's favourite, and nothing was too good for him, with the result that the allowance for the three children's establishment was increased by £3,000 a year. All this time the bills of their French apothecary, M. le Mire, remained unpaid.10

II

In 1631 Charles's wet-nurse was replaced by a Mrs Christabella Wyndham, a West-country woman, whose husband was a soldier. She remained with him for four years, and he became deeply attached to her. Apart from the fact that she continued to influence him after her departure and that she was inclined to presume upon her position, little is known of her. No complaints of her work were made by Lady Dorset or by the Prince's physicians when, in May 1633, he had his first serious illness, one that nearly cost him his life. This began with teething trouble and was at first treated by Dr Chambers, who attributed it to the carelessness of the Prince's attendants, but not specifically to Mrs Wyndham.

The King, who was about to leave for Scotland, had sent for Prince Charles and the Princess Mary to come to Greenwich. As the weather was very fine, he kept the little boy with him in the park till after sunset. Charles then insisted on standing with one of his rockers to watch his father at an open window, 'with no hat upon his head or neck-cloth upon his neck', until Dr Chambers, 'passing by, reproved the rocker', who put him to bed. Next day, when the King had left, the Prince developed a bad cold. The frightened nurses sent for Chambers, who found His Highness 'very heavy and drowsy, inclining his head to one side', and refusing to eat. All that night the fever rose and Chambers, now seriously alarmed, called in Dr Mayerne and Dr Lister. They reassured him. 'Nature begins to dispel the humour by stool,' said one, and suggested that they should 'suspend judgement until the following day'. They advised Chambers to share his responsibilities with five more physicians, who all examined Charles. These attributed his condition to a boil on his neck, to which they applied ointment, with no result. They then gave him 'a cooling drink', which he immediately vomited, 'the like whereof,' Chambers reported, 'I did never see come from a child of his age'. After further consultation the eight experts agreed that more drastic measures must be taken, and milk clysters, 'to refresh his intestines and assuage his pain', were administered. The screaming child, now in agonies, began to vomit blood, but the doctors persisted and he was made to swallow chicken broth, with a purge of senna and rhubarb. The smell in the sick-room was appalling; naturally, no windows were opened – fresh air might have been fatal; and to the doctors' amazement the fever continued.

Suddenly Charles's instinct to survive asserted itself, and his fever gradually diminished, although he was still racked by nausea and diarrhoea. More broth was forced down, 'with every good success'. A few days later he was asking for food, and in a week's time he 'eat heartily, and would have done much more if he might'. For nearly a month he remained languid and depressed. One of his courtiers attributed this to over-coddling. 'That spirit of his,' he wrote to the King's secretary, 'must be reflected with variety, which otherwise is over-apt to fall into musing.' In July, when the King returned to Greenwich, Charles's spirits shot up, and he welcomed his father 'with the prettiest innocent mirth'. By the end of August he had entirely recovered; but he could not forget those days of pain and terror, nor the hideous effect of the fashionable remedies. Henrietta Maria, who was expecting her fourth child and alternated between Richmond and Greenwich, does not appear to have visited him. As soon as he was well again she sent for him and the Princess Mary to Richmond. Without them, her husband's secretary reported, 'a great part of the King's chamber mirth is suspended'.[11]

Soon after Charles's fourth birthday he made his first public appearance at his father's Court, and was taught to imitate the stately courtesy for which his parents were celebrated. Although no lady, not even the Princess Royal, sat down without leave in his presence, the King received his guests with impressive graciousness. He got up from his dais to greet foreign ambassadors and uncovered at the beginning of their audiences;[12] but his composed gravity, his dislike of strangers and his avoidance of discussion enhanced the formality of all his receptions. Henrietta Maria was more approachable because she at once responded to flattery; the King simply accepted it as his due. When he was alone with her and his children he relaxed; the contrast between his father's public and private manner was thus early impressed upon Charles; when he was summoned to Whitehall he found himself isolated from the general company, moving and speaking to rule. Very soon his natural liveliness made him rebellious of the system.

The remoteness of the King from his subjects was in no way lessened by his tastes, which were those of a cultured country gentleman. Even in the hunting-field he seemed set apart; and at race-meetings he was on the look-out for undesirable characters. 'Let that ugly rascal, that whore-master, be gone out of the park, or else I will not see the sport,' he said, when he noticed 'a great lover of pretty girls' on the course.[13] This strict-ness and the unpopularity resulting from it did not affect his children's love for him – the younger ones would have gone to him rather than to the Queen in any difficulty – but they may have become apparent to Charles when his father reproved him, which he did publicly and often. The Prince was seldom punished and never beaten – that would have amounted to an assault on the divine regality; but the King's 'high notions of the majesty and rights of princes'[14] enforced a standard irksome to a spirited child whose instinct was to make friends with everybody. As he grew older Prince Charles must have seen that his father neither knew nor cared to know the common people, although he spent a great deal of time and energy in arranging, much to their annoyance, every detail of their lives in regard to religion, trade, dress, travel and social customs. To mingle with them, however momentarily, as James I and the Tudors had, would never have occurred to him. He was intimate only with the Queen, to whom he told all the state secrets, to the disgust of his ministers. So the little Prince became accustomed to feeling himself estranged from, al-though not hostile to, his severe and melancholy father and his moody, excitable mother.

He may also have been aware of the disagreements between them about the reception of such persons as Panzani, the Vatican emissary – whom the King, at his wife's instigation, admitted against his will – and his German Protestant cousins, Rupert and Maurice; especially because in 1635 Mrs Wyndham left his service and he spent more time with his parents. He seems then to have been in Lady Dorset's sole charge, and his Court moved to Richmond. He had no tutor during this period, although

His Majesty's advisers thought it was high time he should be 'taken out of the hands of the women'.[15] The King, as so often, could not make up his mind. He consulted but did not follow the advice of several experts, one of whom, Sir Robert Le Grys, may have prolonged his hesitation by drawing up an extremely ambitious programme for the Prince before he had learnt to read. Latin, said this gentleman, should be His Highness's *linguam vernaculum* – 'not clogging his memory with tedious rules after the common, pedantic fashion, but by way much more easy'. If Sir Robert might only have sole care of the child till he was seven, 'the nimblest Latinists would find him their match'. Of course he would at the same time learn to read and write Spanish, French and Italian. 'On the least discernible weariness,' Le Grys went on, 'I should wait on him to some exercise or recreation, feeding his mind with variety of narratives ... such as the history of the Bible, from Genesis to Acts, and what is worth observation in historians. (I have not yet met with anyone who has read more than myself.) At other times I would entertain his fancy with tales of the poets, and philosophy ... and make him familiar with arithmetic, geography and the art of War.'[16] This stupendous scheme was rejected. The Prince learnt the three Rs, and nothing else, during the next three years.

When Charles was six Lady Dorset retired, and again the reconstitution of his establishment had to be considered. The King wanted Brian Duppa, later Bishop of Chichester, to be his tutor; but Duppa evaded the responsibility. It was suggested that the Earl of Newcastle should become the Prince's Governor; still no definite offer was made, even after His Highness's new 'little' household had been settled, with the result that he came under his mother's influence just at the time when her chapel in Somerset House was opened by her public attendance at High Mass. (This ceremony was preceded by Henrietta and the King going on a shopping expedition and thence to Bethlehem Hospital, 'to see the mad folks, where they were madly entertained'.)[17] As the better educated citizens were anxious to see the beauties of the chapel – the King had commissioned Rubens to paint a Virgin and Child for the high altar – Henrietta Maria persuaded him to relax the restrictions on those attending Roman Catholic services, and herself took Prince Charles to worship there. When this became known there was an outcry, and the King announced that his son's visits must cease. The Queen and Panzani managed to talk him round, and for the next year (1636–7) the Prince continued to go to the chapel. By the time his father finally decided to stop what everyone felt to be Henrietta Maria's determination to proselytize the heir, the mischief had been done; anti-Catholic feeling was further strengthened by the leniency with which Catholics were now being treated, while the Puritans were further penalized. At that time it would have been very difficult indeed to convince the unsophisticated public that Charles I was in fact completely loyal to the English Church and that he had merely indulged his wife's caprices in his usual vacillating way. Years afterwards, when Charles II rather snobbishly remarked that Presbyterianism was not a religion for a gentleman, his Scottish subjects recollected those visits to the Somerset House chapel and again became suspicious.

Henrietta Maria then circumvented her husband's embargo by secretly organizing parlour games for his courtiers, for which she gave prizes of relics, crucifixes and sacred medals. Prince Charles was allowed to join in, and no doubt enjoyed himself immensely. When the King came upon one of these parties he refused to play and told his son that he must give up the presents he had won.[18] Once more, feeling against the Queen became violently bitter. Thereafter the games, the Mass, the visits to the Chapel Royal were remembered, and the King's belated interference forgotten. Popery – popery! Surely it was creeping in ... The majority of the English people began to believe themselves in almost as great danger as in the days of the Gunpowder Plot and the Spanish Armada. Fear and hatred of foreigners and priests, ceaselessly exploited by skilled and popular preachers, became hysterical.

The King ignored these demonstrations. He and Archbishop Laud were engaged in improving their beloved Church, and they proceeded to do so, casting money-lenders and shopkeepers out of the aisles, setting stone altars under east windows (Sun-worship! Idolatry!), mending medieval glass and replacing figures of saints and martyrs in niches which had remained empty since the reign of Edward VI. Their intentions were admirable, their methods rather high-handed. But the King knew that he was right – how could the crowned and anointed representative of the Almighty be wrong? Meanwhile, his son was absorbing the atmosphere of a Court which would now be described as High Anglican in its general tone, with an openly tolerated substratum of Roman Catholicism.

NOTES

1 Mme de Motteville, *Mémoires*, vol. I, p. 200.
2 Clarendon, *History of the Rebellion*, p. 31.
3 *Cal. D. S. P.*, Aug. 17th and 27th, 1630.
4 *Letters of Henrietta Maria* (ed. Everett Green), pp. 17–18.
5 Strickland, vol. IV, p. 191.
6 *Cal. D. S. P.*, Aug. 19th, 1630; Jan. 10th and March 25th, 1631.
7 *Historical Monuments*, vol. II, p. 341.
8 *Cal. D. S. P.*, Jan. 10th and Oct. 27th, 1631.
9 O. Airy, *Charles II*, pp. 6–7.
10 *Cal. D. S. P.*, March 31st, 1633.
11 *Cowper MSS*, vol. II, pp. 11, 12, 15, 17, 18, 26.
12 E. Law, *A Short History of Hampton Court*, vol. II, p. 114.
13 J. Aubrey, *Brief Lives*, p. 214.
14 Carte, *Ormonde*, vol. II, p. 355.
15 W. Knowler, *The Earl of Strafford's Letters and Dispatches*, vol. II, p. 57.
16 *Cal. D. S. P.* (n.d.), 1633.
17 Goodman, vol. II, p. 244.
18 J. Mackay, *Little Madam*, p. 137.

CHAPTER THREE

DUTIES AND PLEASURES

I

IN December 1635 the Princess Elizabeth was born; eighteen months later Henrietta Maria gave birth to her fifth child and third daughter, Anne, and both were established with the Princess Royal and the three-year-old Duke of York at St James's, now the nursery palace of the royal family. Prince Charles's household moved from there to Oatlands or Richmond. As he reached his seventh year he spent less time with his brother and sisters. He was then joined by George and Francis Villiers, the orphaned sons of the Duke of Buckingham, whom the King had adopted a few months after their father's murder. Their mother seems to have handed them over to him when she married the Earl of Antrim and went to live in Ireland.

The second Duke of Buckingham was two years older than the Prince; Lord Francis, a posthumous child, was Charles's senior by thirteen months. The appearance of both brothers contrasted strongly, indeed painfully, with that of their young master, for they had inherited their father's radiant beauty and fresh colouring. The little Duke's hair was light brown; his eyes were grey; Lord Francis was blond and blue-eyed. Both were in advance of their age and Buckingham was brilliantly clever. His intelligence and his two years' seniority gave him a hold over Charles which, throughout many fluctuations and estrangements, lasted all their lives. Another reason for this domination was the Duke's capacity for amusing and fascinating anyone over whom he chose to exercise his powers. How soon and how effectively he impressed the Prince may be guessed at by the contemporary account of a masque in which the three children appeared before the King and Queen at Richmond. Buckingham was eight, Francis Villiers seven and Charles six when they gave this performance.

The Prince and his friends had been brought up on Court masques. From the age of four Charles had seen his parents and their courtiers gorgeously dressed as marine deities or mythological potentates, seated on thrones descending from the skies into 'horrid Hells' which then turned into forests or giants' castles. Sea-storms, temples, darkness yielding to sunbursts, silver chariots, river palaces, tropical gardens and costumes glittering with jewels were the commonplaces of these productions, which lasted for seven or eight hours and cost thousands of pounds. The anonymous composers of the Richmond masque adapted their ambitions to the age of the principals; the entertainment cannot have lasted for more than three hours, and the cast comprised some twenty persons.

The scene opened on a rural setting, in which Charles and a troupe of boys appeared in a country dance. When they had finished and were seated, a fantastically dressed and bearded Gentleman Usher came on, brandishing his staff and exclaiming, 'Stand by there! Give place, bear back!' Some 'countrymen', pushing past the Usher, clamoured to speak to the Queen, and after some extremely flat rustic dialogue, were allowed to kiss her hand. Against a series of drop-scenes, which included a forest glade, an armed camp and several symbolical tableaux, the cast danced, sang and recited verses while dressed as shepherds, Romans and Druids. Charles, as Prince Britomart, entered in a costume of blue and crimson taffeta, of which the tunic was 'cut into scollops after the Roman fashion'. The show ended with an 'Adventurers' dance' in which all joined.[1]

Charles, although appearing in heroic guise, had no speaking part. While he danced and sang and held the place of glory in a triumphal arch, the Villiers boys took the floor, in a style which he might have liked to emulate and must have admired. Twelve years later all three were in very deed adventurers, with a price on their heads – homeless and penniless outcasts.

II

Van Dyck's romantic attitude towards his sitters seems to have been the basis of his inspiration, as perhaps also of the energy which enabled him to cover acres of canvas with a series of nobly elegant, gracefully melancholic figures. His transcendent genius shows the Court of Charles I as the King himself saw it and wished it to remain – superb, remote, exquisite and yet almost imperceptibly uniform, in spite of its variegated magnificence. If the background of Charles II's childhood was as Van Dyck and his school recorded it – and there is no reason to suppose that it was not – then he was brought up in an atmosphere of conscious rectitude and highly sophisticated taste: what we should now call an ivory tower, in which simplicity and luxury were perfectly blended and complacently accepted. Just as the great artist invariably stressed the most agreeable attributes of his characters – long slender hands, flawlessly delicate skins, richly curling hair – so his patron enforced a routine which shut out even the suggestion of unpleasantness. When Charles I said, 'The English are a sober people,' he epitomized a state of self-delusion (for no nation was ever more unmanageable) which may have been reflected in the triumphs of his protégé.

Yet even Van Dyck seems sometimes to have felt the need of placing his Cavaliers and their ladies in settings which gave his virtuosity a greater freedom – as when he painted Charles I in armour or on horseback, his courtiers with their dogs, and their bejewelled wives and daughters against gleaming draperies or autumnal landscapes. Prolonged study of these portraits gives the impression that armour, animals, jewels, dimly seen trees and yellow, green or blue satins and velvets have become more important than their possessors who, accepting the painter's tribute to their own beauty, are content to be subordinated to its trappings.

The microcosm thus created was only shattered when very young people sat to Van Dyck. In one of his paintings of the children of Charles I he seems to have resisted what, in a lesser artist such as Lely, became wearisome conventions. In the most famous of these family pictures Prince Charles is dressed in rose-pink satin – surely an unfortunate choice for a sallow-skinned child – and, far from being subjugated, appears to be bursting out of the pose, his eyes bright with amusement and interest. He has forgotten the huge dog yearning up at him, just as he has forgotten his brother and sisters, who stare patiently into space from the background. This picture symbolizes both Charles's attitude towards his surroundings and the effect that attitude had on those in charge of him. It was, surely, something more than sycophancy or even loyalty which attached his servants to him from infancy onwards and made them stay with him in his exile.

The exuberance, sometimes amounting to revolt, observed by Van Dyck and by those who could not induce Prince Charles to give up taking his wooden billet to bed with him, was also noted by the newly appointed Venetian ambassador, when in January 1637 he was received at Hampton Court. The Prince, the Princess Royal and the Duke of York, seated below the throne, got up as Correr and his gentlemen came in; after saluting the King he bent to kiss their hands in order of precedence, and was interrupted by His Majesty 'gently reproving' Prince Charles for the off-hand hauteur (*sussiego*) with which he received homage.[2] On another occasion the King, sitting in chapel with his sons, became aware that Charles was smiling and laughing at the ladies opposite. This time he was really annoyed, to the extent of rapping the boy on the head with his cane and speaking to him with cold severity.[3]

The rhythm of life in the royal palaces followed the pattern illustrated by such incidents as these. It was unalterable, strenuous, and extravagant in the sense that neither the King nor his administrators had the faintest notion of financial control. While minor officials sometimes remained unpaid for months or even years, £2,000 would be spent on a single masque. Cooks, writing-masters and apothecaries often faced ruin; their employer continued to live in the 'excess and luxury' deplored by the practical Hyde, who achieved power too late to begin the reformation of these abuses.

Although the King himself was abstemious (he had never been drunk in his life and was a small eater, as indeed was Henrietta Maria), it would not have occurred to him to simplify either the meals themselves or the ceremonial accompanying them. His courtiers' and his family's diet was based on that which had been his when he was Prince of Wales, and followed an inexorable routine. Thus from the moment that he ceased to be a child in arms Prince Charles started the day with an early breakfast of bread, mutton, chicken, beer and buttermilk. At dinner, which was served between midday and two o'clock, according to the season, these dishes reappeared, supplemented by wine, game, rabbit pies and sweet tarts. Supper was an informal meal, and the range was similar but more varied, including three or four different kinds of fish, custards and a favourite concoction of pigs' and chickens' livers fried with ginger and hard-boiled eggs.[4]

Dinner and supper were served on gold and silver plate. The Prince entered the dining-room with his hat on, removing it while his chaplain said grace. He then replaced it and sat down. A kneeling page held out a silver-gilt ewer and a napkin. When the Prince had washed and dried his hands each dish was shown him in turn and he made his choice; this was laid before the carver, a gentleman of high rank; he dealt out a helping, which he tasted and sent back to His Highness. Another kneeling page offered bread cut in thin slices; a cup-bearer, also on the knee, presented wine and a third attendant held a vessel under the Prince's chin to keep the drops from falling on his tunic while he drank. All three then bowed and retired till he was ready for the next course, when the procedure was repeated.[5]

When Charles dined in public with his parents the ceremonial was more elaborate and a large number of spectators was admitted; although all three were surrounded by courtiers, ewerers, tasters and carvers, some of them of royal blood, none shared their meal. The nearest the courtiers might get to conversation was by standing behind the King's chair and waiting for him to speak to them. In the banqueting-hall the table was placed near the hearth; the King and Queen sat in the centre with their backs to it, and the Prince at the right-hand end. In one banqueting-hall – possibly that at Richmond Palace – the royal party is seen, according to a contemporary artist, against a background of carved panelling, high windows in deep embrasures and black-and-white marble flooring. At one end of the huge room a flight of steps leads up to a pillared gallery; here, at a respectful distance, courtiers and guests lean over the balcony, watching the procedure. At the other end stands a circular service table covered with plates and vessels. On the floor is a silver wine-cooler containing three bottles. Dogs, mostly of the pet spaniel variety, are running about. Servers are coming in with covered dishes. Some fifteen or twenty privileged ladies and gentlemen stand between Their Majesties and the great chimneypiece, one or two (those of the highest rank) holding dishes, napkins or crystal beakers. Charles I wears his plumed hat: his son is uncovered. The general effect is one of great stateliness, with a tinge of informality, as if showing a glimpse of the King's graciousness emerging from the magnificence of monarchy. In the adjoining rooms the courtiers sat down to eighty-six tables and a choice of sixteen dishes. The royal menus provided a selection of two dozen dishes at each meal.[6]

Ceremonious meals and elaborate masques were a subsidiary part of the Prince's training; he was taught not only how to become a pleasing show figure, but also to realize his responsibilities as the future head of his Church. Thus he stood godfather to the Princess Anne a few weeks after Brian Duppa consented, rather reluctantly, to become his tutor.

Although Charles's sense of drama and of the picturesque might well have been roused by his visits to the Queen's chapel, there is no evidence that he was drawn towards Catholicism at this time; he was primarily influenced by Duppa, whose jurisdiction over him was mild and agreeable, with the result that his pupil's piety, hitherto superficially fostered, was considerably strengthened. As soon as this became apparent Henrietta Maria's Grand Almoner, de Peron, started a fresh campaign for the Prince's conversion, through the Bishop, whom he tried to influence first. When these unsuccessful efforts were reported to Laud, he protested to the King, who again forbade his wife to take Charles to her chapel, where the parade of fashionable converts had much increased and was bitterly resented. Henrietta, aware that she could not withstand her husband's authority on this point, made a scene with Laud, who once more complained to his master. 'You will find my wife reasonable,' was all the satisfaction he got, followed by one of His Majesty's catch-phrases – 'I mean to be obeyed.'[7]

As soon as Charles had passed his sixth birthday the King again asked Newcastle to be his tutor and this time the Earl, who had refused on the grounds of the jealousy his appointment might cause, accepted. Once more the Prince's establishment was reconstituted, as for a grown person, with Gentlemen of the Bedchamber, equerries and cup-bearers. The Marquess of Hamilton became his Master of the Horse at £476 a year, and a new cook was engaged at £9 5s. As his general education was somewhat in arrears, a French tutor and French page were attached to his household, and the King commanded Wenceslaus Hollar to give him drawing-lessons.[8] Meanwhile, Buckingham and Lord Francis Villiers were to remain with him, sharing all these amenities. Duppa objected to this arrangement: he had been engaged to teach the Prince alone. He was overridden, and by the spring of 1638 the three boys had settled into Richmond Palace with a staff of some four hundred persons.

Charles, who at once became devoted to Newcastle, was completely happy until, in the winter of that year, he had another attack of fever and was ordered to recommence the regime of purges and clysters of five years before. He refused. The physicians were helpless. They dared not use force, and His Highness ignored all attempts at persuasion. In despair, they appealed to the Queen, who at once wrote,

Charles, I am sore that I must begin my first letter with chiding you, because I hear that you will not take physic. I hope it was only for this day and that tomorrow you will do it, for if you will not I must come to you, and make you take it, for it is for your health. I have given order to my Lord of Newcastle to send me word to-night whether you will or not, therefore I hope you will not give me the pains to go ...

When this letter reached the Prince he decided to appeal, in his turn, to Newcastle, who was temporarily absent from the Palace: Charles was still no great hand with the pen; his letters had to be written between ruled lines. This having been done for him, he wrote to his Governor,

My lord, I would not have you take too much physic; for it doth always make me worse, and I think it will do the like with you. I ride every day, and am ready to follow any other directions from you. Make haste to return to him that loves you.

Charles P.[9]

Thereafter, nothing more was heard about the Prince taking medicine. He had not openly disobeyed his mother; but their ensuing correspondence shows that Newcastle was prepared to support him within reason – and his charge was nothing if not reasonable and good-tempered – in all circumstances. This was Charles II's first diplomatic victory.

NOTES

1 *King's and Queen's Entertainment at Richmond, 1636.*
2 *Cal. S. P. Ven.*, vol. XXIV, p. 100.
3 F. Turner, *James II*, p. 46.
4 *Ancaster MSS* (H.M.C.), 'Diet of Charles I', p. 2.
5 S. Hoskins, *Charles II in the Channel Islands*, p. 448.
6 Law, vol. II, pp. 121–3.
7 S. Gardiner, *History of England*, vol. VIII, pp. 240–2.
8 Hearsey, p. 148; Knowler, vol. II, pp. 148, 166.
9 H. Ellis, *Original Letters illustrative of English History*, series 1. vol. III, pp. 285–91.

CHAPTER FOUR

THE RISING STORM

I

WHEN Newcastle became Prince Charles's Governor he was forty-six. His appointment was combined with that of Privy Councillor. He had some hesitation in accepting the post, and indeed relinquished it three and a half years later, but the impact of his personality on Charles was permanent. Long after his death his pupil was acting and thinking on the lines his Governor had laid down for him.

Newcastle's appearance was pleasing but unremarkable. In her memoir his wife describes him as slightly under middle height, fresh-coloured and neatly made. A magnifico of what will always be known as the old school – that school which exists only in nostalgic visions of an imaginary past – Newcastle's greatest asset was his integrity, coupled with an acute and rather cynical attitude towards human affairs. His range of accomplishments and hobbies was enormous, and his powers commanded respect even from those who deplored his refusal to rise to occasions where his personal interests were not involved. A passionate monarchist, he accepted his wife's complaint that he loved the Prince better than her or their children. 'I care not,' he said. 'Whether he love me again or not, I am resolved to love him'[1] – and he would never, from the moment he took over the household, hear a word of criticism of his charge.

In return, Newcastle's tastes and opinions were at once adopted by Charles; in this notable man he found the perfect companion, teacher and hero. Newcastle's lively, natural manners, his original outlook, his scorn of pedantry, priggishness and fanaticism, his splendid courtesy, and above all, his brilliant horsemanship, fascinated the boy whose parents' point of view was limited and commonplace, and whose outdoor activities were circumscribed by tradition.

The Earl began by treating his pupil as if he were a young man (it was at this time that the famous wooden billet seems to have been discarded) and concentrated on athletic pleasures, with the result that in two years Charles became a graceful dancer, a skilled fencer and could ride 'leaping horses, and such as would overthrow others ... with the greatest dexterity'.

Newcastle, one of the finest experts in Europe on the art of *manège*, was consulted by trainers and owners from all over the Continent. As soon as he entered his great stables at Bolsover or Welbeck, he was greeted by the 'trampling and neighing' of his 'rejoicing' stud, whom he treated individually, noting their differences of temperament with a care and observation he did not always use for his fellow-ministers. ('Spanish horses are like princes,' he used to say.[2]) In fact, Newcastle cared little for general popularity, although he was well aware of its importance in the Prince's case. Having long deprecated King Charles's inability to achieve it, he impressed on his heir that the love and support of his future subjects was of far greater value than learning (that should be lightly and elegantly worn), or a too fervent dedication to his Church (good Bishop Duppa was in charge of that anyway), or the obsession with the visual arts on which His Majesty spent so much time and money. Yet Newcastle was rather a man of the world than a worldly man. He thought little of mass movements, was bored by religiosity and considered dissipation and excess, whether at the table or in the alcove, tedious and undignified. A dilettante, with standards as high as they were varied, he urged his eager pupil not to become 'too studious, for too much contemplation spoils action', adding, 'I confess, I would rather have you study things than words, matter than language.' No advice could have been more welcome to an energetic, over-disciplined eight-year-old, all the more when it was reinforced by Newcastle's wish that he should concentrate on history (but not for too many hours a day), foreign tongues (as long as he took care not to become 'a living dictionary'), short prayers, good manners ('to women you cannot be too civil, especially to great ones') and consideration of the feelings of all classes. ('How easy a way is this to have the people.') Newcastle was in favour of ceremonial, as befitting a well-ordered Court and a disciplined populace – but, 'though you cannot put on too much King, yet even there sometimes a hat or a smile in the right place will advantage you'. This cool-headed patrician would have smiled at the judgment of his most distinguished contemporary, the practical, virtuous, middle-class Hyde, who found him useless in war and amateurish in peace, although he accorded him some qualified praise. 'He was a very fine gentleman,' the lawyer remarks condescendingly, '... active and full of courage, and most accomplished in ... horsemanship, chemistry, dancing and fencing ... besides that he was amorous in poetry and music, to which he indulged the greatest part of his time ... He loved monarchy, as it was the foundation and support of his own greatness; and the Church, as it was well constituted for the splendour and order of the crown; and religion, as it cherished and maintained that order and obedience that was necessary to both ... '3

Newcastle's abstemiousness – he often dined off an egg and a glass of ale – set Charles, whose appetite was that of a greedy schoolboy, an excellent example. During his exile the Prince showed an indifference to rich food which he must have learnt from his ascetic Governor. In fact, so many of Newcastle's characteristics were later reproduced in Charles that contemporary accounts of the Prince's tastes and habits might be descriptions of the Earl's – with this difference, that Newcastle's circumstances never caused him to develop cunning, ruthlessness or duplicity. He strengthened his pupil's attachment by giving him little presents. 'My lord,' Charles wrote in the first month of their relationship, 'I thank you for your New Year's gift; I am very well pleased with it, especially with the brass statues. On Monday by three of the clock I shall be glad to meet you at Lambeth.'4

As Charles continued to model himself on Newcastle, he was again withdrawn from his parents, although he shared their piety. Newcastle, noting this – 'You are in your own disposition religious,' he observed – was determined that he should not share their bigotry. 'Beware of too much devotion,' he advised, 'for one may be a good man but a bad king.' As loyal to his master as to his Church, the Earl was now aware of the unpopularity of the one and of the dangers threatening the other. At the same time, he perceived a lack of application in his pupil which might be turned to good account. If the Prince were to become, as Newcastle hoped, all things to all men, then he must avoid extremes in intellectual pursuits, as in religion. 'For books,' he went on, ' ... the greatest clerks are not the wisest men ... Neither have I known bookworms great statesmen ... The reason's plain; for divinity teaches what we should be, not what we are.' Although these precepts did not appear in print till after the Restoration, they formed the basis of Newcastle's training, as is shown by Charles's behaviour from the moment the Earl took charge.

The first year of Newcastle's governorship culminated in his pupil's becoming Knight of the Garter and Prince of Wales. The ceremony took place on May 12th, 1638, at Windsor. The Prince then returned with Newcastle to Richmond, and his parents removed to Whitehall, having informed the Earl that he was responsible to them alone; thus they made it clear that any criticisms of, or suggestions for, the Prince's education would be disregarded.5 None was made; at this time Newcastle's Anglicanism was above suspicion.

A year later the King decided to transfer Charles's household to Hatton

House in Holborn, which he proposed to buy from Lady Hatton. She refused to sell, and when the property was confiscated brought a suit against the Privy Council in the Court of Requests. An enthusiastic gardener, she had surrounded Hatton House with 'the best fruit, vines and flowers that could be got', which she uprooted as soon as she realized that she might lose her case. When the newly appointed Lord Privy Seal announced, 'Upon my honour, I must decree against my lady,' she retorted, 'Good my lord, be tender of your honour, for 'tis young – and for your decree, I value it not a rush, for your Court is not the Court of Record,' and proceeded to bring another action, with the result that the King abandoned his claim, thus making himself look foolish and unpopular to no purpose.[6] So Lady Hatton was left to restore her garden and Prince Charles remained at Richmond, where he was joined in June 1639 by his private troop of horse; he learnt to drill them under Newcastle's direction.

In this busy, happy time the Prince still missed his nurse. He kept in touch with her through Bishop Duppa, who told Colonel Wyndham that he often asked for her. 'He hastens apace out of his childhood,' added the tutor, 'and is likely to be a man betimes.' Duppa was concerned, nevertheless, about certain influences, although he was careful not to name whose they were. His pupil promised to become 'an excellent man,' he reported, 'if ... flattery and humoring him (the bane of Princes) do not spoil him'.[7]

II

Some eighteen months before Newcastle became Prince Charles's Governor, his father's prestige and authority had begun the decline which was to end in his execution. In 1638 the Scottish Parliament signed the Covenant which established Calvinism as the national religion; the King's first unsuccessful attempt to root out their chosen faith by enforcing the English Prayer-Book on the Scots coincided with the Prince's ninth birthday and a gala performance of *Sir John Oldcastle* in the Cockpit at Whitehall. Three months later His Majesty was receiving congratulations from all over the Continent on the peace with Scotland. This was in fact an armistice; the King, while ostensibly accepting the Covenanters' terms, had merely withdrawn in order to advance again with superior forces, although it was obvious to all but himself that his ill-equipped and mutinous troops could not be relied on unless a complete reorganization of the army was effected.

These set-backs were not recognized by Charles I; he was more removed from reality than his heir, playing at soldiers in the gardens of Richmond Palace; for in May 1640, a year after the King's virtual defeat by the Covenanters, the Prince was used by his attendants to express their disapproval of his father's policy.

That section of Prince Charles's household which would later be described as Parliamentarian began by frightening him with descriptions of what he himself stood to lose from the King's mistakes. The ten-year-old boy, believing the worst, cried during the day and was tormented by nightmares when he went to bed. Feeling that they had perhaps gone too far, some of the women tried to soothe and reassure him. It was useless; at last his state of mind became apparent to the King, who asked him what the matter was. 'Your Majesty should have asked me that sooner,' Prince Charles replied. 'Tell me,' said the King. 'My grandfather,' Charles blurted out, 'left you four kingdoms – and I am afraid Your Majesty will leave me never a one.'

This was the moment when the King should have given his remarkably intelligent and sensitive son an explanation. He coldly asked, 'Who have been your tutors in this?', received no answer and turned away.[8] A few months later, when the rumour went round that His Highness was in danger of being kidnapped, perhaps murdered by his father's enemies, and his guard at Richmond was reinforced, the Prince's confusion of mind must have been disagreeably increased, although he was now seen to be in excellent spirits; his manners were much improved by Newcastle's training. When the celebrated Mr Ferrar of Little Gidding was given an audience, there was no question of His Highness lapsing into the ungraciousness noted by the Venetian ambassador three years before.

At about the time of Charles I's accession John and Nicholas Ferrar had retired with their families to Little Gidding in Huntingdonshire, where they established an Anglican centre for charitable works, prayer, meditation and the arts and crafts. The ladies of the household shared in these activities, which included printing and book-binding of a very high order. Charles I, hearing from Archbishop Laud that the Ferrars specialized in sacred books, ordered an edition of the Four Gospels; he was so pleased with the result that he then commanded a Concordance of Chronicles and Kings. 'I have often spoken to many of my chaplains about this thing,' he said, 'but they have excused themselves from it as a difficult work.' He was assured that the matter would be put in hand, and in due course the Archbishop brought John Ferrar to Whitehall to present the book. His Majesty and Mr Ferrar then had an agreeable chat on book-binding and illustration, passing on to the stammer with which both were afflicted. The King gave his guest some sound advice: singing was a help; pebbles in the mouth were quite useless. The Concordance (now in the British Museum) was then produced; it was bound in purple velvet with raised gilt ornamentation. 'This – this is a jewel in all respects!' the King exclaimed. Later on he showed Prince Charles the book, and, Ferrar reports, the boy 'would have begged it of the King'. 'I may not part with this rich jewel,' said his father, 'but Mr Ferrar will give you another.'

Eventually, the Prince's book, a Bible, was ready, and again Ferrar was taken by Laud to Whitehall, where he found the King standing with his gentlemen by the fireplace. 'What?' said His Majesty in his most gracious manner, giving Ferrar his hand to kiss, 'Have you brought with you those varieties and jewels you told me of?' – and the Bible was taken out of its box. 'Here is a fine book for Charles indeed!' said the King, 'I hope it will soon make him in love with what is within – for I know it is good.'

Mr Ferrar then begged His Majesty's leave for an audience with the Prince, whose Court was at Richmond. He and Laud set off and were presently ushered into the presence chamber, where Charles, the Duke of York, Lord Francis Villiers, the Duke of Buckingham and Bishop Duppa were standing. After the kissing of hands Ferrar, with a low bow, presented the Bible. 'Here's a gallant outside!' Charles exclaimed, and showed the volume to his tutor, who read out the title and dedication. 'Then,' says Ferrar, 'the Prince took it, and turning it over, leaf by leaf, said, "Better and better!"' A courtier interposed with, 'How liketh Your Highness that rare piece?' 'Well, well, *very*,' said Charles emphatically. 'It pleaseth me exceedingly – and I wish daily to read in it,' he tactfully added. The eight-year-old Duke of York, feeling rather out of it, now put in, 'Will you not make me also such another fine book? I pray you do it.' 'I will not fail to make one for Your Grace,' Ferrar replied. 'How long will it be before I have it?' the child pursued. 'With all good speed,' was the rather unsatisfactory answer. 'But how long time will that be?' the little Duke persisted – and as Ferrar hesitated, he went on, 'I pray you, tell the gentlewomen at Little Gidding I will heartily thank them if they will despatch it.' At this all the courtiers burst out laughing. The Duke, Ferrar says, 'would have no nay, but a promise speedily to have one for him like his brother'.

After some further talk the Prince and his brother went to dinner, which Ferrar ate with the twelve-year-old Duke of Buckingham and Lord Francis. He then rejoined James and Charles, to whom Duppa described the King's Little Gidding acquisitions. 'Ah! I would you had brought them, so that I might also have seen these rare things,' said the Prince. When it was time for Ferrar to leave His Highness took off his hat as the visitor knelt to kiss his hand, and said, 'I am much beholden to you for the jewel you have given me, and for the contrivement of it – and,' he added, as if recalling his Governor's precepts about courtesy to ladies, 'to the Gidding gentlewomen who have taken so much pains about it to make it so curious.' He then offered Ferrar a purse of £20. As his guest modestly drew back, Charles reassured him. 'Nay, I do not give you this as any reward in recompense of your book,' he explained, 'for I esteem it in every way above much gold, and prize it at a far greater rate. Only, you shall take this as a testimony of my acceptance of it. I shall let all know how much I deem of this book,' he went on earnestly. So urged, the delighted Ferrar took the money, and, completely entranced, returned to Little Gidding with a glowing account of His Royal Highness's charms. The Duke of York never received his present; by the time it was ready, he and his family had left Whitehall.[9]

Already the unfamiliar shapes of rebellion and danger were rising round the precincts of the palace, as if to enforce the warnings which had alarmed Prince Charles, in spite of the fact that the elaborate and costly routine of theatricals, receptions, hunting and card-parties was sustained as usual. The King appeared serene and carefree. He ordered new sets of tapestries for Hampton Court; Sir William Davenant, his Poet Laureate, produced, after three months' rehearsal, the seven-hour masque of *Salmacida Spolia*, in which Charles watched his parents appear from the clouds to vanquish the evil spirits of unrest. The King sat late at basset, while his secretaries hung about waiting for him to sign his letters. Henrietta Maria had recovered from the difficult birth and immediate death of her fourth daughter, Princess Katherine, and was pregnant again. In July 1640 her third son, Henry Duke of Gloucester, was born at Oatlands, where the King kept the oaken staff on which were recorded, in silver, the heights of his children. A month later the Prince, standing godfather at the christening, observed his mother's absence from that Protestant ceremony.

Then arose the question of his betrothal: should it be to the Infanta of Spain, or to the Princess Maria Anna, the Emperor's daughter? Nothing came of either proposal: but the national fear of a Catholic alliance, especially one entailing closer connection with their ancient enemy, so worked upon the English people that there were riots in London and the provinces: while the dark and menacing figures of John Pym and Thomas Wentworth Earl of Strafford rose to begin the struggle in which the Prince was to play a minor part.

Complaints about ship-money, Scotland and Ireland increased. When the Lord Keeper Finch declared at the opening of Parliament that no country had ever yet been blessed with so good a King, so virtuous a Queen or so hopeful a band of royal progeny, and asked for subsidies to crush the Covenanting rebels, he was coldly received and objections to his master's policy were renewed. The King called out the train bands against the rioters, hanged and quartered one leader and put another to the torture. On May 5th, 1640, he dissolved what he described as his 'mongrel' Parliament; the Long Parliament was called in November; Laud's canons endorsing the Divine Right of Kings were followed by another widespread Puritan revolt and the impeachment of the Archbishop in December.

That the Prince took in the significance of, or the connection between, these events, is unlikely; his conversation with his father merely indicates the uneasiness he shared with the nation. In September this was increased by the arrest of his Scots chef, who had threatened to kill him, and the removal of his household from Oatlands to Hampton Court. Then, just before the Christmas festivities began, sorrow came to the Stuart family. The four-year-old Princess Anne was dying.

In accordance with custom, she was informed of her condition, and required 'to call upon God, even when the pangs of death were upon her'. She replied as became her station and upbringing. 'I am not able,' she said, 'to say my long prayer ' –she meant Our Father – 'but I will say my short one.' Folding her hands, she proceeded, ' "Lighten mine eyes, O Lord, lest I sleep the sleep of death." ' 'This done,' says the witness who records the scene, 'the little lamb gave up the ghost.'[10]

So the year ended in mourning and anxiety for some, in fierce and relentless resolution for others. On one point all were agreed. In the lively, good-tempered, genuinely pious little Prince of Wales they saw their best hope for the future.

NOTES

1 M. Newcastle, *The Duke and Duchess of Newcastle*, pp. 208–42.
2 Ibid.
3 Clarendon, p. 493.
4 Ellis, series 1, vol. III, pp. 285–91.
5 *Calendar of Clarendon State Papers*, vol. II, pp. 7–8.
6 R. A. Coke, *Detection*, vol. I, p. 389.
7 *Cal. D. S. P.*, Sept. 18th, 1639.
8 Op. cit., May 21st, 1640.
9 J. Mayor, *Two Lives of Nicholas Ferrar*, pp. 115–294.
10 Strickland, *Lives of the Tudor and Stuart Princesses*, p. 249.

CHAPTER FIVE

THE FIRST REBUFF

I

EARLY in 1641 Mr Edward Hyde, who had given up the law for Parliamentary business and the chairmanship of several committees, was leaving the House of Commons with his friend Henry Marten. Hyde had been much annoyed by the 'indecency and rudeness' of the Member for Huntingdon, Mr Oliver Cromwell, whom he had reprehended. 'If you proceed in the same manner,' he told him, 'I shall presently adjourn the committee and complain of you to the House.'

Hyde was thinking over these and similar matters, when Marten suddenly said, 'You will undo yourself by adhering to the Court,' presumably referring to Hyde's association with Archbishop Laud and the fact that the King had just sent for him. 'I have no relation to the Court,' said Hyde, 'I am only concerned to maintain the Government and to preserve the law – ' and gave Marten a lengthy discourse on these lines. The other waited patiently till he had finished – a habit which most of Hyde's friends were forced to adopt – and then replied, 'I do not think one man wise enough to govern us all.'

For once, Hyde was speechless. 'It was the first word,' he says, 'he had ever heard any man speak to that purpose.' Next day he had his audience with the King, who praised him for his loyalty in the House, thanked him for his affection to the Church and dismissed him 'with very gracious expressions'.[1] From that moment Hyde became one of his master's most valuable advisers; a year later he was in fact, although not in name, the Prince of Wales's Governor. For the next two decades their relationship was that of teacher and pupil, to the slowly mounting dissatisfaction of both parties.

All that spring and summer Hyde was too much absorbed in Parliamentary affairs to take much interest in the Prince as an individual; the boy was to him, as to most courtiers, the appendage to his parents; and the forthcoming trial of the Earl of Strafford for high treason, manipulated by Pym and his supporters and symbolic of the whole struggle between King and Parliament, occupied Hyde's attention as it did that of everybody else.

As it became clear that the trial must take place, Charles I wrote to Strafford assuring him 'on the word of a King, you shall not suffer in life, honour or fortune' and signing himself 'your constant, faithful friend'.[2] When the proceedings opened on March 22nd the King and Queen were present in a box. Prince Charles represented the monarchy sitting alone on a dais, covered and wearing his George.[3] On the evening before he made this, his first important public appearance, he and the Duke of York had waited at the head of the great staircase in Whitehall to welcome Prince William of Orange, the fifteen-year-old bridegroom of the Princess Royal.

During the next three weeks – from April 20th to May 12th – the marriage festivities coincided with Parliament's struggle about Strafford's life. Prince Charles, alternating between Westminster and Whitehall and sure at first, as his father was, of Strafford's eventual acquittal, watched Pym closing in, discounting one line of defence after another. This occupied most of the day; in the afternoon and evening he attended the betrothed couple through the intricacies of Court ceremony and marriage rites – a strange and bewildering experience for a boy of his age. In those strenuous, tragically contrasting days he must have begun to put aside childhood and to see, for the first time, that to be a king and wear a crown is not all glory: that those who serve may be betrayed by their masters; that a king's word must, sometimes, be broken; that an ignoble yielding can be preferable to a brave defence; and that every now and then it is expedient that one man should die to appease the fury of a mob.

He never afterwards spoke of that time except obliquely; that avoidance is the proof of a full and fearful awareness which then, as later, was concealed beneath a gay and graceful participation in the ceremonies accompanying a royal alliance. So, before he reached his teens, Charles learnt to wear a mask. The accounts of the wedding show that he wore it with the ease of an accomplished performer.

The Princess, a pretty, fair-haired child of nine, had been corresponding with her betrothed and was much looking forward to his arrival; unfortunately she had been allowed to attend the trial with her parents – on one occasion she remained in their draughty box for six hours – with the result that she caught cold and her face swelled. The King, apologizing for her absence, told Prince William that she was bilious and advised him not to see her until she recovered. William gallantly insisted on visiting her in bed, escorted by Prince Charles; he declared himself delighted with her appearance and manner.[3]

On the afternoon of the next day the bill of attainder against Strafford passed through the House of Commons. The miserable King's signature was then required; in a penultimate appeal he wrote protesting to the Houses and suggesting imprisonment. This letter was ignored. A week later his daughter's marriage took place privately in the chapel at Whitehall. Prince Charles and the Duke of York escorted her to the altar, and after the ceremony walked on either side of their brother-in-law to the wedding breakfast. The royal party then went for a stroll in Hyde Park, returning to Whitehall for supper and a dance. At ten o'clock the bedding of the Prince and Princess was inaugurated by the King bringing Prince William into the state bed-chamber, having first helped him to change his court suit for a dressing-gown and slippers. The little Princess, already disrobed, was waiting for her husband in the huge bed, which was surrounded by the ladies of her household, the Queen standing at the foot. The bridegroom, assisted by Prince Charles, then removed his dressing-gown and entered the bed – 'very gently', according to an eye-witness. 'He kissed the Princess three times,' goes on the narrator, 'and lay beside her for about three quarters of an hour in the presence of all the great lords and ladies of England.'

The King then indicated that this part of the ceremony was over and Prince William, after kissing his bride three more times, got up, put on his dressing-gown and knelt for Their Majesties' blessing. He was escorted by the King and Prince Charles to his own chamber.[5]

The ensuing week, spent by Strafford in prayer and meditation, was one of parties and present-giving at Whitehall. On May 10th the King assented to the bill of attainder; the execution was fixed for the 12th; the mob, who suspected that Charles might reprieve the Earl, threatened to storm his palace. The building was not suitable for defence, and there was a danger of the royal family with their Dutch guest and his attendants being lynched. The King, ignoring the screams and sobs of his wife's ladies – Henrietta Maria behaved with great courage – and the white faces and drawn swords of his courtiers, sent a last appeal to the Houses on the next day. To sentence Strafford to imprisonment would be, he wrote, 'an unspeakable contentment to me. C.R. P.S. If he must die, it were charity to reprieve him till Saturday.' He was about to dispatch the letter when the Queen suggested that Prince Charles should carry it in person, unattended. Surely the spectacle of the nation's darling coming alone to beg mercy for his father's servant would save the situation and the King's honour. The coach was summoned and Charles set off, driving by back ways. He reached the House of Lords in a few minutes. His father's letter was returned, unopened. Then, rather abruptly, His Royal Highness was dismissed.[6]

On the 10th the King signed the warrant. Two days later 'Black Tom Tyrant' was beheaded on Tower Hill in the presence of some ten thousand gloating people.

No comment was made, except by the foreign ambassadors, on the strange discourtesy of the House's treatment of the Prince. For Charles himself, hitherto cheered, admired and flattered wherever he went, it was the first step in his progress through sneers, insults and cold withdrawals to the depths of a prolonged and merciless humiliation. Within a fortnight of his eleventh birthday it was brought home to him how a king could be used: and that a group can be stronger than an individual, however sacred, however outwardly revered.

A fortnight after the execution he escorted Prince William to Gravesend. After a further exchange of presents the bridegroom announced that if the Princess did not follow him immediately he should come back to fetch her. There were tears and farewells, last compliments and firing of cannon. The same crowds that had howled with delight as Strafford's blood streamed over the scaffold cheered and applauded. In the evening Charles and his mother left for Oatlands.

II

After Strafford's execution the King pursued a policy of appeasement towards Pym and his party, using changes in Prince Charles's education as a sign of his good intentions. He replaced Newcastle and Duppa by Lord Hertford and the Reverend Dr Earle. Hertford was dull, respectable and bookish; Earle's volume of 'characters', *Microcosmographie*, shows some originality of mind. Neither was suited to his post and both seem to have been amiably ignored by their charge.

Parliament believed that Newcastle was affiliated with the Army Plot to rescue Strafford and seize the Tower. They considered the inoffensive Duppa a pro-Laudian and perhaps even in favour of an Anglo-Catholic understanding with Rome. Their greatest fear for the Prince was, as ever, caused by his mother's influence.

Henrietta Maria's inroads on the national sensibilities had been so many and so deeply felt that the King's attempts to smooth matters over were received with contemptuous distrust. In the first place, her mother, Marie de Medici, had been established in London with her Catholic household of six hundred persons since the autumn of 1638.[7] She now departed; but the mischief believed to have been effected by her Jesuits – and they had made a number of converts – was done. Prince Charles's visits to Henrietta Maria's chapel had long ceased; yet they could not be forgotten. The Vatican envoy was dismissed; the fact that the King and Queen parted with him on affectionate terms and took care to protect him from anti-Catholic demonstrations was, to the majority, a proof that the King not only tolerated but encouraged his wife's co-religionists. He was not preparing to discourage popery as he was preparing to stamp out Calvinism in Scotland and dissent in England. That must mean that his heir was still in danger of being converted.

These feverish suspicions rose with increasing speed. When in June 1641 Prince Charles broke his arm riding in Hyde Park and retired to Richmond to recuperate, it was said that this was a ruse to conceal his departure with Newcastle, to command – at eleven years of age – a force against the Scots. When it was discovered that this was not so, his leaving Richmond to convalesce at Oatlands with the Queen caused an outcry: why did he not remain at Richmond with his Protestant household? There was some talk in the Commons about the King's abdication in his son's favour: the boy would reign as a puppet sovereign under Parliament's jurisdiction. This idea was not long or seriously considered.

At the end of October Pym organized a debate on the danger of His Highness's apostasy. It was proposed that he should be entirely removed from his mother and handed over to Hertford, who would be required to prevent all contact between them except such as might arise on formal occasions. The King countered this by announcing that negotiations for Charles's betrothal to the Princess of Orange had begun; when they fell through he was thought, with some reason, to have deliberately deceived the public. The King then removed Prince Charles from Oatlands to St James's. A fortnight later the boy returned to Richmond; from there he was sent for by the Queen to Oatlands, where his brothers and sisters were living.

Parliament at once commanded Hertford to bring him back. Henrietta Maria immediately dispatched him to Richmond, where she and the Princess Elizabeth joined him. To the Commons' objections she replied that all the Prince's attendants were Protestants, that he was merely spending a short time with her and his sister in order to celebrate the Princess's birthday, and that she had kept and would continue to keep her promise to the King not to attempt the conversion of any of their children. Naturally she believed what she said; her basic belief – that the Church of England was a rubbishy affair and that in her own faith lay the only way to salvation – could not possibly have been subordinated, as her subsequent behaviour proved. And the contemporary judgment that she had 'an immoderate desire of power', while continuing to enslave her husband, could not be gainsaid, even by her supporters.

These disputes, the imprisonment of her confessor, the imminence of civil war, the outbreaks during Strafford's trial and thirteen years of difficult and dangerous births had destroyed Henrietta Maria's beauty. She was still graceful and lively; but she had become sallow, grey-haired and emaciated; her protruding teeth, and the long, drooping nose and too heavy chin inherited by, and exaggerated in, all her children, were now painfully conspicuous. Not even Van Dyck could disguise the fact that, with the exception of the Princess Mary and the eight-year-old Duke of York, the royal family were a plain lot. Prince Charles's vitality and intelligence, his graceful bearing and the brilliance of his black eyes made up for his dark skin and coarse features; but no one, however charmed by his address, could have described him as a handsome child.

Meanwhile, his education was culturally and intellectually in abeyance; the general atmosphere of disturbance, coupled with his being perpetually on the move, made it impossible for him to concentrate on his lessons. Newcastle's warning – 'take heed of too much book' – was fully, if inadvertently, obeyed; for England was now on the brink of civil war, and the Prince's schooling about to enter another sphere.

NOTES

1 Clarendon, p. 937.
2 L. Aikin, *Memoirs of the Court of King Charles the First*, pp. 130–40.
3 C. V. Wedgwood, *Thomas Wentworth First Earl of Strafford*, p. 337.
4 Strickland, *Tudor and Stuart Princesses*, p. 253.
5 Ibid.
6 *Cal. S. P. Ven.*, vol. XXV, p. 151.
7 Strickland, ibid.

CHAPTER SIX

THE END OF PEACE

I

IT was characteristic of Charles I that while seeming to be on fairly good terms with the Covenanters – who received him in Edinburgh during the autumn of 1641 – he was maturing his plans for defeating both them and his enemies in England by the enforcement of religious uniformity and of his own absolutism throughout the kingdom. The fact that he had had to sacrifice Strafford merely strengthened his conviction that he had made a mistake out of weakness. He often told Prince Charles that he had been undone by his concessions.[1] The effect of this statement was in some respects the opposite of what he intended. While Charles I maintained his habit of pretending to submit in order not to do so, his son soon learnt to accept the inevitable (as he had when the Lords refused to read his father's letter) and to substitute one scheme for another.

Prince Charles not only loved but was entirely loyal to his father; yet at some point early in life he seems to have realized that the King was hopelessly misguided, not so much by deceiving those who trusted him, as by deceiving them so ineptly that they saw through him before he could use them. Thus the Prince's policy of not lying until it was essential and then lying in such a manner as not easily to be detected, may have been formulated during the months preceding the Civil War.

The King returned from Scotland to the enthusiastic welcome of the City fathers, who feasted him, the Queen and their three eldest children at the Guildhall. Those in Court and Parliament circles knew well that further trouble lay ahead. In the first week of January 1642 the King attempted and failed to arrest Pym and four other members of the Commons for high treason. Their escape and Parliament's triumph emboldened Lord Newport to suggest that the Queen and Prince Charles should be 'secured' as hostages for the King's good faith. The King replied by leaving Whitehall, preparatory to taking the field against his rebellious subjects. He was not to see it again till the morning of his execution. Both he and the Prince – who returned to it after eighteen years of war and exile – believed that they would be resuming life there in a few months, when the struggle was over and Parliament subdued. They left in such a hurry that when they arrived at Hampton Court Palace nothing was ready; Charles and his parents had to sleep in one bed;[2] so the contrast between this and other moves was poignantly, perhaps frighteningly, emphasized. In that perfectly ordered household such a thing had never happened before.

The King and the Prince then left for Greenwich, where they were joined by the Queen of Bohemia's sons, the Elector Palatine, and Prince Rupert, newly released from his Austrian prison. Prince Charles was immensely impressed by the younger, better-looking, rather solemn German cousin, who had had so many adventures; from that moment their friendship was established.

The King then took the Prince to Theobalds, leaving Hertford, whom Parliament trusted, at Greenwich. There the Court remained until March, when Pembroke was sent by the Lords to ask the King to give Parliament control of the army 'for a time', to which he replied, 'By God, not for an hour!'[3]

By now the Royalist progress northwards had been decided on, and both sides were preparing for war. The breach between King and Parliament was complete. The Queen left for Holland with Princess Mary. Prince Charles and his suite were to accompany the King to York, via Cambridge, Huntingdonshire and the Midlands.

Prince Charles was in the highest spirits. He had entered the world of action; his lessons were virtually at an end; there could be no doubt about the speedy and victorious conclusion of his father's cause; and wherever he went he was not only acclaimed with rapture but treated as a grown person. No public duties, however solemn and prolonged, seemed tedious. His visit to Cambridge was a series of triumphs, and he enjoyed every moment of it.

He arrived at Peterhouse on the morning of March 21st, with a suite which included his cousin the Duke of Richmond and Lennox, the thirteen-year-old Duke of Buckingham, Lord Francis Villiers and Lord Hertford. The Vice-Chancellor received him with an address in Latin and gave him and the Villiers their honorary degrees. Charles was presented with one pair of gloves by the Vice-Chancellor and another by Dr Comber; he then proceeded to King's, where the Provost made another Latin speech and gave him a Bible. During the service in King's Chapel the Prince appeared unaware of the staring undergraduates; he did not cover his face with his hat when he knelt to pray; this unconventional behaviour was considered rather charming.

He was then conducted to Regent House, where he sat under a canopy on a throne and listened to a number of orations. After dinner he went on to Trinity. Here the undergraduates played *The Guardian*, which Cowley had written for the occasion. 'You are our morning star,' the Prologue began, 'and shall be our sun.' The play lasted three hours, and even the performers found it so dull that they were in some anxiety as to His Highness's reception of it. He applauded vigorously, and 'gave', says an eye-witness, 'all signs of acceptance which he could, and more than the University dared expect'. Another play, Vincent's *Paria*, followed, and was received by the Prince with the same enthusiasm. The delighted audience then surged out of the hall to escort him to his coach, and he left to join the King at Newmarket, where they spent Sunday quietly together.

On Monday Prince Charles and his father entered Cambridge and stopped at Trinity, where the King was greeted by shouts of '*Vivat Rex!*', a Latin speech and the gift of a Bible. Preceded by the beadles, who in their excitement carried their staves upside down, they walked from Trinity to St John's, where a stand-up meal was awaiting them. Two more speeches were made, and it was then observed that Prince Charles was wearing the gloves given him by the Vice-Chancellor – and the echo of Newcastle's voice is recalled. ('Certainly, Sir, civility cannot unprince you, but much advantage you.') The King ate almost nothing, but took some of the sweetmeats from the trays which were being handed round and told his son to put them in his pocket for the journey into Hunting-donshire. As soon as he left the hall the courtiers fell upon the remains of the feast and finished up everything.[4]

As the King left Cambridge his coach was surrounded by the towns-folk, 'humbly and earnestly' begging him to 'return to your Parliament, or we shall be undone'. These pleas were, naturally, ignored by the ruler who 'thought the difference between him and his subjects so great that he would not condescend to humour his Parliaments, and could so ill brook any contradictions from them ... that he chose to part from them in anger'.[5]

II

It was at about this time that the epithets of 'Cavalier' and 'Roundhead' came into everyday use. The first had a slightly sinister connotation, for it derived from the Spanish *caballero*, which the Parliamentarians chose to mean a Roman Catholic trooper and persecutor of Protestants. The

Royalists retaliated by associating their enemies with the crop-headed London apprentices, whose rioting and storming had marked every stage of the conflict between King and Parliament, and whose murderous violence was partly the cause of his leaving the capital.

When Charles and his father left Cambridge for Huntingdonshire the opprobrium attached to their followers' nickname was forgotten; and their troop of richly dressed riders, among whom were the Elector Palatine and the Duke of Richmond and Lennox, epitomized the romantic aspect of the Cavalier as seen by Van Dyck and later reproduced in pictures of a more naively sentimental school. ('When Did You Last See Your Father?')

At some point in their progress the King realized that they would pass Little Gidding, where another 'great book' had been ordered for his son, and he decided to pay the Ferrars and their ladies a surprise visit. He reached the house a little in advance of the Prince, who galloped up as his father was holding out his hand to be kissed. 'Seeing that,' Nicholas Ferrar recalls, 'he did the like.'

The royal party first visited the chapel. Returning to the house, His Majesty asked to see the Prince's book which, not quite finished, was produced and laid on a table. 'Sir,' said Richmond, 'one of your strongest guard will but be able to carry this book.' 'Well – it is very well done,' said the King, as he opened it. 'Charles, here is a book that contains excellent things. It will make you both wise and good.' Turning over the pages, he began to explain the illustrations, which were copies of famous pictures, many of them in his own collections. The Prince said nothing; his bright dark eyes were fixed on the book. 'It is a jewel only for a prince,' his father went on; 'Charles, make good use of it.' 'Sir,' added his Palatine cousin, 'you will be master of the gallantest great book in the world,' and the Duke of Richmond put in, 'It is a most admirable piece.'

The King then shut the book and put it back on the table. 'Charles,' he said, 'this is yours –' but did not hand it over. 'But Sir,' the boy burst out, 'shall I not now have it with me?' One of the Ferrars intervened. 'If it please Your Highness, the book is not on the outside so finished as it is intended.' 'You must content yourself for a while,' remarked the King.

The visitors then inspected the alms-houses where the King left five gold pieces for distribution. From there they were conducted to the parlour; the Prince Palatine and the Duke followed the ladies to the buttery, where apple pies and cheesecakes were laid ready. Returning with these to the parlour, they found the Prince of Wales waiting for his father, who was in another room. 'Sir, will Your Highness taste?' said one. 'It is as good apple pie as we ate.' The Prince laughed, but did not eat till wine was brought and he was served on the knee. Then the King reappeared. 'It grows late,' he said. 'The sun is going down, we must away.'

At the doorway he turned, held out his hand and took off his hat. Ferrar saw that he was troubled. 'Pray,' he said, 'pray for my speedy and safe return again.' So they all rode away into the dusk.

As they crossed the park the King saw a sitting hare and called to Richmond for his fowling-piece. He shot and wounded the creature, who set up a pitiful crying and ran a little way, then fell. Immediately the Prince jumped from his horse, waded through a couple of ditches, found the animal and put it out of its misery. Then he returned, laughing at the little adventure, to his father. As their hosts watched them go one decided to ride after them as far as the village. Here the people ran out of their cottages to cry, 'God bless Prince Charles!' There was no greeting for his father; yet he had not parted from them, as from his Parliament, in ange .[6]

The King's pessimistic mood had nothing to do with the outcome of what he had to face. Naturally, the Royalist party would be victorious – but he himself must lead them into battle; and this might result in the kingdom's being ruled by Henrietta Maria until Prince Charles reached his majority. He was not afraid to die; but the possibility of his being killed created a situation of which the Prince was the central figure. The twelve-year-old boy must now learn to lead his people in war: yet his safety was vital to his father's cause. This also applied to the little Duke of York. The King had to arrange for both children to share in the struggle while eliminating all risk of their being wounded or, worse still, captured and used against him.

For the advanced group whose intention at this time was to reform the structure of the monarchy, the possession of Prince Charles's person was equally important. Throughout the political fluctuations of the Civil War and the Protectorate there existed a minority whose aim was to install him, not even as a puppet king, but as a constitutional ruler, trained to co-operate as well as to command. Thus, before he reached his teens, Charles became aware of his own potentialities and of the use he might make of them, not only by subservience, but by diplomacy and intrigue.

Newcastle's advice about what James I called kingcraft reads like an accompaniment to the northern progress when Prince Charles, now always at his father's side, saw him receive an empty homage. The people's acclamation, Newcastle had said, was sometimes like a mist which hides resistance. 'Authority,' he explained, 'doth what it list, I mean power that's the stronger, tho' sometimes it shifts sides. Therefore the King must know at what time to play the King and when to qualify it.' It was as if New-castle, far away in the city that bore his name, had seen his master at York when Sir Thomas Fairfax, kneeling to present him with a petition, was rebuffed by the King turning his horse so sharply that Fairfax was knocked over and badly bruised.[7]

Here the Prince was made Captain of his father's Guard and given a regiment of cavalry. From York the Royalist army went to Nottingham, where the King held a chapter of the Garter and raised the royal standard. After opening negotiations with the Prince of Orange for Prince Charles's marriage with his eldest daughter, he proceeded to Shrewsbury and Chester; both cities presented His Highness with a purse of £100. Charles then left his father and went to Raglan in Hertford's charge.

Here he was received by Lord Worcester and Sir Hugh Vaughan at Raglan Castle. All the rooms were hung with tapestry, 'full of lively figures and ancient British stories'. A banquet was served in which 'metheglin and other British drinks were plentifully afforded'. Then the procession of those bringing gifts began.

In this wild place there was nothing available to give the Prince but what the inhabitants, simple or noble, already possessed. Some brought antique pieces of plate, on which their own arms were engraved; the more prosperous commoners appeared with 'young kids, sheep, calves, fish, fowl and fat oxen'. Sir Hugh Vaughan then rose amid this mêlée of offerings to address His Highness. 'We have no happiness nor hope but what we derive from your gracious aspect,' he began, and after a short discourse on these lines, concluded, 'The Prince we now behold with tears of joy.'

There was a pause. All eyes were fixed on the slight boyish figure under the canopy. Then Prince Charles stood up to make the first speech of his career.

'Gentlemen,' he said, 'I have heard formerly of the great minds, the true affections and meanings of the ancient Britannies – but my kind entertainment hath made me confide in your love, which I shall always remember. I give you commendations, praise and thanks for your love, your bounty and liberal entertainment. I know' – did he hesitate for a moment? – 'you desire nothing but thanks. You shall be sure of that, and of my favour, as long as I am Prince of Wales.'[8]

Thereafter his progress through Radnorshire was a triumph. He showed himself, says an eye-witness, 'very gracious and loving' to everybody. The country people wept to see him go.

NOTES

1 Bishop G. Burnet, *History of My Own Time*, vol. I, p. 53.
2 Law, vol. II, p. 128.
3 *Cal. S. P. Ven.*, vol. XXV, p. 272.
4 A. Cooper, *Annals of Cambridge*, vol. III, pp. 321–2.
5 Carte, *Ormonde*, vol. I, p. 355.
6 Mayor, pp. 149–50.
7 Carte, vol. I, p. 357.
8 J. R. Phillips, *Memoirs of the Civil War in Wales and in the Marches, 1642–1649*, vol. I, p. 118.

CHAPTER SEVEN

FOUR YEARS OF WAR

I

'BEFORE the Civil War,' Aubrey noted, 'the fashion was for old women and maids to tell fabulous stories night-times, of sprites and walking of ghosts ... When the wars came, and with them liberty of conscience ... the phantoms vanished. Now children ... are not checked with such fears.'[1]

As the antiquarian jotted down that rather sweeping statement (for when did nursemaids cease to frighten children?) he was re-creating the mythical good times to which elderly persons return in fancy; then, all issues were clear-cut, all losses and gains definite, and all young people properly disciplined.

Neither the Earl of Newcastle, nor the Marquess of Hertford, nor kind Dr Earle, nor even the doting Mrs Wyndham had ever invoked the aid of the supernatural to overawe their charge; in that circle, such methods were already out of date. In a practical sense, he grew up fearless and remained so. But in his thirteenth year he was thrust into the confused, uncertain battle of Edgehill, in which both sides were to claim a victory which neither achieved. So he became vaguely aware of the phantoms of doubt and irresolution rising about him. Before that misty October morning of 1642, when he saw the rebel army massed below the slope of the pleasant Warwickshire fields, Charles had heard the herald stumble over the words of his father's illegibly corrected proclamation; he had seen the Royalist standard, blown down by the wind, lying unheeded in the mud; and he had waited for his little brother of York to return, humiliated, from a futile attempt to occupy Hull, now a Roundhead stronghold. All that time he had been subjected to restlessness, indecision, changing of plans – while nothing happened. There was no fighting, except for his cousin Rupert's sensational routing of the Parliamentary horse at Powicke, no news of final triumph or disaster. To an eager, excitable, increasingly belligerent schoolboy, those months must have seemed endless and intensely bewildering. No war in his history books was like this one, not even that of the Roses. The enemy hovered, infiltrated, then disappeared;

the Cavaliers argued, acknowledging no single authority; the Royalist troops were ill armed, badly fed and increasingly discouraged; and his father seemed 'more concerned in the drawing of a paper than in fighting a battle'.[2]

Then at last, King Charles, halting for the night at Southam on his march to London, received a message from Rupert of the Rhine. The enemy was some seven miles away, in a plain 'convenient for a battle'. The twenty-three-year-old general had already proved his system of attack. Now it must be carried out on the grand scale.

On the morning of the 23rd the trumpets sounded, and the camp became a mass of hurrying men, plunging horses and creaking cannon. The King left his tent and mounted his charger. Slowly the magnificent array formed and began to stream across the flat wooded country. First came the cavalry, clanking, splendid, elaborately accoutred, then the foot, then a brilliant scarlet banner, 'larger than ordinary', to advertise His Majesty's presence and leadership. He was attended by his cousins of Richmond and d'Aubigny and his standard-bearer, Sir Edmund Verney. The little Princes rode just behind him and were followed by a plumed and glittering cavalcade – Seymours, Montagues, Sackvilles, Howards – their curled lovelocks flowing over their damascened breast-plates and the point-lace cravats which Rupert had just made fashionable. Behind them, preceding the bulk of the army, came the soberly dressed, inconspicuous figures of Dr William Harvey and Dr John Hinton.

The ensuing delay must have further irritated and puzzled Prince Charles. Again, nothing happened till three in the afternoon, when Rupert's horse charged and routed the Parliamentary right wing. The reserve Royalist cavalry, seeing this, pursued them, with the result that the King and his sons were abandoned by all but the foot; in the fighting their ranks became confused and they began to retreat. Before riding in to rally them, the King told Sir William Howard to retire with the Princes; according to a Royalist eye-witness, 'the great bullets often fell near the King and them, and some passed over their heads, [so] that His Majesty was often importuned to draw off further, but by no means would, and presently rode away into the head ranks.'[3]

Before entering the fight the King told the Duke of Richmond to remove, with the Princes, to the top of the slope. Richmond refused; he would not give up his share of the battle. Desperately, the King turned to Dorset, who 'answered him with an oath. "I will not be thought a coward for the sake of any King's sons in Christendom," he said, "and therefore humbly desire Your Majesty to commit that charge to some other man." ' Finally the boys, with Dr Harvey, took refuge, first in a barn, where several wounded men were lying, and then under a hedge.⁴

As soon as they were out of sight of the enemy, Dr Harvey ('always very contemplative and curious in anatomy') took a medical book from his pocket and became absorbed. Then a bullet tore up the ground at his feet, and he removed his charges to a field – much to Charles's disappointment, for he was armed with a pistol and had counted on using it.⁵

At this point the Royalist foot began to retreat, having endured the Roundhead attacks for some three hours. Dr Hinton, returning to look for the Princes, saw that Charles had mounted his pony and was alone, facing an enemy troop of horse, who now bore down upon him. Hinton managed to cut them off and ordered the Prince to withdraw. By this time the Roundheads were within shooting distance. Charles's moment had come. 'I fear them not!' he shouted, and, wild with excitement, dragged out his pistol and levelled it at the oncoming horsemen. Hinton seized the Prince's rein and interposing himself between him and the enemy, fired into the centre of the troop. As one fell, they hesitated; then another man advanced. Hinton wounded him and he dismounted. Still the rest came on: and still the Prince was struggling with his weapon. Then, to Hinton's speechless relief, they were joined by one of the Gentleman-Pensioners, who with his pole-axe charged the Roundhead squadron and beat them off.⁶

A general retreat of both armies followed, while the panting physician dragged His Highness from the field and returned him to Dr Harvey. An hour later the King joined them in the village of Edgecot. He then returned to inspect the camp, 'where he stayed all night, giving order ... as occasion required'. As darkness fell he sent instructions that his sons should retire to their lodgings at Kineton. On the following afternoon they returned to the field of Edgehill.

So Prince Charles had his first sight of death and agony. Of the six hundred casualties the majority were lying where they had fallen; most of the wounded were waiting to be carried away. And the Roundhead army was still there, weakened but by no means routed. 'We found all things preparing for another battle,' says Lord Bernard Stuart, who accompanied the Princes, ' ... and the enemy ... expected us again ... But His Majesty thought it better for that time to draw away his army.'

In theory, the King should have attacked; indeed, Prince Rupert urged him to do so. The state of his troops, shivering, discouraged and half starved – for the commissariat had been shockingly mismanaged – made this impossible; and he was in any case still hoping for an agreement

CHARLES I AND HENRIETTA MARIA

THE CHILDREN OF CHARLES I

CHARLES II AT FOURTEEN

which would end the war. The deaths of d'Aubigny, Richmond's younger brother, and of Sir Edmund Verney may have enforced his desire to avoid killing any more of his subjects and to effect a compromise by outwitting or winning over the men who had sent them to fight against him, and who now had control of London, Hull and the navy. It was well for him that Lord Essex, whose generalship of the Parliamentary army had been dogged but uninspired, was equally unwilling to advance again.

Having knighted Dr Hinton and made him physician in ordinary to the Prince, King Charles continued his march on London, now fortified against him. After some fierce but indeterminate fighting at Brentford and Turnham Green, the Royalists withdrew to make Oxford their winter headquarters. In November the King and his sons went to Reading, where Prince Charles developed measles. His father waited for him to recover and then returned to Oxford. Here Dr Harvey, who had been much disturbed by the destruction, during the occupation of Whitehall, of all his notes for his new book of medical discovery, resumed his experiments undisturbed. And here the Prince, reunited with both parents – for Henrietta Maria had returned from Holland with arms and money – came under the influence of three persons, all temperamentally opposed and bitterly antagonistic to one another, with the result that their domination of his development became one of the prizes in their private war.

II

Apart from the fact that he was quicker witted and more intuitive than most boys of his age, Prince Charles was not phenomenally advanced; when he entered his teens there was no sign of the far-sightedness and self-control so brilliantly exercised as he reached manhood. His first apprenticeship as a diplomat and a leader began just before his thirteenth birthday and lasted for the next three years; by the time he was sixteen he had, as it were, passed his preliminary test with honours and become extremely capable, more so indeed than anyone about him realized. To those who had known him since childhood he was still the enthusiastic, light-hearted boy whose development as a Christian gentleman and a great King was inevitable and fore-ordained: the child of hope, of fervent prayer and of belief in the future.

Those who first came to know the Prince at this time found him spirited, amenable and as responsive to pleasure as to any other new experience. His reputation among persons who knew him only as a state figure was very high; many of his father's most obdurate enemies believed that in him lay their best hope of a peaceful and properly organized government. Nothing that he did or said between 1642 and 1646 caused them to change this view.

Thriving, as was natural, on this general esteem, Charles was gradually drawn away from family influences, partly because he saw very little of his mother, and partly because his father was too harassed and preoccupied to do more than use him as a figure-head. The King was devoted to his eldest son, as to all his children, of whom the seven-year-old Princess Elizabeth seems to have been his favourite; but he had no time to train him, and so left him in charge of those whom he instructed to 'unboy' his heir. Of these, Edward Hyde, now knighted and some years later Chancellor of the Exchequer, was the first choice, and Hertford the second. The Prince passively accepted Hyde and turned away from Hertford; he became subjugated by his cousin Rupert and, to a lesser degree, by George, Lord Goring, who had recently risen to a higher command.

During the twenty-odd years of his relationship with the Stuart family Hyde's political genius was recognized by himself, but not always by them. Indeed, most of his circle considered him trustworthy, indispensable, authoritative and dominating, but no more. Hyde's own account in his *History*, his autobiography and his correspondence gives the impression that he suffered from an ineradicable sense of grievance, one which was fully justified; he was constantly undervalued, even by his most loyal supporters. This was partly because his tactlessness and insensitivity to the feelings of others amounted to a disease. His energetic and many-sided intelligence found expression in ceaseless disquisitions on all subjects. Tireless and verbose, he could not understand that some of his hearers would never be convinced, however eloquently he spoke. He knew – and invariably pointed out – that he was right, because in nine cases out of ten he had been proved so. His grasp of a situation, his goodwill and his unassailable integrity were such that the Prince not only respected and liked him, but put up with his lectures and defended him against his enemies. As Charles saw more of Hyde and less of his father, the secretary began in some ways to take the King's place; for a time his relationship with his young master was serene.

George, Lord Goring cut a very different figure. Dissipated, reckless, arrogant, gross in his appetites and crudely cynical in his defence of them, he yet had what is now called personal magnetism, and this came into play in times of suspense and discouragement. To the bewildered, restless boy, who had been prevented, at the last moment, from taking an active part in his first battle, Goring appeared a dashing, attractive figure, who could make light of heroics as soon as they became tedious. This irresponsible fine gentleman both enjoyed and liked talking about women, eating and drinking; he could sing a catch with the best and was an accomplished swordsman; and he had a bold, careless way of getting out of awkward situations by acknowledging his own negligence which impressed, even while it may have shocked, the observant Prince.

The dislike and distrust aroused by Goring in Sir Edward Hyde paled before the contempt felt by Prince Rupert for him when Goring disobeyed his orders and they ceased to be allies. Haughty, bad-tempered, passionate and rude, Rupert had two useful virtues: he was utterly fearless, and deeply serious about his profession; there was little he did not know and could not practise in military matters. He left nothing to subordinates, never spared himself, was trusted by officers and men and incapable of intrigue, deceit or wanton cruelty, even when he was forced to be ruthless. These qualities were combined with striking and unusual beauty of person, great elegance of bearing and a range of talents stretching far beyond those of a prince or a soldier. He spoke six languages, was well read, a good artist, and knowledgeable in science and mathematics; in a word, it must have seemed to his young cousin – there were eleven years between them – as if there were nothing Rupert could not do: and the fact that his enemies called him Prince Robber and Rupert the Devil added to his legend. Above all, Rupert was completely, sometimes brutally, unconventional; and Charles, whose upbringing had been bounded by formality and etiquette, was stimulated by the harsh mockery, the discourteous interruptions and abrupt fault-finding which spared neither rank, age nor authority when the elder Prince chose to speak his mind.

Rupert grew very fond of and encouraged Charles, whom Goring flattered and amused; Hyde loved him, first for England's and his father's sake, and then for his own. Each of the three had a group of allies who during the early period of the Civil War centred on the King, then gradually turned towards his son. So their varying influences converged, combating one another.

These inner conflicts contributed to the process of disillusion. Although Prince Charles never ceased to feel that he represented a righteous cause, he became increasingly aware that some of those about him were completely self-interested, that others were prepared to change sides and that general agreement on tactics was out of the question. The case of Richard Feilding, Deputy Governor of Reading, not only showed Charles the divergence between Rupert and the King, but illustrated his own potentialities.

In May 1643 Colonel Feilding was found guilty of surrendering the city, and court-martialled. The King insisted on his being sentenced to execution. Rupert and Hyde considered the evidence insufficient and protested, with the result that Feilding was sent to the scaffold and reprieved at the last moment. Again the King asserted himself, and again Feilding went to the block. This time Rupert told Prince Charles to intercede with his father, which he did so eloquently that Feilding was finally released.[7]

So it was that when he and the King joined Henrietta Maria at Wroxton before returning to Oxford the Prince had been made to feel his power; a month later he was again treated as a child, while helplessly contemplating disaster. From August 10th Gloucester was besieged by the Royalists; there seemed every chance of their capturing the city before the Roundhead relief arrived. The King spent the day with his army, sometimes sleeping under canvas. Charles and James were sent to Matson House, a few miles away. On one occasion their host had to leave them alone there. He ushered them into an upper room and departed, after locking the door and barring the windows; here they remained the whole day, with nothing to do – no books, no games; so they got out their daggers and carved their initials all over the panelling. These depredations were long treasured by the owners of Matson House.[8]

On September 5th Gloucester was relieved and the Royalists retreated. A few days later the King, resting by the roadside on his way back to Oxford, sat silent between his sons. They were alone; and the sense of defeat overcame his optimism. One of the little boys said, 'When are we to go home?' The King replied, 'We have no home.'[9]

Neither Charles nor James appears to have referred to that moment in after years. Its effect, whether that of fear, disbelief or simply bewilderment, must have been emphasized when, six weeks later, they were told that Parliament had discontinued their revenues. In November, Henrietta Maria, now in the highest spirits and convinced that these set-backs were momentary, began negotiations for Prince Charles's marriage with Louis XIV's first cousin, Anne-Marie de Montpensier, La Grande Mademoiselle. This scheme was as unsuccessful as all her other plans for her eldest son; undaunted, she pursued it for the next nine years. By April 1644 she was seven months pregnant and withdrew to what was then the comparatively safe area of Exeter. The King and Prince Charles escorted her as far as Abingdon; here this tragic couple parted in tears, never to meet again. In June the Queen gave birth to her ninth child, the Princess Henrietta Anne.

Within a few weeks of Prince Charles's fourteenth birthday the King

suggested that he should become nominal head of the Western Association. Rupert objected to this, on the grounds that it would entail Charles's
being sent to Bristol and put in charge of the youngest Palatine Prince,
Maurice, then in command of that city. Rupert, who was devoted to his
brother, felt that this new responsibility would be too great; he preferred
to keep Charles under his own eye. He was supported by the Prince, who
refused, for the first time in his life, to obey his father. 'My cousin Rupert
left me my lesson,' he said, and told one of his gentlemen, a Mr Elliott, to
write to Rupert, now recruiting in Wales, that no one could love him
better than he did and that he was not going to give way. 'He will enterprise nothing,' Elliott added, 'wherein he has not Your Highness's approbation.' Charles's and Rupert's decision was supported by Richmond, and
the King yielded, merely remarking that Elliott had 'too much credit' with
his son.[10]

After a brief visit to Weymouth Charles returned to Oxford; from
there he, Richmond and the King passed unseen through the enemy lines
to Burford on their way to Worcester, where Charles fell ill. A few weeks
later he and his father were reunited at Oxford; then the King left for the
north. In the first week of July news came to Prince Charles that the
Royalists had been defeated at Marston Moor by the men whom Rupert
described as Cromwell's Ironsides. In the following week York was taken
by the Roundheads, Essex advanced on Exeter and Henrietta Maria fled
to France. Then the King, summoning Prince Charles, advanced to meet
Essex's army in Devonshire. At a great gathering on Dartmoor he introduced his son to the people as their future leader. Charles was rapturously
received, but no recruits came in. Essex retreated, and the King then
turned eastwards after dealing with a rebellious group of Cavaliers, who
wanted him to make peace and abdicate in the Prince's favour. Lord
Wilmot, afterwards Earl of Rochester and father of the poet, was their
spokesman. The King accused him of intriguing with Parliament, ordered
him to leave the country and put Goring, who was now drinking heavily,
in his place. Meanwhile, Henrietta Maria, despairing of Cardinal Mazarin's
consent to her son's marriage with La Grande Mademoiselle, again asked
the Prince of Orange for his sister's hand and was politely snubbed.

All this time Charles's lessons were at a standstill. Hertford was in the
field, and no one filled his place till the Earl of Berkshire was appointed as
the Prince's Governor. When Hyde pointed out that this nobleman was
totally unsuited for the post, the King replied that he himself would be responsible for his son's education and that Berkshire's appointment was
honorary.[11] In fact, the boy had entered a school in which his father would

not have passed the first grade. Prince Charles's lessons were infiltrated rather than taught, every day and every hour that he spent with the Cavaliers or travelling about the countryside. As he began to perceive his value, he said nothing, and made few gestures of independence; already he had learned to watch and wait till the moment came for him to assert himself; now he knew how to use his own mistrust of those about him, and how to exploit treachery and vanity. So, unwittingly, he passed beyond his father's teaching and began to discount the King's opinions.

Early in 1645 the King opened negotiations for Prince Charles's marriage to the Infanta Catherine of Braganza. Then he began to curtail Rupert's powers as Generalissimo of the Royalist forces by arranging for him and Charles to form a separate command in the West. Rupert disapproved of the plan; Charles was eager to go. The King decided that his son should hold his Court at Bristol under the jurisdiction of Hyde, Richmond, Berkshire and the Earls of Hopton, Capel and Colepepper. He was not to 'engage himself in any martial action', but to recruit in Dorset, Devonshire and Cornwall while officially taking over Rupert's command; in fact, he would be his cousin's pupil. This scheme not only added unnecessarily to Rupert's responsibilities, but permanently split the Royalist party. The King then announced that he could not finance his son's Court; the expenses would fall on his Council; he himself could only spare three hundred horse as an escort.[12]

So it was that within three months of his fifteenth birthday Charles achieved manhood and independence. On March 5th he left Oxford in pouring rain and slept at Faringdon. Next day he reached Devizes, passing through Bath on his way to Bristol. He never saw his father again.

NOTES

1 Aubrey, pp. 8–9.
2 Burnet, *History*, vol. I, p. 86.
3 Ellis, series 2, vol. III, p. 304.
4 J. S. Clarke, *Life of James II*, vol. I, p. 12.
5 Sir John Hinton, *Memoirs*, pp. 7–13.
6 Gardiner, *Civil War*, vol. I, p. 151.
7 Sir Nathaniel Wraxall, *Historical Memoirs*, vol. II, p. 288.
8 Gardiner, *Civil War*, vol. I, p. 206.
9 E. Scott, *Rupert Prince Palatine*, p. 142.
10 Clarendon, p. 455.
11 Aikin, vol. II, p. 449; Scott, p. 159; Hoskins, pp. 305–6.
12 Gardiner, *Civil War*, vol. I, pp. 181–2.

CHAPTER EIGHT

DEFEAT IN THE WEST

I

THE first weeks of Charles's command were comparatively happy. In the portrait painted of him at about this time he seems to radiate cheerfulness and determination, while revelling in his martial pose and the symbols of victory shown by Anarchy sinking beneath his feet and the smoke of battle fading in the distance. He shared his father's belief that the rebels would shortly be defeated, as did Newcastle, now exiled in Germany. 'It is no small comfort,' he wrote to Charles, 'that ... we have lived to see you a man; and could I see but peace in our Israel, truly then I care not how soon death closes my eyes.' The proudest and most independent of the Cavaliers ended his letter on the note that was to become part of a wearisome chorus in his pupil's correspondence. 'But whilst I crawl here in this uneven world ... it is your turn to take care of me.'

There could be no answer to such an appeal. The Prince's Council were in despair about his finances; none of the supplies promised them had come in; and they spent the greater part of the time arguing about tactics and intriguing for position. Hyde insisted that His Highness should attend these discussions 'to mark and consider the state of affairs and to accustom himself to speaking and judging upon what was said'. The boy fulfilled his hopes when he gave audience to the Somerset commissioners who came to complain of the 'riots and insolences' of Goring's troops. 'I am very sensible of these disorders,' he said, adding that he would put things right as soon as the commissioners obliged him with men and money.

A summons for a general meeting at Bridgwater for April 23rd was then sent out, and it was suggested that Charles should spend the intervening days in Wales, where he was eagerly expected. Rupert, who was recruiting there, advised him to stay where he was, with the result that the elder Prince's enemies in the Council said he was afraid of his young cousin's popularity. 'Such is the jealousy of great princes, though the house be on fire,' wrote one, and others professed themselves disgusted at Rupert for urging a negotiated peace when he visited the King at Oxford.[1]

On April 11th Rupert reached Bristol to find everyone at loggerheads

71

about their respective duties, while complaints of Goring's troops continued. Advised by Hyde, Charles gave Goring's command to Sir Richard Grenvile. At first Goring refused to obey; then he sent his foot to join Grenvile at Taunton; he withheld his cavalry, while he himself retired to Bath for a cure. 'Well, you generals are a strange kind of people,' said Hyde contemptuously; he then told Charles that Goring was jealous of Rupert, while making it clear that he himself disapproved of all Rupert's schemes.[2]

During the week he spent at Bridgwater Charles renewed his relationship with Mrs Wyndham, whose husband was Governor there. His former nurse – who had nothing of the woman about her, Hyde observed, but a fleshy exterior – at once took advantage of the Prince's affection by thrusting herself into his company and showing off her power over him in public. She kept him away from Council meetings and spoke 'negligently and scornfully' of his advisers. The Prince appeared not to heed these criticisms; he may have found them amusing, nevertheless; and he did listen to her pleas for grants of land, in spite of the fact that he was not supposed to promise anything without the consent of the Council. Hyde urged him to stand firm; Mrs Wyndham, hearing of this, proceeded to make further mischief by tale-bearing and back-biting, so that quarrels about places and precedence grew daily more enraged. Then she began to insinuate to the Prince that his father was responsible for all their disasters; he appears to have heard her without comment; Hyde failed to find out whether he believed her or not. The horrified Council reported her to the King, who desired his son to return immediately to Bristol. Here Charles was approached by Goring, who asked for an overall command in the West, Sussex and Kent; he was given a half-promise of consent on condition that he reformed his troops; a few weeks later they were behaving as badly as ever. The Prince then had to soothe a deputation of volunteers, who complained that they had been underpaid and brutally treated. He did this very well; he was becoming an adept at making promises; no doubt he was still under the impression that he would be able to fulfil them.

Meanwhile some of the Council had decided to deprive Goring of his command; warned by his friends, he at once made his plans. Drunken and lazy though he was, he could still persuade and wheedle, still present himself as an invaluable officer; this was partly because the licence he allowed his troops and his courage in action had made him popular in the ranks; and he knew that if he did not remain with his men they would desert. He therefore began by making up his quarrel with Prince Rupert;

he then managed to persuade the King that he should be reinstated, and crowned this triumph by forming an alliance, against the Prince of Wales's Council, with Sir Richard Grenvile, formerly his rival and successor.

That Goring's machinations – carried on between bouts of drunkenness and equally incapacitating courses of physic – should have been even temporarily successful, now seems inexplicable. Yet such was the case. One of the most curious aspects of the situation was the power he exercised over Grenvile, a similarly arrogant and corrupt intriguer, who remained with the Royalists for what he could get out of them. In fact, their professional relationship was like that of a married couple who, while quarrelling incessantly, cannot, for practical reasons, do without one another. Goring ruled the roost; as far as Prince Charles was concerned, there was little to choose between him and Grenvile. Yet they had to be employed because there was no one else the troops would follow and whom Prince Rupert could spare.

By the beginning of May Charles was beginning openly to rebel against his father's orders. Hyde's insistence on his working daily with the Council and with the officers under their command had given him a clearer insight than the King could ever have developed; although he knew and understood the general situation, Charles was still obedient and respectful; he took no steps without his father's permission. But when his requests were refused or ignored he now, as the King bitterly observed, grumbled at having to yield, and did not attempt to conceal his displeasure from the Council. So it was very natural that some of his advisers began to believe that he would consent to take his father's place. If they persuaded him to do so, they could then treat with Parliament and end the war.

Their first opening came when Charles, having left Bristol because of an outbreak of plague, settled at Barnstaple. Here he could ride and sail almost at will. Idolized by the people, he was in high spirits – until, on May 10th, Goring appeared with a letter from the King revoking every arrangement that had been made. The Prince's request that John Grenvile, Richard's brother, should become one of his gentlemen was refused, no reason being given. Goring and Sir Richard Grenvile were to have equal command of the army, while Goring was to give orders to, instead of receiving them from, the Council; and Charles himself was no longer to have even a nominal command but to be immured in a garrison, preferably one in the neighbourhood of Bristol.

The Prince's desire to employ John Grenvile, which may have been partly inspired by Hyde, shows a certain prescience; for this member of a famous family not only remained devoted to the Royalist cause until the Restoration, but became one of the few efficient agents for it during Charles's exile. John Grenvile had been left for dead during the second battle of Newbury; when the Prince left England he continued to work for him at the risk of his life and without any reward. They were not now to meet again for some fourteen years.

The lamentations and complaints of the Prince's advisers, although loud and prolonged, were not those of rebels. The King's commands were being obeyed when ten days later he wrote again, ordering Goring to join him in Northamptonshire, transferring his command to Lord Hopton and commanding the Prince to remove at once to Bristol. A reply was sent pointing out the risk of returning to that city and asking that Goring might stay in the West in order to besiege Taunton. This letter did not reach the King, who was now on his way north, so the Council instructed Goring to march on Taunton, where he failed to raise the siege. Again there were furious complaints of his troops and again he was ordered to control them, with no result.

On June 14th, 1645, the Royalist cause suffered final defeat at the battle of Naseby. When the news reached Charles's Council they did not grasp the whole extent of the disaster, partly because several weeks passed before they heard the details, and partly because they were dealing with a plot to set the Prince against the King.

Bishop Duppa, now one of the Prince's chaplains, complained to the Council that a young man called Wheeler, who had somehow got leave to enter Charles's private apartments, must be dismissed; he was dissipated, insolent and suspected of homosexual tendencies. When examined, Wheeler retaliated by giving away three of his confederates, one of whom had said he was ready to kill the King in order to put Charles in his place. The charge was denied, Charles imprisoned Wheeler and reported the whole matter to his father, who was now in Hereford.

After further angry correspondence with Goring and Richard Grenvile Charles wrote to the King asking for full powers, replaced Grenvile by Sir John Berkeley and summoned Grenvile to meet him and the Council at Liskeard. Defiant and sullen, Grenvile alternated between asking for a court-martial and refusing to give up his powers. 'What authority have you now to command?' said Charles sternly. 'I am high sheriff of Devon.' Grenvile at once joined Goring, who took him under his protection, reinstating him without the Council's leave. Then Charles received the first of a series of letters from the King in which the consequences of total defeat were revealed.

'Charles,' he began, 'it is very fit for me now to prepare for the worst ...
Wherefore know that my pleasure is, whensoever you find yourself in
apparent danger of falling into the rebels' hands, that you convey yourself
into France, and there to be under your mother's care; who is to have the
absolute full power of your education in all things, except religion; in
that, not to meddle at all, but to leave it entirely to the care of ... Bishop
[Duppa].' The King required instant obedience, 'without grumbling', and
signed himself 'Your loving father, Charles R.'[3]

II

Shortly after the battle of Naseby Rupert joined Prince Charles in the
hope of making a stand in the West. He himself felt that a negotiated peace
was the only solution; for Fairfax's army was now gradually closing in,
with the result that Charles retreated to Launceston, where he spent 'a
tedious cold winter', trying, unsuccessfully, to raise recruits. He hated
this inactivity and urged the Council to let him advance on Fairfax with
such troops as remained, but they would not let him risk capture, and
preferred that he should go to Exeter to have it out with Goring, who had
ignored their letters and was making no attempt to carry on the campaign.
While Charles and Hyde were on their way there one of the King's
letters advising his son's flight to France was captured by the Roundheads,
who publicized it as a proof that the Royalist cause was lost.[4] A few weeks
later Rupert surrendered Bristol, upon which the King deprived him of
his command and told him to leave the country.

After a fruitless interview with Goring, who was now posing as an
invalid, Charles and Hyde returned to Launceston, where it was agreed
that negotiations with Parliament should be opened. Charles wrote to his
father to this effect, and to Fairfax, suggesting that Hopton and Colepepper should mediate. Meanwhile Bishop Duppa begged the King to
comply with some, at least, of Parliament's demands, if only for his son's
sake, whom he described as 'the darling and little eye of this kingdom',
comparing his piety to that of Edward VI. 'For his sweet sake,' he concluded, 'I am to beseech Your Majesty for a speedy accommodation.' The
King did not reply to these appeals – he may not have received them –
and Fairfax sent Charles's letter to Parliament, who ignored it, while
instructing him to crush the remaining Western resistance. The Council
were then warned by one of the Royalist exiles that if the Prince went
abroad it would be 'the certain ruin' of his cause.

In November Goring handed over his command to Lord Wentworth,

one of his boon companions, and left for France. When interviewed by
Charles and the Council, Wentworth, who was drunk, insulted Hyde and
refused to take their orders. 'Then I will take the command of the army
upon myself,' said the Prince. Wentworth began to apologize. 'Will you
submit or not?' said Charles sharply, and Wentworth muttered an assent.
Charles then left Launceston for Falmouth where he took a hand in forti-
fying Pendennis Castle, to the delight of the citizens; their only criticism
was that he seemed too lenient and easy-going; he even spoke in a friendly
manner to the Roundhead prisoners.[5]

All this time Fairfax had made no move towards a negotiated peace. In
December he wrote to Prince Charles, suggesting, in respectful and
affectionate terms, that he should affiliate himself with Parliament and
agree to depose his father. Charles was enraged. None of his Council had
ever seen him so angry. 'Rogues! Rebels!' he exclaimed. 'Are they not
content to be rebels themselves, but would have me in their number?' and
collected his scattered forces to advance on Fairfax from Tavistock.[6] The
Royalist night attack failed. By the middle of February 1646 Fairfax had
taken Dartmouth, Torrington and Launceston, while Charles, with a
handful of mutinous, starving troops, had retreated to Truro. Now he was
in imminent danger of being captured. He must fly – but where? Finally it
was agreed that he and his little Court should take refuge in the Scilly
Isles. Harassed, exhausted, but still calm and cheerful, he arrived there
within two months of his sixteenth birthday. His exile had begun. For
five years he did not return to the mainland.

NOTES

1 Carte, *A Collection of Original Letters and Papers*, vol. I, p. 77.
2 Gardiner, *Civil War*, vol. II, pp. 198–200.
3 Clarendon, p. 547.
4 Ibid.
5 Bulstrode, pp. 150–3.
6 *Portland MSS* (H.M.C.), vol. I, p. 328,

PART TWO

The Outcast

(MARCH 1646–JUNE 1650)

Thus hath the course of justice whirled about,
And left thee but a very prey to time;
Having no more but thought of what thou wert,
To torture thee the more, being what thou art.
Richard III

------◆◆◆◆◆------

CHAPTER ONE

TWO ISLANDS

I

THE voyage from Penzance to the Scillies lasted from the evening of March 10th to the morning of the 14th.[1] Charles's Councillors, crowded into the *Phoenix* frigate and enduring the miseries of sea-sickness, prayed for a following wind and escape from the Parliamentary fleet. The Prince, who was a good sailor, no doubt enjoyed the trip. Life on St Mary's might prove to be simple, even rough; but within those rocky confines he would at least be freer than on the mainland. At the moment of departure he was joined by Sir Richard Fanshawe, who had been one of his Council in Bristol. The King having forbidden any women to frequent his son's Court, Lady Fanshawe had then been left at home; now she and her gentlewomen boarded the *Phoenix* and stayed with the Prince in the medieval fortress-castle on top of the hill.

In her memoirs Lady Fanshawe, a spirited and uncomplaining person, makes it clear that the hardships of Scilly were worse than any of the exile. To begin with, the weather was appalling; when it rained the water came through the roof. The castle contained some half-dozen barely habitable rooms, and there was no fuel to warm them. She and Sir Richard had to climb a ladder in order to sleep in a loft where dried herrings were kept. The islanders, scraping a living from the soil, seldom ventured out to fish, and showed not the faintest interest in Prince Charles, or indeed in anything that was happening on the mainland. He received no welcome and very little food, and was constantly flooded out of the castle.

Hitherto his daily life, although perturbed and sometimes uncomfortable, had not been short of necessities; now he was often soaked and always hungry, but he did not complain. The Council, who had arrived with the intention of making a long stay, wrote to the Queen for provisions from France. Fairfax, guessing what the Prince's straits were, sent a messenger to suggest that he should return and discuss a treaty. The General's letter, Hyde thought, read like 'a summons rather than an invitation'. Parliament followed it up with what they described as 'a loving and tender' appeal to His Highness to come to London, where he would be well received, 'and reside in such place and have such attendants and counsellors ... as should be approved by both Houses'. In order to show that he would do well to accept, they sent a fleet to invade and capture the island. On the morning of April 14th Charles woke up to see some two dozen ships standing off St Mary's. A few hours later they were dispersed by a storm.[2]

A Council meeting was held, during which the question of leaving St Mary's for Jersey was discussed. Charles said nothing until everyone had finished speaking. Then he produced the King's letter, hidden since the preceding June, nine months ago, in which he was ordered to keep out of Parliament's hands at all costs, even that of his father's life.

Hyde was amazed – was this the only secret the boy had kept from him? He believed so: but he could not help feeling slight disapproval. Then Charles, 'with great earnestness', urged immediate departure to Jersey. This was agreed on, and he and Hyde withdrew to compose a reply to Parliament's invitation. This letter, a combination of vague promises, half-truths and diplomatic reassurance, was the first in a process of deception which lasted fourteen years. 'We have a great and earnest desire to be amongst you,' it began, 'if we might have any assurance that it might prove an expedient towards a blessed peace ... We are ... removing to Jersey, as being nearer to you and so fitter for correspondency.' The Prince added that he had no intention of leaving the kingdom (he was still considering departure to Ireland, whence he had been told that he could invade with an army of some 12,000 men) and asked for a safe conduct to the Channel Islands. The Houses described the letter as 'artful' and refused the safe conduct. By that time, Charles, followed by some three hundred Royalists from the mainland, had arrived in Jersey.[3]

The Prince and his Council sailed in *The Proud Black Eagle*, a frigate of a hundred and sixty tons, accompanied by their servants and six clergymen. The other vessels carried his Court, which now included tailors, cobblers, laundresses, carvers, doctors, four horses and a mass of stores. On the evening of April 16th the little fleet stood in to St Aubyn's Bay, where they were to disembark near the mole leading to Elizabeth Castle. None of the Council had ever set foot on the island. The extent of their preparations indicates that they expected Jersey to be a poor refuge, little better provided than the Scillies.

Within a few hours of landing they found themselves in a perfectly organized, fervently loyal community, run on semi-feudal lines, yet without squalor, cruelty or oppression. The fishermen and farmers were pious, hard-working and respectfully independent. The richness of the soil and the bays teeming with every kind of fish provided a varied and hearty diet for all classes. The second most important industry, knitting, occupied the women's leisure hours. The gentry, a respectable and highly civilized group, comfortably housed in medieval or sixteenth-century manor-houses surrounded by well-stocked gardens and streams running down to the sea, shot rabbits, plovers and hares; they took pride in their great libraries, their oak-panelled parlours and fashionable dress; for what the island could not provide was imported from England, France and Italy. Silks and velvets from Lyons, jewels from Paris and Rome, Buckingham-shire laces were set off by the stately manners of the great Queen's golden age and made the basis of an almost idyllic existence. All these amenities were displayed against a wild yet exotic background of grey, crimson and orange rock, purple seaweed, tropically luxuriant woodland and slopes strewn, at this time of the year, with primroses, periwinkles, eyebright and orchis. Jade-green waves broke over cream-coloured sands, fine as Egyptian dust, and fierce, blackish-brown archipelagos of toothed rock; yellow-eyed gulls, black-backs and kittiwakes beat in from the Atlantic, harshly complaining, or perching, arrogant and aloof, on the peaks below the gorges. Inland, the stretches of heath were grim, bleak and flat; but they were deserted.

In such a place, the older Cavaliers, yearning for the half-imagined, lost, good times, could realize their dreams; and in those dreams the slender, smiling, dark-haired Prince moved like the hero of a fairy-tale. The people rushed out of their white-washed cottages to kiss his hands, his feet, his stirrups, when he rode along the shore, calling to him in their clumsy French patois, cheering, crying for joy as he raised his plumed hat and bowed; the children's excited screams drowned the sea-birds' protests against this invasion. All, from the Carterets who had ruled for the English monarchs since the days of King John, to the poorest fisherman leaving his nets to stare at the great folk, had hoped that one day he might visit them; they had never expected that he would come to them in his distress, relying on their bounty and devotion. They poured out both, rejoicing in the presence of this delightful boy and in the magic of royalty. Because they had never seen a king or a queen, they welcomed their king's son as if he were a god. And he responded as freely, as warmly – yet with a touch of the melancholy Stuart dignity that was beginning to grow on him – as if he had always known them. It was natural to Charles to be adored. For a time – till he grew weary, impatient and bored – he was at home, contented, friendly, energetic and gay. But that time was short. There was nothing in Jersey which could contribute to his father's cause.

And presently his mother summoned him. The Louvre, the Tuileries, the Palais Royal ... What boy of sixteen would stay in the Channel Islands if he could go to Paris?

II

The seven weeks Charles spent in Jersey began in an atmosphere of relief and hope. Here he was safe; although all but a minute portion of England was in Parliament's hands, and the King had been forced to turn to the Scots for military aid, the ultimate triumph of the Cavaliers, however long delayed, still appeared inevitable. This triumph, some thought, would not necessarily be Charles I's; he might have to abdicate in the Prince's favour; this would result in monarchy being established on a new and improved basis and thus satisfying all but the minority groups in the country.

At this time, it occurred to no one in Prince Charles's circle – or indeed to any Royalist – that certain elements in Parliament might establish a government without monarchy. Such a metamorphosis was impossible and unimaginable. Thus, the first duty of the Prince's advisers was to organize a counter-invasion, preferably in his rather than in his father's name. Meanwhile the majority in Parliament believed that one of the best ways of consolidating their victory was through Prince Charles, whom they would establish much as the Whigs established William III sixty years later – rather as a controlled head of the state or a privileged civil servant than as a *roi fainéant* or a figurehead. The power of this majority was threatened by a section who felt that England should be ruled by a republican oligarchy selected and partially represented by themselves.

The underlying divisions in both Parliamentary and Royalist parties made their agreement impossible; this deadlock was strengthened by the fact that each underrated the other's appeal to the people. The most serious split in the Royalist group had been partly caused and was now being widened by the Queen. Henrietta Maria regarded the English as a heterogeneous mass of heretical rebels who, having been crushed into obedience, must then show their gratitude not only by an abject submission to monarchical absolutism, but, eventually, by their reconciliation to the true Church. It did not signify how this was achieved – as of course it would be. Her little Court at St Germain contained a number of English noblemen who subscribed, or made her believe they did, to this view; naturally it was one which horrified and disgusted such Royalists as Hyde, Colepepper and Hopton.

Meanwhile the King's attitude alternated between vague hopelessness and unreasoning optimism. At one moment he believed that the Scots would restore him; then he foresaw his own destruction and the collapse of his cause. And all the time he suspected that his wife was planning to convert the Prince of Wales. So she was: but in such a way that it was difficult, if not impossible, to accuse her of deliberately breaking her word. If she had been asked whether she was proselytizing her son, her answer would have been, 'No. But if he discovers the true faith for himself, which he is bound to do, it will not be for me to prevent his salvation.'

As the miserably anxious King reiterated his commands about the Prince's religion in his letters to him and the Queen, Charles's Anglicanism appeared impregnable and fervent – and here, once more, Newcastle's advice appears to have been followed throughout his pupil's stay in Jersey. 'How many [kings],' Newcastle observed, 'will history represent to you that in seeming to gain the kingdom of heaven have lost their own; but if you be not religious, and *not only seem so but be so*, God will not prosper you.' Newcastle then points out that 'reverence as to prayers' is of course essential, 'even were there no heaven or hell', for the successful government of a people. 'If you have no reverence, what will the people have [for you], think you?' In Jersey Charles's church-going was of the kind Newcastle would have recommended. The day after his arrival he went to morning service in St Helier, where great preparations had been made. Flowers and sweet herbs covered the route from the shore to the church porch.[4]

He arrived on horseback attended by a hundred splendidly mounted Cavaliers and the local militia with muskets, banners and drums. The church was crowded; those who could not get places waited in the cemetery. Between two of his chaplains Charles sat in the choir in a chair of state. A few hours later his devout behaviour was the talk of the island. He then rode along the shore and visited the rose-red medieval fortress of Mont Orgueil, where he was received by Colonel Philip Carteret, whom he knighted, and his wife, a rather formidable lady, with a Greek profile and a large bust. He reviewed the Jersey troops, distributed largesse and to a salute of guns departed to Elizabeth Castle, where he dined in public and then held a levee. His 'gracious and loving' manners captivated everyone: his greatest triumph was with the Jersey ladies who, some months earlier, had been commanded by the Governor to hide all their jewels in the event of an invasion. When Charles heard of this (did some charming creature complain?) he gave orders that during his visit these adjuncts to beauty and elegance were to be restored to their owners; this gallant thoughtfulness not only ensured the devotion of the sex but made it clear that there was nothing to fear as long as the Prince and his followers were in Jersey, although their installation had caused some inconvenience.[5]

Prices rose, until profiteering was stopped by Sir Philip's regulations. The Fanshawes, who had had to take lodgings in a stocking shop on the quay, ceased to think about their discomfort when they saw how happy and busy their young master was. He now further endeared himself to the islanders by taking lessons in the management of a pinnace from Captain Mainwaring, a sixty-year-old mariner, who had first hauled a rope under the great Sir Walter Raleigh, the builder of Elizabeth Castle. Charles's life-long passion for sailing was created at this time; he liked nothing so well as to steer his boat in and out of the rocks of St Aubyn's Bay under Mainwaring's direction. He determined to have a yacht of his own, and orders were sent to St Malo for a twelve-oared craft to be built for him.[6]

For a time this new pleasure absorbed him, and he seemed moderately content – until Parliament sent a message to Sir Philip desiring him to deliver up the island. The Governor replied, 'I do not intend to make myself a villain by betraying my trust,' a Council of war was called and the defences were strengthened under Charles's direction. He inspected the fortifications of the famous 'violet bank' (so called because of its amethyst seaweed) near Elizabeth Castle. In these last four years he had learnt enough to know what should be done, and his suggestions were carried out.[7]

So outwardly his visit continued in a satisfactory manner; at the Council meetings there were fierce divisions and bitter disagreements about His Highness's next move. Should he stay in his island kingdom, or go to France in order to raise an army against his father's enemies? The Queen required his presence. Cardinal Mazarin had promised – although rather vaguely – French support; and the King was now writing from Newcastle that Charles would be safer with his mother; he did not believe that Jersey could hold out against an invasion.

The low-ceilinged, narrow Council Chamber in Elizabeth Castle has not changed much since those days of anxiety and dispute, when the harsh voices of Charles's advisers jangled against one another, drowning the cries of the gulls and rising above the crash of the waves on the rocks below. In that group of middle-aged men he must have appeared startlingly youthful; but there was nothing immature about his observant impassivity. He remained silent, while Hyde, Capel and Colepepper argued with the volatile and impetuous Digby who, with the Queen's special emissary and favourite adviser, Lord Jermyn, had arrived to urge the Prince's instant departure. Digby and Jermyn were supported by the

Earls of Wentworth and Wilmot, whose leadership of the Royalist troops had been fatally incompetent and who had taken refuge in France several months earlier.

Wilmot and Wentworth were negligible; Jermyn, a gross and cunning self-seeker, had too much influence with the Queen to be discounted; Digby was a man of great personal charm, whose strength lay in his powers of persuasion. 'He always concluded,' says Hyde, 'that that was fit to be done which his first thoughts suggested to him.' Digby now declared that the Prince was wasting his time in Jersey and should at once leave for Ireland so as to invade in force. Charles made no definite answer; next day, having sent Jermyn, Capel and Colepepper to confer with his mother, he said, 'It would be very incongruous now to go into Ireland before my messengers return from Paris.' Digby burst out, 'That is a pernicious counsel!' and offered to convince the Queen in a letter. As the Prince would not be moved he took Hyde aside and again urged departure to Ireland. Hyde agreed that French help could not be relied on – but were not the Irish equally untrustworthy? Digby said, 'I will carry the Prince into Ireland even without and against his consent.' 'That would be impossible,' said Hyde, but Digby went on, 'I will invite the Prince on board the frigates to a collation, and as soon as he is on board I will cause the sails to be hoisted up and make no stay till I come into Ireland.' 'That neither agrees with your wisdom nor your duty,' said the horrified Chancellor, and Digby flung out of the room, announcing that he would go himself to Paris to put his plan before the Queen.

Hyde, recalling that Henrietta Maria had said she would hand over the Channel Islands to any foreign power in return for their services, warned Charles against the French. 'They talk, but do not act,' he said, and reminded him that so far they had sent him neither men nor arms.[8]

When Capel and Colepepper waited on the Queen at St Germain they found that Jermyn had forestalled them. (Henrietta Maria, who had expected Jermyn to return with Charles and had prepared the Prince's rooms, burst into tears when Jermyn appeared alone.) She listened to the other two emissaries graciously enough. Then she said, 'I have the King's commands to have the Prince in France. I doubt the insecurity of Jersey.' They reassured her, adding, 'His Majesty, when he is fully informed, will rest well satisfied with His Highness's longer abode in Jersey.' She told them to come again next day, when she had had time to consider. Before their second interview Jermyn came to them. 'The game is to be played out by the French,' he said coolly. 'The Queen can no longer support His Highness where he is. If he comes into France he will be given 14,000 pistoles for his maintenance.' 'Until the French declare war on His Majesty's behalf,' Colepepper protested, 'it is not reasonable His Highness should put himself under their power – if His Majesty is taken prisoner, then he might do so,' and Capel put in, 'The French themselves do not urge the Prince coming over.' 'I know very well,' Jermyn replied, 'that the French will not engage heartily till the Prince is in France,' and continued to uphold French goodwill.

After some further discussion they went to Henrietta Maria, whom they found in a temper. Digby was with her. 'I am resolved to send for my son,' she exclaimed, 'I have the King's commands. If you think that place secure, why do you desire aid? Nothing can be done without French assistance.' Digby added that he was now of Her Majesty's opinion, and the argument continued with increasing heat. A few days later Henrietta Maria, who had told her ladies, 'I am fully resolved and nothing shall divert me,' sent for Capel and Colepepper, showed them the King's letter describing his own danger and ordering Charles to France and said triumphantly, 'Now – what is your opinion?' 'My opinion,' Colepepper replied, 'is that the Prince should come into France if His Majesty were made prisoner – and by this letter I conceive him to be so, therefore I am sorry for the Prince's coming.' 'Speak,' said the Queen, turning to Capel. 'I am sorry the Prince should move out of his father's dominions,' said that nobleman stoutly, 'until there is an excusable necessity for it. If the Prince should put himself under a foreign power, the kingdom will apprehend a new embroilment [i.e. with Catholicism] and thus Your Majesty will render yourself irreconcilable to the whole nation.' 'I cannot help that,' replied the Queen, 'if it be for the King's service.' Capel then apologized for his frankness, adding, 'It would be against my honour and duty to the King to attend a foot of this fatal journey.' Henrietta Maria dismissed them courteously; she could afford to do so. When she reported her success to Anne of Austria, her sister-in-law, now Queen Regent for Louis XIV, that lady expressed her horror at the thought of her nephew's heresy. 'He drank in the faith with his mother's milk,' she said, adding, 'If he comes to Paris he must not worship with Huguenots.'[9] A few days later Colepepper, Capel, Jermyn and Digby returned to Jersey to confer with the Prince.

III

While he waited for his ministers to return from France Charles sailed with Mainwaring and went shooting with the Carterets and other Jersey notables, in the intervals between carrying out his duties as a public figure.

All this time Hyde continued to train him, not in Newcastle's manner, but in the pompous, fault-finding style so unacceptable to young people. The other courtiers noted that the Chancellor treated the Prince like a schoolboy, approached him without formality and snubbed him whenever he tried to assert himself.[10] Charles appeared not to resent this, just as, in childhood, he had submitted to his parents' strictures while preserving his independence of mind. In a long letter to Jermyn Hyde unwittingly revealed the Prince's attitude, while defending himself from the imputation that he dominated His Highness. 'No man in his wits,' he protested, 'can think fit that the Prince should bury himself in this obscure island from action. I wish action were as ready for him as he is for it; but the question is only, whether it is more honourable to be without action in this island or in France.' He went on to stress Charles's 'piety and devotion'.

Naturally the Prince was eager to take the field against his father's enemies. Nearly four years had gone by since Sir John Hinton had dragged him out of the fight at Edgehill, and ever since then he had been sent from one stronghold to another, escaping capture and yielding to superior strength. This was not war, as Charles, once General of the Western Association, saw it; nor active service, as his hero, Rupert of the Rhine, had taught him to understand the words. If he could not lead the Cavaliers into battle and bring back his father in triumph, then he must seek out those who would lend him the means to conquer his rebellious people with the help of foreigners and mercenaries. Meanwhile he had no companions of his own generation in whom he could confide. James, Henry and Elizabeth were in the charge of the Earl of Northumberland; the Villiers boys, whom he had last seen in 1642, were travelling in Italy with their tutor. And Jersey had, it appears, the average quota of pretty girls.

During the weeks of inactivity which followed the celebration of his sixteenth birthday, Charles may have begun to look for feminine society. No rumours of his attachment to any particular young woman were circulated, then or later; but more than two hundred years after his death a correspondence purporting to have taken place in the 1670s between him and the Jesuit College in Rome revealed the existence of a son, 'James de la Cloche', born in 1647, of a Jersey lady (*des plus qualifiées de nos royaumes*) whom the King received secretly at Whitehall, and who himself became a Jesuit priest.[11] This story has since been disproved; and it is to be noted that throughout Charles's exile none of the Parliamentary spies who seized on and reported every discreditable incident in his daily life, mentioned either this liaison or its outcome. So that first romance has become apocryphal. Yet the fact that it was written of at all and the existence of those mysteriously worded (and highly uncharacteristic) letters give the impression that in the summer of 1646 the young Prince discovered the pleasures of the alcove. The Stuarts were not laggards in love; and for some three hundred years Charles II has epitomized that aspect of the family temperament. If it can be assumed that he enjoyed women at an early age, then it follows that he might have begun to do so during those idle weeks in Jersey, although contemporary reports of his behaviour reveal no interests of this kind; indeed he seems to have been entirely absorbed in his future plans, which were made in the now familiar atmosphere of bickering and intrigue.

The Council met in Charles's bedroom. They had first to consider that Guernsey was in danger, as the Governor had asked to be relieved of his command, and then that the Parliamentary invasion, which was to have taken place on May 28th, had been abandoned through the mutiny of the sailors. They passed on to the latest letters from the King and Queen, in which both commanded Charles to go to France. 'See that you go no whither without her or my particular directions,' wrote Charles I, and Henrietta Maria added, 'Your coming ... is the security of the King your father, therefore make all the haste you can to show yourself a dutiful son.'[12]

Hyde then stressed the advantages of Jersey as being 'a corner of His Majesty's kingdom', adding, 'In France you will be a foreigner, begging your bread.' 'There is no argument for debate,' said Jermyn sharply, and Colepepper, turning to the Prince, put in, 'You should not suffer anybody to debate what the King and Queen have positively commanded.' Still Charles said nothing, and Hyde resumed, 'As soon as His Highness appears in France it will be said that he goes to Mass with the Queen, even if he does not – hitherto he hath been free from the least taint or blemish that way.' He added that this would prejudice Holland and Denmark against the Royalist cause, and concluded, 'It will be most pernicious and fatal for him to go.'

Jermyn then asked the Chancellor to withdraw, so that he might reason with him privately; they returned to find that Charles had dismissed the Council till the next day, when the argument was renewed. 'We should wait to hear [again] from the King,' Capel began. (He did not know that Charles I had written secretly to Parliament offering to send the Prince back to London – a characteristic piece of underhand dealing.) He went on, 'The French are not to be trusted, they have not sent Your Highness a pass.' 'When you were in the West,' Hyde put in, 'they promised 5,000 foot, who never arrived – ' and was interrupted by Digby's and Jermyn's assurance of French support.[13]

At last the Prince, hitherto ignored, said quietly, 'I am resolved to comply with the commands of the Queen.' The voices of the Council broke out again; he continued, 'There must be no more debate upon this point.' As the anti-French party still protested, he repeated, 'There can be no dispute upon the thing. I conceive it a command, and am resolved to obey it as soon as may be. Provide all things for the journey.' In a tone which must have come as a shock to his seniors, he added, 'There must be unity in your counsels – ' and stood up to go.[14]

Hyde, Capel and Colepepper then announced that they could not accompany him. The Prince accepted this, to them, heartbreaking decision, without comment, and held out his hand. As they bent to kiss it, he said, 'I shall be gone tomorrow by five o'clock in the morning – ' and left the room.

By this time Charles's yacht had been delivered; he decided to man her with Jersey seamen and set sail for St Malo; but the islanders refused to take him to France, and he had to appeal to Carteret, who found him a crew. Then the wind changed and sailing was postponed. While the Prince waited in a fever of impatience – he allowed no one to go to bed in case the wind, now very high, became favourable – the tradesmen sent in their bills, clamouring to be paid. Although reassured by those of the Council who were to remain on the island, they refused to supply the Prince with provisions for his journey; eventually these were collected by the Fanshawes and others. So four days passed, most of which Charles spent on the shore, surrounded by his anti-French ministers trying to persuade him to change his mind. He listened to them so sympathetically that Jermyn and Digby began to feel alarmed; their anger rose, with the result that they and their antagonists met only for meals and did not speak to one another.[15]

At five o'clock in the evening of the fifth day the wind, although still contrary, dropped a little, and Charles went down to the shore for the last time, accompanied by Jermyn and Digby and followed at a short distance by Capel, Colepepper and Hyde; the Chancellor was in tears, and presently his companions began to cry too. While they waited the Prince walked up and down the bowling-green; Hyde and his allies sat sadly on the rocks. Then, as the rowing-boats approached, Hyde saw that Digby and Jermyn had taken hold of the Prince's arms and were marching him along, as if afraid that he would change his mind.

He had no intention of doing so; but that sudden mistrust was characteristic of much that followed in his relationship with his courtiers. The more astute had begun to perceive that His Highness so disliked scenes that he would go to any lengths to avoid them. This slipperiness was caused, Hyde said loyally, by his sweet and gentle nature; he could not bear to see long faces about him, or to disappoint the least of his servants. So no one was ever quite sure what the Prince had decided, or what he really wanted, except when he made it clear that he did not mean to be troubled. Then his ministers would suddenly realize that while they were disputing he had disappeared.

Charles and his diminished Court reached St Malo on the evening of June 26th. Next morning they began their journey to St Germain. Hyde did not see the Prince again for two years. When Charles I heard that the Chancellor had refused to accompany his son, he was much displeased.[16] But Sir Edward knew he was right: and so indeed it proved. The Prince had made the wrong decision. His punishment – a gradually intensifying process of humiliation – lasted for fourteen years.

NOTES

1 Lady Anne Fanshawe, *Memoirs*, p. 61.
2 Clarendon, pp. 505–619.
3 W. Harris, *Charles II*, vol. I, pp. 24–5.
4 Hoskins, pp. 351–448.
5 Ibid.
6 Sir Henry Mainwaring, *Life and Works*, vol. I, p. 313.
7 Hoskins, ibid.
8 *Beaufort MSS* (H.M.C.), pp. 16–19.
9 *Cal. S. P. Ven.*, vol. XXVI, p. 254.
10 *Cal. Clar. S. P.*, vol. II, p. 277.
11 Lord Acton, *Historical Essays and Studies*, pp. 85–122.
12 *The Letters, Speeches and Proclamations of Charles I* (ed. Sir Charles Petrie), p. 175; *Cal. Clar. S. P.*, vol. II, p. 230.
13 Clarendon, pp. 550–74.
14 Hoskins, ibid.
15 Clarendon, ibid.
16 *Cal. Clar. S. P.*, vol. II, pp. 236–40.

CHAPTER TWO

A FAMILY GATHERING

I

IN 1644, a year after the accession of Louis XIV, Henrietta Maria, arraigned by Parliament of high treason, had been received at the French Court. With her youngest child, the Princess Henrietta Anne, she was now settled in the Palace of St Germain, where she lived as a pensioner and a refugee.

Her spirit was high and undaunted. Misfortune had strengthened her resistance, and she was busy with plans for the reinstallation of her husband and the punishment of his enemies. Her optimism about the future sprang partly from the conviction that she knew exactly what to do, and partly from her belief in the goodwill of Cardinal Mazarin and Anne of Austria. Her anxiety for the King was mitigated by the certainty that God would help them to victory as long as she continued to work for him and their children; of these the Prince of Wales came first. He must be financed on a scale which would enable him to invade England in strength; as it would be difficult, if not impossible, for the French to fit out and pay the required troops, he must be provided with a large private income through marriage.

The young woman selected two years earlier by Henrietta Maria remained the best choice, for she was the greatest heiress in Europe. Although the Queen's efforts to marry La Grande Mademoiselle to Prince Charles had hitherto been unsuccessful, she was still hopeful and determined. She assumed that her niece would be not only willing but eager to marry a penniless outcast three years younger than herself. Mademoiselle had ideas of her own about her future which she did not divulge to her aunt. Her upbringing had been unusual, her circumstances were happy and by the age of nineteen she had achieved a certain independence. She had been a very important person in her own and everyone else's eyes ever since she could remember.

Anne-Marie-Louise de Montpensier was the only child of Marie de Bourbon, Duchesse de Montpensier, and Gaston, Duc d'Orléans, younger brother of Louis XIII. Her mother, a distant cousin of the reigning house, died when Mademoiselle was a week old, so that she inherited her titles and the vast estates of which her father enjoyed the revenue, but which remained her own property. As Sovereign of Dombes, Princesse de Joinville and Laroche-sur-Yon, Duchesse de Montpensier, Châtellerault and St Fargeau, Dauphine d'Auvergne and Comtesse d'Eu, she grew up in an atmosphere of courtly subservience; her household, directed for a short time by her grandmother, Marie de Medici, was larger and more splendid than those of the Queens of England and Spain, and second only to that of Louis XIII and Anne of Austria, whom she condescendingly referred to as *petit papa* and *petite maman*. Her father, a frivolous, selfish intriguer, made it his business to flatter and spoil her, with the result that she adored him and remained blind to his faults. Naive, limited and supremely arrogant, Mademoiselle was neither stupid nor irresponsible. She took herself and her position very seriously, and was not always taken in by the sycophants and toadies who had surrounded her since infancy. She was affectionate and generous – when Gaston d'Orléans married again she made pets of her half-sisters – and ambitious only in the sense that she knew it her duty to make a magnificent marriage, one worthy of the granddaughter of Henri Quatre. In 1645 the question of her marrying Philip IV was considered and rejected by Mazarin, so that when the Prince of Wales arrived Mademoiselle was once more on the look-out for a suitable husband. If not Queen of Spain, why not Queen of England? The Prince's Bourbon descent made him worthy of her, in spite of his circumstances; but she did not care for the idea of leaving France to reign over a half-civilized and heretical nation, and was contemptuously aware of Henrietta Maria's eagerness to secure her wealth. Yet these disadvantages did not quite outweigh two assets – those of gaining a throne and helping Prince Charles to restore his fortunes. There was something chivalric and noble in that aspect of the situation which appealed to her. She assumed that her cousin would immediately throw himself at her feet, not only because she had so much to give, but because she was herself desirable: in fact, a beauty. Whenever she looked in the mirror she was struck afresh by her own perfections.[1]

There she saw the face and figure of a young woman who would now be described as the Teutonic type – tall, robust, blonde, fresh-coloured and blue-eyed. Her nose was large, her chin heavy, and although well proportioned she was already beginning to put on weight. She had no taste in dress, was not interested in fashions and sometimes appeared unkempt, even grotesque.

Mademoiselle's temperament and upbringing had combined to deprive her of the faintest sense of irony; and her circumstances barred her from any knowledge of the world outside the Court circle. Nor was she accomplished, for she spoke no language but her own and a little Italian, and was not well read. She liked light music, picnics, cards and guessing games; her hobby, indeed her passion, was etiquette in all its elaborations as practised at the Louvre, Fontainebleau and the Tuileries; she was an expert on precedence and protocol. Her greatest virtue – one not fully appreciated at the Court of Mazarin and the Queen Regent – was her truthfulness. She seldom told a lie, even to spare someone else's sensibilities; her frankness was childlike and, ultimately, the cause of all her misfortunes. She did not know what it was to be shy, and although highly emotional and sometimes observant, was quite incapable of entering into the feelings of others. When she first met Prince Charles she was living in a Corneillean drama, of which she was the triumphant rather than the persecuted heroine. Grand, absurd, vulnerable and courageous, she was – and would have been in any age – hopelessly out of date, for mentally she belonged to an epoch which existed only in romances and plays.

This inexperienced spinster was now contemplating marriage with a secretive, anxious and disillusioned youth, who in some respects might have been twice her age, and whose knowledge of the world, compared with hers, was that of a middle-aged man. Charles's taste in women was then unformed; but he knew the kind of woman he did not like. Mademoiselle regarded all men, young and old, as aspirants or courtiers, unless they happened to be of higher rank or greater wealth than herself.

Prince Charles reached St Germain at the beginning of July 1646. There he remained, with the two-year-old sister he now saw for the first time, his moody, excitable mother and those of his Court who had rooms in the palace. Jermyn was indispensable to the Queen and saw her every day. Digby, Wentworth, Wilmot and the eighty gentlemen who had accompanied them from Jersey had to find lodgings near by or in Paris. Charles, who knew what Henrietta Maria had planned for him, was given ample time to realize the accuracy of Sir Edward Hyde's prediction. Although he was Louis XIV's first cousin and his guest, he now knew himself a foreigner, begging his bread. For five weeks he remained with his mother and sister, unrecognized, ignored, aimlessly waiting, while the Cardinal, the Queen Regent and their advisers discussed the various aspects of his future treatment and what honours could safely be given him. Louis, his younger brother Philippe d'Anjou, Mademoiselle and Gaston d'Orléans seem to have shared in these debates and were eventually allotted their respective parts. When the decisions had been made and announced to all

the Courts of Europe, Charles's French relations took the stage and the
family gathering was set in motion. Only one member of the cast fell
below the standard ordained. The star performer was the eight-year-old
King.

Since his accession at the age of four and a half, Louis XIV had appeared
daily in public, taken his place at official ceremonies (he made a short
speech to his first Parliament before he was five) and was accustomed to
being treated with cringing reverence. His mother's methods were dis-
ciplinary; but even she accorded the son for whose birth she had waited
twenty-three years, the respect of a subject, while she instilled into him an
abiding sense of duty. He was never allowed, and did not in fact want, to
forget his position; at no moment, whether hunting, playing or at his
lessons, was he approached as a child. Such an upbringing might have put
too great a strain on a sensitive or delicate boy; Louis was neither. Healthy,
intelligent and serious, he never took his greatness for granted; his ambition was to increase it and to become, as a king and as an individual,
impregnable and supreme.

The Cardinal's subtle flatteries and ostentatious modesty impressed the
Queen Regent, who became completely dependent on him. By the time
Prince Charles arrived, Louis – Mazarin's pupil and rival – was already
looking forward to the time when he would be able to dispense with the
services of this brilliant, avaricious and dominating minister. From
Mazarin he learned to work as few kings have ever worked, how to
conceal his emotions and to exploit those of others.

Louis was aware of his English cousin's political importance at this
time, and of the marriage planned for him by Henrietta Maria; although
he was not personally grasping, he did not want La Grande Mademoiselle's
fortune to go to the Royalist cause. He, his mother and Mazarin were
therefore agreed on the necessity of receiving Charles honourably but
distantly. The Queen Regent was inclined to be sentimental about her
exiled nephew; Mademoiselle was curious and a little excited; Louis and
the seven-year-old Duc d'Anjou, an over-indulged, rather unpleasant
child, were not much interested in the guest who was to appear as a
suppliant and a refugee.

It had been agreed that at Charles's first meeting with his cousins he
should arrive informally and incognito; in this way it was made clear
that French support, if given at all, would be unofficial and not necessarily
renewable. Such an arrangement prevented his being received in the
capital and entailed his coming upon Louis XIV and the Queen Regent
'as if by chance', in the forest of Fontainebleau.[2] So when the coach

containing the royal family drew up in the appointed glade, they remained inside it till that of Charles and Henrietta Maria was seen approaching. Hosts and guests descended simultaneously. Henrietta Maria went up to Anne of Austria, leading the Prince, whom she presented first to the King and then to her sister-in-law. When he had kissed their hands the Queen Regent kissed him on the cheek; he was then presented to the Duc d'Anjou, Gaston d'Orléans and Mademoiselle, in that order.[3] After a few moments' conversation the French party re-entered their coaches, while Charles and his mother returned to St Germain.

Next day, in order to show their appreciation of this fortunate encounter, Charles and Henrietta Maria set off for the palace of Fontainebleau. They were greeted by the young King, who happened to be strolling about in the forest, the exact distance of his coach from the palace having been duly worked out and recorded. They joined him, and he conducted them to his mother's apartments, where the ritual became a little more complicated.

Anne of Austria stood up to receive them. Charles handed her to a chair, and Louis XIV did the same for Henrietta Maria. As the two boys took their seats the King not only indicated that Charles should sit on his right (an honour which caused some comment and might have been excessive) but gave him a chair exactly similar to his own, one with arms. All this time – about a quarter of an hour – Henrietta Maria's chair remained outside the royal circle. She now got up and was conducted by her son to his chair, in which she sat next to the Queen Regent, while Charles and Louis stood immediately behind them, flanked by the other members of the royal family, who were themselves encircled by the most privileged courtiers and their ladies.

A short time was then allotted to conversation, after which Louis suggested to Charles, as if the idea had that moment struck him, that they should go for a walk in the grounds. At this point everyone in the outer circle was agog to see what honours the Prince would receive. Some were disapproving and rather taken aback when Louis, having preceded Charles, not only desired him to put on his hat, but kept him at his right hand during their parade through the gardens. Next day Charles was admitted to his cousin's *petit lever* – entry to the *grand lever* would have been more usual and less complimentary – and again given a chair with arms. Louis and his mother then visited their guests at St Germain, where the same procedure obtained. They were accompanied by Mademoiselle, who had received a favourable impression of her English cousin, as had Madame de Motteville. These ladies' descriptions of the Prince balance one another. They thought him tall for his age and very well made. His dark complexion suited his brilliant black eyes and richly waving hair. Mademoiselle admired his 'fine head', but Madame de Motteville found his mouth so large as to be downright ugly; this defect was made up for by his graceful bearing and agreeable manners.[4] During the three days of the Fontainebleau visits Mademoiselle's early impressions were sustained. Then, as she and Charles were brought together, he fell from favour. She began to criticize him, mentally at first, then openly, and finally to his mother. Henrietta Maria, seeing her hopes in ruins, became distracted. She had never visualized her son's response to the bride she had chosen for him – what was to be done?

II

'The private apartments of kings,' says Madame de Motteville, 'are as theatres where plays are acted which affect the whole world; some are merely comic; but others are tragedies, in which the big scenes always spring from trivialities.' The acute and kind-hearted lady was not thinking of Prince Charles and Mademoiselle de Montpensier when she made that statement; yet it perfectly illustrates the ironic comedy of their first meetings, in which Charles's deviousness and Mademoiselle's self-absorption were displayed to a rather puzzled audience.

In her famous memoirs Mademoiselle gives a brief and merciless account of her cousin's failure – which was in fact a refusal – to approach her in the proper manner. A voluble egoist, she was nevertheless willing to listen, above all when addressed in a complimentary or gallant strain. Charles not only remained silent, but when she spoke to him, indicated that he did not understand a word of his mother's language, one in which he had conversed with his pages and his writing-master since his sixth year. 'This,' says Mademoiselle, 'was most inconvenient.' (It did not occur to her to help matters by learning a few phrases of her cousin's barbarous tongue, or to suggest that he might give her lessons in it – what would he have done if she had?)

The French spoken and written by Charles in the later years of his exile does not accord with this ingenious dumbness. He could not have acquired his knowledge of that language suddenly, after the age of sixteen; and he had heard his mother, her ladies and their priests talking French throughout his infancy. Though he had had no practice in it during the first four years of the Civil War, he could not possibly have forgotten every word, or have failed to recapture some facility during the two years he spent at

LA GRANDE MADEMOISELLE

PRINCESS MARY OF ORANGE

the French Court. His apparent inability to achieve a social relationship with Mademoiselle must therefore have been based on a firm resolve not to become involved with a lady he found personally unattractive and politically undesirable, if not actually dangerous, to his cause; for within a very short time of his arrival at St Germain anti-French feeling in England had been so expressed as to make it obvious that he would be extremely foolish to commit himself irrevocably to a Catholic ally – who might, in the last resort, fail to support him. If he had proposed to and been allowed to marry Mademoiselle, he would have acquired wealth, but not necessarily power or independence. At the same time, it was essential not to offend his mother or his French relatives. He therefore assumed the role of the speechless admirer: so well indeed, that Madame de Motteville was also deceived, and pitied the poor boy for his awkwardness, which sometimes resulted, she observed, in a stammer, when he was trying to get out a few words. (There is no other record, throughout his life, of Charles having inherited his father's disability.)

None of the English courtiers then living in Paris or St Germain made any comment on Charles's incapacity to speak French. He and they hunted, talked and danced with their hosts throughout his stay; if he had so failed, it would certainly have been reported in their letters to the other Royalists. His mother, who could have tutored him when they were alone, appears to have accepted the situation. In fact, all the evidence points to Charles adopting an attitude towards Mademoiselle which eliminated any question of contact, let alone intimacy, while he attended her with the impressive courtesy of an aspirant to her favours.

'He was paid,' Mademoiselle rather resentfully goes on, 'much attention. During the three days at Fontainebleau he enjoyed the pleasures of the chase, and any others there available; he visited all the princesses.' (Her Bourbon and Condé relatives.) 'It was clear to me,' she then explains, 'that the Queen of England wished me to believe that he was in love with me.'[5]

This desperate resource was engendered by Henrietta Maria's being unable to influence her son. If he would not or could not speak to Mademoiselle himself, then she would be his mouthpiece. So she rushed headlong into the breach, while Mademoiselle, cynically observing her agitation, replied with polite nothings to her aunt's reports of the Prince's real feelings. 'He talks to me of you all day long,' the poor Queen declared. 'If I did not hold him back, he would be in your apartments at all hours. He finds you much to his taste. He is in despair at the death of the Empress [of Germany] because he fears that they will marry you to the Emperor

[Ferdinand III].' Mademoiselle withheld her judgment; as an heiress, she knew very well when young men were serious in their intentions.

By the time the Court, followed by Charles and Henrietta Maria, returned to Paris, the Queen perceived that she was not making headway with her niece. She therefore approached their common friends, the Duchesse and Mademoiselle d'Épernon, whom she instructed to repeat her propaganda to Mademoiselle, as if on their own initiative. These efforts were received with the same courteous incredulity. Mademoiselle then says naively, 'I do not know, *if he had approached me himself,* what success he might have had; but I do know that I did not take much heed of what people told me on behalf of a man who could not speak for himself.'

Henrietta Maria did not abandon her campaign. At balls, at private and public theatricals, assemblies and hunting-parties, she made Charles stand next to Mademoiselle and conduct her to her coach. This he did charmingly, refusing to put on his hat in her presence, whatever the weather. 'His politeness,' says Mademoiselle, 'was shown in the smallest details.' Then came what seemed to Henrietta Maria a wonderful opportunity. The Choisys – he was Gaston d'Orléans' Chancellor – were to give a ball, to which all the royal family, French and English, were bidden. The Queen announced that she herself would dress Mademoiselle's hair, so often neglected, for this great event, and that Prince Charles would accompany her to his cousin's apartments and hold the candelabra, as if he were a page, or a gentleman in waiting, thus advertising to the Court the chivalrous fervour of his devotion. Charles amiably agreed. Mother and son then set off for the Tuileries, and were ushered upstairs.[6]

The principal actors in that celebrated scene, so characteristic of seventeenth-century *amour courtois*, were an odd-looking trio and must have appeared rather absurd to those in attendance in Mademoiselle's gilded and mirrored dressing-room. The eager Queen, absorbed in her preparations and long since heedless of her own appearance, has been described by one of her Palatine nieces as 'a little woman with long, lean arms, crooked shoulders and teeth protruding from her mouth like guns from a fort.'[7] Mademoiselle's large features and bold colouring were of the kind best seen in artificial light. In her ball-dress sewn with diamonds and dotted all over with bunches of black, white and rose-coloured ribbon, she gazed at her reflection in an ecstasy of approval. 'My fine figure, glowing looks and golden hair,' she recalls, 'more than equalled the splendour of the ornaments with which I was covered.' She wore, and could well support, not only the historic jewels of France, but those lent her by Henrietta Maria, who, having put the finishing touches to her niece's hair, fastened in it three feathers matching her ribbons and attached to a weighty diamond circlet.

And all the time Prince Charles stood behind the two excited women, the great silver-stemmed flambeau in one long brown hand, the other on his sword-hilt, his dark face darker in the shadow: enigmatic, submissive, ironically withdrawn. His shoulder-knot, chosen and arranged by his careful mother, repeated the colours of Mademoiselle's ribbons; he wore his Garter and carried a diamond-hilted sword. So he was to lend himself, throughout his tempestuous career as exile, pensioner and beggar, to others' whims, seemingly indifferent to censure and disdain. It was then, surely, in that candle-lit room, that he began to learn how to give in over a triviality and abase himself as a means to an end; how to be the *cavaliere servente* with the minimum of effort; how to play his part with a group of fumbling amateurs whom he finally acted off the stage.

All that evening he went through the motions, gracefully and convincingly, of the humble servant of his bouncing heiress, seeking her favour, hoping for a smile, a nod, a touch of the hand – and all without a word: a remarkable achievement for a boy of sixteen. He preceded Mademoiselle to the Choisys'; there she found him, in the portico, waiting to hand her from her coach, with just that melancholic, pleading look which most appeals to a condescending great lady. Surprised and delighted, she went before him into the first ante-room, where she paused in front of a mirror to rearrange her hair. Immediately the Prince took a flambeau from the nearest attendant and held it behind her. Then he followed her into the ballroom and never left her side – 'very unusual behaviour for him,' remarks Mademoiselle complacently; she was beginning to believe that she had made a genuine conquest of this impassive suitor.

They were then joined by Prince Rupert, who had just arrived in Paris and was presumably unaware of his cousin's tactics. Anxious to put Charles at his ease, he proposed to interpret between him and Mademoiselle. 'And then,' she says, apparently rather surprised, 'he understood all I said, although he himself could not speak French.' In this way the ingenious youth cut their interview short and, desired by King Louis to dance with his cousin, acquitted himself so well that M. de Choisy's critical guests were entranced.

At last the ball came to an end. Mademoiselle got into her coach and returned to the Tuileries. There again, waiting by the lodge gates, was her Prince, hat in hand. She went in; he watched her disappear, then strolled away, his duty done for that evening. 'His gallantry,' Mademoiselle recalls, 'was carried to such lengths that it caused great comment.'[8] Comment was what was needed and what Henrietta Maria required. Charles continued to create it by his behaviour to Mademoiselle during the autumn and winter of 1646. He showed no weariness; perhaps he was enjoying himself; only so would it have been possible to accept the bad news from England.

First, a Puritan gang stormed Whitehall, broke into the Queen's chapel, flung the Rubens Madonna into the Thames and took away the wafers and the pyx, which they threw on a bonfire. The Queen's distress was somewhat assuaged when one of her Jesuits told her that at that point the pyx burst open with a bang, soared into the air and was no more seen.

The House of Commons then declared that they would 'make Prince Charles repent' for having joined the papist-traitress Queen. His father wrote to him at length of the 'iniquity of these times', and again implored him to maintain his faith, 'not only in relation to conscience, but ... for the necessary subsistence of the crown,' adding, 'next to religion, the power of the sword is the truest judge and greatest support of sovereignty.'[9] The King's sword had been taken away; he was now the prisoner of the Scots at Newcastle.

All this time Prince Charles's promised allowance was not forthcoming; he had to live on, as well as with, his mother. He was cut off from his English attendants, then spied on and followed by Mazarin's agents, who treated him with a familiarity bordering on insolence. His courtiers quarrelled; the fiery Digby challenged Prince Rupert; Charles managed to prevent them fighting and the dispute was patched up. Then Charles I, realizing that it was his person rather than his office which Parliament would not accept, proposed abdication in the Prince's favour; his plan was to rule through his son, using him as a screen. Meanwhile everyone in Paris, the foreign ambassadors, the courtiers, the Queen Regent, admired and praised the Prince. Gratified, impatient, anxious, hopeful, Henrietta Maria pursued her plans for the capture of Mademoiselle.

NOTES

1 Mlle de Montpensier, *Mémoires*, vol. I, pp. 126–8.
2 *Cal. S. P. Ven.*, vol. XXVII, p. 269.
3 Montpensier, ibid.
4 Ibid.
5 Ibid.
6 Ibid.
7 Electress Sophia of Hanover, *Memoirs 1630–1680*, p. 12.
8 Montpensier, ibid.
9 *Letters* (ed. Petrie), pp. 205–6.

CHAPTER THREE

AMENITIES OF EXILE

I

I N the early autumn of 1646 the eighteen-year-old Duke of Buckingham and Lord Francis Villiers finished their continental tour and joined Prince Charles in Paris. They were accompanied by their tutor, William Aylesbury, who wrote to their cousin, Lord Denbigh, 'I am sure you will not let them lie longer there than is necessary, especially now the Prince is there.'

Aylesbury's wish to separate his charges from their old playfellow sprang from a vague fear that somehow the three boys would together get into mischief, or that the Villiers would place themselves at the Prince's disposal and so return to take part in the Civil War. After they had run away from Cambridge (at the ages of fifteen and fourteen) to fight under Prince Rupert, Aylesbury was instructed by their guardian, the Earl of Northumberland, to keep them out of danger and thus restore them to the favour of the Parliamentary Commissioners who had confiscated their estates in 1643. They remained in Paris till the summer of 1647, their lands having been given back to them early that year. So Prince Charles renewed his companionship with his most intimate friends, who not only had a good deal more money to spend than himself, but who for the last four years had been leading a highly social, cosmopolitan life. The young Villiers were now fashionable and accomplished men of the world, at ease with everyone. They had done all the things Charles longed to do – run away from their tutors, stormed Lichfield Close in the siege of that city and stayed in luxurious splendour with the great families of Florence, Venice and Rome.

Thus the Duke and Lord Francis – handsome, gay, sophisticated and completely irresponsible – must have appeared to their former comrade as in the children's masque at Richmond Palace. Once more, George Villiers dominated, took a leading part and set the example. The result, according to Bishop Burnet, was that Charles was 'corrupted' by Buckingham, who himself had 'already got into all the vices and impieties of the age'. It may have been so; what is more likely and, from the point of view of the Prince's development, more important, was that Buckingham's mockery of the most serious aspects of Charles's situation changed the younger boy's attitude towards the older Royalists and perhaps even to their cause. The Duke's derision spared no one; then, as always, he made a joke of everything – religion, politics, the whole hierarchy of the state. His mimicry, his satire, his rhyming quips, afterwards so famous and so fatal to his own interests, may have been crude and silly enough when he and Charles met in Paris; but his merciless irreverence (he even made fun of Charles I's solemn and anxious letters to his son) diverted the Prince, who was beginning to tire of the formalities of his cousin's Court and of having to flatter the ineffably correct little King. (At the age of eight Louis XIV never so far forgot himself as to smile or to laugh in public; he and Charles, having nothing in common, marched about together in almost total silence, exchanging bows and courteous gestures as if they had been wound up to do so.)[1]

So it was that, breaking into the Prince's taxing and constricted existence with the dash and brio of an inspired comedian, Buckingham, who now shared his lessons with Dr Earle, and brought the great Thomas Hobbes to Charles to teach him mathematics and philosophy, began to influence him against his father. That monarch's stiffness became – perhaps it had already been – 'a perpetual subject of raillery' with the Duke. Meanwhile, according to Burnet, 'under the pretence of instructing him with mathematics [Hobbes] laid before him his schemes both as to religion and politics, which made a deep and lasting impression on [Prince Charles's] mind, so that the main blame of [his] ... bad morals was owing to the Duke.' The less prejudiced Hobbes – whose *Leviathan* Charles never attempted to read – described the Duke as exceptionally brilliant; in a grossly indecent anecdote recorded by Aubrey, he made it clear that George Villiers was not a desirable influence.[2] Then, and until the end of his life, Charles found Buckingham irresistible, and forgave him all his many enormities.

If Charles did manage to slip away from his mother and his tutors to find diversion outside the residences of the monarchy, he could have had no more agreeable companion than the Duke and no more variegated hunting-ground than that provided by seventeenth-century Paris, where medieval grimness and Renaissance splendour were inextricably interwoven; where the austere and forbidding outlines of the Louvre were set off by the soaring elegance of the Tuileries and the Palais Royal; where to turn away from some magnificent colonnade was to find oneself trapped in a series of stinking, narrow alleys and overwhelmed by a mingling of noise, filth and the prowling, tattered, wolfish figures of the most dangerous people in Europe. When Charles first came to Paris fifteen to eighteen persons were killed every night in the haunts of those living within a few hundred yards of King Louis's palaces. It was almost certain death to enter them without an armed bodyguard. 'There is less risk,' wrote an English traveller, 'in crossing a virgin forest than walking through the streets of Paris when the candles and lanterns are put out.'[3] This comparatively small city contained some 50,000 thieves and cut-throats who emerged as the curfew rang and were divided into bands – the Red, the Grey, the Plumed Hats – the better to war against one another when they were not stabbing and robbing the passers-by, and who were attended by groups of prostitutes as savage and rapacious as themselves.

Yet here as elsewhere in the capitals of Europe poverty, vice, disease and crime ran like underground rivers beneath the delicate and luxurious refinements of pleasure, of expensive and carefully-thought-out means to the 'simple life', pastorally set in arbours and summer-houses. Every evening at dusk the four tree-lined avenues of Cours-la-Reine were filled with coaches of great ladies and their cavaliers driving out to Chaillot to sup, rustically, in forest glades, or to picnic by the river.

In this glittering kaleidoscope Prince Charles's tastes were partially formed; here he found the freedom, variety and contrast he had never known in the ordered stateliness of his father's Court; here beauty and wit were boldly allied and the graces were undraped and the hours glided past ... There was a nucleus of dullness and constraint in the Palais Royal, where in the Queen Regent's apartments a heavy, Hispano-Austrian etiquette prevailed; and in the Tuileries, where Henrietta Maria sat writing long, tear-stained letters or conferred with depressed, rather shabby English exiles. And then, suddenly, that inner gloom would be dispersed by invitations to an assembly, a play or a ball – as when, in March 1647, Cardinal Mazarin entertained the Court in the private theatre of the Tuileries which he entirely redecorated for the occasion. Here, once more, Charles and Mademoiselle were thrown together and publicly honoured.

II

Mazarin's party began with Monteverdi's *Orphée*, for which two celebrated Roman singers had been engaged. For six hours Signora Leonora and Signor Torelli, aided by the efforts of choruses and scene-shifters, carolled away against a series of elaborately changing backgrounds. When the opera was over the guests mounted the stage, which was hung with new tapestries and *trompe-l'œil* paintings and lit by huge crystal chandeliers.

In the middle at the back was a golden throne, raised by a flight of five steps. Benches for those not dancing were placed on either side of the auditorium.[4]

Louis XIV, who had desired Prince Charles to lead in Mademoiselle, was still in mourning for his aunt the Empress (his black satin doublet was so thickly sewn with pearls that only a few inches of the material could be seen) and therefore did not dance.[5] He indicated that the Prince should precede him to the dais, which Charles, according to custom, politely refused to do. Louis insisted. This formalized dispute might have lasted indefinitely if Mademoiselle had not seated herself on the throne. 'I remained there,' she says, adding that the King and her cousin then sat on the steps. 'No one could have been more magnificently attired than I,' she goes on, 'and there were plenty who told me so ... I was not in the least shy of sitting there ... It well became me ... I was destined for just such a place, not merely for the length of a ball, but for always.'[6]

As she gazed down the room, her famous white, black and carnation draperies flowing about her, Mademoiselle's ambitions reached their apotheosis. Her thoughts turned from the rather nebulous vision of the English crown to an imperial diadem – for she knew that Ferdinand III must marry again; and was she not born to be an empress? 'I then looked down on the Prince in more than one sense,' she recalls, 'for I had it in mind to marry the Emperor and was so taken up with the idea that a Prince of Wales became, merely, an object of pity.' (The object of pity remained thankfully silent and was presently able to enjoy a good supper.)

As Henrietta Maria became aware that her son was making even less progress than usual with his courtship – indeed, he appeared to be taking an interest in one or two other ladies at the ball – she took the first opportunity to reproach Mademoiselle. 'You are thinking of the Emperor,' she added crossly. Mademoiselle denied it; nor did she tell her aunt that the Cardinal seemed to favour the match with Ferdinand. The day after the party her father, the only person whose opinion she valued, and who had been warned by Mazarin that Mademoiselle's fortune must not go out of the kingdom, said to her, 'I know that the idea of marriage with the Emperor appeals to you. That being the case, I will do all I can to forward it, but I am sure you would not be happy in that country,' and went on to speak about the Emperor's unattractive appearance and middle-aged habits. 'You would be happier in England if matters improve there,' he added. 'I prefer the Emperor,' pleaded Mademoiselle, 'I beg you to agree to the marriage. I don't care for youth or gallantry. It is the position I am thinking of, not the person.' Gaston d'Orléans said no more, and neither did the Cardinal. A few months later the Emperor married one of his Austrian cousins.

Shortly after Mazarin's party Henrietta Maria received a letter from Parliament in which she was offered £100,000 never to set foot in England again; the Commons asked the Prince to return.[7] She then declared that she would retire into a convent; her husband's distress put an end to this scheme. Meanwhile Prince Charles was once more considering invasion from Ireland. When he was told that his father had 'pledged his word' that he should go back to England on Parliament's terms, he ignored the statement, as no doubt he was intended to do. He then got into touch with the Earl of Newcastle, now established in Paris, where he was running a school of *manège* and doing quite well out of it.[8]

A Royalist conference was held at St Germain during which Newcastle suggested that His Highness should go to Scotland. Henrietta Maria immediately lost her temper. The Scots were traitors. 'You are too quick!' she exclaimed, and the meeting broke up.[9] By this time Prince Charles had decided to join the French army and fight the Spanish under Gaston d'Orléans in Flanders. When the Queen heard that he had written for his father's leave to do this without consulting her, she made another scene, appealing to the Queen Regent to support her. The Royalists in Jersey also expressed their disapproval, and Charles remained at St Germain, studying with Dr Earle and amusing himself with the Villiers in Paris. His relationship with his mother was becoming strained; yet in a sense it had not changed since his ninth year, when she had ordered him to take his physic and he had ignored her and appealed to his Governor. It was at about this time, when he had just celebrated his seventeenth birthday, that he began to evolve his invariable system with demanding and hysterical women: that of agreeing to everything they said, granting all requests and then going his own way. His courtesy to Henrietta Maria never failed; he remained respectful, protective and affectionate; but he made his own decisions and stuck to them. 'Without doubt,' wrote Hyde to Sir Edward Nicholas, Charles I's Secretary of State, 'he hath a sweetness of nature not easy to be corrupted.'[10] Although the Chancellor was worried about his young master and would have liked to join him, he would not go to France. (Besides, he was busy with his *History of the Rebellion*, which was coming on at the rate of sixty pages a day.) And he could not leave Jersey till His Highness's debts were paid.

So the months passed in the usual round of formal and informal entertainment, while the Royalist prospects deteriorated. Mazarin began to wonder whether he had not better abandon Charles I's cause, and the

politicians and statesmen started to talk about that General Cromwell who
had apparently achieved final victory in the Civil War – was he to be
reckoned with or not? Since the Covenanting Scottish party, headed by
the Marquess of Argyll, had sold the King to Parliament, it had been impossible for Mazarin to commit himself to either side; and now matters
were further complicated by the Royalist Scots, represented by Montrose,
making advances to Prince Charles, whose value, from the Cardinal's
point of view, was thereby increased. He began to look on his young
guest as if he were a hostage, with the result that the Prince became increasingly restive, and considered appealing to Holland or Denmark for
help. Charles shared his mother's distrust of the Scots; it was one of the
few points on which they were agreed. 'If I go to Edinburgh,' he said,
when that question arose, 'I shall be sold, as my father was,'[11] and for a
time he made plans to go to England to treat with Fairfax and Cromwell
in person.

Meanwhile Henrietta Maria, not yet despairing, told Mademoiselle that
Charles had been too much discouraged by the talk of her marriage with
the Emperor to pursue his courtship. Mademoiselle was inclined to believe
this until, at a ball given in the Prince's honour, she saw him footing it
merrily with the beautiful Duchesse de Châtillon – Bablon was his pet
name for her – and then with Mademoiselle de Guerchi, one of the
Queen Regent's ladies; and this before he had asked her to dance with
him! Mademoiselle was very angry, and prepared to refuse him with
cutting disdain. As the evening wore on and he did not come near her, she
complained to Prince Rupert, who said something about his cousin's
youth and ignorance of etiquette. Mademoiselle would have none of it;
she was disgusted. A few weeks later she began to make plans for marrying
Ferdinand's brother, the Archduke Leopold; these were at once frustrated
by her father and Cardinal Mazarin.

Throughout the spring and summer of 1648 Charles's rather hesitant
negotiations with the Scots continued. 'He is ready for action and longs
to be at it,' wrote one of their emissaries, adding that His Highness had
no funds for the journey and that the French were preventing his departure.[12] And if he were allowed to leave – should he go to Ireland, Scotland,
or the Low Countries? Finally Charles decided to go to the Hague and
plan his campaign from his sister's and brother-in-law's Court. Having
tried, unsuccessfully, to prevent a duel between Prince Rupert and Lord
Percy, in which the latter was wounded, Charles made a rendezvous with
the Duke of Hamilton at Helvoetsluys.

Then suddenly news came that the greater part of the English fleet had broken away from Parliament and declared for Prince Charles. On June 25th, 1648, he left Paris for Calais. Parliament voted him a traitor and there was talk of setting a price on his head.[13] But Charles was jubilant. After six years, victory was in sight. With the English navy and the Scots army behind him he was sure to triumph.

NOTES

1 De Motteville, vol. I, p. 390.
2 Aubrey, p. 384.
3 P. Amiguet, *La Grande Mademoiselle et son Siècle*, p. 15.
4 De Motteville, vol. I, pp. 312–15.
5 Ibid.
6 Montpensier, vol. I, pp. 126–8.
7 *Cal. S. P. Ven.*, vol. XXVII, p. 306.
8 *Cal. D. S. P.*, Addenda, May 1647.
9 Newcastle, pp. 73–4.
10 *Cal. Clar. S. P.*, vol. II, p. 319.
11 *Cal. S. P. Ven.*, vol. XXVIII, Feb.–March, 1648.
12 *Hamilton Papers* (H.M.C.), p. 171.
13 *Cal. D. S. P.*, May 28th, 1648.

CHAPTER FOUR

THE NAVY AND THE SCOTS

I

FROM Calais Prince Charles sailed to Helvoetsluys, arriving there on July 9th, 1648, accompanied, among others, by Prince Rupert, Lord Hopton and Lord Colepepper. At Honslaerdyke he was met by the fifteen-year-old Duke of York, who had just escaped from England in woman's clothes and had already become the centre of an intrigue manipulated by Lord Jermyn and his agent Dr Goffe. Jermyn wanted to make the younger Prince titular Admiral of the Royalist fleet with a view to controlling it himself – although he had not the slightest knowledge of naval affairs – and had sent Goffe to put his plan before the sailors, who were in favour of James, but became doubtful when Goffe said, 'You should all petition the Lord Jermyn may be made your Admiral. He will be able to supply you with money and whatever else you want.'[1] Their officers distrusted Jermyn and felt that the King and the Prince of Wales should be consulted first; when Prince Charles, the Duke of York and the Prince and Princess of Orange all met at Helvoetsluys, the fleet was on the verge of mutiny. Charles's presence reassured them, and by the 16th a plan of action had been made, a few provisions found and the seamen satisfied by Charles and Rupert taking command.

During that week of preparation Charles and York spent a few nights at the Hague with their sister and brother-in-law. A devoted family, they were all very happy together. At some point in that brief visit Charles became the lover of a young woman called Lucy Walter. Their relationship was to be disastrous, not only to themselves, but to their son James, born the following April and created Duke of Monmouth fourteen years later. Lucy's hold over Charles was of the kind that is difficult to break. Of all his mistresses, she was the most important; indeed, she may have been the only woman he ever really loved; certainly she was the one he treated worst.

Lucy Walter, only daughter of William and Elizabeth Walter of Haverfordwest in Pembrokeshire, was born in 1630. Her parents were of good family; through her mother she was related to the Earls of Carbery, and her father was heir to Roch Castle, near St David's, although he could not afford to live there. When Lucy was eight the Walters quarrelled, each accusing the other of infidelity. They then moved, with Lucy and her brothers Justus and John, to London. Two years later William Walter abandoned his wife and children, and Mrs Walter took refuge with her mother and her sister Margaret in a house at St-Giles-in-the-Fields. Margaret was married to a Dutch merchant, Peter Gosfright. They could do little for Mrs Walter, who in 1640 brought an action for maintenance against her husband in the House of Lords, eventually obtaining £60 a year from his estate. In 1644 Algernon Sidney, then a colonel in Cromwell's New Model army, who was recovering from wounds received at the battle of Marston Moor, met Lucy on one of his visits to London and gave her 'fifty broad pieces' (about £60) to become his mistress. He took her with him to the Hague, where they lived together for a short time. He then passed her on to his brother Robert, who in 1648 became groom of the bedchamber to Prince Charles. Within a few days of the Prince's meeting Lucy, Robert Sidney 'willingly' gave her up to his young master. 'Let who's have her, she's already sped,' he is reported to have told the Prince. Charles ignored this warning. By the time he left Holland his son had been conceived and Lucy, now known as Mrs Barlow, was his public mistress.[2]

The imperfectly authenticated portraits of Lucy, probably painted in her middle twenties, do not quite correlate with Evelyn's famous description of her as 'a bold, brown, beautiful but insipid creature'. They seem to indicate that her experience as the mistress of two men several years older than herself was enhanced by sexual magnetism of a very high order. Her beauty was not of the kind that endures, or one that would have been admired in any age but her own; but she had a strong, indeed a violent personality (the cultured and fastidious Evelyn found her insipid because she was unintellectual to the point, almost, of illiteracy). She was not the kind of favourite who is easily discarded or kept in the background. Her instinct was to assert and parade herself, while granting her favours to any man who took her fancy. Today, her type throngs the police courts and is then submerged. Lucy's career was more sensational – and equally sordid.

When these eighteen-year-old lovers had their first parting neither could have been unduly cast down. Charles was at last within reach of the action which had been denied him since the battle of Edgehill; and Lucy was the acknowledged mistress of a king's son. Indeed, at some moment – probably when he returned to the Hague two months later to find her pregnant – the evidence points to Charles having promised to marry

Lucy: for she was practical, and he was easy-going. So a mysterious situation was created which has not yet been made clear.

On July 22nd the Prince's fleet sailed for the Downs and he himself was on board the *Satisfaction*. Here he had been joined, from the Hague, by the Duke of Buckingham, who had barely survived the consequences of an abortive rising led by himself, Lord Holland and Francis Villiers. Holland was now in prison and under sentence of death; Francis Villiers had been killed in a fight near Surbiton Common. Buckingham, apparently unaffected by these disasters, which were followed by the sequestration of his estates and by a price being set on his head, had once more surpassed his former fellow-pupil; for he had killed the Roundhead captain of horse who pursued him after the battle, escaped with a posse of Cavaliers and hidden in London before escaping to Holland.

Buckingham now took part in preparations for a sea fight and in the disputes between Prince Charles, the Council and the Earl of Lauderdale, who was expected from Scotland to arrange the terms of an alliance with the Prince. These negotiations continued during the whole course of Charles's attempted invasion; all those concerned, including the seamen, had a share in them; it was taken for granted that these complicated and far-reaching discussions should accompany an equally intricate naval expedition.

Lauderdale, an apparently uncouth but extremely cunning and accomplished politician, represented only one of the three parties into which Scotland was divided and which the Prince was trying to unite behind him; if he succeeded, victory would be within his grasp. The first was that of the Royalists led by the Marquess of Montrose and recently defeated by the other two; this had resulted in Montrose's banishment; he was now trying to raise forces for the King in Denmark. The second and most powerful was that of the Marquess of Argyll, opposed to Montrose and to the Duke of Hamilton and Lord Lauderdale. Hamilton, Lauderdale and Argyll were all Presbyterians; but the difference between Argyll's policy and that of the Hamilton-Lauderdale party lay in their attitude towards the fanatical puritanism of the Covenant which represented the dictatorship of that grim organization, the Kirk of Scotland.

Argyll was heart and soul for the Covenant, because he realized that only so could he himself become master of Scotland. Hamilton and Lauderdale, although they also had signed the Covenant, were now working against its power and that of Argyll and the Scots clergy, with a view to reinstating the rule of the nobles; yet both they and Argyll were determined to destroy Montrose and his faction. Hamilton and Lauderdale had a majority in the Scottish Parliament, but not the backing of the nation as a whole. In December 1647 these two noblemen and Charles I, then a prisoner in the Isle of Wight, had entered into a treaty known as the Engagement, in which the King agreed to allow Presbyterianism in Scotland for three years and security to those who had already taken the oath of the Covenant (he did not, of course, intend to stick to his share of the bargain) in return for Hamilton's invasion of England. Argyll had no part in this scheme. While Prince Charles was at sea Hamilton started his invasion; so the military issue was in the balance when the negotiations with Lauderdale began.

To Charles, it must have seemed strange that Argyll and the Engagers, who had united in signing the Covenant, were rivals and enemies. The reason for this lay in clan warfare, that legacy from the past. Argyll, having eliminated Montrose, had to find a presentable excuse for defeating Lauderdale and Hamilton in the struggle for power. He and the Covenanting ministers, his most influential supporters, therefore condemned and abused the other two noblemen, because they had made the Engagement with Charles I, whom they rightly described as the would-be destroyer of Presbyterianism in Scotland. The ministers were sincere. Argyll was not; he simply wanted Hamilton and Lauderdale out of the way, and the Engagement was as good a stick to beat them with as anything else. Hamilton and Lauderdale, equally determined to loosen Argyll's hold over Scotland, were using the Prince as their weapon. So both parties, while outwardly vying for Charles's favour and apparently working for Cromwell's defeat, were in fact only concerned with their own ambitions. As soon as Charles realized this, he began to play off the Engagers against Argyll, while keeping in touch with their common enemies, the Scottish Royalists.

Lauderdale had been instructed to make clear to the Prince (who had already written warmly to Hamilton) that the Engagers would only invade from Scotland if he abandoned those of his party who were known to be antagonistic to the Covenant – Prince Rupert and Montrose were among those named – and used the Presbyterian form of worship; he would have to abjure the Prayer-Book and all 'episcopal ceremonies', and must dismiss his chaplains, of whom there were three on board his frigate.

While Charles was considering the letter embodying these terms his fleet was forced into Yarmouth Roads. As soon as they realized what had happened the citizens sent a deputation to greet him, but begged him not to land, as they were afraid of Parliamentary reprisals.[3] The Prince ignored this request and sent ashore a party of horse who were cheered by the people. The bailiffs called out troops to arrest them, and seven men had been disarmed and were being marched off when the townspeople intervened and released them. The Royalist party then returned to their ships with a present of provisions, and the Prince's fleet set sail for the Downs. Here Lauderdale joined them, and came aboard the *Satisfaction*.

Charles, apprised of his terms, was hoping to get round them by a series of vague promises and the assurance of his good intentions. He agreed to leave behind those of his Councillors to whom the Scots objected, and evaded the more difficult issue of attending Presbyterian services. In a few hours he had won over Lauderdale by talking to him privately of his eagerness to be among his Scottish subjects. 'We are like to be very happy in him,' Lauderdale reported to Lanerick, Hamilton's younger brother, '[his] inclinations I found as good and earnest ... as possible.'⁴ When the Council was called Lauderdale's hopes were dashed by their insistence that the King must be consulted before anything was settled. Lauderdale 'flatly', as he told Lanerick, refused to consider this, but was persuaded by Charles to have an informal discussion in his cabin with Prince Rupert, Hopton, Colepepper and several other lords. When the Earl appeared he was received with impressive courtesy. 'Sit down next to Prince Rupert,' said Charles, and a long debate ensued. Charles's secret plan – which he did not divulge and which is recorded in a letter he never sent – was that when he appeared in Scotland he would 'prevail with them to depart from the strictness of their purposes'.⁵ In fact, he was using the same tactics as he had with La Grande Mademoiselle, those of appearing to comply while not committing himself and relying on the combination of his status and his personal charm to win over the people who had sold his father and whom he himself disliked and mistrusted.

Charles was too intelligent to be conceited; but he had the self-confidence and optimism natural in a boy of eighteen leading, as he thought, an expedition which was bound to succeed; and he was completely deceived by Lauderdale, whose repellent exterior, dirty habits and thick, almost unintelligible accent created a false impression, not only on Charles but on the more experienced Buckingham. The Duke who, with Rupert, was still the strongest influence in the Prince's Court, described Lauderdale as 'a man of blundering understanding', and thus encouraged Charles to think that he was dealing with a half-witted savage.

Lauderdale also was taken in; he believed that Charles was eager to comply with his terms and was being held back by his Council. It did not occur to him that this gallant and agreeable youth was not putting all his cards on the table. During the course of their discussion Charles drew him aside and begged him not to insist on the exclusion of Rupert in that Prince's presence. Lauderdale agreed, upon which Charles struck out, 'with his own hand', some of the points on which the Council had refused to give way, at the same time assuring Lauderdale that he would arrange everything satisfactorily as soon as he reached Scotland. 'I must go first to Holland,' he added, 'as I cannot divide the fleet.' In that case, Lauderdale said, he should leave. Charles persuaded him to stay and the meeting broke up.

Next day the Councillors told Lauderdale that he should not have insisted on any agreement with His Highness without the King's consent. 'This,' Lauderdale told Lanerick, 'I eluded ... but ... it was impossible to obtain more in religion from the Prince.' Charles then sent for Lauderdale and said, 'I have accommodated the business smoothly concerning Prince Rupert – but write to your private friends and say that it is my earnest desire that that restraint be taken off.' Lauderdale would not commit himself; he promised Charles 'honour, safety and freedom' in his Scottish kingdom. 'Truly, I am aweary of wagging at sea,' he told Lanerick, 'I had far rather be at cuffs with you.' A few days later he tried to force the Prince's hand by threatening to break off negotiations, upon which Charles suddenly announced that he was ready to accept all the Scottish conditions. While Lauderdale was wondering what to believe he found himself involved in a different and much more dangerous dispute.[6]

II

'The seamen,' says Sir Edward Hyde, 'are a nation by themselves, a humorous and fantastic people; fierce and rude in whatsoever they resolve or are inclined to, unsteady and inconstant in pursuing it and jealous of those tomorrow by whom they are governed today.'[7]

The sailors of the Royalist fleet were at least steady in their resolve to attack Parliament's navy, not only because of their devotion to Prince Charles, but because they believed that Hamilton's invasion would be successful. When Captain William Batten, in command of the *Constant Reformation*, went over to Charles and was knighted, they were more than ever sure of victory, although they considered, rightly, that he was an incompetent officer. Further encouraged by the capture of several Parliament ships, one of which was an East Indiaman carrying a valuable cargo of cloth, they proceeded to blockade the mouth of the Thames. What they chiefly desired was to fight, and so far they had not seen the enemy.

From the Thames Charles sent Parliament a letter offering to sell them the merchantman and appealing to them to restore the King and the liberties of the people. In the debate held on this communication it was declared that the Prince was 'his father's own son, and as like him as can be', and should be outlawed as a rebel and a traitor. Those who had aided him were pronounced guilty of high treason.[8]

As they could not afford to lose the merchantman, Parliament had to enter into negotiations with Charles, who eventually parted with her for £12,000, and was thus in a position to pay his crews; but he was not able to land and buy provisions. The seamen became increasingly discontented and, encouraged by Rupert, announced their intention of taking the Roundhead blockhouses, which they did, leaving in them such men and arms as could be spared; these were recaptured by Parliament, who then sent out a fleet under the Earl of Warwick, instructing him to occupy the Lee Roads.

Charles's fleet had now been at sea for five weeks and supplies were very low. 'We had not drunk for three days, we had not provisions for four,' one of his chaplains reported. The seamen offered to go on half rations rather than retreat. Lauderdale and Colepepper were heard urging the Prince to return to Holland, upon which a posse of sailors burst in upon the Council and threatened to throw the two noblemen overboard. They then rushed to Charles, who went on deck, and implored him to attack. As he hesitated – for he knew that they might find themselves without food or drink before they reached Warwick's fleet – one said, 'If we go without you, we shall have no Prince.' 'If a contrary wind should come,' Charles replied, 'we may be all starved', but they refused to consider this and fell to cursing Lauderdale and Colepepper.[9]

Charles then went below to consult Rupert; they agreed that to sail for the Lee Roads was to risk losing all that had been gained; but the ships' companies were on the point of mutiny. What was to be done? None of the Council dared approach them again, so Charles returned to the deck and appealed to them to obey orders. 'Will you not go with me wherever I go?' he asked, and after some further argument they agreed to do so.[10]

At this point Warwick's fleet was sighted. The drums sounded for action stations. As the Royalist ships advanced Warwick retreated. Charles was still on deck. The Council, supported by the sailors, implored him to go below. 'I will not hear of it,' he said. 'My honour is more to me than my safety.' As they continued to persuade him he interrupted, 'Do not speak of it any more,' and remained where he was.[11]

The pursuit continued till nightfall, when both fleets were forced to cast anchor. As day broke Warwick sent a message to the Prince, desiring him to yield, and signing himself Lord High Admiral. Charles replied, 'None but the King can make a Lord High Admiral of England. But I will give pardon and pay if you will come over to me, and will receive you with all sincerity and affection.'[12]

Warwick ignored this overture, and at last battle appeared inevitable. The sailors cheered and threw up their caps. Then, as both fleets made ready to close, a violent gust of wind drove them apart. This was followed by a storm which lasted several hours.

There was now nothing for it but to return to Holland. As they were doing so another fleet was sighted which Rupert said was the Portsmouth squadron. Charles, who was steering, gave orders for action. Batten expostulated. 'Sir, whither do we steer? Will Your Highness run out of the way for every collier that you see?' and persuaded him to keep his course. As it was a very hot day, Batten had wound a white scarf round his neck with which he mopped up the sweat. Prince Rupert took it into his head that Batten was signalling to the enemy in this way. 'By God!' he said to Charles, 'if things go ill, the first thing I will do is to shoot him.'[13] By this time the half-starved sailors had lost heart and the retreat continued, while Warwick followed them at a distance. On September 1st Charles's fleet stood off Goree. As soon as they landed he gave orders for refitting and provisioning. The crews, now completely demoralized, spent their time ashore, drinking and fighting among themselves. Some were shot, others thrown overboard. These measures had no effect. As an active force, the Royalist navy had ceased to exist.

So ended Prince Charles's second attempt to fight his father's enemies. Six years had passed since he charged the Roundhead troop at Edgehill and was held back by Sir John Hinton, who now reappeared as a messenger from the English Royalists.[14] Cromwell had completely routed Hamilton's forces in Lancashire. Parliament had announced that, as 'the office of a king ... is unnecessary, burdensome and dangerous to the liberties of the English people,' Charles I should be tried for high treason. The Prince of Wales and the Duke of York were also summoned for trial 'upon pain of being declared incapable of governing, and sentenced to die without mercy, if found in England or its dominions'.[15]

In his humiliation Charles, who had so rejoiced, according to Hinton, 'to cut a caper' at sea, now had no one to turn to but the Scots. First he had to go through the farce of a formal reception from the Dutch, who brought him and his courtiers to the Hague in a train of thirty coaches, and there 'solemnly feasted and entertained' him, while announcing that they would allow him a thousand guilders a day for just over a week; after that he would have to shift for himself. He stayed at the Hôtel de Ville and had his meals with the Prince and Princess of Orange.

One aspect of the situation held a little hope, and that was that the Hamilton-Lauderdale party's defeat might prevent their insisting on the Prince's acceptance of the Covenant and on the dismissal of his chaplains before leaving for Scotland. A few days after his arrival at the Hague he called a Council, which was attended by Sir Edward Hyde and his friend and ally, Lord Cottington, now Treasurer to the Royalist exiles. The Chancellor, who had not seen the Prince for two years, was so concerned about his alliance with the Presbyterian rebels that he did not observe how much he had gained in authority and diplomatic cunning.

When Lauderdale was summoned to read out his commission and the Scots' conditions, he concluded with the hardest – that only 'godly' men would be admitted as His Highness's chaplains.[16]

Charles said, 'If you have no more to say, you may withdraw, that the Council may debate the matter.' Lauderdale angrily refused. 'Do not be unreasonable,' said Hyde, and a violent dispute ensued, interrupted by the Prince. 'It is unreasonable that you should be present,' he said coldly, 'I command you to withdraw.' Lauderdale did so, muttering and cursing, 'with much indecency', according to Hyde. Charles then said, 'News of the victory over the Scots has come and Duke Hamilton is taken prisoner. We will meet again next morning to consult what is to do. In the meantime, the intelligence will be more perfect, and we shall see whether my Lord of Lauderdale will take any notice of it.'[17]

Next day Lauderdale took up the same attitude. When asked whether he knew of the defeat, he began to bluster. 'I know well what the news is, and hope it is not true,' he said, and again urged the Prince to come to Scotland on the terms of the Engagement – which would have amounted to the betrayal of the Royalist cause. Once more Charles tried to arbitrate between the older Councillors and those in favour of accepting Lauderdale's conditions. In the weeks that followed Lauderdale, despairing of pinning down this evasive young man, returned to Scotland, 'with as much rage and malice against the Council,' says Hyde, 'as against Cromwell himself'.

Charles now had to deal with two more complications: that of his mother's interference with his and his Council's decisions, and the intrigues centring on the Duke of York. He had already discharged a Colonel Bamfield who had helped the Duke to escape – Bamfield was 'a man of a turbulent and intriguing temper' – and who had urged the seamen to mutiny before they left Helvoetsluys.[18] During the dispute over the admiralship, which Charles now gave to Rupert, he had also dismissed a Captain Griffin; this officer, having announced his intention of cutting Lord Jermyn's throat, had suggested to York that he should defy his brother rather than give up the command of the fleet. Now Charles had to soothe York's jealousy in the intervals of reading – he does not seem to have answered them – the mass of letters from his father which had accumulated during his absence, and also mediate between Hyde and Henrietta Maria; for the Queen had gone over to the Covenanting party although warned by the French ambassador in Scotland that they were not to be trusted. Her plan was that Charles should give in to all the Scots' demands, use their armies against the Parliamentary forces and then break the promises he had made. Her letters embodying this scheme were inspired by Jermyn and what the Council described as the Louvrian party in Paris. Meanwhile, there was Lucy Walter, now pregnant by the Prince, planning to entrap him into marriage; and Sir Robert Welsh, one of his gentlemen, was bent on attacking Lord Colepepper, who, he said, had slandered him to the Council. Welsh and three of his friends entered Colepepper's lodgings with drawn swords, forced him outside and after walking 'civilly' with him into a secluded street, knocked him down. Colepepper was not seriously hurt, and Charles dismissed Welsh. The fact remained that Colepepper was disliked by everyone, and continued to make mischief.[19]

Warwick's fleet now appeared off the Dutch coast; it was feared that he might try to kidnap the Prince, which would amount to an invasion. The Dutch, who were beginning to feel Parliament's power, sent a deputation begging Warwick to withdraw. He replied that he would do so if the Royalist ships came over to him. Charles then went down to the harbour and held a meeting with officers and men, with the result that those whose loyalty had been shaken decided to remain where they were; next day Warwick left for England. Once more an intrigue was started to give the naval command to the Duke of York, and thus to Jermyn. Charles was firm, and instructed Rupert to take command and sail for Ireland; for the Irish, so Ormonde had informed him, were ready and eager to invade. York then joined Henrietta Maria in Paris.[20]

In October Charles had smallpox, and for a few days was very ill. As soon as he was able to deal with his correspondence, he began trying to raise money from anyone who might lend it – the Queen of Sweden, the Prince de Condé, the King of Denmark, Anne of Austria – and answer the piteous letters of the disabled seamen and their wives, whose scrawled, weirdly spelt communications poured in daily. 'For his hines the Prince of

Wales,' wrote one, 'Your hines veri well knows that my husband has done veri much sarvis for the King your fath in the wors...'[21]

Meanwhile, Charles I, meticulous and painstaking as ever, was writing to the Prince at enormous length about duty, misfortune, religion and the imminence of his own martyrdom. One of these letters ran into some 20,000 words and dealt with kingship in all its aspects. Another outlined, at similar length, the whole history of the King's disagreements with Parliament. Both were full of advice and conscious rectitude, exquisitely phrased, superbly resigned and imbued with a total and magnificent disregard of the facts. On every page the King adjured his son never to desert the Church of England, for which he himself was now preparing to die.

> I had rather you should be Charles *le bon* than *le grand*...This may be the last time we speak to you or to the world publicly. We are sensible into what hands we are fallen... So order affairs... that you shall not need to fear or flatter... or... you are undone... I know God can – perhaps He will – restore me to my rights. I cannot despair, either of His mercy, or my people's love and pity... I shall but go before you to a better kingdom, which God hath prepared for me and me for it, through my Saviour Jesus Christ... Farewell, till we meet, if not on earth, yet in heaven...

No answer to these communications survives; perhaps none was made. After Christmas, when news came that the King had been moved to Windsor and was to be tried for high treason, Charles heard no more from him. He then wrote – from Breda, where he was living unattended so as to save money –

> Sir, having no means to come to the knowledge of Your Majesty's affairs, but such as I receive from the prints (which is altogether uncertain) I have sent this bearer [Henry] Seymour to wait upon Your Majesty... I do not only pray for Your Majesty according to my duty, but shall always be ready to do all which shall be in my power to deserve that blessing which I do most humbly beg of Your Majesty.[22]

Charles then appealed to the Dutch to save his father's life, at least. They sent an emissary to Parliament, who was politely received and told to go about his business. The Prince wrote to the Scots, imploring them to rescue their King and his; to Montrose, now in Brussels, who replied, 'I never had passion on earth so strong as that to do the King your father service;' and to Fairfax, begging him for a report on his father's 'health and condition'. He also asked about the rumour that the King was to be tried and beheaded, 'the thought of which,' he wrote, 'seems so horrible and incredible'. He begged the Parliamentary Council not to be authors of 'misery unprecedented by contributing to an action ... repugnant ... to the principles of religion ... and destructive of all security'.[23]

No answer came to these appeals, and it was said that the King had come to an arrangement with the Parliamentary Council. In the third week of January 1649 Prince Charles dispatched three copies of his famous *carte blanche*, a paper on which was written his signature and nothing else, accompanied by a letter asking Parliament to place above it whatever terms they desired in return for the King's life. One of these was given to Charles I a few hours before his execution; he burnt it, so as not to compromise his son. Another was presented to Cromwell by a Royalist relative, Colonel Henry Cromwell, and also destroyed. The third survived and is now in the British Museum.[24] Charles then returned to the Hague.

On February 4th William of Orange was sailing near the Hague, when his yacht was hailed by a fishing smack on its way home. The captain boarded the Prince's ship and told him that the King of England had been executed on January 30th. William returned to the palace and broke the news, first to his wife and then to the new King's chaplains. It was decided that Dr Goffe should ask for an audience and tell him what had happened.

For some time the wretched chaplain blundered on, speaking at random. Then he began a sentence with 'Your Majesty – ' and broke off. There was an appalling silence. Charles burst into tears, with the loud, agonized sobbing of a frightened child. Then he rushed out of the room and shut himself in his bedchamber. There he remained, alone, for many hours.[25]

Several weeks later Charles I's last words were printed and smuggled out to the Hague. 'For the people, truly I desire their liberty and freedom as much as anybody whomsoever. But I must tell you, their liberty ... consists in having government ... *It is not for their having a share in the government; that is nothing pertaining to them.* A subject and a sovereign are clean different things.'

The political and religious contradiction of this statement was the next lesson Charles II had to learn. It was the bitterest of his life – and the most destructive. Being forced to come to terms and to share his power with the people so altered his outlook as to change his character, and that for the worse. Knowing now that he could not live like a king – and that he probably never would be able to do so – he saw that to behave like one would be fatal and absurd. He therefore applied himself to the methods he had used since his exile, those of 'accommodating everything smoothly', while pursuing his own ends. Of this art he was to become the greatest exponent in the civilized world.

NOTES

1 Clarendon, pp. 648–9.
2 A. Fea, *King Monmouth*, p. 5; E. d'Oyley, *James, Duke of Monmouth*, pp. 4–10; G. Steinmann, *Althorp Memoirs*, pp. 80–116; G. Montagu-Douglas-Scott, *Lucy Walter – Wife or Mistress?*, p. 57.
3 *Hamilton Papers* (H.M.C.), pp. 233, 237, 244.
4 Ibid.
5 *Clarendon MSS*, vol. XXXI, fol. 2858.
6 *Hamilton Papers* (H.M.C.), p. 244.
7 Clarendon, p. 646.
8 Op. cit., pp. 655–7.
9 *Clarendon MSS*, vol. XXXI, fol. 2881.
10 *Cal. Clar. S. P.*, vol. II, pp. 414–15.
11 Op. cit., vol. I, p. 438.
12 Hinton, p. 23.
13 S. Pepys, *Diary*, vol. IV, p. 141.
14 Hinton, ibid.
15 Gardiner, *Civil War*, vol. IV, p. 235.
16 Clarendon, pp. 659–61.
17 Op. cit., pp. 672–3.
18 *Nicholas Papers* (ed. G. F. Warner), vol. I, p. 64.
19 *Clarendon MSS*, vol. XXXI, fol. 2004.
20 Clarendon, pp. 672–3.
21 *Cal. D. S. P.*, Jan. 22nd, 1649.
22 *Letters* (ed. Petrie), pp. 239–73.
23 C. J. Lyon, *Personal History of Charles II*, p. xvi.
24 Baroness van Nyevelt, *Court Life in the Dutch Republic*, p. 132.
25 Gardiner, *Commonwealth and Protectorate*, vol. I, p. 17.

CHAPTER FIVE

THE FIRST SCOTS COMMISSION

I

IN the five centuries that preceded Charles I's execution four Kings of
England had been secretly murdered, one killed by accident and another in battle. If he had been privately assassinated few would have
felt surprise and not many pity for a monarch who had made a series of
fatal mistakes in his dealings with a barbarous people. But that an anointed
king should have been publicly tried and judicially (although illegally)
condemned seemed, to an incredulous Europe, so terrible, so hideously
alarming, that many rulers were frightened into treating with Cromwell,
while others appear to have felt that sympathy was all they could safely
give his successor. The Tsar of Russia set a high standard by ordering all
the English to leave his dominions, while continuing to trade with their
country.[1] Other European potentates expressed their horror with less
force but more eloquence. A Dutch lady who was in labour when told the
news was so appalled that her child was born dead; another woman died
from shock and a third became so ill that her life was despaired of, although only for a time. Montrose fainted, reviving to write one of his
most celebrated poems – 'Good, great and just … ' – and the young
King's Court were 'almost bereft of their understanding'.[2]

Charles himself was stunned. Although long aware of his father's
danger, he seems to have hoped for a last-minute reprieve; now he remained bewildered and dazed, unable to accept – even, at times, to take
in – his loss. He fell, according to Hyde, 'into all the confusion imaginable
… sinking under the burden of his grief' and heedless of his courtiers, who
'besought him to reserve so much courage as was necessary'. In such times
of misery and despair the treasured past is despoiled; the present appears
at the same time unreal and unendurable: and the future a long dark
passage leading into further depths of sorrow. For Charles to take up the
load of his diminished inheritance, of duties and public appearances was
temporarily impossible. He did not even write to his mother, who behaved with great fortitude, although for many hours after hearing the
news she had been unable to weep or speak or move from her chair.

Eventually Hyde drafted a letter to her which Charles signed, presumably without reading it. 'Your Majesty,' it began, 'will rather wonder that after this horrid and deadly blow, I have so soon recovered my spirits as to present my duty ... nothing but my reverence and devotion to Your Majesty being able to awaken me out of the deep amazement and condition I am in.' The letter concluded with some pious reflections and a polite request for Henrietta Maria's advice. The Queen replied in the same strain, but not so distractedly as to disguise her determination to dominate. 'Dearest and most unfortunate son,' she began, 'Your most loving letter with all its force of reason to console your most wretched mother would have disinvolved the misfortunes of my life – but my horizon is too far from the poles ... I have no other rainbow but that of remembering that I am your mother ... Declare yourself a Catholic ... *as you have so often promised me* ... Only so can you win Ireland.'[3]

By the time he received this letter Charles's rooms had been hung with black and he and all his Court provided with mourning at William of Orange's expense. He then 'bravely cheered up' and roused himself to ask for money, 'in our royal father's name', from the King of Denmark and other powers.

The lack of response to these appeals was partly made up for by the indignant and practical sympathy of the Scots, who now expressed their resolve to crown Charles and avenge his father – but under the conditions already presented by the Engagers. While considering how to combine their forces with those of Montrose and Argyll without committing himself to the Covenant, Charles received the condolences of the States General with graceful dignity, and a strong hint as to his expectations. 'My sole comfort among so many disasters,' he said, 'is to find myself among you, with whose help, under God, I look for my restoration.'[4] Meanwhile he was secretly proclaimed in London and publicly in Edinburgh.

The Scottish proclamation partially reassured Charles's cautious and unwilling Dutch hosts, who had been much alarmed by Warwick's descent on their shores; a few weeks after their visit of condolence they made it clear that they would prefer him to leave. In this they were opposed to William of Orange, whose powers, as Stadtholder of the province of Holland and head of the army, were confined to those posts. His Court was a Franco-Dutch colony, where only French was spoken, and he and the Princess were completely out of touch with the life of the Netherlanders, although they shared in the pleasures of their miraculous Golden Age.

To Charles, who at intervals had to thrust himself upon the fortunate creators of a unique and highly developed civilization, those pleasures meant very little. He had not inherited his father's knowledge of the arts, nor his feeling for order and cleanliness; so the villas and palaces of the Dutch merchant princes, with their glorious and variegated content of pictures, silk carpets, painted ceilings and gilded leather hangings – their gardens, their libraries, their splendid arrays of Chinese porcelain and Venetian glass – caused in him neither envy nor appreciation. He enjoyed, when he could afford them, their enormous meals, their coffee-houses, the skating, ball games and theatres; but promenading up and down long avenues, boating on sluggish canals and then sitting down to a solemn feast of hot-pot, sour beer, rice-pudding and waffles were distasteful to a young man used to wild hunting, fast tennis, French wines and English roasts; and there was a portentous respectability, an enclosed self-satisfaction about these dour potentates which made them unsympathetic to those who did not share their views or way of life.

Among these was Mary of Orange who, insisting on her English title of Princess Royal and deeply chagrined by her husband's unfaithfulness – his numerous love-affairs were at one time the subject of a play performed in Amsterdam[5] – never ceased to pine for England and her family. She was devoted to her brothers – as indeed, was William, whose generosity to them never failed – and perfectly indifferent to her own unpopularity. Since the outbreak of the Civil War this rather low-spirited, discontented girl had surrounded herself with English exiles, many of whom were now her attendants; she spent a great deal of time with her aunt, Queen Elizabeth of Bohemia, and that lively lady's clever, unconventional brood, of whom the youngest, Princess Sophia, was Charles's favourite girl cousin, and whose marriage to him had been considered in 1644.

Sophia was a very pretty girl, and although she had always been penurious, she had strong views about her own status and value. She was much taken with Charles – they were born in the same year – whom she describes at this time as 'richly endowed by nature, but not sufficiently so in fortune to allow him to think of marriage'. With him she attended the English services at the Hague – to the horror of William's mother, the Presbyterian Princess-Dowager Amalia – and they were 'on the best of terms, as cousins and friends'. Sophia considered that Charles was too easily influenced, and disapproved of his open frequentation of 'Mrs Barlow'. (By this time, Lucy's hold over her latest lover was deplored by most of his friends.) Also, Princess Sophia had the feeling that if the King did ask for her hand it would be in the hope that her richer relations might lend him money. Her suspicions were confirmed when he sent two of his gentlemen to call on her and then asked her to walk with him in the Voorhout during the evening promenade. She accepted and Charles, after paying her a number of compliments, suddenly said, 'You are handsomer than Mrs Barlow '– adding, 'I hope some day to see you in England.' As nothing was said, either to the Princess or her mother, about marriage, the acute young lady came to the conclusion that her cousin's intentions were dishonourable; she then heard that his courtiers had encouraged his advances in the hope that Lord Craven – a wealthy admirer of Queen Elizabeth – would be persuaded by Sophia to finance him. 'I was much offended,' she goes on, 'but the Queen, who had noticed His Majesty's marked attentions, was just as much delighted, and blamed me for not going on the promenade the following evening.' (Elizabeth adored her nephew and was more inclined to indulge him than her daughters, who sometimes got on her nerves.) 'I made the excuse,' Sophia continues, 'of a corn in my foot, which prevented me from walking. My real reason ... was to avoid the King, having sense enough to know that the marriages of great kings are not made up by such means.'[6]

Charles accepted his cousin's rebuff philosophically; his rather casual advance had been a momentary distraction from the furthering of a number of schemes in which marriage with an heiress came last. At this time he first considered asking for the hand of William of Orange's sister, Henriette Catherine, whom he found quite as attractive as Sophia, and whose mother favoured the match; but the Princess Dowager did not mean to part with her daughter till she knew what the King's prospects were.

These seemed hopeless enough. Three weeks after his father's execution Parliament confiscated Charles's property, refused his request for the late King's George and Garter, condemned him, Rupert, York and his Councillors to death and sold their goods, with the result that on February 22nd Charles reopened his negotiations with Scotland.

Although he must have known that he would be censured for his backing of Montrose, Charles made the Marquess Governor of Scotland and Lieutenant-General of all its forces. Argyll, ignoring this seemingly pointless gesture, sent a commission to the Hague to discuss the terms of the Covenant. Meanwhile Montrose, a courageous, forceful but rather vain man, continued to work for Charles in the belief that he would receive his support. He had the King's written promise to that effect – just as Strafford had had that of Charles I.

Charles II's circumstances differed from those of his father in that inexperience, penury and exile combined to make him the prey of Scottish cunning and fanaticism before their negotiations began. Although he was severely handicapped, he now had no illusions; he started the duel – it was no less – by adopting, in his correspondence with Scotland, a mild, winning tone, as of a person anxious to co-operate, and willing, indeed eager, to understand their point of view. These tactics were not apparent to the Council. Hyde, Nicholas and Cottington deplored His Majesty's weakness in consenting to receive Argyll's Commission, while doing all they could to prevent the only alternative, that of appealing, through Henrietta Maria, to France. In the first week in March, just before Argyll's Covenanting Commission arrived at the Hague, the Chancellor was trying to stop Jermyn coming from Paris to bring back the King on the Queen Mother's behalf, in spite of the fact that Charles had said he did not want to go to France if he could possibly avoid it. The danger of Henrietta Maria converting her son was paramount in the minds of this group of Royalists, and to prevent him even meeting her was their first thought. In any case, he ought not to be in France but in Ireland, whence he could invade without the help of those treacherous and hateful Covenanters.[7]

Charles's own plan was practical, if not very straightforward. He intended to encourage the Covenanters' hopes of his agreeing to all their conditions, while waiting to see what Montrose would be able to do for him in Europe and Scotland, and for the outcome of Ormonde's Irish venture. If Montrose and Ormonde both failed him, he would have to fall back on the Scots, but not necessarily be forced into observing all their terms. He might promise and not perform. In fact, his scheme was to keep the whole situation fluid, while playing off one Scottish faction against another and raising money on the Continent; only so would he be able, at the last moment, to evade the Covenanters' conditions.

These were hard. They contained, as Hyde pointed out, all the most extravagant demands required of, and originally refused by, Charles I. In signing the Covenant Charles II would promise to establish Presbyterianism throughout his kingdoms, thus depriving the Catholics of their Mass and the Protestants of the Prayer-Book. He himself, having dismissed his chaplains and all his Anglican Councillors, must conform to the Presbyterian form of worship for the rest of his life. Montrose must be permanently exiled and Henrietta Maria forbidden to enter her son's dominions.

Charles believed that he could handle this situation. From Kinsale Rupert wrote that he had taken several prizes. Ormonde and Montrose were optimistic. And the Engagers, as represented by Lauderdale and the new Duke of Hamilton (his brother was executed on March 9th), were also on their way to the Hague, with the backing of the Scots Parliament. What Charles and the Scots did not know was that the most formidable of his so-called Scottish allies, the 'master-fiend' Argyll, had made a secret pact with Cromwell, in which he promised to prevent the King landing in Scotland and thus laying on the English Parliament the burden of an invasion. Argyll had not been able to stop Charles being proclaimed; but he promised Cromwell to insist on terms that would enforce his refusal to come over; thus the attack from Scotland would fall through and Argyll, with Cromwell's approval, would become the dictator of that country. Argyll's other plan, which he concealed from Cromwell, was that the King should marry his daughter the Lady Anne Campbell, in the event of Argyll changing his tactics and making Charles the puppet monarch of Scotland.[8]

By the time the Covenanters arrived Charles alone was confident and hopeful. 'I wish they will not deceive his expectation,' was one Royalist's comment, and Hyde noted that the announcement of the terms upon which they were approaching His Majesty was 'more like [that] of ambassadors from a free state ... than like subjects'. Yet the Chancellor had great faith in his new master's powers. 'He is more likely to find friends abroad as well as at home, than his father,' he concluded, as he observed the King's beguiling ways and tireless efforts at establishing his cause. Charles was learning patience and method. Every week his letters went out to all the European Courts and to his own dominions, including the Virginian colonies. He kept in touch with anyone likely to help him.[9]

On March 27th the Covenanting Ministers, all in deepest black, were ushered into Charles's bedchamber at the Binnenhof Palace of the Hague. They were greeted by a very tall young man – he was six foot two – dressed in the purple mourning of royalty, with the silver star of the Garter on his breast. He was clean-shaven and wore a short cloak and doublet; his rather bony wrists were partially concealed by large ruffles. His dark hair, falling in waves over his cravat, was parted in the centre; the right-hand lock, longer than the rest, fell below his laced and tasselled neck-band, in the French fashion.[10] He carried himself with easy grace and seemed to welcome them more as friends than as emissaries.

The principal speaker, Robert Baillie, opened the conversation with the reminder that they came 'upon condition of His Majesty's good behaviour, and observation of the Covenant', and the dismissal of his chaplains. Hyde, appalled at this insolence, could hardly contain himself; he said nothing. Baillie then formally condemned the late King's execution – but he spoke, Hyde noted, 'without horror ... as if it had been an ordinary accident'.[11] 'We desire,' the Scottish minister continued, 'the restoration of Your Majesty, and here present the letter of our Church –' handing Charles the statement of their terms. He and his companions then said that Montrose (whom they referred to as James Grahame) was 'the most bloody murderer of our nation', and asked for his instant removal. They concluded by assuring the King of their loyalty and support.

Charles listened without comment; he appeared amiable but impassive; and Baillie was impressed by his behaviour, non-committal though it was. They were then told that His Majesty would consider their terms; they kissed his hand and withdrew.

Next day they received a rather disconcerting note from the King. 'I desire and expect,' it ran, 'that you deliver all the propositions you are instructed to present to me before I make an answer to any particular one, being resolved to consider of the whole before I declare my resolution on any part.' The Covenanters repeated their specific demands. Charles replied, 'I do insist upon my former answer.'[12]

On April 2nd Baillie, having interviewed Charles alone and late at night, wrote to his superiors in an ecstasy. His Majesty was one of 'the most gentle, innocent, well-inclined princes ... A trim person, and of a manly carriage: understands pretty well: speaks not much: would God he were amongst us! ... He is of a very sweet and equitable disposition ... and judicious.' Unfortunately, the King's loyalty to his own Church remained a barrier; yet Baillie could not but admire his integrity and frankness. 'I think he might be as good a king,' he wrote, 'as any these hundred years.' At their next meeting Charles suddenly said, 'I cannot force the Covenant on England.' Baillie protested. The King made no reply. 'It were a thousand pities,' the disappointed minister then reported, 'that so sweet a man should not be at one with all the people.'

So Charles played for time, sometimes appearing to agree, sometimes even consenting to everything required – but never definitely or in writing. Several weeks passed in this manner, and still he and the Covenanters had come to no agreement. (This was because nothing had been heard from Ireland.) The Scots were hopeful. Eventually this gracious and intelligent young man must be convinced, and then everyone would be happy. Nevertheless, the delay was a little worrying; so they asked the Queen of Bohemia to influence her nephew on their behalf. To their horror, the outspoken lady declared her adherence to the faith in which she had been brought up, and – worse – her admiration for Montrose, whose portrait by Honthorst hung in her room. She had put it there, she said, 'to fright away the Brethren' – and Montrose was now at the Hague!

The Brethren left her with long faces; they were beginning to feel very anxious.[13]

Charles, realizing that he could not use these delaying tactics much longer, wrote to Ormonde urging him to press on with his Irish plan, and asked the States General for money, which they refused. If he found time to visit Lucy, it was secretly; she was now in her Gosfright uncle's house at Rotterdam; there, on April 9th, 1649, their son was born. In the following year another mistress, Lady Shannon, bore Charles a daughter.

II

Charles now tried to deal with the divisions in his Council. The party led by Hyde, the seventy-five-year-old Lord Cottington and Sir Edward Nicholas (formerly Charles I's Secretary of State) was not on speaking terms with those in favour of the King's signing the Covenant. These were headed by Lord Percy, Colepepper and the Duke of Buckingham, all young men. Both parties were rivals of Henrietta Maria's advisers, whom they still called the Louvrians; and all of them seem to have detested Jermyn. Hyde, Cottington and Nicholas believed that their master could only be restored by Montrose's Scottish Royalists and Ormonde's Irish Catholics, and were prepared to wait for their victory. The younger set, desiring immediate action, thought that if Charles did not close with the Covenanters, their enthusiasm would cool; these advisers had little or no feeling about the religious aspect of the situation, partly because they could not visualize, as the older men could, the effect his apostasy would have in England, where his father's execution had increased the number of Royalists, helpless and ruined though they were. This section of the Council underrated the powers of the Engagement-Hamilton-Lauderdale group, perhaps because Argyll's Covenanters opposed them.

The basic weakness of all the English parties lay in their lack of leadership and their inability to work with, or trust, one another. Charles's own preference was for the Buckingham-Colepepper-Percy faction, and for Ormonde and Montrose; he continued to charm the Covenanters, who still believed that he would come to Scotland as the pupil and protégé of Argyll.

Meanwhile, the King's need of money was so desperate that he decided to send a mission to the Spanish government, whose financial support seemed his best hope. Cottington, who had lived in that country for many years and was *persona grata* at King Philip's Court, suggested, first to Charles and then to Hyde, that he and the Chancellor should go there together.[14]

Charles was much taken with this scheme; for Hyde's disapproval of his negotiations with the Scots had become very irksome. He told the Chancellor that he would have to visit his mother before leaving for Scotland or Ireland. Hyde said something about Sir Edward Nicholas, who was then in Rouen, coming to the Hague. 'I desire Nicholas should meet me in France,' said the King, 'I have promised my mother.' 'I fear,' the Chancellor went on, 'that the old Council' – he meant Jermyn's group – 'will govern all.' Charles made no reply, and Hyde pursued, 'Have you a good opinion of Secretary Nicholas?' 'I have a very good opinion of him, and it shall be in nobody's power to do him harm,' replied the King, and then broached the question of Hyde and Cottington going to Spain. 'Is it to be rid of me?' asked the Chancellor. 'On the contrary,' was the answer: but Hyde remained suspicious.[15] Hyde then spoke at his usual length about the integrity of the older Councillors. Charles agreed, so heartily that the Chancellor's fears were soothed. 'Upon my conscience, he doth love all honest men,' he wrote to Nicholas, adding that the Louvrians would never prevail.

The King's next step was to interview Montrose, who, with Hamilton, begged him to reject the Covenant. Later, Lauderdale said, 'Grant all that is asked as far as Scotland is concerned, and comply with the Covenant – *when in Scotland.*'[16] Charles was considering this advice when a private audience was requested of him by another of Argyll's emissaries, the Reverend James Wood, whom he so worked upon that the minister wrote to his wife that their talk had been most fruitful. His Majesty was on the point, Wood thought, of signing the Covenant. Then Charles said something about Ireland. 'God will not bless Your Majesty if you join with Irish Papists!' Wood exclaimed. The King received this reproof courteously. 'I was very free with him,' added the complacent minister.[17]

At this point Montrose asked leave to return to Denmark to raise men and money. Charles agreed, thankfully, for he was being pressed for the Marquess's dismissal by the Covenanters. Then all his plans were thrown into confusion by the arrival at the Hague of Dorislaus as Parliamentary ambassador to the States General. This man, of Dutch origin, had been one of the lawyers who drew up the charges against Charles I. Now he was received by the Dutch as an honoured guest, on one occasion in the new King's presence.

Dorislaus had been living at the Hague for about a week when a party of Cavaliers, led by a Colonel Whitford, entered his house while he was at supper. The Colonel 'cleaved his head with a broadsword ... and quietly departed'.[18]

The Royalists could not contain their satisfaction, and spoke warmly of 'the deserved execution of that bloody villain'. The States were enraged – as was Charles, by his followers' stupidity; for the Dutch now required his instant departure. His brother-in-law advised him to comply and managed, somehow, to raise the £20,000 necessary for the embassy to Spain and for Charles's journey. Charles then asked for an interview with the States General, whom he assured of his toleration of Presbyterianism in Scotland. 'I desire that you will give me your advice as to which of my kingdoms I *shall* repair,' he added rather desperately, 'and that you will give me all necessary assistance.' Both requests were ignored.[19]

Charles then saw Hamilton and Lauderdale alone; after that, he and William had a talk with the Council, to whom the King announced his intention of leaving for France. 'You have received no condolement from France, nor invitation to go there,' said Hyde. Charles disregarded this snub. William suggested that he should see his mother incognito, outside Paris, and then leave for Ireland – for the Irish news was now very promising – and offered to lend him two warships. Charles accepted, and made arrangements to forward his heavy luggage to Ireland, adding, 'If I make France my way, I will make all possible haste and go with as light a train as I can.'[20] He then told Hyde and Cottington to undertake their Spanish mission 'cheerfully', and sent for the Covenanters for, as he thought, the last time. 'I will comply in Scotland,' he told them, 'but I must refer the extension of the Covenant to a free Parliament in England.'

The Scots were horrified and amazed. 'This is the advice of that fugatious man, James Grahame!' exclaimed one, and after some further condemnation of His Majesty's 'evil councillors' they left – much to his relief, for Ormonde's letters had convinced him (he was not quite nineteen) that his and Rupert's invasion would succeed.

In the last week in May Charles, accompanied by Elizabeth of Bohemia, the Princess of Orange and his personal suite of fifty gentlemen with their servants and chaplains, left for St Germain via the Spanish Netherlands. Breda, Antwerp and Brussels were to be his stopping-places. So that he might travel as became his rank, William of Orange lent him a troop of forty horse.[21] At Breda he was visited by the Spanish ambassador. He then parted from his aunt and sister and went on to Antwerp, where again he was magnificently received. A silver-mounted coach and six was waiting outside the gates to bring him in; this present from the Spanish government was followed by one of six pure-bred Neapolitan horses and another of 25,000 gold crowns. In return Charles wrote to the King of Spain assuring him of his continued 'grace and favour' to all Catholics in his dominions, asked for more money and sent his compliments to the Nuncio. This letter had to be conveyed with the utmost secrecy, for any hint of it in England or Scotland would have ruined his cause; but this was not the moment for scruples.[22] Two days later he arrived in Brussels, where he was lodged in the royal palace and waited on by Spanish officials. After four days the French began the siege of that city, so he had to move on. He was followed, privately and at a distance, by Lucy Walter, who had left their son in charge of the Gosfrights at Rotterdam.[23]

Meanwhile at St Germain Henrietta Maria and Lord Jermyn were planning Charles's second approach to La Grande Mademoiselle. This time they were certain of success. At twenty-two, Mademoiselle should long since have been married. Surely she could not refuse the King of England.

NOTES

1 J. Heath, *Brief Chronicle*, p. 472.
2 *Nicholas Papers* (ed. Warner), vol. I, p. 115; Clarendon, pp. 704-8.
3 *Letters* (ed. Everett Green), pp. 350-7.
4 *Cal. D. S. P.*, Feb. 22nd, 1649.
5 P. Zumthor, *Daily Life in Rembrandt's Holland*, p. 319.
6 Electress Sophia, p. 18.
7 Clarendon, pp. 704-8.
8 Ibid.
9 Op. cit., pp. 699, 707.
10 F. Peck, *Desiderata Curiosa*, p. 577.
11 *Cal. Clar. S. P.*, vol. II, pp. 4-6.
12 R. Baillie, *Letters and Journals (1637-1662)*, vol. III, p. 86.
13 *Cal. Clar. S. P.*, vol. II, p. 476.
14 Clarendon, pp. 911-15.
15 *Nicholas Papers*, vol. I, pp. 123-6.
16 Gardiner, *Commonwealth*, vol. I, p. 62.
17 *Laing MSS* (H.M.C.), p. 247.
18 Heath, p. 469.
19 Clarendon, pp. 711-15.
20 Ibid.
21 B. Whitelocke, *Memorials of English Affairs*, vol. III, p. 54.
22 *Cal. Clar. S. P.*, vol. II, p. 481.
23 J. Evelyn, *Diary*, p. 280.

CHAPTER SIX

TEMPTATION AND BETRAYAL

I

WHEN the sixteen-year-old Duke of York joined his mother at the Louvre, and Mademoiselle came to pay her visit of condolence, she was much struck with his fair colouring, good figure and pleasant manners; these and his fluent French were in marked contrast to his elder brother's tongue-tied awkwardness and sallow skin. 'Nothing,' she says, 'detracts from a man so much as not being able to converse; and the [Duke] talked very well.'[1]

Henrietta Maria made a less agreeable impression. Her mourning was inadequate; and she was remarkably self-controlled; on such an occasion tears and lamentation would have been more suitable, 'considering,' Mademoiselle thought, 'how devoted the late King had been to her'. Later on she realized that the Queen Mother was concealing her grief for her sons' sake; this became apparent when Henrietta Maria renewed Charles's courtship of his cousin. She, Lord Jermyn and the Duc d'Orléans's confessor, the Abbé de la Rivière, prepared the way some weeks before Charles arrived.

De la Rivière said to Mademoiselle, 'The Queen of England has done everything she can to persuade Monsieur to consent to your marriage with the King, and Milord Jermyn has come on His Majesty's behalf to plead with him. It is for you to make up your mind. Monsieur will speak to you about it.' Mademoiselle found her father characteristically non-committal. After a rather maundering speech about assets and liabilities, he said, 'The Queen of England has spoken to me of what the Abbé told you – you see what you have to do.' 'I will obey you,' Mademoiselle replied. 'You know, better than I, what is right. I have no will but yours.' No more was said till Lord Percy arrived from the Hague with Charles's compliments to Louis XIV and his request to be received. Percy then called on Mademoiselle and, backed up by Jermyn, begged her to look graciously on their master's suit.

By this time Mazarin and Anne of Austria, while negotiating with Cromwell, had come to the conclusion that Charles's situation was promising; his agents in Ireland and elsewhere had convinced them that his restoration was a matter of months. They were therefore prepared to help him – with Mademoiselle's money. 'I love you,' the Queen Regent told her, 'as if you were my own daughter. But if I did not think this alliance would benefit you, I should not suggest it. You know that the Queen of England is one of the best creatures in the world, and that she is very fond of you. Her son is passionately enamoured, and begs for marriage.' 'He does me too much honour,' replied Mademoiselle dryly, 'but as his circumstances are such that his restoration requires support – ' she broke off, as if to make it clear that she was not to be fooled, and added, 'Nevertheless, I will do what you and Monsieur desire.'

Anne of Austria said nothing more till Lord Jermyn was present; then she began teasing Mademoiselle about her new admirer; Jermyn joined in, and Mademoiselle found herself blushing. A few weeks later de la Rivière said, 'Milord Jermyn has been to see the King, in Holland. His Majesty would be glad of a definite answer, because he will soon have to leave for Ireland. If you accept him, he will come here [to the Tuileries] for two days. He will then marry you, and thus you will take precedence of the Queen Regent. Then you and he will go to St Germain, to the Queen of England. But he will not stay there long, and you will be able to return to Paris, which you prefer.'

'That is impossible,' Mademoiselle said sharply. 'I would rather accompany the King to Ireland, if he so desired. If he does not, I would stay with his mother, or remain quietly in one of my own palaces. I do not care for gaieties – and for a person in my position they cost too much. For I would have to save in order to send him money – and also, I could not but be anxious, knowing that he was at war.' As the Abbé demurred she went on, 'In fact, if I marry him, I shall have to make up my mind to do what is very hard. I should have to sell my estates to help restore him.' As she said this Mademoiselle's heart sank. 'I was frightened,' she says. 'Having always been used to wealth, these ideas alarmed me.' 'You may be right,' said the Abbé, noting her expression, 'but you must remember that there is now no other suitable match for you in Europe. Both the Emperor and the King of Spain are married.' Mademoiselle tried to laugh off this threat. 'The Empress is pregnant, and she might die in childbirth,' she said, adding, 'If Monsieur wants the King of England to marry me sooner or later – if he really thinks I should do so – I would rather marry him while he is unfortunate, because then he would be under an obligation to me, and thus, when he is restored to his kingdom, he will think of me and my House as having been his chief support.'

Next day the Orléans family moved to Amiens. Mademoiselle took the opportunity to confide in her stepmother. She dreaded the thought of marrying a penniless exile, and begged the Duchesse to tell her father so, which she did. Jermyn followed them. He harried the flustered heiress with innumerable questions – 'What do you feel? Does not the King love you?' – and so on. Mademoiselle was not deceived. 'I knew,' she says, 'that milord Jermyn was afraid of getting into trouble with the Queen of England, and that she had told him I must be won over, because I always made my own decisions. And it's true indeed, that if one has any sense, it ought to be applied to such a matter as this, the most important in the world.' Jermyn then spoke rather too frankly of the pleasures of the married state, Mademoiselle took exception to his tone and on her return had it out with him and Henrietta Maria.

'I honour Your Majesty,' she said, 'and, if I may say so, I am very fond of you. But I cannot change my religion. If the King is really attached to me, it is for him to surmount that difficulty.' Jermyn said, 'His Majesty cannot and must not become a Catholic,' and explained why this was so. With some adroitness, Mademoiselle pretended not to see his point, and a long argument ensued. As Jermyn left he said, 'I hope that your objections will be overcome,' in a tone she found very alarming; it was as if she were going to be forced to marry Charles. To her great relief, the subject was abandoned until he himself arrived.

In the first week of June Mademoiselle was with the Queen Regent and Louis XIV when the courier announcing Charles's entry into French territory was received. Anne of Austria said with a smile, 'Your suitor is on the way,' and de la Rivière repeated the words.

Suddenly Mademoiselle felt strangely agitated. A suitor – she had never had one. That was because of her position, of course; no ordinary aspirant had dared approach her. For the first time in her life, she began to think she had missed something – and that the King of England might supply it. As soon as they were alone, she said to the Abbé, 'I long for him to say sweet things [*douceurs*] to me.' She went on to explain, with naive complacency, 'I do not know how it is, but no one has ever ventured to do so – not because of my rank, but because of my nature, which everyone knows is not that of a coquette. But I could, without coquetry, encourage a king whom I am supposed to marry. So I hope he will say sweet things to me.'[2]

Charles and his mother were to meet his French relations in the forest of Compiègne. That day Mademoiselle got up much earlier than usual and spent some time at her dressing-table; her hair was curled and arranged in the height of the fashion. As she got into the Queen Regent's coach that lady said archly, 'Someone is expecting a suitor – look at those ringlets!'

Mademoiselle was very angry. She nearly said something sharp, but thought better of it, and they drove on to the meeting-place to wait for the Queen of England's coach. As they all descended and Charles kissed his aunt and cousin and then turned to her, Mademoiselle was considerably shaken. Her suitor – could he be that? – was no longer a gawky youth, but a distinguished and graceful man, tall and elegant in his purple mourning and his Garter star – how he had changed! He was not handsome: but he had an air ... And if his manners and conversation came up to the standard of his appearance – but now they were all settled in the coach, driving through the glades to the palace for dinner.

In accordance with etiquette, everyone waited for the ten-year-old Louis to speak first; he turned to his guest and asked him about the Prince of Orange. 'What hounds has he? What is the hunting in Holland?' Charles answered agreeably, and in excellent French; Mademoiselle's hopes rose. Then Anne of Austria asked her nephew how his plans were working out, and what his intentions were. Charles did not answer. His mother pressed him with more questions; the Queen Regent did the same. At last he replied, 'You Majesty must excuse me – I do not speak your language.'

Mademoiselle was horrified. How could she contemplate marrying a young man who did not even know what his own circumstances were, and who made such stupid excuses? She came to the conclusion that he was like many of the Bourbons – frivolous and idle.

When they sat down to dinner she received another shock. Among the innumerable dishes set before Charles was one of ortolans, another of mutton, and an enormous joint of beef. Without hesitation, he 'flung himself', Mademoiselle disgustedly observed, on the beef, ate largely and then attacked the mutton; he did not so much as glance at the ortolans. This lack of delicacy was deplorable. 'I was ashamed,' Mademoiselle records. Worse was to follow.

After dinner the Queen Regent isolated Charles and Mademoiselle. For a quarter of an hour she waited for him to talk. He remained speechless. She began to make excuses for him; for by this time she was almost convinced that he was in love with her. His silence was therefore caused by respect, perhaps even timidity. She decided to help him out – 'though I must say,' she adds, 'that I could have put up with a little less respect.' She beckoned to a passing courtier and told him to sit down with them – and the moment he began to talk, the King replied. Soon they were chattering away, as if Mademoiselle did not exist. As she got up and walked off the Abbé de la Rivière approached her. 'He did not remove his eyes from you all through dinner,' he said, 'and still he is looking at you.' 'It is all very well for him to look,' Mademoiselle replied tartly, 'but he does not utter.' 'You choose to ignore the sweet things he has said to you,' the courtly priest replied. Mademoiselle's irritability burst out – did they all take her for a fool? 'Pray forgive me,' she said, 'but if you will come and sit with us, you will see how he behaves.' When they were seated she began to make conversation: had His Majesty any news of So-and-So? And what had happened to her other English acquaintances? Charles replied courteously, 'but' – records poor Mademoiselle – 'he did not say any sweet things to me.'[3]

It was now time for Charles to return to St Germain. Having made his farewells to his hosts, he went up to Mademoiselle; Jermyn was with him. With a daunting and mechanical gallantry, he began, 'Monsieur Jermyn, who speaks better French than I, will have told you of my intentions – and of my hopes. I am your most obedient servant.' 'And I am yours,' Mademoiselle coldly replied. The ever-ready Jermyn stepped into the breach with a flood of complimentary speeches; Charles stood by in sardonic silence. He had said what his mother required of him, and that must suffice. He then kissed Mademoiselle's hand and departed. During the next few weeks she determined not to think about him, and nearly succeeded; as he remained with his mother at St Germain and she was at the Tuileries, she did not see very much of him. Nor was she aware that Lord Wilmot was in charge of – and apparently waiting on – the beautiful Mrs Barlow, whom Evelyn, now on one of his continental tours, discovered in Wilmot's coach when he was driven by his lordship to the Louvre. Evelyn thought her dull; and no doubt pretty Lucy found the solemn diarist equally so.[4]

Charles's first days with his mother were gloomy enough. They spoke much of his murdered father and wept together. This relieved Henrietta Maria, and she began to catechize her son about his plans. He replied with great respect, but in such a manner as to make it plain that she was to have no share in them, and that her advice was not wanted. She persisted, became angry and then reproachful. He did not even apologize, and when she again cross-questioned him, remained silent. The Queen Mother at once made a terrible scene, of the kind Charles had seen his father endure and had himself learned how to deal with as a child. He waited till she paused for breath, and then said, with cold formality, 'I will always perform my duty towards Your Majesty with great affection and exactness – but in my business I must obey my own reason and judgment. Do not trouble yourself in my affairs – ' and walked out of the room.[5]

At this point Hyde and Lord Cottington arrived. Henrietta Maria sent for the Chancellor and told him that she had not been consulted about their mission to Spain, nor about Ireland. Worse still, when she sent to tell Charles that she wished to see him, he would reply that he was too busy to admit her. And now the odious Thomas Elliott – a man the late King had disliked and removed from his son's entourage – had rejoined him, and they were always together.

Hyde was sympathetic. 'Elliott,' he said, 'is a bold man, and speaks all things confidently.' (To Cottington he had already observed, 'Mr Elliott has not that reverence for the late King that he ought, and less for the Queen, to whom he is insolent.') The Chancellor's disapproval heightened when he realized that Elliott, who was now married to the daughter of Charles's old nurse, Mrs Wyndham, had brought his wife and his father-in-law to St Germain, and was persuading Charles to make Colonel Wyndham his Secretary of State. 'He is an honest gentleman, but marvellously unequal to that province,' Hyde pointed out, as soon as he and the King were alone.

Charles seemed not to hear this criticism. He began to talk about his mother, at length and with violent irritation – she was behaving impossibly. He could no longer put up with her attempts to dominate and interfere. 'You must speak to her,' he told Hyde, and dismissed him.

The Queen Mother received Hyde with unusual graciousness. She began, 'The King is unkind to me – ' and burst into tears. The Chancellor attempted to console her. She would not be comforted. Charles was rude; Elliott was insolent, and had influenced him against her; Wyndham ought not to have the secretaryship. 'He will be sure to join with the other to lessen the King's kindness to me,' she sobbed out. Hyde discoursed soothingly of His Majesty's real affection and respect, and then returned to the King. When he had lectured the goaded young man for some time, Charles said patiently, 'I desire nothing more than to live well with the Queen. I will never fail towards her in my duty – as far as is consistent with my honour, and the good of my affairs.' (He was referring to Henrietta Maria's attempts to convert him and her suggestion of complying with the Covenant in order to reject it later.) 'If I do not seem desirous of her company,' he went on, 'it is only when she grieves me with importunities in which I cannot satisfy her. Her exception against Elliott is very unjust. I know the man to be honest, and I love him well. The prejudice the King my father had against him was only the malice of Lord Digby.'

Hyde was appalled. 'Does Your Majesty intend to make Wyndham Secretary?' he asked. 'I have not promised to do it,' said Charles evasively; then he added, 'But I intend to do it.' 'I am glad you have not promised it,' said the Chancellor, 'I hope you will never do it. He is an honest gentleman, but in no degree qualified for that office –' and mentioned Sir Edward Nicholas. 'I think Nicholas to be a very honest man,' said the King, 'but he has not title to that office more than another. Mr Wyndham hath not any experience,' he went on rather defiantly, 'but he will quickly be instructed. He is a very honest man, for whom I have never done anything, and I have nothing else to give him. I doubt not but in a short time he will make himself very fit.' 'Hear me again,' the Chancellor implored, 'before you make a final resolution.' Charles agreed in his most amiable manner. (Hyde had not yet got to the point of recognizing this tactic.) The King went on, 'I will live with the Queen with all kindness and freedom – that she may be in a good humour.' He added, 'But I will not hear a word against Wyndham –' and went out.[6]

Hyde would have continued to lecture and reason with Charles, thus increasing his determination to have his own way. Lord Cottington, a man of the world, a wit and what is now called a character, had a better plan. This nobleman's early years had been spent at the Court of the great Queen, and his judgment of human nature was subtler and more imaginative than Hyde's, who revelled in his company and admired his 'custom of never smiling while he made others merry'.

One day, when Elliott and Wyndham were absent and Charles was talking with his courtiers, Cottington approached him and solemnly began, 'I have a humble suit to Your Majesty.' Having obtained everyone's attention, he went on, 'It is on behalf of an old servant of Your Majesty's father, whom, I assure you, your father loved as well as any man in that condition in England. He has been, for many years, one of his falconers – and I do really believe him to be one of the best falconers in England.' With the utmost gravity Cottington then launched into a discourse on hawking, in which he was an expert, while everyone stood round wondering what this was all about: for the King had given up the sport since his exile. At last Cottington paused, and Charles said, 'What would you have me do for him?'

'It is very true,' said Cottington sadly, 'that Your Majesty has no falconers – and the poor man is grown old, and cannot rule as he used to do. But he is a very honest man, and can read very well, and hath as audible a voice as any man needs to have.' He waited, and then said very earnestly, 'I beseech Your Majesty to make him your chaplain.'

Charles smiled, beginning, as he thought, to see what was coming. Cottington's jokes, although rather long on the way, were always enjoyable. 'What do you mean?' he asked. With an immovable countenance the old lord replied, 'The falconer is in all respects as fit to be Your Majesty's chaplain as Colonel Wyndham is to be Secretary of State.'

There was a moment's silence. Then the courtiers burst into peals of laughter. Charles, still too young to take a jest against himself, flushed darkly and turned away. When the falconer story was repeated to Wyndham, he saw that if he got the post of secretary, he would be laughed out of it; he and Elliott made no further efforts, and the situation was saved.[7]

The exiled Court needed such diversions as these; for the group attached to the King, who had not expected to remain in France for more than a fortnight, now found themselves vainly waiting for better news from Ireland. As the weeks went by they became increasingly isolated; the French nobles no longer troubled to visit St Germain. 'This,' remarks Madame de Motteville, 'was not surprising. Misfortune was their lot; they could benefit no one.' So the younger men bickered among themselves, in the intervals of seeking what pleasures their circumstances allowed – cheap and sordid dissipations, from which their elders turned in disgust. Charles, who had to listen to the complaints and schemes of both, was always patient, sensible and good-tempered: too good-tempered sometimes, Nicholas thought; people were inclined to underrate him; his 'sweetness of disposition' was misleading.[8]

Then the Royalists in Ireland heard that 'a fair lady' was detaining His Majesty in France. This version of his mother's attempts to marry him to Mademoiselle did not do Charles much harm; nor did Lucy's establishment in Paris affect his reputation; and when inactivity drove him towards obscurer diversions, Madame de Motteville was almost the only person who deplored the change. At this time Charles was not – he never really became – a heavy drinker; nor could he afford to gamble. When Jermyn advised him not to go to Ireland, he burst out, 'I must go there, or die – since I am ashamed, as a prince, to go elsewhere!' 'This discourse,' says Madame de Motteville, 'was apparently sincere ... But young men descend easily from those heights of virtue ... Then they put up with abuses which formerly seemed insupportable, and the pursuit of pleasure is the cause ... This prince ... inclined towards women's society; and many years of his life, both in France and elsewhere, were wastefully passed.'

Meanwhile Nicholas was much struck by his new master's judgment. 'He is a great observer ... and makes good distinction between ... hearty

... and half-hearted,' he wrote to Ormonde.[9] Certainly Charles appreciated, as he had to use, the whole-heartedness of such Cavaliers as Montrose, with whom he was in constant touch. In every letter – some personal, some official – he assured James Grahame of his loyalty and support. Neither the King nor the most high-minded and heroic of his servants visualized the outcome of these declarations. As Cromwell advanced and Ormonde retreated Charles's letters increased in frequency and warmth; for in Montrose's projected Scottish invasion lay his better hope; and when, on August 10th, he heard that Ormonde's forces had been utterly routed at Rathmines, it was his only one. As he had not come to any arrangement with the Scots, he decided to go to Jersey; by the beginning of September everyone, even his mother, wanted him to leave; nevertheless, he might have stayed, if Mazarin had not made it clear that he must once more move on, and that he would be paid to do so. Monarchy had been abolished by Cromwell; Irish Royalism was crushed; Scottish loyalties were divided; the King of England had becomed a taxing liability.

As soon as Charles's departure was announced the nobility hastened to visit him, and a number of farewell entertainments were planned – tennis-matches, banquets, bull-baiting and so on. When Mademoiselle called at St Germain to say goodbye the Emperor was again a widower; this inspired Henrietta Maria to make another effort on her son's behalf. 'I must congratulate you,' she said acidly, 'on the Empress's death. The match will probably not fall through this time.' 'I have not thought about it,' Mademoiselle replied. The Queen Mother turned to Jermyn and burst out, 'Here is a man who believes that a King of eighteen' – presumably she took a year off Charles's age to make him appear more desirable – 'is better than an Emperor of fifty with four children. But my son is too awkward and unfortunate for you.'

Charles was standing at the other end of the room with an English lady, 'with whom,' says Mademoiselle, 'he was in love'. (This was almost certainly Lucy.) Henrietta Maria pointed to them and said, 'He is afraid you will find out – see how embarrassed he is –' as the young couple moved away. She then led Mademoiselle into her cabinet, shut the door and went on, 'My son desires your forgiveness for having troubled you with his offer at Compiègne. He is in despair, he is always thinking of it. I did not want to tell you, but he so implored me that I am obliged to – because you are right, you would have been miserable with him, and I am too fond of you to want you to share his misfortunes. All I can hope for is that his expedition will be successful, so that later on you may feel kindly towards him. That would be the best thing that could happen to him.'

Much confused, Mademoiselle murmured something evasive; she was rescued by the Duke of York, who came in to ask her if she would accompany him on a visit to the Abbey of St Dominique at Poissy, returning to St Germain the same day. She agreed, and the co-operative youth suggested that Charles should come too. Mademoiselle said that she did not mind going unchaperoned with a schoolboy; the King of England was another matter; so Henrietta Maria joined the party.

When they were all in the coach the Queen Mother began, 'When my son the King marries he will be the best of husbands. He will love none but his wife,' and continued to expatiate on Charles's domestic virtues. At last she stopped. With great solemnity, His Majesty then remarked, 'I do not understand how it is that a man who has a sensible wife can love another woman. For myself, when I do marry, there will be no one else.'

This pronouncement was received with silent incredulity by Mademoiselle. When the visit came to an end Charles conducted her to her coach. As his mother and brother dropped behind he said something polite – 'but' – she noted – 'that was all – no sweet things. In any case, it would have been useless, as my mind was set on the Empire.' [10]

After her husband's death Henrietta Maria always described, and sometimes even signed, herself as *La Reine Malheureuse*. Her eldest son's treatment of La Grande Mademoiselle seems to emphasize the aptness of the description.

II

Just before Charles left St Germain it was discovered that a Puritan fanatic was planning to assassinate him. In the same week Parliament issued a warrant for the arrest of 'Charles Stuart, eldest son of the late King, by name Charles II'.[11] So he was provided with an escort of sixty horse, six coaches and 3,000 pistoles for his journey. Meanwhile, Jermyn took advantage of his departure to pawn the Queen Mother's jewels without asking Charles's leave; naturally some of the money stuck to his fingers. He was protected by Henrietta Maria, to the great indignation of Nicholas who, reporting the incident to Charles, allowed himself to criticize Her Majesty's indulgence of her treasurer. 'It is a notable juggle,' he complained. The King turned upon him and said sternly, 'You do very ill to breed differences with the Queen my mother – it shall not be in your power, or any man's, to effect it.' [12]

Charles's loyalty to, and patience with, his mother made him more than ever determined to prevent her wrecking his plans, as much for her sake as for his own. Having failed to convert him, she was now trying to proselytize the more malleable York; so Charles took the boy with him to Jersey, much to her annoyance. Morosini, the Venetian ambassador at the Louvre, thought that he did this more to irritate Henrietta Maria, 'with whom there is little love lost, [rather] than because prudence required it'. Morosini had not a notion how dangerous to her son's cause the poor lady could be, partly because Charles himself criticized her only when appealing to Hyde to help him control her. When Morosini asked him why he was removing York, Charles said briefly, 'The French mean to deceive – that is why.' He went on to speak of his hosts with great bitterness, as if he suspected them not only of playing a double game with himself and Parliament, but of using his brother in any way that suited their policy. He then said, 'The Turks have offered me money, but I will not accept it because I am loyal to the Venetians.' This strong hint was not acted on by the ambassador; in his report to the Senate he made it clear that, although fascinated, he was not deceived by Charles's winning ways. 'The step taken by this young and very talented king,' he wrote, 'has reference certainly to his own interests,' adding that the Queen of Sweden had answered Charles's begging letters with a present of money and cannon. The Senate replied that Morosini was not to 'go too far' in his friendship with the enemy of their business associates.[13]

On September 27th, 1649, Charles and York set sail from Cotainville in a Jersey flotilla, of which Charles steered the flagship. They were pursued by a Parliamentary fleet, but arrived safely in the afternoon of the next day and were rapturously greeted. Although they were the Carterets' guests, the islanders produced £600 for their maintenance.[14]

In the weeks that followed it was observed that Charles had changed a good deal since his accession. Although more poised and impressive and always gracious, particularly to women and young people, he looked depressed. As he and York walked or rode about the island – York in black with a violet and silver shoulder-knot, Charles in his purple doublet and hose – he seemed pale and preoccupied, except when he roused himself to receive an ovation. Then he would smile, rein in his horse and bend from the saddle to speak to those nearest him. When he had reviewed the island militia he waited to let the officers kneel and kiss his hand; when Lady Carteret gave birth to a daughter whom she called Carolina, he stood godfather; and when he and his brother were asked not to walk or go shooting alone and unguarded, he submitted with his usual amiability, returning to Elizabeth Castle, where he occupied himself with drawing a map of the island.

He was anxious – and hideously bored. His affairs seemed to be at a standstill. Ormonde now advised him not to think of landing in Ireland. The three Scottish parties – Montrose's, the Engagers and Argyll's Covenanters – implored him to come to Scotland, while fulminating against one another. So he fell back on his old tactics of offering himself to each, privately, and as if eliminating the other two, in the belief that somehow he would be able finally to co-ordinate their forces. At this time he still wrote most often to Montrose, whom he considered, mistakenly, to be his strongest ally. This was partly because the Marquess's integrity was beyond question. Charles knew very well that the others were corrupt and self-interested. He detested Argyll and the Covenanters, not only because they had sold his father, but because he found their Calvinist fanaticism odious and absurd. He was yet to learn that their powers were the greatest and the best organized.

On January 1st, 1650, the Duke of Buckingham arrived with a train of gentlemen – 'a very handsome young man in black, silver star and purple Garter' – just in time for the New Year party at the Castle.[15] By this time Argyll's Covenanters, headed by Winram, Laird of Libberton, and Silas Titus (an English Presbyterian, afterwards famous as a Royalist agent and pamphleteer) had arrived to discuss the negotiations. Charles's letter suggesting that they state 'exactly' what they required of him had been so agreeable that they were sure of coming to an immediate agreement. Now, with Buckingham at his elbow, Hyde and Cottington about to leave for Spain and Nicholas in Paris, the King found it easier to commit himself. He agreed to go to Breda in order to come to terms with the Covenanters before embarking for Scotland, and implied, if he did not actually promise, that he would sign the Covenant. This change of front was partly caused by Buckingham's influence; the Duke was the only person in Charles's circle who had no beliefs at all, although at this time he knew better than to admit it. In Buckingham's opinion all religious persons, of whatever creed, were foolish – and therefore to be used – in proportion to the fervour of their faith. This supremely cynical, overconfident young man saw the hard-headed Winram as a tool and Argyll, of whose subtlety and unscrupulousness he had not an inkling, as a go-between, to be suitably rewarded when they had helped Charles and himself to come into their own.

This attitude and its effect on the King horrified the other Councillors, who disliked George Villiers, resented his derisive arrogance and were bitterly jealous of him. There were many disputes between English and Scots; but their 'heats and animosities' were 'smoothly accommodated' by Charles, whose 'moderation, patience and judgment' went hand in hand with his secret support of Montrose. ('I will do nothing without consulting you' – 'Proceed vigorously and effectively' – 'I will only agree with the Scots on honourable terms' – 'We will not anything contrary to that power and authority we have given you.') Meanwhile, he was telling Winram that his demands seemed reasonable and encouraging the Spaniards to believe that he was not only prepared to tolerate his Catholic subjects, but that he himself was drawn towards their faith. When he suddenly announced that he would neither go to Scotland nor sign the Covenant, his intention was to frighten Winram into thinking he had failed in his mission and would thus get into trouble with the all-powerful Argyll.[16]

Charles then made preparations for departure, touched some of the afflicted islanders for the King's Evil, gave Carteret the Smith Islands off the Virginia coast and found time to write to Prodgers, one of his gentlemen of the Bedchamber, now at the Hague, about his clothes. 'I would have, besides the embroidered suit ... a plain riding suit, with an innocent [clean] coat, the suits I have for horseback being so spotted and spoiled that they are not to be seen out of this island ... I do not remember whether there was a belt or a hat-band ... You must not forget them.'[17] He left behind him a jack-boot, his map of the island, and his purple velvet holsters and saddle; these treasures, kept against his promised return, are still in Jersey. When he said goodbye to the Duke of York, the boy burst into tears.

Charles sailed from St Helier in the middle of February, having sent Buckingham to Paris to tell Henrietta Maria that he would meet her at Beauvais in order to say goodbye before leaving for Scotland via Breda. He and the Queen Mother were now in accord. She thought that he should go to Scotland as soon as possible, either before or after signing the Covenant, because subscribing, if only outwardly, to Presbyterianism, would so disgust him that he would then turn to her faith; in her view the Church of England differed very little, if at all, from any other heretical organization. She therefore set out to meet Charles in excellent spirits; later, she told Mademoiselle, 'My son is incorrigible; he loves you more than ever – I have had to scold him.'[18]

After a voyage in which he was nearly shipwrecked, Charles reached Rouen, to be received by Lady Ormonde and her daughter; he travelled to Beauvais in her coach, remaining there for a week at his mother's request. At first all went well. The King was observed to be 'very courteous' to Henrietta Maria, as to Jermyn, whom he made Governor of Jersey, much to York's disappointment. Charles seemed to agree when the Queen Mother urged him to 'dissemble' with the Scots; she added that he should conceal his affection for the Catholic faith until he attained power. 'You must not think it necessary to keep any treaties,' she said, 'further than they may serve your ends.'[19] Then again she began to dictate and interfere in such a way as to advertise Charles's Catholic sympathies. When Nicholas joined them he told the King that his mother had 'converted' the six-year-old Princess Henrietta Anne.[20]

Charles was very angry; he behaved with restraint. When he reminded Henrietta Maria of her promise to his father, she quoted, inaccurately, the articles of her marriage, flew into a rage, declared 'I am resolved' and finally threatened to place the princess in a convent. Charles pointed out that 'Minette's' apostasy would do him irrevocable harm in Scotland and England; Henrietta Maria was not to be moved, and he had to yield, as he could not himself get in touch with his little sister. This dispute, coming on top of his anxieties in Jersey, led him, not unnaturally, to seek diversion in the taverns of Beauvais; he and his courtiers went on a series of drinking bouts, and made themselves conspicuous by their gallantries with the local girls.[21] On the day of Charles's departure he, Henrietta Maria, Nicholas and Jermyn dined together in a house lent them by one of the canons of the cathedral. Nicholas and the King then remained alone with Henrietta Maria for three hours. A violent quarrel ensued, of which the cause was not revealed. The courtiers waiting for Charles saw the Queen Mother come out 'red with anger and much unsatisfied', and the King walking beside her in cold and silent rage. He handed her into her coach; then, abandoning his usual courtesy, turned and walked away before she drove off.[22]

Next day he reached Ghent and here, it seems, Lucy joined him. Perhaps on this account, or possibly because of his forthcoming association with his Presbyterian allies, he was denied lodgings by the Spanish Governor. Charles retaliated by refusing to receive anyone, although the townspeople flocked to see him. The local nobility then sent him a present of wine, which he would not accept; his courtiers stopped the bearers on their way out and drank it without telling him.

On March 16th he reached Breda; from there he wrote to Montrose, who was now about to sail for the Orkneys, 'I will never fail in ... friendship,' and sent him the Garter, to which Montrose replied, 'The joy of your prosperity and greatness ... shall ever be my only passion and study.'[23] 'So early,' remarked one of the older Royalists some years later, 'was he embarked in a course of hypocrisy ... This seems to have laid the foundation of that unthinking kind of life which afterwards His Majesty too much observed.'[24]

In one respect this criticism is unjust. At the time of his second meeting with the Covenanters Charles's behaviour was the reverse of thoughtless; every move was calculated, as far as religion and politics were concerned. His temperament was not, and never became, spiritual or selfless; yet it does not follow that, within two months of his twentieth birthday, he had sunk into an irresponsible and heartless intriguer, only concerned with bettering his own fortunes.

The complications of Charles's responsibilities have no parallel. At the age of twelve he had been thrust into a position of authority, without preparation or training, by parents who had brought him up to believe that he would inherit an orderly and prosperous kingdom. In the ensuing eight years of war and exile his father had been murdered, his mother proscribed and ruined, two brothers and a sister imprisoned and his own life threatened. Furthermore – and this may have most affected his outlook – he had been reduced to a degrading penury, which he could neither alleviate nor escape. Having spent his childhood in the most luxurious and extravagant court in Europe, where a single night's entertainment might cost thousands of pounds, which moved in splendour from one great palace to another and whose ruler had been described as the happiest king in Christendom, Charles now had to sponge and cringe in order, not to keep himself – he could have abdicated and lived very well as a mercenary in the French or Spanish forces – but to represent a cause left him as a sacred trust. Also, he had partially to support all those who had worked and fought for himself and his father, at the same time sustaining a certain state. Just as a modern business executive must sink his capital in a 'good' address and well appointed premises, so Charles had to appear before those whose help he needed attended by some forty or fifty persons, with their servants and hangers-on. If he had cut down the resultant expenses, he would have been passed over, and the Royalists in England would have lost heart. He had three, sometimes four, chaplains. (The atheistical Buckingham, who was much better off, employed two.) If he had dismissed one, not only would the poor man have starved or deserted to his enemies, but Charles himself would have been accused of spiritual negligence.

His difficulties, already insurmountable, increased with every month of his exile. Each time he was desired to move on, his expenses accumulated; and whatever approach he made, either to the Catholic or the Protestant powers, he was suspected of selling himself. That the majority of his younger courtiers – all of whom were older than he – were frivolous and self-seeking, was not his fault; and the fact that his more responsible and experienced advisers could not understand, let alone tolerate, their juniors' dissipations, turned Charles towards his own generation; with them he could relax and enjoy himself when his circumstances became unbearable.

As a warm-hearted and thoughtful son and brother, he had to control and look after a family in which each member took for granted that his or her welfare was his chief concern. Finally, he was still emotionally involved with a girl set on trapping him into marriage, whom, as the mother of an idolized son ('the King loved Monmouth as he did his eyes', said one Royalist after the Restoration[25]), he dared not offend; for the lovely Mrs Barlow soon made it clear that she was capable of using the child against the father if she did not get her way.

It may therefore be suggested that for a lively, pleasure-loving, not highly intellectual youth of nineteen, Charles had not, up to now, done so badly – except, possibly, in his treatment of Montrose. But here again, his inexperience combined with the Grahames' optimism to deceive him. When Montrose announced that as soon as he – not Charles – appeared in Scotland, the whole country would rise, the King believed him, and made his plans accordingly; this involved keeping in touch with Montrose's rivals, in the manner of all seventeenth-century statesmen. When he realized that Montrose was fatally mistaken, it was too late to reverse his policy.

Charles's heaviest handicap lay, paradoxically, in his greatest asset; that of being able (sometimes, perhaps, without realizing it) to fascinate nearly everyone he met. This gift made his prospects appear more hopeful than they really were; and so he was often outwitted by cunning, unscrupulous and fanatical persons – specifically by the Scots Covenanters, whose racial and endemic conceit inspired them first to use and then to sacrifice a young man they did not hesitate to place in an invidious and humiliating position, in spite of the fact that he himself only wanted to work with and lead them. Charles was neither fooled nor flustered by these self-satisfied and ignorant bigots. He began by trying to understand their points of view; finding this impossible, he then copied their methods without the help of their weapons; he ended by being forced to fight his own allies with one hand tied behind him.

The generous, affectionate, enthusiastic and genuinely pious Prince of Wales was now an embittered, worried, over-worked, uncrowned King; yet when he reached Breda in the spring of 1650 he was still resolute, hopeful, and morally, at least, undefeated.

The connection between Charles and Lucy Walter lasted for ten years – from July 1648 till the early summer of 1658 – and may be divided into two sections. The first, in which they became lovers and their child was born, ended in October 1651, when Charles returned to the Continent after an absence of a year and three months; during the next seven years he was trying to pension her, and to obtain possession of his son.

If, in the early part of their relationship, Charles and Lucy went through some kind of marriage ceremony, it could not have been legal; and that she herself seriously supposed it to be so is unlikely. Whatever papers were the fruit of that so-called contract were kept by her and used to blackmail Charles. They have now disappeared. The evidence concerning them is therefore conjectural and can only be supported by the statements of those who were witnesses to what they themselves described as a marriage, but which was almost certainly nothing of the kind. In February 1696, eleven years after Charles's death and some thirty-eight after Lucy's, the Archbishop of Glasgow wrote in his journal that a certain 'Sir J. Corke' told him that the Earl of Newburgh (a close friend of Charles during the latter part of the exile) had told Corke that he had been one of the witnesses of the marriage of Charles II and Lucy Walter. Newburgh added that Edward Prodgers, an even more intimate associate of the King's, and another, unnamed person, were also witnesses.[26] In 1680 the story that Charles and Lucy were married in an inn at Liège and that the innkeeper and his wife were witnesses was disproved.[27] Finally, on May 26th, 1905, Sir Frederick Barnwell wrote to a lady whose *nom de plume* was G. D. Gilbert and who had translated Madame d'Aulnoy's *Mémoires de la Cour d'Angleterre*, as follows:

> A good many years ago the late Sir Bernard Burke whom I knew very well and who was intimate with the late Duke of Abercorn told me that he (the Duke) had told him that he had heard from the late Duke of Buccleuch [the direct descendant of Monmouth] that he one day, looking through papers in the muniment room at Dalkeith, came across the marriage certificate of Charles II and Lucy Walters [*sic*], that after considering the matter for some time he decided to destroy it and thereon threw it into the fire and it was burned ... '[28]

In the seventeenth century a marriage certificate – and this one was reported at fourth hand – did not necessarily mean very much. But if some kind of rite was celebrated, it could be accounted for by Lucy's demands, by the fact that Charles was, for a year at any rate, deeply in love with her, and by his habitual and fatal attitude of 'peace at any price' when nagged and bullied by insistent women.

For a short time Charles and Lucy seem to have lived together under the same roof. Although it is impossible exactly to date or determine the length of this honeymoon period, it probably falls into the year 1650, some time between February and June. Charles left Jersey on February 13th, arriving at Beauvais on the 21st. He left Beauvais for Breda on March 5th, where he remained till he sailed for Scotland on June 10th. During this time it would have been difficult for him to slip away and be alone with Lucy, because he seems to have been in almost daily communication with the Scots Covenanters; nevertheless, he might have done so.

While he and Lucy were living together she had a maid, Anne Hill, whom she afterwards dismissed and who gave evidence against her when, during a visit to London in 1655, Lucy was arrested and sent to the Tower. Anne Hill's statements are naturally suspect; but two of them are so trivial and innocuous as to be of the kind that is not worth inventing. Charles and Lucy, she said, 'lived very closely in their lodgings yet very plentifully in their diet' (Charles's hearty appetite was noted by La Grande Mademoiselle), and hired a coach every week. The maid heard Lucy say, 'I have bespoke a coach, and will have it lined with red velvet and have a gold fringe on it.' [29] On several other occasions she said, 'I hope Charles will quickly have England.' Commonplace and seemingly unimportant, these two remarks, all that have come down to us of Lucy Walter's conversation at that time, do create a picture of a childish yet predatory young woman, one whom Clarendon might well describe as 'of no good fame, but handsome', the severer Evelyn as a strumpet and the *Mercurius Politicus* of 1656 as passing 'under the character of Charles Stuart's wife or mistress'. [30]

Three pieces of evidence about her marriage to Charles can be dismissed. In 1655, Lucy's mother and her aunt Margaret Gosfright said they had seen a declaration of marriage between Charles and Lucy 'under the King's own hand'. Naturally it was in both ladies' interests to believe in and publicize Lucy's claim. [31] A second lies in three letters, written in 1654 by Mary of Orange to Charles, in which she mentions 'your wife', three years after Charles had parted from Lucy, and which seem to refer to some lady to whom Charles had made advances. [32] The third is the *Heroic Life* of the Duke of Monmouth, a work of propaganda put out to prove that unfortunate young man's legitimacy, and completely unreliable. Charles publicly denied that he had ever been married to Lucy, and there is no reason to disbelieve him. She died many years before he made this statement.

Unsatisfactory and inconclusive though any account of Charles's relationship with Lucy must be, it is worth consideration, partly because of her rather sinister recurrence throughout the exile, and partly because his dealings with her spread and darkened the stains on his reputation. He was fortunate in that their connection was concealed from Argyll's Covenanters during the three months of the Scots' second visit to Holland in the summer of 1650.

From Jersey, Winram had jubilantly reported that as Charles and his brother had not a shilling between them, he was sure to sign the Covenant without hesitation, unless his 'pernicious and devilish Council' allowed him to starve rather than yield to the only persons able to help him. Charles's position was not quite as bad as Winram chose to believe; he could afford to temporize, while the Scots' need of his presence was urgent, or so they thought; for Cromwell's victory at Drogheda had given them the impression that they must be ready to withstand him immediately; and they could not rally the country until they had crowned Charles and made him, if only in name, their leader. The Scottish fear of Cromwell was the sole card Charles had to play; the Covenanters held all the rest.

Their meeting with Charles took place in his bedroom at Breda on March 29th. The Covenanters were headed by the Earls of Cassilis and Lothian, who were supported by three ministers, four lay advisers and their secretaries. Charles's reconstituted Council, much disapproved of by Nicholas and Hyde ('God help us,' Nicholas exclaimed, 'when Mr Long, Newcastle and Buckingham rule in Council!' [33]), also included Wentworth, Wilmot, the Duke of Hamilton, and William of Orange as arbitrator and intermediary.

Cassilis opened the proceedings by telling Charles, 'It is not our purpose to flatter, but to be faithful and free.' [34] He was followed by a minister, Livingstone, who spoke censoriously of the late King and of the Stuart family in general. Charles listened in cold silence; his Council were disgusted, not only by the content of Livingstone's speech, but by the insolent and hectoring manner of the speaker. In the ensuing discussion Newcastle, enraged by the Covenanters' insistence on Charles's dismissal of Ormonde and Montrose, broke into furious objections, and was reproved by Cassilis for swearing. The same ground was gone over and the same terms insisted on by the Scots at the next meetings. Meanwhile, Charles managed so to impress the Covenanters that they sent back glowing reports of his character. 'We found the King,' Livingstone wrote, 'of a courteous and tractable disposition.' By interviewing the clergymen privately, in pairs, and allowing them to argue as long as they liked, Charles succeeded in setting them against one another. In these talks he would raise theological questions and repeat their answers at the general meetings. 'This,' said Livingstone, 'made some of us suspect that if all of our number had dealt alike ... the King had granted us all our desires.'[35]

As the Scots' fear of invasion increased Charles began to correspond with Argyll, whom he begged not to believe the reports of his loyalty to Montrose. 'I depend upon your assistance and advice in all things,' he added.[36] To a Royalist in England he wrote, 'Advise [the Catholics] not to be startled with anything ... put out here in my name, which I assure you and them [is] forced and constrained.' By this time Montrose had received Charles's letter telling him that he might have to disband his forces and withdraw from Scotland. Montrose, already in the Orkneys, realized that he was betrayed, and replied that he would 'abandon still my life to search my death for the interests of Your Majesty's honour and service.'

In April Charles said to one of the Council, 'I perfectly hate the Scots [Covenanters], but I may have to give in to them,' and at the next meeting suggested referring all their disputes to a free Parliament in Scotland as soon as he arrived there.[37] The Scots refused to consider this, with the result that William of Orange, who was being pressed by the States General to get rid of his brother-in-law, advised him to sign, as did Buckingham and Newcastle. As Charles continued to procrastinate, his position deteriorated. The Queen of Sweden and the King of Denmark refused further help and also advised him to sign. His difficulties were then increased by the arrival of a personal envoy from Argyll, suggesting that he should marry the Lady Anne Campbell. Charles replied that he could not accept without his mother's approval – for which he took care not to ask – and made a final appeal for the reconciliation of all the Scottish parties. When the Covenanters refused to consider this, he lost his temper and threatened to break off negotiations.

In the silence that followed this announcement Charles stood up and rated the Scots 'with great passion and bitter execration'. 'We find in you only lightness and vanity,' retorted one of the ministers, and Charles dismissed them. He was then set upon by Buckingham, Hamilton and Newcastle, who pointed out that as he had not yet taken his coronation oath, he was not bound to keep his word when he gave it; therefore, let him agree to everything – what did it matter? 'It is sometimes needful,' said one, 'to hold a candle to the devil,' and another reminded him that his Huguenot grandfather had found Paris worth a Mass.[38]

In the evenings Charles broke away, 'balling and dancing', to the horror of the Scots, who continued to exhort and lecture him during the day, begging him to 'humble himself before God,' for his father's sins and his mother's idolatry. Meanwhile the Princess Sophia, secretly hoping that he would resume his rather shady courtship, perceived that he avoided her in the presence of the Covenanters, and decided to think no more of him.[39]

Nicholas, whom Charles had dismissed from the Council at the request of the Scots, was very unhappy; he could neither understand nor forgive His Majesty's methods. 'He hath not resolution enough to discountenance those he knows to be false,' he wrote to Hyde, ' ... I doubt past cure in him,'[40] but Hyde had better hopes of his pupil. It was Charles's great weakness 'not publicly to detest what privately he abhors, and if I did not hope that he would shortly outgrow that deformity, it would break my heart,' he wrote from Madrid, adding that the Scots would get the best of the King in the end.[41]

At last Charles said that he would agree to the Covenant, but not till he arrived in Scotland. The Scots, who no longer trusted him, said that he must agree to it before he left and sign it when he got there. While he hesitated, his mother wrote urging him to sign, and the English Parliament offered the Covenanters a large sum to break off negotiations.[42] The Scots now felt themselves in a position to reject this approach, for they knew that Charles had heard nothing from Montrose and had received no support from the continental powers. On May 7th, in full Council, Charles told the Covenanters that he would dismiss his chaplains, allow the establishment of Presbyterianism throughout his dominion, enforce the penal laws against Catholics and sign the Covenant as soon as he arrived in Scotland. He then accepted the Scots' formal invitation to be received and crowned by them, the assurance of his own safety, honour and freedom and the promise of full restoration to his power and authority.[43]

In the days that followed Charles's distress was painful to see. He thought much, as he later confessed, of his father's last instructions.[44] At meals he sat silently brooding. His bitter melancholy so struck Jaffray, one of the ministers, that he asked to see him alone. Jaffray had grown very fond of 'that poor young prince', and was now of the opinion that he should not have been forced to sign a Covenant 'which we knew ... he hated in his heart'. 'Do not subscribe to it if in your conscience you are not satisfied,' he said. Charles made no reply, and Jaffray went sadly away.

'He ... sinfully complied with what we ... pressed upon him ...' he wrote in his diary. 'Our sin was more than his.'[45] Everything now seemed to be settled. But the Covenanters had tasted blood; they were not yet finished with Charles. A few days before his twentieth birthday they heard that he was about to receive the Sacrament – kneeling. Immediately they asked for an audience.

Charles received them with his usual courtesy. Livingstone, who seems to have regarded all social amenities as part of Sassenach decadence and falsity, began an oration on what John Knox had condemned, more than a hundred years ago, as the Table Gesture. Kneeling to receive the Host was idolatrous. 'We have come to you,' he said, 'to show the sin of so doing, and what inconveniency it may bring on your business, and what scandal to such as are honest – ' with a great deal more about what the Scriptures (to which his persuasion alone had the key) had ordained.

Charles, to the delight of his Council, side-tracked the main issue in order to gain time. 'How do you know,' he asked, 'that the Scriptures are the Word of God but by the testimony of the Church?'

Livingstone was momentarily staggered by this appeal to an episcopal and therefore crypto-papist organization. He and the other ministers insisted that Charles should not communicate. He replied that he had nothing more to say. 'We will leave you,' said Livingstone sternly, 'to think upon it till after supper – ' and they marched out.

They returned to find him 'tenaciously resolute'. 'My father,' he said, 'used always to communicate at Christmas, Easter and Whit Sunday, and I must do likewise. I do it to procure a blessing from God on my intended voyage.' 'It is provocation against God,' Livingstone thundered, 'to procure the blasting of all your designs.' 'I shall stick to my resolution,' Charles replied, and indicated that the audience was at an end.[46]

The Covenanters now began to feel that their triumph was marred; their uneasiness increased when the King sent for them next day and calmly proposed to 'qualify' their agreement; he again suggested that the Covenant should not be forced on the English people. 'We cannot receive your oath if you add any one word to the words read,' was the reply. 'I ought to do so,' persisted Charles; but he gave in after a long argument.

The ministers left him in deepest gloom. 'We are bringing the plague of God to Scotland,' said one. 'His word is useless,' another added. They then reported this disastrous development in a letter to Argyll.[47]

As Charles prepared to leave Breda for Terheyden, whence he was to sail in a ship lent him by his brother-in-law, he received a letter from Henrietta Maria, who had suddenly grasped what the Treaty of Breda implied. He must have opened this one with more than usual dread, for it was immensely long; his mother's vast, slanting, rather illegible hand gave the impression, now more than ever, of someone writing in a state of semi-hysteria. She rated him for having yielded to the Scots. 'I always said you should never have accepted the Covenant,' she declared, and expatiated on the distress caused her by 'the horrid particulars' of his apostasy. Charles ignored this characteristic volte-face, which so astonished his mother's ladies that one of them ventured to ask her if she had not originally supported His Majesty's actions. 'God forbid,' the weeping Queen replied, 'that I should have had a hand in persuading him to sacrifice his honour and conscience.'[48]

In the first week of June Charles reached Terheyden, pursued by the lamentations and reproaches of those he was leaving behind, whom he promised to reinstate on his restoration. There he heard of Montrose's capture and execution. 'This,' said one of the Covenanters, 'is for Your Majesty's service.'[49] Charles found it very difficult to write an adequate letter of condolence to the new Marquess. Eventually he scribbled a few lines, assuring the young man that 'I shall have the same care of you as if he were still living, and as able to serve me as ever.' It is perhaps the most heartless of all his letters; yet he was appalled, although he would not admit it, by what he had done.[50]

On the 10th, having smuggled two of his proscribed chaplains on board, Charles and his party of undesirables, or malignants, as the Covenanters called them, set sail. Among these were Wentworth, Wilmot, Buckingham, Hamilton, and Lauderdale. Those Catholic powers who had refused to help him expressed horror and disgust. A Cromwellian spy, who had been reporting all the negotiations with the Scots, remarked with grim satisfaction, 'They must not be ashamed to beg that cannot dig – they needs must go whom their fates drive – ' adding, 'Charles Stuart will stroke them till he is in the saddle, and then he will make them feel his spurs.'[51]

It was well for Charles that he had not the least notion of what the fates had in store for him.

NOTES

1 Montpensier, vol. I, pp. 209–11.
2 Op. cit., p. 223.
3 Ibid.
4 Evelyn, pp. 280–2.
5 Clarendon, pp. 718–22.
6 Ibid.
7 Op. cit., pp. 721–2.
8 *Nicholas Papers*, vol. I, pp. 135–6.
9 Carte, *Original Letters*, vol. I, p. 296.
10 Montpensier, vol. I, pp. 232–5.
11 *Cal. D. S. P.*, Aug. 25th and Sept. 29th, 1649.
12 *Nicholas Papers*, vol. I, pp. 152, 156.
13 *Cal. S. P. Ven.*, vol. XXVIII, p. 119.
14 Hoskins, pp. 307–89.
15 Ibid.
16 *Cal. D. S. P.*, March 22nd, 1650; Carte, *Original Letters*, vol. I, p. 356; Gardiner, *Charles II and Scotland*, p. 8; *Clar. MSS*, fol. 39, no. 20.
17 H.M.C. Report 10, App. IV, pp. 146–8.
18 Montpensier, vol. I, p. 319.
19 Gardiner, *Charles II*, p. 256.
20 *Cal. Clar. S. P.*, vol. II, p. 528.
21 Gardiner, *Charles II*, p. 291.
22 Ibid.
23 *Cal. D. S. P.*, March 26th, 1650.
24 Carte, *Ormonde*, vol. II, p. 88.
25 Bulstrode, p. 391.
26 D'Oyley, p. 13.
27 Harris, vol. I, p. 175.
28 D'Oyley, ibid.; Montagu–Douglas–Scott, p. 49.
29 Harris, ibid.
30 D'Oyley, p. 12.
31 Ibid.
32 Ibid.
33 *Nicholas Papers*, vol. I, p. 173.
34 Gardiner, *Charles II*, p. 40.
35 Lyon, *Personal History of Charles II*, pp. 16–23.
36 H.M.C. Report 6, vol. 5, pp. 12–14.
37 Gardiner, *Charles II*, p. 63.
38 Carte, *Ormonde*, vol. II, pp. 129–33.
39 Electress Sophia, p. 48.
40 *Nicholas Papers*, vol. I, p. 171.
41 *Cal. Clar. S. P.*, vol. III, pp. 13–15.
42 Lyon, pp. 16–23.
43 Scott, *The King in Exile*, p. 129.
44 Carte, *Ormonde*, vol. II, pp. 129–33.
45 A. Jaffray, *Diary*, p. 32.
46 Lyon, pp. 26–30.
47 Ibid.
48 *Nicholas Papers*, vol. I, p. 173.
49 Clarendon, p. 743.
50 Scott, *The King in Exile*, p. 156.
51 Gardiner, *Charles II*, pp. 74, 109.

PART THREE

The Wanderer

(JUNE 1650–JULY 1654)

For though God hath leaden feet and is slow in
punishing, yet He hath iron hands, and strikes
home in the end.

BULSTRODE: *Memoirs*

CHAPTER ONE

PAYING THE PRICE

I

THE majority of Charles II's contemporaries deplored, when they did not condemn, his signing the Covenant; and most historians have followed their example. Neither group seems to have visualized the alternative. Charles must have done so, and thus seen the consequence of refusing to sell his honour and betray his friends as another and more delayed form of treachery – that of remaining abroad and wandering from one place to another indefinitely, while his followers starved or deserted and the Royalists in his rebellious dominions ceased to believe in, or struggle for, a king who did nothing to help himself.

So once more, as when he left Jersey for France four years earlier, Charles made the wrong decision. In the decade that elapsed between his departure for Scotland and his restoration the results of his mistake – as some of the Cavaliers put it, his sin – were brought home to him daily. It never occurred either to him or to the most far-sighted and acute of his advisers that to wait, in semi-inactivity, was the right, the only policy; and to reject Scottish help in 1650 would have been to do exactly that. In his twenty-first year Charles therefore submitted, with loathing, self-disgust and in fear of his life, to a process of humiliation in which he was spared nothing.

In one respect the effect of that process on Charles himself was the reverse of what might have been expected. Hitherto, his experiences had driven him into silence and withdrawal; he now became talkative, even voluble (a habit he retained till his death), whether as the result of his separation from the older Cavaliers and his family, or because unhappiness forced him to talk in order not to think, is uncertain. Those who had seen him darkly brooding at Council meetings or courteously reserved at formal entertainments, would have been amazed by the change. This metamorphosis may have begun with his renewed hopes of the future, and also with his anticipation of the active service which had been denied him for eight years – nearly half his life. Now, at last, he was on board his frigate again, on his way, as he believed, to acclamation, fulfilment of his functions as a monarch, and almost certain victory. As the flat dimness of the Dutch coast sank away, and Buckingham and his gay companions joined him on deck, the King's spirits rose; during the first part of the voyage guilt and shame were thrust aside.

Meanwhile Argyll, realizing that Charles was now in his power, instructed his emissaries partially to abrogate the Treaty of Breda by enforcing higher terms. These embodied the dismissal, among others, of Hamilton and Lauderdale; a more sinister clause established Scottish freedom from any obligation. Inspired by Argyll, Kirk and Parliament declared that they would not invade England unless it appeared 'lawful and necessary', while His Majesty must submit to such further demands as they chose to make.

Brodie, Jaffray and three other ministers pursued Charles's frigate with these conditions, but did not catch up with him till the weather caused his and their ships to cast anchor off Heligoland. On June 23rd they came aboard to present the new terms.[1]

Charles was enraged. 'I will not grant them,' he exclaimed. 'Rather, I will land in Denmark, and lay aside all thought of coming into Scotland.' As they argued, the wind changed and his threat was exposed; to land would be to abandon any chance of his restoration. He gave orders to sail, hoping to persuade the Covenanters to compromise during the rest of the voyage. When the coast of Scotland was sighted they were in dispute. By this time the Scots had the upper hand. On July 3rd, having anchored off the mouth of the Spey, Charles consented to swear to the revised oath. Just as he was about to do so, he said, 'What I do should not import any infringement of the laws of England,' going on to explain that Presbyterianism had not been legally established there.

The infuriated Covenanters refused to proceed, a violent quarrel ensued and finally the King yielded. Jaffray, aware that their victim would not hesitate to break an oath so enforced, recorded his disapproval in his diary. 'Our guiltiness was the greater,' he observed, just as four English Parliamentary ships left the harbour.[2]

Under cover of a thick mist the King then prepared to disembark, while some of the watchers on the shore recalled that a century earlier his great-grandmother had been similarly protected from Queen Elizabeth's fleet. 'I pray God he prove more fortunate!' said one, and another added something about ill omens.[3] So, having shed the last rag of honour, Charles entered the kingdom which was virtually the property of Argyll. From that moment he became the prisoner of the great Marquess, whose emissaries,

THE DUKE OF MONMOUTH
AS A CHILD

THE MARQUESS OF ARGYLL

LUCY WALTER?

binding him with silken cords, made his position clear within a few hours of his arrival.

That kingdom, two hundred years later the paradise of delighted tourists and discreetly grasping purveyors of outdoor amusements, was then a wilderness partially inhabited by illiterate savages, whose loyalty to their chiefs was so exploited as to keep them in perpetual warfare: living like beasts and fighting like demons, superstitious, tormented and hideously cruel, the clans had long submitted in atavistic terror to the voice of the Kirk, whose ministers, after a century of frenzied effort, had achieved power over nobles, Parliament and the Stuart dynasty. Although the mystique of that dynasty and its appeal to the people were renewed with the appearance of a proscribed and uncrowned king, the influence of the clergy was so formidable, so capriciously and cunningly exercised as to throw up a barrier between Charles and his subjects whenever they chose to create it. Like malicious witch-doctors, believing only in themselves and identifying their own hates and desires with those of the deity invented by John Knox and long since turned into a Moloch through their loathing of all beauty, happiness and common sense, these imitation Old Testament prophets had brought conceit, hypocrisy and tyranny to a fine art; their vanity was boundless, their ranting eloquence as tedious as it was repetitive, their horror of natural instincts and healthy enjoyment ludicrous and disgusting. For such as these, the tempestuous grandeurs, the violent and dramatic contrasts of colour and outline, the wild glories of glen and moor, of streams and forests and mountains, in which their slaves would have been content to live primitively, yet with gaiety and hope, were merely a setting for the infiltration of fear, pompous self-examination and nauseating exhibitions of repentance for sins freshly discovered on each occasion. Through the influence of these maniacal egotists, any human emotion, any simple courtesy or act of kindness could be looked upon as sinful; this was the Covenanters' favourite adjective, one they had imbued with a terrible and all-embracing significance. To love one's children, to care for dependants, to show hospitality to strangers or devotion to the chieftain – to laugh, to dance, to sing, to play games – might, at any moment, be pronounced a sin.

The simplicity, amounting to a bare subsistence, in which the poorer classes lived, not only made this bitter dictatorship secure, but helped to tighten its hold on the clans and so on the authority of the nobles, who had to subscribe, whether sincerely or not, to the tenets of a Calvinism bordering on lunacy. Campbells, Grahames, Maitlands and many more—all were in the grasp of the Kirk; and so their leaders, many of them highly educated, widely travelled, sophisticated and intellectual persons, whose surroundings and manner of life reflected European culture and cosmopolitan taste, persuaded themselves, or decided to pretend, that their God was that of the Covenanters; like the priests of Baal, they too were prepared to howl and weep and cut themselves with knives in degraded ecstasies of self-abasement before their awestruck followers, whose subjugation was thereby complete. By the time Charles II reached Scotland, church-going had become a vice, sermons a disease and religion a monstrous canker in the body politic, enfeebling the ancient virtues of courage, truthfulness and self-respect. If it had been otherwise, he might have entered into his inheritance in 1650, instead of ten years later.

Meanwhile, the sight of the young King raised, if only for a time, the ministers' embargo on any form of rejoicing. The people, thronging about him, danced and sang; so many bonfires were lit that the citizens of Garmouth on the Spey had to replenish them with their few sticks of furniture.[4] The Covenanters retorted by ordaining a 'solemn fast'; but the crowds drank themselves into the gutters of the town, where many of them remained until the next morning. Charles, who had had to sign the revised Covenant before being allowed to land (so ran Argyll's instructions), was hurried on to the Bog of Gicht, where he was told that he must at once dismiss all but two of his courtiers – Henry Seymour and the Duke of Buckingham. Seymour was negligible; the versatile Duke's 'godliness' had so impressed the ministers that he was regarded as the single good influence in his master's entourage. At twenty-two, George Villiers's powers of charm and deceit had reached their height; and he was determined to submit himself wholly to Argyll.

Although Charles was ready to accept humiliations, he could not control his resentment at Hamilton's and Lauderdale's dismissal; he had counted on uniting their forces with those of Argyll. 'Your Majesty must prepare yourself for things of a harder digestion,' Hamilton told him. 'At present I can do you no service. The Marquess of Argyll is now in absolute credit. Study to gain him, and give him no cause of jealousy on my account.' He added, 'When Your Majesty's affairs are in a better posture, you will not forget your faithful servants.' He then retired to his island of Arran ('for the most part inhabited with wild beasts')[5] while Lauderdale took refuge in another stronghold.

Still Charles, encouraged by the rapturous welcome of the people, hoped to win over the detested Marquess and so regain some of the advantages he had signed away. Argyll himself was suddenly at a loss. It had not occurred to him that the King would submit to conditions expressly designed to prevent his entering Scotland. Now that Argyll's secret agreement with the English Parliament was broken, all he could do was to play for time, delay Charles's coronation as long as possible and make it clear to Cromwell, whose armies were about to cross the Border, that he would do nothing towards the King's restoration.[6]

So he began by adopting an attitude of coldness and reserve which amounted to insolence. He was not waiting for Charles at the Bog of Gicht, but at Pitcaple, while the King was made to feel his own helplessness in various ways. When Charles entered Aberdeen, he was shown, nailed up over the main gateway, the right hand of Montrose; at Edinburgh, the betrayed Marquess's skull grinned down at him from the Tolbooth; and wherever he went he had to listen to abuse of his most faithful servant. Charles sustained his serenity; the scenery, he tactfully, if untruthfully, remarked, reminded him of 'dear England'.[7] At St Andrews, having attended morning service, he visited the Reverend Robert Blair and congratulated him on his four-hour sermon. Mrs Blair ran to fetch a chair for His Majesty, but was halted by her husband. 'My heart,' said the minister, 'he is a young man, and can wait on himself.' Charles submitted to the discourtesy with a smile, and sat down to an afternoon meal with the Blairs.[8] When the citizens presented him with a sum of money which was at once confiscated by the Covenanters, he made no comment on their announcement that all such gifts must be administered by themselves.

Before Charles reached Pitcaple he was entertained by Sir James Livingstone, with whom he raised the question of advancing on Cromwell. Following Argyll's instructions, Livingstone advised delay, and suggested coming to an agreement with the enemy. Once more the King controlled his anger, and said merely, 'I hope you would not wish me to sell my father's blood.'[9] A few days later he arrived at Pitcaple. A hogshead of claret was commandeered from a local fair, and a banquet given for him, Buckingham and Argyll by General Leslie. During the course of the feast Charles, whose loathing and dread of the Marquess had increased with every step of his progress, received a violent shock. His resistance was undermined: his plans for defeating the Covenanters were overthrown. He was completely subjugated by Argyll.

II

Archibald Campbell, eighth Earl and first Marquess of Argyll, was forty-three when he and Charles met at Pitcaple. Now that his long feud with Montrose – who had defeated him twice, and destroyed five thousand of his men in 1645 – was over, he was not only the acknowledged master of Scotland, but its most remarkable statesman. 'A man,' says Hyde, 'of craft, subtlety and falsehood, who wanted nothing but honesty and courage to be a very extraordinary man, having all other talents in a great degree.'[10] His appearance was not impressive; slight, dark, squinting and lame, Argyll at once made a conquest of the young King by a combination of respectful subservience, amusing talk and intelligent sympathy with Charles's difficulties. Here at last was someone in whom he could confide, and who 'entertained him', according to Hyde, 'with very pleasant discourses, with such insinuation that the King did not only very well like his conversation, but often believed that he had a mind to please and gratify him ... There was never a better courtier.'

The honeymoon period lasted throughout the journey from Pitcaple to Falkland, the palace of the Scottish kings, where Charles was installed on July 9th. In this magnificent Renaissance building Argyll set up his victim and protégé as a monarch in name only; by degrees, with the utmost correctness, yet ruthlessly and in steady pursuit of his own ends, he made it clear to the King what his position was. He was luxuriously housed, given an allowance of £9,000 a year, superb hunters and elaborate meals. The etiquette surrounding him was strict and formal; so much so that he found himself waited on with watchful reverence by Argyll's servants, who were also spies; those of his English attendants who had refused to leave were put into lodgings some way from the palace and only allowed to approach him with the Marquess's permission. Lord Lorne, Argyll's elder son, seconded by the Earl of Eglinton, was Captain of his Campbell bodyguard; Mr Blair replaced his English chaplains; his secretaries, Long and Sir Edward Walker, were sent away; one of his gentlemen, Daniel O'Neile, was imprisoned and put under sentence of death because he was an Irish Catholic; others found it advisable to return to Holland. Of his whole entourage all but Seymour and Buckingham had disappeared. He was as much a prisoner as if he had been captured by the English Parliament and shut up in the Tower.

The only group to which Argyll's embargo did not apply was that of the Covenanting ministers. They had access to the King at any hour, and would appear in his bedroom unannounced. Instructed by the Marquess, they approached him 'in the humblest postures', bowing three times when they entered his apartments and kneeling till they had his leave to rise. But from the moment they came into the room – they were apt to arrive in pairs – they held forth in a series of tutorials on their faith and His Majesty's neglect of it. After sandwiching these lectures between immense and sometimes hysterical prayers, they would then issue their orders. Charles was required to attend their services every day, and four times a day on the Sabbath.[11]

That Sabbath, still a nightmarish institution, involved Charles's hearing sermons which succeeded one another almost without intermission (one fast day he endured six, each lasting from three to four hours), and in all these discourses he had to listen to violent abuse of his parents, his Stuart grandfather and great-grandmother and all his Catholic ancestors.[12] He was not allowed to walk out of doors, or to ride, or to play games (not even golf, which he detested anyway), or to smile, or to show any sign of gaiety. If he rebelled, or even protested, the eloquence of the chaplains became more furious and lengthy. When, finally, the wretched young man appealed to Argyll, that nobleman, hitherto so agreeably co-operative, 'gathered up his countenance', and left the room.[13]

Charles fell back on his best and most characteristic weapons – cunning and self-control. He swallowed the insults and diatribes, set in hand plans for escape and for the defeat of Argyll – possibly by calling on the treacherous Buckingham and the comparatively powerless Seymour – and once again began to practise the tenets of Newcastle's early training.

'If any [of your subjects],' says Newcastle, 'be Bible mad, over much burnt with fiery zeal, they may think it a service to God to destroy you, and say the spirit moved them, and bring some example of a king with a bad name in the Old Testament.' After a passage on the danger of Utopian ideals – or, in fact, of any ideals at all – the Earl advises Charles to avoid ill-natured talk ('*seem* to dislike it') and to be friendly with everyone, no matter what his real feelings. The King followed these precepts almost too well. When reviewing the troops on the links at Leith he made himself so agreeable that the soldiers prepared to follow him rather than Argyll's faction, with the result that he was not allowed to attend the Council of State (whose decisions, carefully edited, were communicated to him later), was forced to ask Lorne's permission for every move and kept away from the army. The soldiers' welcome had alarmed the Covenanters, who described them as 'too much inclined to put their confidence in the arm of flesh', and re-doubled their warnings against His Majesty's winning ways.[14]

Nevertheless, the Covenanters' support of Charles so offended the extreme Presbyterians that five of the western counties broke away and made an alliance of their own against Argyll. Thus Charles was nominally at the head of four opposing forces – the Royalists, the Covenanters, the Engagers and the Extremist westerners. These divisions weakened Argyll's power and his hold over Charles, and had a fatal effect on the army, now under the command of General Leslie. Meanwhile the King, who had managed to keep in touch with the English Royalists and was told that he might expect support from the City of London, continued to behave with urbane serenity and to exercise his charm over everyone he was allowed to meet. Few women could resist his easy yet dignified address. One, Anne Murray, who had organized the Duke of York's escape from England, describes her first meeting with him in ecstatic terms.

Having received a message that His Majesty would be pleased to see her at Dunfermline, Anne Murray arrived to find herself in the midst of a large assembly. When she was pointed out to the King, he 'looked favourably' at her – she was young and pretty – and smiled; he did not send for her to speak to him. After he left the presence-chamber to go into dinner, she complained to his chaplain – why had she not been given an audience? – and burst into tears. As soon as Charles reappeared the chaplain spoke to him; then she saw that instead of sending for her, he was walking towards her with his long rapid stride. As she gazed up at him, he began, 'Mrs Murray, I am ashamed I have been so long a-speaking to you, but it was because I could not say enough for the service you did my brother. But if ever I can command what I have a right to as my own, there shall be nothing in my power I shall not do for you.'

Anne Murray was speechless; she pressed both hands on her chest. Charles laid his long brown fingers on hers and continued to look at her. She withdrew, curtsied, kissed his hand and replied, 'I have done nothing but my duty, and have recompense enough if Your Majesty accept of it as a service, and allow me your favour.' The King paused; then he bent down and kissed her cheek. A glance and a smile were interchanged, to the horror of the attendant ministers. All in a flutter, Mistress Murray curtsied again and stood back. Charles supplemented this interview with a present of fifty pounds when, a few weeks later, he heard that she was nursing the Scottish wounded.[15]

Shortly afterwards the King said to one of his ecclesiastical attendants, 'I am something troubled at the dismissal of my servants – ' hastily adding, 'The wholesome advice of the Kirk shall ever have great weight with me.' Almost at the same moment he was writing to Hamilton, 'I am sure there is nobody that is more concerned with the rigidness of this Kirk and State towards you than I am, and I desire you to let me know if I can do anything that take off their cruelty ... I am very much grieved ... Your most affectionate friend.'[16]

As the result, perhaps, of his interview with Anne Murray, Charles was rated by the ministers for his falsity. 'Your Majesty's whole deportment and private conversation,' he was told, 'show a secret enmity to the work of God.' They then suggested to Argyll that the King should be excluded from any share in the administration of the Government. Argyll now had to compromise; it was becoming increasingly difficult for him to subvert the influence of this agreeable young man, who accepted all reproofs without protest and 'wrought himself into as grave a deportment as he could', sitting through the Covenanters' sermons and prayers with stoical patience. Once more, some of them began to feel that he might be going to reform; meanwhile he secretly interviewed Dr King, the Royalist Dean of Tuam and the emissary of Ormonde, who had been very much disturbed by the reports of His Majesty's Presbyterianism. He was shown into Charles's bedchamber at one o'clock in the morning. Aware of the Irish clergyman's distrust, Charles at once began, 'Mr Dean, I have received a very good character of you, and do therefore give you assurance that, however I am forced by the necessity of my affairs to appear otherwise, yet I am a true child of the Church of England, and a true Cavalier and shall remain firm to my first principles.'

Dr King fell on his knees. 'God Almighty bless Your Majesty!' he exclaimed, 'and continue you in that resolution, and make you a nursing father to His Church.' As Charles signed ,to him to rise, he went on, 'Your Majesty now sees how inconsistent the ecclesiastical Government here is with monarchy.' 'Mr King,' said Charles vehemently, 'the Scots have dealt very ill with me – very ill.' After a moment's thought he went on, 'I understand you are willing to go into Ireland. My Lord of Ormonde is a person that I depend on more than anyone living. I much fear that I have been forced to do some things which may prejudice him. You have heard,' he continued rather uneasily, 'how a declaration was extorted from me, and how I should have been dealt with if I had not signed it.' After begging the Dean to reassure Ormonde, he went on, 'Although I cannot at present reward you, yet if God shall be pleased to put power into my hands, I will remember it unto you.' With his newly acquired volubility, Charles then reiterated his messages to Ormonde, expressed regret that he had lost touch with him, and added, 'But I have been ill dealt with. The circumstances are too long to acquaint you with – Robin Long will inform you.' At some length he assured the Dean of his loyalty to Ormonde and the Irish; then he said, 'Remember me to my lord Clanrickard. He is a good man.'

At last the Dean was able to get in a word. He said, 'Clanrickard has been extremely loyal to preserve Your Majesty's interest in that kingdom.'

'It is to their interest as well as mine,' said Charles abruptly. After another pause, he asked, 'Let me see – who do I know in that kingdom?' 'Lord Viscount Dillon?' suggested the Dean. 'I know him very well,' Charles agreed. 'Remember me to him. I hear that he and his family are great sufferers for me. I pray remember me to my Lord of Castlehaven. I know my Lord of Muskerry too – remember me to him.' The Dean said, 'Sir Richard Blake hath been a faithful servant to Your Majesty.' 'That is he who is Speaker?' said Charles eagerly. 'Remember me to him also,' and the Dean was dismissed.

Later on Charles saw Dr King again, and began, 'Tell my Lord of Ormonde I would by no means have him come here. Robin Long will tell you what I have been forced to do concerning Ireland.' Once more he repeated his messages to the Irish nobles, some of whom were Catholics, adding, 'And tell them, I prefer their particular safeties to any interest of my own in that kingdom. It was not only an error, it was a misfortune, that I came not thither when my Lord of Ormonde invited me.'[17]

Dr King went away in perfect trust, leaving his master to compose, with Argyll's help, a declaration to the Scottish army. 'We shall ... be ready to hazard our life (nay, our crown)', it ran, 'for God, the Covenant and the honour and freedom of this hitherto unconquered kingdom.' At about the same time Hamilton received another smuggled letter in which the King described the odious behaviour of the 'severe Christians' by whom he was surrounded, the enthusiasm of the soldiers and his removal from their assemblies. 'They are so watchful over me that I do nothing but they observe it,' he concluded. 'I desire you to direct me, because I do not know whom to employ without suspicion ... I fear that our masters have some design against your person ... Have a great care.' A few days later Charles managed to convey a message to the Pope, assuring him of his 'goodwill' to all Catholics in his dominions.[18]

Truly Argyll had an apt pupil, one worthy of his talents. Already Lord Lorne had been captivated by his charge's engaging manners, and now allowed him to see certain of his Royalist followers privately. Yet, devious and untiring though Charles was, he needed certain diversions that even the witty Buckingham could not supply. Forced into idleness, he fell back on what one of the more sympathetic and intelligent ministers described as pleasures natural 'to a prince of his age and vivacity' – with dire consequences.

At Dunfermline it was sometimes possible, perhaps with Buckingham's and Seymour's connivance, for the King to receive privately not only his Royalist supporters, but also their wives. As this became a habit, he grew careless. One day, when he had concluded a long interview with the Moderator and other ministers in his bedroom, a lady was announced. The weather was warm, and during the course of an agreeably intimate conversation Charles and his visitor drifted towards the open window, forgetting that the covey of black-clad divines must pass that way. As they did so the ministers looked up. There was His Majesty, 'toying and fondling with one of his fair mistresses' – and this just after they had been praying together! When the Covenanters reached the meeting to which they were bound, the King's 'indecent and sinful' behaviour was described to those who had not seen it, and a long discussion took place. Their leader then commanded silence and called upon the Almighty – whom he seems to have looked on as a kind of chairman – to advise them as to what punishment would be most suitable. The answer was prompt and satisfactory. The King must be publicly reproved and lectured and then undergo a penance, also in public. As they were gloating over this prospect the Moderator, Robert Douglas, objected. To expose and degrade a guest, however deplorably behaved, whom they had accepted as King would be to lower themselves and the Kirk. He suggested privately reproving Charles, and after some further argument the assembly agreed that he should do so.

Douglas, who had been disgusted by the arrogance of his fellows, asked for an audience with Charles and bluntly began, 'I come upon a very impertinent errand from the Brethren, which I think needless to communicate.' He went on in a more courtly tone, 'I humbly beg Your Majesty of your princely goodness to pardon my presumption.' As Charles desired him to proceed, he said smiling, 'There is an old proverb, which imports, "When one is inclined to kiss his neighbour's wife, it is proper to shut all the doors and windows."'

Charles burst out laughing. 'I agree,' he said, and he and Douglas parted on excellent terms. A few days later a stricter – or perhaps less desirable – lady saw the King and Buckingham playing cards on the Sabbath and told the Commissioners. They decided to take a strong line with this incorrigible young man by so humiliating him that he would never again dare to transgress their commands.[19]

Some thirteen months later, Charles, describing the horrors of his stay in Scotland, said, 'It was a miserable life. I saw no women – and the people were so ignorant that they thought it sinful to play the violin.'[20] These deprivations must have been enforced after the window and card-playing incidents. On August 16th they were followed by the drawing up of a new declaration, in which the King was required publicly to condemn, and repent for, the sin of his father's marrying into 'an idolatrous family', his own 'ill education and former wickedness', and his regret for having made agreements with papists – i.e. the Irish.

Although his ability to lie and prevaricate had now become instinctive, Charles was not yet utterly corrupted. At twenty, there was still something in his temperament of the ten-year-old boy who had so delighted in the fine new Scripture book produced by good Mr Ferrar, and whom Newcastle had observed to be naturally pious. Intermingled with these damaged remnants of religious feeling were reverence for his father's memory and care for his mother's sensibilities. Now, required to betray and vilify both the dead and the living, he indignantly refused to submit. The Covenanters, headed by Argyll, were equally determined; and for three days the battle continued.[21]

Charles began his resistance by calling a Council, in the hope that some among them, such as Douglas and Jaffray, might see what a monstrous and evil imposition they were forcing on him. It was useless. He was told that if he did not sign, the Scottish Parliament would deny his rights and cast him out; thus all his previous humiliations would be wasted and himself thrown back into the miseries of exile. Desperately, he appealed to Argyll. 'I can never look my mother in the face if I pass it,' he said, to which the Marquess coldly replied, 'It is necessary for your affairs.' The King spoke of the dishonour done to his father; not unnaturally, the man who had sold Charles I to the Roundheads remained unmoved.[22] A Parliamentary conference was then held at Edinburgh, in which Charles was formally repudiated, while it was privately made clear to him that if he signed the declaration the ban would be lifted. Still he stood firm, in spite of the fact that this threat was implemented by a sermon in which he was abused for deceiving his only loyal supporters, and described as 'the root of malignancy and an utter enemy to the kingdom of Christ'.[23]

For the last time the miserable King turned to Argyll. 'If you will protect me from the Covenanting party,' he said, 'I will make you a duke and a gentleman of the bedchamber when I come into what is mine,' and added a promise of £40,000.[24] The master of Scotland remained non-committal, but left to interview the ministers (who, he told Charles, were 'in great indignation'), and persuaded them to modify the manner, although not the content, of the clauses in the declaration referring to Charles I and Henrietta Maria. He then sent the King the revised copy, with a note, which ran, 'When you come into your kingdom, you may be more free – but, for the present, *it is necessary to please these madmen*.'[25]

Madmen – yes! That was what they were. And might not promises made to such persons be discounted, above all when signed by a King who had not taken his coronation oath? Argyll's advice, the epitome of his present and his pupil's future diplomacy, was a brilliant stroke. Charles agreed to meet the ministers and declared himself ready to sign.

When he confronted them, there was something in his look which disturbed the less besotted members of that grim assembly. Suddenly the Reverend Mr Gillespie said, 'If Your Majesty is not satisfied, do not sign – even for the sake of your three kingdoms.' The King's saturnine impassivity remained unbroken. 'Mr Gillespie,' he said, 'I am satisfied' – and signed.[26]

Next day he left for Perth, to find that even the easy-going Henry Seymour had shown his disgust, and been dismissed for speaking in violent terms against the declaration. So, of all Charles's intimates, Buckingham alone remained. The Duke had always considered that a great to-do was being wrought about a trifle – until he was crowned, Charles might sign anything. 'You will be in a capacity to recover all, in the end,' he assured him. In the end ... towards that, now, Charles turned in hope. Once more, he was sure of victory. Meanwhile, in the manner that had become a habit, he dashed off a letter of reassurance to Sir Edward Nicholas, who was waiting anxiously for news in Holland. 'Nothing,' it concluded, 'could have confirmed me more to the Church of England than the treachery and hypocrisy of the Kirk.'[27]

1 *Cal. Clar. S. P.*, vol. II, p. lxi.
2 Jaffray, p. 32.
3 Scott, *The King in Exile*, p. 162.
4 *Cal. S. P. Ven.*, vol. XXVIII, p. 150; Whitelocke, vol. III, p. 219.
5 J. Nicoll, *Diary of Public Transactions*, p. 17.
6 Clarendon, pp. 745-7.
7 Lyon, p. 41.
8 Op. cit., p. 43.
9 Op. cit., p. 41.
10 Clarendon, p. 747.
11 J. Willcock, *The Great Marquess*, pp. 222-74; Lyon, p. 39; Carte, *Ormonde*, vol. II, pp. 129-33; Gardiner, *Commonwealth*, vol. I, p. 235.
12 Burnet, *History*, vol. I, p. 86.
13 Clarendon, pp. 746-7.
14 Op. cit., p. 271.
15 A. Murray, *Autobiography*, p. 59.
16 *Hamilton Papers* (H.M.C.), p. 254.
17 Carte, *Original Letters*, vol. I, pp. 391-2.
18 Whitelocke, vol. III, p. 234.
19 Cameron, *Memoirs*, p. 91.
20 Montpensier, vol. I, pp. 319-29.
21 Lyon, pp. 65-7.
22 Burnet, *History*, vol. I, pp. 102-6.
23 E. Walker, *Works*, p. 166.
24 Gardiner, *Commonwealth*, vol. I, p. 338.
25 *Cal. D. S. P.*, Aug. 28th, 1650.
26 Ibid.
27 Lyon, p. 79.

CHAPTER TWO

KING OF SCOTLAND

I

SHORTLY after Charles's hypocrisy had been so developed by the Covenanters' treatment as to equal their powers of self-deception, the Roundhead forces were approaching Dunbar. The ministers (urged on by Argyll, who was still Cromwell's most valuable ally) chose this moment to purge the army of 'malignants', with the result that a hundred officers and 3,000 men were dismissed. The new recruits were then required to sign the Covenant; many of them did so in their own blood, howling and sobbing.[1]

Because it was necessary for the Scots outwardly to maintain Charles's rights, they moved the regalia from Stirling to Perth, as a guarantee that he would shortly be crowned; but when he offered to lead them into battle, they replied that 'the Lord would never bless the army as long as he, the chief of the malignants, was in it'.[2] So Charles continued to correspond with the English Royalists, who declared themselves able to rise in strength; he wrote to William of Orange for money, men and arms – in vain. His too generous brother-in-law's private fortune was nearly exhausted; and the Dutch would have no part of his schemes. Charles therefore remained inactive and under restraint at Perth till September 4th, when Argyll arrived with the news that the Scots had been utterly routed at Dunbar. The English had suffered the minimum of loss: the Scottish dead numbered some 3,000: and Cromwell was still, although slowly, advancing.

In this defeat Charles perceived the lessening of the Covenanters' power. He indiscreetly expressed the hope that his jailers would be forced to call in the Engagers, and even the Royalists, rather than risk the English occupation of Edinburgh, which was Cromwell's next objective. The ministers replied by reproaching God for deserting them; they ordained a general fast, a day of repentance and the burning of several witches. They drew up another declaration, in which the King was required to express his remorse for his own sins and for those of his remote ancestors, as being partly the cause of the English victory. Charles complied without demur, sardonically remarking, 'I think that I should repent too, that ever I was born – ' as he did so.

In the weeks that followed the extreme Covenanters began to hint that Charles ought to be 'laid by' and deprived of his powers – whatever they may have amounted to – as King, until he gave real and convincing proof of his repentance. His Scots chaplain conveyed this message, which he described as 'uncharitable. But,' he added, 'there are many sad truths in it which I humbly call Your Majesty to remark.'

The Extremists' alarm had been roused by the change in Argyll's attitude towards his prisoner, who he knew was in touch with the Scots Royalists, his own bitterest enemies. While some among the Extremists considered seizing and murdering the King, and the Royalists on both sides of the Border were preparing to rise for him, the Marquess, aware that Charles might slip through his net, produced his trump card. 'I cannot serve Your Majesty as you desire,' he said, 'unless you give some undeniable proof of a fixed resolution to support the Presbyterian party – which I think would be best done by marrying into some family of quality that is known to be entirely attached to that interest. This,' he added, 'would take off the prejudice upon your mother.'³

Although unprepared for this flank attack, Charles replied in a polite and non-committal manner. Argyll, having made it clear that he might go over to Cromwell if His Majesty did not co-operate, explained that his daughter, the Lady Anne Campbell, was the King's destined bride.

Charles answered encouragingly, and asked for time to think over the proposal. He then managed to get in touch with, and ask the advice of, an English Royalist, Colonel Legge, who told him not to risk offending Argyll and to put him off with promises. Charles sent a messenger to Paris to ask his mother's permission to marry the Lady Anne, having instructed him to prolong his journey indefinitely. Argyll's spies informed him of these manoeuvres. A few days later Colonel Legge was arrested and imprisoned in Edinburgh Castle.

At about the same time, one of the Lauderdale-Hamilton group, Lord Carnwarth, who had been allowed to visit the King, told him, in Argyll's presence, that he could do so no longer. 'Friends must part,' he said significantly, and turning to the Marquess, went on, 'This is your doing – but I value it not.' A few days later Carnwarth was arrested.⁴ If Legge had been a Scottish subject, he would have met with the same fate; it was well for him that Argyll, who did not forget the possibility of a Royalist victory, later found it prudent to release him. In fact, 'His

Majesty's condition,' concluded Sir Edward Walker, who, at considerable risk to himself, was following Charles from a distance, 'is most sad and dangerous.'[5]

At this point news came of the death of the fifteen-year-old Princess Elizabeth, at Carisbrooke Castle. The poor child, who was tubercular, had never got over her father's murder and that last, terrible interview; she was found lying as if asleep, her cheek resting on the Bible he gave her two days before his execution. The Duke of Gloucester, now in his eleventh year, who had been imprisoned with her, remained in the Castle with his tutor. Cromwell, who was sorry for the boy, talked of apprenticing him to some trade, but nothing came of it. Little Master Harry, as the Royalists called him, was completely cut off from his family; he had not seen Charles since January 1642.

And now at last the King, beset on every side, became desperate. He decided to steal away, join the Scots Royalists and defy Argyll and the Covenanters. His escape – later known as the Start – was planned for the afternoon of October 4th.

The Start was not so wild a venture as it subsequently appeared. During the months that elapsed between Cromwell's advance from Dunbar and his occupation of Edinburgh in December, the Covenanters' dependence on Charles, if only as a figurehead, became more apparent to themselves. They disliked and mistrusted him, the Royalists and the Engagers: all were malignants. But they so hated and feared the English Parliament that they were prepared to support Charles against Cromwell in order to drive the Roundheads out of Scotland and, eventually, convert England to Presbyterianism (they refused to admit that the English Presbyterians were a minority group) under a monarchy controlled by themselves. They now began to realize that in one sense Charles might be more necessary to them than they were to him; for if the Scots Royalists allied themselves with the Engagers, then the Covenanting party would be fatally weakened, and Charles would desert them for one or both of the other two factions. So Argyll, deciding to persuade rather than force the King into an alliance, gave him greater freedom and allowed some of his entourage – among whom were Henry Seymour, Prodgers, Lord Wilmot and the Earl of Newburgh – to return to his Court at Perth.

Through the bolder of these, Charles continued his communication with the Scots Royalists, who promised him 10,000 men as soon as he appeared to lead them. All he had to do was to join them in the Inverness– Morayshire area, where the clans would gather. Then they would align themselves with the Engagers and drive out the English before crushing the Covenanters. They believed that many of these would join them in their advance on Cromwell. The whole scheme must have appeared more than feasible, especially to a young man thirsting for action, who knew that wherever he went the common people would support him. Then Charles made one irremediable mistake – he confided in Buckingham.

This again seems egregiously rash, in view of the fact that the King had known Villiers all his life; and Charles was not only intelligent, but already a fair judge of character. He must have realized how unreliable the Duke was; and he also knew that Buckingham was still loyal – in so far as he was capable of being loyal to anyone – to Argyll. The King's assumption that Buckingham would join in the Start was based on their shared hatred and mockery of the Marquess, his Covenanters and everything they represented, and also on the Duke's connection with the Stuart family, who had adopted and cared for him since his third year. There was yet another factor: the fascination which Buckingham exercised over Charles, then and always. Long after the King had grasped the whole extent of the Duke's treachery and duplicity, he continued to receive him, to revel in his jokes and to lend him money, refusing to punish or ostracize him. To Charles, George Villiers remained irresistible, when he was not dominant. In 1650 he was both.

Buckingham's attitude was that of the gambler who, having placed his stake, refuses to withdraw it at the last moment. On the afternoon of October 2nd he and Charles went out riding, and he was told of the King's intentions. He at once made some excuse to return to Perth, where he repeated the information to Wilmot. When the King joined them Buckingham and Wilmot united in trying to make him change his plans. The Duke argued, stormed and, it seems, threatened to betray his master to Argyll, knowing that Wilmot had already done so. Charles refused to give in, and a long and heated discussion ensued.

That Buckingham was proved to be right had nothing to do with his motives, which were characteristically discreditable. Charles, very much taken aback by his friend's defiance, decided that, as he was committed to the Royalists, he must pretend to agree with Buckingham. He therefore promised to stay where he was.

On the morning of October 3rd the King was informed that all the officers of his bodyguard were to be dismissed and cashiered. His remonstrances were ignored; in a fury, he became more than ever determined to join the Royalists. On October 4th he dined early and then announced that he was going hawking. Buckingham said he should not leave the castle, and another argument developed; once more, Charles appeared to yield. Half an hour later he, Prodgers and two other gentlemen left by the garden entrance and rode towards Fife at headlong speed.

As soon as they realized he had gone, Buckingham and Wilmot rushed to his cabinet which, in his hurry, he had left open. There they found indisputable evidence – supplemented by a paper he had thrust into the privy – that Charles had outwitted them and was on his way to the Highlands. They gave chase, and having failed to overtake him, appealed to the Covenanting authorities, who sent Colonel Montgomery and six hundred horse in pursuit of the King.

Meanwhile Charles had crossed the Tay, and was met by Lauderdale, who said, 'Return, before it is too late.' In bitter contempt, the King rode on to Lord Airlie's house, where he was greeted by some eighty Highlanders. He then changed horses and proceeded to Clova, where he hoped to meet the Royalist (and Catholic) Earl of Huntly. As Huntly did not appear and no fresh horses were to be found, the King took refuge in a farm-house, after riding forty-two miles.

And now, but for the faithful Prodgers, he was alone. His guard had dispersed; none of the clans, nor their leaders (sixty of whom had promised him their support) were to be seen: so much for Highland loyalty. He and Prodgers climbed into a hay-loft, hoping that their pursuers would pass by and thus enable them to continue their flight. Hungry, exhausted and shivering, they waited, crouched in the straw. At last they heard horse-hoofs and voices. Then messengers from the Committee of Estates appeared. With respectful courtesy they implored His Majesty to return, and trust himself to his faithful servants; Colonel Montgomery promised indemnity to his supporters. 'Do not trust them,' urged Prodgers. Charles said, 'I have been warned that you would give me up to Cromwell.' Montgomery denied it. 'I will live and die with Your Majesty,' he added, and again begged the King to return. Otherwise... the implication was not only sinister, but obvious.

Charles, whose common sense had begun to prevail over his loathing of Argyll and his faction, saw that to persist would only end in further humiliation – perhaps in his own murder. He descended, ate some oatcake and meat, and – haggard, unshaven, defeated – rode back to Perth, once more the prisoner of the Covenant and the McCallum Mor.[6]

II

Charles and his escort reached Perth on Sunday the 6th, just a little too late for morning prayer. Exhausted and broken, the King entered his bedroom to find a minister waiting for him, who immediately launched into a lecture on his rash and wicked behaviour. He was then required to attend three services in succession.[7]

Thereafter, Charles adopted a completely and openly cynical attitude towards the religious issue. He repeated, parrot-like, every statement the ministers made, and agreed with all their diatribes, whether directed against himself, his family or his Church. These tactics defeated them, They could no longer argue with or preach at him, for there was nothing left to say; and the fact that he made no pretence at sincerity reduced them, for perhaps the first time in their lives, to uneasy silence. At the meeting called to discuss the Start and its consequences, His Majesty stood up, and in glib and expressionless tones, announced his regret. He went on, in what seems to have been a recitative, 'I was advised by the evil counsels of some who have deluded me. I trust in God it will be a lesson to me all the days of my life. As I am a Christian, when I first went out, I had no mind to depart. I acknowledge that what has befallen me is just from God for my sins.' Required to put his repentance in writing, he at once dashed off a short and, as his persecutors realized, totally valueless statement. 'We are grieved,' it ran, 'that we should have listened to the suggestions of wicked persons. We now discern the folly and madness of it ... We have religion, the Gospel and the Covenant, against which hell shall not prevail.'[8]

The Scottish people now began to grasp the pointlessness of thus humiliating Charles and the dangerous absurdity of the ministers' attitude. 'Behold a fearful sin!' wrote one, himself a so-called penitent. 'The ministers ... knew well enough [our repentances] were but counterfeit ... If this was not to mock the ... all-knowing God to His face, then I declare myself not to know what ... hypocrisy is.'[9] So the more enlightened classes made it clear that they would not support the clergy against a King who ought long ago to have been crowned instead of being treated like a criminal. The ministers, appalled at the prospect of losing their power, declared that 'the kingdom hath been betrayed to the enemy by want of confidence in His Majesty', and went on to censure General Leslie and Argyll.[10]

As Cromwell advanced towards Edinburgh it was decided to raise a new army, including in it those Royalists who would accept the Covenant. This alarmed Argyll, who, abandoning his usual courtesy, protested to Charles. 'You have done wickedly,' he said, 'in admitting malignants to power.' 'I know not what you mean by malignants,' the King blandly replied. 'We are all malignants to God.'[11] The Marquess, defeated by a quotation from his own creed, was forced, a few days later, to allow the

King to receive Hamilton and Lauderdale, interview the burgesses of Perth, attend the Council meetings, and reorganize the army, of which Charles and Leslie were to have joint command. The King then persuaded Parliament to repeal the cruellest acts against non-Covenanters. His triumph was complete when some of his father's Royalist supporters were given commissions.

Shortly after the coronation had been announced for January 1st, 1651, news came of the death of William of Orange. Charles's nephew, later William III, was born ten days later. In some anxiety, but with justifiable hope, the King proceeded with his plans for an English counter-revolution, to be combined with his invasion from Scotland. On Christmas Eve Cromwell occupied Edinburgh.

Charles believed that this disaster would help to unite the four disputing factions and further weaken Argyll. One of his English attendants warned him that the Marquess was still to be reckoned with, and must, if possible, be persuaded to believe in His Majesty's promises. Charles knew this to be virtually out of the question; and his interviews with Argyll became even more awkward when his mother's reply about his marriage to the Lady Anne Campbell reached him at Perth. For once, Henrietta Maria's tactics were sensible. Her letter was amiable and non-committal. She seemed, although vaguely, to approve of the match, but thought that the contract should not be drawn up till the King's affairs took a more hopeful turn. Buckingham then asked Argyll for his daughter's hand. This impertinence, which again increased Charles's difficulties, was ignored. The Duke continued 'wholly Argyll's' – to the point, indeed, of refusing to speak to Hamilton and Lauderdale when they came into the presence-chamber. The Lady Anne, a beautiful and elegant girl, died unmarried eight years later.

Meanwhile, the people's devotion to Charles had been heightened by an attempt on his life from a man who admitted to having tried to poison him as a dangerous malignant.[12] In the last week of December, another problem arose: should Hamilton and Lauderdale be allowed to have commands in the army? Finally it was agreed that they should if they made a public repentance for having signed the Engagement with Charles I.

On December 31st, 1650, Charles and his Court were established in Gowrie House on the Tay. This medieval mansion, now destroyed, had sinister associations. Here, half a century earlier, the Earl of Gowrie and his brother Alexander Ruthven had imprisoned and, it was thought, tried to murder Charles's grandfather James I, then a boy of sixteen, who managed to give the alarm, with the result that in the ensuing struggle both the wicked Earl and his brother were killed. Long afterwards Charles's English attendants recalled the gloom of the place and the forbidding aspect of the Scottish nobles. 'Who but so good a King,' said the devoted Sir Edward Walker, 'would have exposed himself to such men's trust in so dangerous a time?' Charles himself appears to have been unaffected by the atmosphere.[13]

The outer courts of Gowrie House led into the ancient palace of Scone, where all the Scottish kings had been crowned since the reign of Malcolm III. Its glories had gradually diminished since that black day in 1297 when Edward I removed its magic Stone to Westminster Abbey. By the time Charles reached it, on the morning of New Year's Day, it was partially ruined, but still contained a state bedchamber, a presence-chamber adjoining the church and what remained of the original structure, once an Augustinian monastery.

In the presence-chamber the King was placed under a cloth of state and the nobles about to take part in the ceremony were presented to him. The Moderator, who was also his Chamberlain, then addressed him at the usual length. 'You are crowned,' he concluded, 'only on condition of supporting the Covenant.' Charles replied with the speech prepared by Argyll. 'I do esteem the affection of my good people,' he began, looking round at the sour-faced chieftains and hostile ministers, 'more than the crowns of many kingdoms. I shall be ready, by God's assistance, to bestow my life in their defence, wishing to live no longer than I may see religion in this kingdom flourish with all happiness.'

He then stood under a canopy supported by six nobles and walked in procession to the church. The spurs, sword and sceptre were carried by the hereditary dignitaries, preceded by Argyll, who bore the crown. This was the most ancient item in the regalia. The original circlet, made for Robert the Bruce, was topped by closed and jewelled arches and a cross, as first worn by James VI and I. In the church two stages had been put up, one above the other, for Charles and his attendants. They took their seats, and the minister began the sermon, of which the text was taken from the Second Book of Kings. 'And he brought forth the king's son and gave him the testimony and put the crown upon him; and they made him king and anointed him; and they clapped their hands and said, God Save the King.' The discourse lasted some three hours and was an exposition on the tenets of the Covenant. The preacher concluded with a condemnation of the holy oil as popish, and the suggestion that Charles should undergo further public humiliation for his own and his family's sins.[14]

It was observed that the King's 'serious and devout' behaviour was sustained throughout the coronation. 'None doubted,' says a delighted eye-witness, 'of his integrity and sincerity.' When the sermon ended Charles stood up and raised his right hand. 'I declare on the word of a King,' he said, 'that I agree to all the terms of the Covenant.' The ministers produced the latest edition of this document, embodying further insults to his parents, which he signed. He returned to the stage, was presented to the people from each of its four corners and greeted with shouts and blessings. As he took his seat in the chair of state he was asked if he would take the coronation oath; he assented, repeating after the ministers, 'I believe the Covenant to be the true Church of God.' He was then invested with the coronation robes and the sword – 'the Covenant,' announced one of the officials, 'being thereby protected.' After the spurs had been fastened Argyll advanced to him with the crown.

There followed an interval, during which the ministers prayed that the crown should be 'delivered from the sins and transgressions of those preceding His Majesty King Charles II'. And then, at last, Argyll placed it on his head.[15]

The trumpets sounded and the heralds proclaimed him. The nobles advanced and declared their allegiance. The Covenant was once more invoked in a lengthy address. Not till then was Charles given the sceptre. There followed another sermon in which the theme of the Covenant was repeated. These ceremonies lasted some seven or eight hours.

Robed and crowned, Charles walked down the aisle and was presented to the crowds outside. He was escorted to a seat, where he listened – in the open air of a Scottish winter – to a third sermon. The procession then re-formed and returned to the palace of Scone. At the ensuing banquet the King replied to his subjects' homage in a brief and formal address, concluding, 'I have much joy in that I am the first Covenanted King of Scotland.'[16]

A few days after the curtain fell on this monstrous farce, the King and his Court, accompanied by Argyll and his family, moved to Stirling; on the following Sunday Charles, having finished supper, was alone in his closet. Argyll appeared, and suggested that they should pray together before going to bed. An extraordinary scene ensued.

The King, perhaps more than usually exhausted by his Sabbath ordeal of sermons, consented to 'pray and mourn' with the Marquess till the small hours. Both shed tears. At three in the morning Argyll returned to his own bedchamber. 'Why are you so late?' asked the Marchioness. 'I have never had such a sweet night in the world,' her husband replied, and dwelt, with apparently sincere rejoicing, on His Majesty's tears of repentance. Lady Argyll did not speak for a moment. Then she said, 'They are crocodile tears – and this night will cost you your life.'[17]

The Marchioness was not of Highland blood; nevertheless, it may have been that her natural perspicacity was enhanced by the second sight popularly attributed to such persons. Nine years and five months later, Argyll, having come to Whitehall to beg the King for his life, was refused an audience, sent back to Edinburgh, and beheaded.

NOTES

1 Lyon, p. 42.
2 R. Blair, *Life and Letters*, p. 235.
3 Burnet, *History*, vol. I, pp. 103–6.
4 Ibid.
5 E. Walker, p. 195.
6 Lyon, p. 97; E. Walker, p. 197; Gardiner, *Commonwealth*, vol. I, p. 334; Clarendon, pp. 788–9.
7 Lyon, p. 97.
8 Op. cit., pp. 87, 97.
9 Sir James Turner, *Memoirs of his own Life and Times 1632–70*, p. 94.
10 Clarendon, p. 794.
11 Willcock, p. 271.
12 Op. cit., p. 270.
13 C. Walker, *The History of Independency*, p. 19.
14 Lyon, pp. 147–57.
15 Ibid.
16 Whitelocke, vol. III, p. 280.
17 Lyon, p. 159.

CHAPTER THREE

INVASION

I

THE effect of Charles's coronation on the Courts of Europe heightened his prestige and changed, in theory at least, his whole situation. As King of Scotland he was no longer considered an exile or a pensioner, and it was assumed that he would be restored in a few months' time. When it was known that he had begun to unite the religious factions and was collecting recruits from all over Scotland, those rulers who knew nothing of Anglo-Scots politics, or of Cromwell's administrative and military genius, visualized a successful Royalist rising exactly timed to coincide with the Scottish invasion.

These assumptions helped to weaken Argyll's and the Covenanters' powers. They were no longer in a position to dictate to Charles; yet he could not make full use of his own authority until Hamilton and Lauderdale had been re-admitted to Parliament and established themselves as repentant, godly and sincere supporters of the revised Covenant.

Twelve days after the coronation 20,000 troops were in training and many Royalist and Catholic chieftains given commands, with the result that Hamilton and Lauderdale hastened to declare their loyalty. They were required to attend a service for which stools of repentance had been provided. Hamilton brought a cushion for his, and as soon as the prayers were over retired to his pew, where he dozed off during the sermon.[1] His request to be re-admitted to Parliament was so phrased as to surprise even Charles, that expert in penitential display. 'The meanest of my subjects,' he said, 'would not have made so low a petition to me.'[2] The King then pursued his recruiting campaign in Forfarshire and Fife. At Pittenweem he was feasted with bannocks (their first sight of these 'great buns' amazed his English entourage), ale and white wine after reviewing the troops. Every day his popularity increased. 'He is very intelligent, industrious and active,' one admirer reported. 'His judgement and activity, both in civil and martial affairs are to a degree as you would not imagine ... adventuring his person upon every show of danger, riding continually and being up early and late. But – ' he added, after attending a staff conference, 'he is too forward ... to hazard his person against the rebels.'

In March Charles returned to Edinburgh for the opening of Parliament. Here he gave audience to three of Argyll's allies, Sir Alexander Hope and his brothers, who suggested that it would be better to come to terms with Cromwell than risk defeat. There was no need, now, for the King to appear acquiescent, or even non-committal. 'I would rather see both you and your brothers hanged at one end of a rope and Cromwell at the other, before I would do any such thing,' he replied. In matters of religion he remained cautious and diplomatic. In his speech to the Covenanting nobles he said, 'If at any time coming you do hear or see me breaking that Covenant, tell me of it, and remind me of my oath.' Everyone was delighted with him; he was so much in demand that he seldom spent more than two or three nights in one city – but he would not practise his golf, although constantly urged to do so.[3]

Buckingham did everything required of him by the clergy, continued to declare his faith in Argyll and reproached Charles for deserting the Marquess (Argyll was still very powerful), although a few weeks after the coronation he was reported to be 'very lascivious' and the father of a number of bastards, locally described as 'Buckingham's birds' – and this in spite of the fact that a Scots colonel had called for a Covenant against 'tobacco, strong waters and whores'.[4] Yet Villiers and the King were still on excellent terms. During the summer the Duke persuaded Charles to give him the southern command in England during the invasion. Charles consented – why not? He had reached the position for which he had been struggling for two and a half years, and could afford to dispense favours which might never materialize. On May 29th he celebrated his twenty-first birthday amid scenes of ecstatic rejoicing.

The improvement in the Scottish situation had been counter-balanced by a family quarrel in Paris, with which Charles had to deal. It occurred to no one, least of all to the King himself, that just as he was preparing for a major campaign, he might have been spared the additional burden of the Duke of York's disputes with Henrietta Maria. James, already chagrined at being left behind to kick his heels at St Germain, had become, as was natural in a rather stupid, highly emotional boy of eighteen, obsessed with his mother's dependence on Jermyn, and suspected her of being unfaithful to his father's memory. 'She cares for him,' he burst out, 'more than for all her children,' and after a series of disputes about money, left to stay with his Aunt Elizabeth at Rhenen; he then moved to the Hague. In her turn, Henrietta Maria complained to Nicholas. York had been odious: Charles was the model son. The King immediately sent off a long, severe but tactful letter to York, desiring him to return to Paris, make his peace with the Queen Mother, consult Ormonde, who had just arrived there, and cut down expenses. Later on, he added, York might go to Sweden as Charles's representative; meanwhile he could spare him a little money, and promised him a share in the invasion as soon as it could be managed. By the same post the King wrote to Mary of Orange asking for details about his nephew and telling her to hasten James's return to France.[5]

As Charles went on with his preparations for war he received complaining letters from Nicholas and Hyde. Why did he not write to them? And was it true that the Covenanters had forced him to treat with Cromwell? Charles ignored these inquiries, convened a general assembly of his troops at Stirling, arranged for the Earl of Derby to meet him in Lancashire and issued an appeal to the English people in rousing terms. 'Cromwell,' he declared, 'is an absolute enemy to the liberties of England ... It is impossible to conquer the [Parliamentarians] with any language but the language of the sword, and with that I intend suddenly to treat.' He concluded with a promise of amnesty for all his adversaries but the regicides and assured his subjects of the liberties and prosperity ('each to sit under his own vine and fig-tree') they had hitherto been denied.[6]

Charles's supporters in Scotland were jubilant. 'He now has absolute power,' Dr King reported, 'his army is accomplished, cheerful, numerous.' Meanwhile, Cromwell had advanced from beyond the Forth and was occupying the southern counties. By the end of July Charles, General Leslie and Argyll had to choose from three courses of action. They could either retreat to the western Highlands, or meet the Cromwellian forces in Perthshire, or strike into England, where, so the King was told, the Royalists would rise in strength and overthrow the government before he reached the capital. Argyll, true to his agreement with Cromwell, urged delay, and when the King refused to consider it, retired to Inveraray. Charles was then advised, presumably by Hamilton and Lauderdale, to arrest the Marquess. He shook his head. 'I am confident,' he said, 'that he will not do anything while the army is entire. If it prevail, he neither can nor will do any harm – and if it is defeated, it is no matter what he does.'[7] Leslie seemed undecided and gloomy. Charles therefore declared for England, in spite of the fact that 2,000 English Royalists, one of whom was his powerful cousin, the Duke of Richmond, had been arrested and imprisoned. On August 6th he reached Carlisle at the head of 8,000 foot, 2,000 horse and sixteen rather antiquated leather cannon. Although

Cromwell was now at his heels with an infinitely superior force, he was proclaimed and rapturously welcomed. Then his most dangerous enemies struck at him from behind.

The Covenanting ministers who, like a cloud of poisonous insects, had shadowed Charles's progress into his kingdom, issued, without his knowledge, a protest against his being proclaimed Head of that odious organization the Church of England, and another against his visits to the Catholic Royalists of the north; they added that he had sworn to enforce Presbyterianism on all his subjects as soon as he was in a position to do so, with the result that many Royalists fled south or went abroad, and no one rose to support him. This alarmed the Scots troops, who began to desert. By the time Charles reached Warrington on August 16th, where his cavalry routed a posse of Lambert's horse, his army had greatly diminished; and Derby had not arrived. Yet there was nothing for it, now, but to press on. His progress from Warrington to the Midlands was marked by an irritating dispute with the Duke of Buckingham.

The two young men were riding together when Buckingham, who was in command of a regiment, launched into a long speech about the morale of the army. 'The business,' he began, 'is now to reduce England to your obedience. Therefore, you ought to do all things gracious and popular in the eyes of the nation – and nothing could be less so than that the army should be under the command of a Scottish general. David Leslie is only Lieutenant-General. It would have been unreasonable, whilst you remained in Scotland, to have put any other over him. But it would be unreasonable, now you are in England, and have hope to increase the army by the access of the English, upon whom your principal dependence must be, to expect that they will be willing to serve under Leslie.' As Charles did not reply, he went on in a more significant tone, 'It will not consist with the honour of any peer of England to receive his orders. I believe very few of that rank will repair to you unless they are secure from that apprehension.'

Charles was so surprised, as he afterwards told Hyde, that he remained silent, trying to make out what his irrepressible friend was aiming at; then he said, 'Who is it that you think fit for that command?' Buckingham immediately assumed a courtly tone. 'I hope,' he said, 'that Your Majesty will confer it upon myself.' Charles, more embarrassed than displeased, called up one of his officers, as if he had just thought of some orders that must be given, engaged him in conversation and so broke off Buckingham's discourse. This hint was ignored by the Duke, who next day approached him once more and began, 'I am confident that what I have proposed to you is for your service. David Leslie himself would consent to it.'

Charles lost his patience. He said, 'I can hardly believe that you are in earnest, or that you can in truth believe that you are fit for such a charge.' 'Wherein does my unfitness lie?' the Duke demanded. 'You are too young,' replied Charles. 'Henry IV of France,' Buckingham persisted, 'commanded an army when he was younger than I.' Charles ignored this rather impertinent reference to his grandfather, said abruptly, 'There will be no generalissimo but myself – ' and spurred on his horse. Thereafter, for several days, Buckingham played Achilles' role. He remained in his tent, refused to wash or change his shirt when he did appear and treated Charles with sulky insolence.[8]

The conclusion drawn by Buckingham from this dispute was characteristic. If he was not to be in command, there was little hope of a Royalist victory. Spitefully, yet convinced that he was in the right, he wrote to the Earl of Newcastle advising him to make his peace with Parliament, and then made his with Charles, fascinating him all over again, as he generally did those who found him irreplaceable. In Charles's case his need of Villiers's amusing talk, high spirits and gift for mimicry grew in proportion to his difficulties, which now increased with every mile of his advance.

Although the King refused to admit it, Buckingham was right about Leslie. He was 'sad and melancholy' and slow in giving orders, which he rescinded as soon as they were given. This disturbed his officers, whose doubts infected the other ranks. At last Charles, after watching Leslie for some time, rode up to him and said impatiently, 'How can you be sad when you are at the head of so brave an army?' The General drew him aside. 'I am melancholy indeed,' he said in a low voice, 'for I well know that army, how well soever it looks, it will not fight.' The King made no reply. He said afterwards that he had discounted and then tried to forget Leslie's warning, because it was too late to do anything else.[9]

This conversation seems to have taken place on the march from Warrington, when news came that Cromwell, returning south by another route, had outstripped Charles and was on his way to join Lambert, now encamped on the Severn just outside Worcester. At a general conference it became clear that the obvious move – that of attacking Lambert before Cromwell arrived – was not to be considered. After twenty-three days' march the troops were not only exhausted, but unreliable to the point of mutiny, in spite of the fact that the citizens of Worcester had greeted them with immense enthusiasm. This welcome had not included recruits;

then, for the first time since leaving Scotland, the King's optimism gave way.

At the Council meeting the few minor triumphs – two satisfactory skirmishes, which had resulted in the Cromwellian prisoners joining the Royalists – had to be set against Cromwell's superior numbers and the abandoned hope of marching on London before he and Lambert united. When it was acknowledged that the Royalists must fight where they were, someone raised the question of quarter. (This had been Charles I's stumbling-block; unwilling to slaughter his own subjects, he had shrunk from attacks in which he might have prevailed.) Charles II, neither then nor later a military expert, had learnt this lesson. 'You may do what you will,' he said. 'For my part, I will not give any, for I am sure I shall have none. For me, it will be a crown or a coffin.'[10]

Encouraged by the report that some of Cromwell's staff feared defeat and believed that he had allowed Charles's entry into England when he might have prevented it, the question of attacking Lambert was again raised and dismissed. Hamilton said, 'We have one stout argument – despair,' and the meeting broke up.[11] Hamilton then retired to his quarters, where he prepared for death in meditation and prayer. Leslie remained abstracted and gloomy. Charles, Lauderdale, Wilmot, Buckingham and Lord Newburgh were hopeful and eager for battle.

On August 28th Lambert crossed the Severn; he was joined by Cromwell next day. Charles then worked out plans for a night attack. If that succeeded – and there seemed every chance that it might – the Royalist advance would sweep on, via Gloucester and Hereford, to the capital.

II

Early in the evening of August 29th, Mr Gives, a Worcestershire tailor and presumably a member of Cromwell's fifth column, swam the Severn and told the Parliamentary generals that the Royalists would attack at nightfall three days later. He was afterwards discovered and hanged.[12]

On the 31st Derby appeared, a wounded fugitive. His troops had been routed at Wigan and himself rescued and cared for by Richard Penderel, Catholic part-owner of the manor of Boscobel, some twenty-six miles from Worcester.

On September 1st Cromwell, advancing from Perry Wood, a mile beyond the city, threw off the Royalist night attack, drew his left wing round the curve of the Severn and formed a bridge of boats, thus securing both sides of the river. Still he did not advance – and neither did the

Royalists. They had decided to hold Worcester till the troops promised them from Wales and the south came to their rescue. Then, as they realized that national hatred of the Scots might delay or prevent this conjunction, they made plans to break out of the city. During the night of the 2nd Charles, in his buff coat and breast-plate, over which were his diamond George and blue ribbon, rode round the emplacements, instructed the officers, talked to the men and saw that everything was in order for the last effort which might yet bring them to victory. On the morning of the 3rd he and his staff met on the Cathedral tower to hold their final Council of war.

The formation of the defences made it impossible for the Royalist troops to attack *en masse*. It was therefore agreed that the main body should divide and advance from separate points, to be followed by Leslie's horse as soon as they penetrated the Cromwellian lines. Half an hour later Charles, with his own regiment of cavalry, left from Sidbury Gate, while General Montgomery descended from the south-east over Powick Bridge.

Waving his sword, the King charged at the head of his troops. The Cromwellians replied with a burst of gunfire. Still the Royalists streamed on, in close formation, piercing the enemy lines, overriding their infantry, apparently heedless of loss. The Parliamentary forces began to fall back. Meanwhile Montgomery's advance continued. The Duke of Hamilton was fatally wounded.

Then Charles's horse was shot under him. One of his Scottish officers managed to shield him while another was brought. A few minutes later the second horse fell. Again he sprang free, and defended himself till a third charger was found. By this time the battle was ranging round, and at some points inside, the walls. Montgomery began to retreat as Cromwell's first reinforcements came up and pushed back the Royalist cavalry, although slowly and with difficulty. Meanwhile, Leslie remained with his reserve troops in the rear, on the southern side of the walls.

Suddenly Charles became aware not only that his men were about to be cut off, but that less than half the Scottish army was engaged. He fought his way back and rode up to Leslie, who was in the saddle, his men behind him, inactive, as if they were spectators. 'In the name of God, charge!' shouted the King.

Leslie did not move. Charles turned, rallied his men and charged again; now his numbers were so diminished that they were thrust back, against the walls. And there were Leslie and his reinforcements, glowering, sullen, motionless. 'I command you – upon your loyalty and honour – charge!' cried Charles. Leslie did not stir.

The King looked round. Behind him, the Cromwellians were advancing. He was turning to threaten Leslie when Lord Cleveland, one of the older Cavaliers, seized his rein and said, 'He hath betrayed you. You must shift for yourself – else you will be delivered up, as your father was.'

With such as were left of his horse Charles withdrew into the city. He decided to collect enough troops to advance again, or, failing that, to make a last stand and die with them. As he rode in, the sun was shining over the dead and wounded; the gutters ran with blood. The streets were piled with screaming, writhing men and horses. Then he was halted by an overturned baggage wagon. As his men broke it apart he tore off his breast-plate and let it fall on the cobbles. With Lord Wilmot, Buckingham and Derby, he got through to his headquarters in Friar Street. There he and his companions re-armed, more lightly (for the heat was intense), and mounted fresh horses.

The King then announced his intention of going from street to street to collect those regiments still in formation in order to attack again. It was all he could think of – all, in fact, he had hoped for, since that day, nine years ago, at Edgehill. To charge again, till the enemy broke before him and fled – so his childhood's hero, Rupert of the Rhine, had succeeded against apparently impossible odds. And so, once more, he returned to the battle.

He was reasonably, desperately, calm. He rode from one regiment to another, calling on each officer by name. As each group broke, or retreated into the houses, or was split into obscenely hideous fragments, he dashed up to those that remained. 'Charge, gentlemen – follow me – I command you!' Suddenly the last outpost gave way, and the Cromwellians poured into the city.

The King was still on horseback and unhurt. Wilmot, Derby, Buckingham, Lauderdale and two of his gentlemen surrounded him. In that frightful turmoil, heedless of the horrors at their feet, and of the oncoming Ironsides, they paused and began to argue. Charles refused to fly. As they realized that the town hall was still holding out, they agreed to make a stand at Barbour's Bridge, on the south side of the outer wall. Here they remained, isolated, yet still on the defensive, till six in the evening. And still Leslie's horse had not charged, although none had been captured and few wounded or killed. Presently they began to give themselves up. Leslie disappeared; no doubt this manoeuvre and those preceding it had been arranged between him and Argyll.

As the shadows lengthened it became clear that the Royalists were in total rout. The King and his party would soon be surrounded by hundreds of Cromwellians, who might take him alive. Buckingham and Wilmot again urged him to escape. There was still time: and their horses were fresh. 'I would rather be shot,' he said. As they continued to plead with him – for if he were taken prisoner and executed, then the Royalist cause was lost for ever – he repeated, 'Shoot me – I will not live.'

Seconded by Wilmot, Buckingham, who had kept his head and behaved with as great courage and gallantry as Charles himself, used his special brand of persuasion. No doubt his arguments were sensible enough. Live to return: escape to conquer: keep the monarchy, that sacred trust, out of the hands of those who would bring it to degradation on the scaffold. Youth, energy, the instinct to survive – perhaps even hope – prevailed. Hardly knowing what he did, the King turned his horse and rode out of the doomed city with his companions. His coach, containing £400 and all his papers, was left behind and taken by the Roundheads.

Now it was dusk. And everywhere, on horseback, on foot, straggling or huddled together, shadowy groups were stealing away over the fields and into the quiet valleys and the sheltering woods. Two thousand Royalists had been killed and three thousand taken prisoner. In the day of battle the Lord God of Hosts had remembered His faithful servant. That 'stiff business', Cromwell's crowning mercy, was accomplished.[13]

NOTES

1 Lyon, pp. 190–1.
2 Clar. MSS, vol. XL, fol. 185.
3 Lyon, p. 170.
4 Op. cit., pp. 162–3.
5 Nicholas Papers, vol. I, pp. 209–12, 232–3.
6 J. Somers, Scarce and Valuable Tracts (4th Collection), vol. I, p. 421.
7 Clarendon, pp. 760–4.
8 Ibid.
9 Ibid.
10 H.M.C. Report 3, vol. II, p. 192.
11 Gardiner, Commonwealth, vol. II, p. 35.
12 J. Hughes, The Boscobel Tracts, p. 36.
13 Cal. D. S. P., Sept. 17th, 1651; MSS in Various Collections, vol. V, p. 53; Cal. Clar. S. P., vol. II, pp. 561–2; Lyon, p. 215; Hughes, pp. 33–8; Gardiner, Commonwealth, vol. II, p. 40; Cook, Titus Britannicus, p. 106; Clarendon, p. 764.

CHAPTER FOUR

FLIGHT

I

THE majority of Charles's contemporaries visualized bravery simply in terms of physical courage. Their reports of his conduct during the battle of Worcester emphasize his dash and gallantry rather than his ingenuity or the resolution which enabled him to attack against odds instead of staying on the defensive. So it was that at the age of twenty-one his reputation reached its highest point ('Certainly a braver Prince never lived ... He hazarded his person more than any officer of his army') and the young King, sword in hand, his black curls streaming behind him, his diamond George a target for his enemies, remained for many years the prototype of a magnificent hero. Those who delighted in this picture did not add that, during the eight hours of his first real active service, Charles must have killed a number of persons and wounded many more, all of them his own subjects; if it had not been so he could not have survived. It is noticeable that in all his lengthy and repetitive accounts of his Worcester experiences (he often told his stories twice and even three times running) he never mentioned that aspect: nor did his hearers ask him about it. In an age when gentlemen of breeding sometimes murdered one another for a triviality and, with the less sophisticated classes, thronged to watch criminals hanged, drawn and quartered or broken on the wheel, this is rather surprising. It might have been expected that Charles and his companions would assess their personal share of the slaughter in the same spirit in which sportsmen enumerate their respective bags at the end of the day, dwelling on their triumphs with each repetition. That they never did so shows a certain sensitivity, in the King at least.

When they heard the story of his adventures after Worcester Charles's adherents could only feel pity, wonder and thankfulness to God. They overlooked, or perhaps took for granted, the presence of mind, unselfishness, patience and good humour which, allied to a splendid physique and a capacity to enjoy the ridiculous, even in moments of the greatest danger, showed the King at his best. Never again, in a dramatically contrasting

THE DUKE OF YORK

THE DUKE OF
GLOUCESTER

THE EARL OF
CLARENDON

THE DUCHESS OF ORLEANS

life of fifty-five years, did he appear to such advantage as between the evening of September 3rd and the morning of October 15th, 1651.

The King and his party did not stop their flight till they were some twelve miles from Worcester. They then halted in order to discuss the best means of escape for him and for themselves.*

That wild ride roused Charles from the dazed recklessness of despair. He no longer wanted to die; and for the first time since his childhood he was not responsible for anyone else. 'I began to think,' he says, 'of the best way of saving myself.' Having turned northwards, they were now some five miles from Kidderminster. 'It is impossible,' said the King, 'to get back into Scotland,' and while those immediately surrounding him began to argue the point, he drew Wilmot aside and proposed making for London. By this time they had been joined by several hundred runaways, any of whom might be frightened into giving him up. 'Though I could not get them to stand by me against the enemy,' he said, 'I could not get rid of them now I had a mind to it.'

Finally Charles, Buckingham, Wilmot, Derby and some sixty horse-men 'that were gentlemen and officers' managed to slip away and reached Stourbridge, where a troop of Cromwellian horse was stationed. No one saw them and they rode on, pausing at a house outside the town. One of the Cavaliers brought the King some food, and there was another con-sultation, which resulted in the postponement of the London scheme, partly because their guide confessed himself lost.

Derby then suggested that the King, Wilmot, himself and their attend-ants should leave the others and find somewhere to rest before it grew light. 'In my flight from Wigan to Worcester,' he said, 'I met with a perfect honest man, and a great convenience of concealment at Boscobel House. It is a recusant's house – and those people are the most like to have the readiest means and safest contrivances to preserve Your Majesty.' 'I will go thither,' said the King, and escorted by Giffard, another Catholic, they set off. 'I humbly propose,' Giffard said, 'to carry Your Majesty to Whiteladies, half a mile beyond Boscobel, where you may repose yourself

---

* In order to avoid a conglomeration of confusing and repetitive references, the con-temporary sources for the collated account of Charles's adventures are here listed under two headings: first- and second-hand. Those who shared in and reported them are the King him-self (as dictated to Pepys thirty years later), Thomas Blount, Thomas Whitgreave, Captain Ellesdon, Anne Wyndham (daughter-in-law of Charles's old nurse), Father Huddleston, Dr Bate, Captain Alford, Colonel Gunter and the anonymous author of Tract No. 1, for which the information may have been supplied by one of the Penderels. These are collected in Hughes's *Boscobel* and Fea's *Flight of the King*. The second-hand reports are to be found in Clarendon's *History*, the *Cal. D. S. P.*, Whitelocke's *Memorials*, Warwick's *Memoirs*, Cook's *Titus Britannicus* and C. Walker's *History of Independency*.

for a while – ' going on to explain that he was the owner of Whiteladies, now let to John Penderel, one of five brothers (two others had fallen at Edgehill), all of whom lived on the Boscobel estate.

The King and his party reached Boscobel at about four in the morning of September 4th. Here they were told that General Leslie had rallied his horse and was on his way back to Scotland. It was suggested that Charles should join them. This, he replied, was impossible. 'The country would all rise upon us,' he said, adding, 'Men who deserted me when they were in good order will never stand to me when they have been beaten.'

Still he considered going to London – 'on foot, in a country fellow's habit'. Wilmot agreed that this would be a good plan, and Mrs Giffard and the other Penderel brothers – William, Richard, Humphrey and George – appeared. Mrs Giffard produced sherry and biscuits for the King and the two noblemen, and they were conducted to an inner parlour. William and Richard Penderel, who had no idea whom they were sheltering, were told to find him a disguise. They were then summoned to the parlour. 'This,' said Derby, pointing to Charles, 'is the King. Thou must have a care of him and preserve him, as thou didst me.' The Penderels knelt and kissed Charles's hand in awestruck silence.

Charles was about to put on his disguise – green breeches, a leather doublet and a grey felt hat – when Derby advised him to rub his hands on the back of the chimney and then over his face. Wilmot cut off his hair with a knife; the result was so grotesque that Richard Penderel insisted on making a better job of it with the shears. 'I prefer your barbering to my Lord Wilmot's,' said Charles, and told him to burn the pile of black hair. Richard could not bring himself to obey; he made some excuse about collecting the locks in a piece of paper; they were later divided between himself and his brothers to be treasured for many generations.

Charles then gave his George, blue ribbon, watch and 'other princely ornaments' to Derby. His buff coat and breeches were thrown into a privy-house, and he put on the disguise. 'Now I am a woodman,' he said as he stood up. The transformation was incomplete – and highly unsatisfactory.

Although Charles was never considered handsome – in middle life he described himself as 'an ugly fellow' – his height, grace, and elegance of bearing justified his contemporaries calling him 'the best bred man of his age'. In youth his dark skin, brilliant eyes and rather coarse features were softened by that mass of thickly waving hair; without it, his heavy nose and chin, pendulous lips and angular figure were so emphasized as to make him extremely noticeable, all the more so perhaps in the country-man's dress, which rather drew attention to than concealed his exotic, southern appearance. Anyone less like an English woodman it was impossible to imagine. In London or some other large city Charles, in livery, might have passed as a nobleman's foreign valet; in the country, where such persons were unknown, he must have appeared freakishly conspicuous, quite apart from the fact that he moved as one trained from infancy to take precedence of others and had no notion, until instructed, of adopting the trudge and the bent shoulders of those accustomed to manual labour. More dangerous still, he was unable, although he did his best, to imitate the almost unintelligible dialect and accent of the Midland peasantry.

Fortunately for Charles, all those persons who took charge of his forty-three days' flight were perceptive as well as practical and courageous. They saw at once that he could not make his way about alone, or even with a single companion; others must speak for him and he must, if possible, be sheltered by a group in order to escape notice.

After some further discussion as to how he should find a ship to the Continent, Derby, Wilmot and their attendants 'took heavy leave' of the King. Still only Wilmot knew that he meant to make for London, and they agreed to meet there. As the others kissed his hand, one urged him not to tell them his plans – 'because I know not what I might be forced to confess' – and the rest, says Charles, 'with one voice begged of me not to tell them of what I intended to do'.

Now that His Majesty had been disguised, the Penderels' and Giffards' next duty was to get him out of the house before it was searched; for Whiteladies had none of the priests' holes commonly found in Catholic manors on which Lord Derby had counted. Carrying an axe, Charles walked out into the woods by which Boscobel was surrounded and sat down under a tree. It began to rain heavily. Meanwhile, Richard Penderel went to his brother-in-law Yates, and told him what had happened. Mrs Yates at once prepared a mess of buttermilk and eggs; she and Richard brought it and a blanket to the solitary figure in Spring Coppice. Charles, rather taken aback at seeing yet another let into his secret, said with a smile, 'Good woman, can you be faithful to a distressed Cavalier?' 'Yes, Sir,' replied Mrs Yates, 'I will rather die than discover you.' Charles, not readily trustful, believed her and having eaten his scrambled eggs, moved nearer the highway. A few moments later a troop of Parliamentary horse – militia, not professional soldiers, he noted – rode by. Evidently the hunt had begun. For the rest of that day the rain continued without stopping.

'But this,' Charles realized, 'hindered them ... from coming into the wood to search.' Presently Richard Penderel joined him.

By this time Charles had begun to change his mind about going to London, and the fact that Richard Penderel knew no one who could help him on his way there, turned his thoughts towards Wales. He and Richard decided to cross the Severn and embark from Swansea. As it was now five o'clock and the King had eaten nothing since early morning, Richard took him into the Yateses' house, Hobbal Grange, where Mrs Yates gave him a purée of milk and apples in a black earthen cup ('I love it very well,' said the King) and found him dry clothes. Charles insisted on sharing the food with Richard, exchanged his axe for a light bill-hook and, under his hosts' direction, practised 'ordering his steps and straight body to a lobbing, Jobson's gait'. It was arranged that he should call himself William Jones and pass as a wood-cutter from another part of the country.

As soon as it was dark Mrs Yates made a fricassée of eggs and bacon, while Charles, watching her, took little Nan Penderel on his knee. They sat down; the Penderels waited for His Majesty to begin. 'Eat – ' said Charles, and when Richard did so he said, 'You have a better stomach than I, for you have eaten five times today already.' Old Mrs Penderel then joined them and having kissed the King's hand said, 'I bless God that he has so honoured my children in making them the instruments, as I hope, of Your Majesty's safeguard and deliverance.' They were about to leave when Francis Yates came forward with the better part of his savings – thirty shillings. Charles took ten. 'Put the other up,' he said, and he and Richard Penderel set forth.

It was now nine o'clock. They walked for some three hours without seeing anyone. As they came to a mill they heard the sound of voices. 'Do not answer if anybody should ask you questions,' said Richard when they saw the white-clad miller sitting in his doorway. 'Who goes there?' he called. 'Neighbours going home,' Penderel replied. The miller stood up, brandishing a cudgel. 'If you be neighbours, stand,' he said, 'or I will knock you down.' 'Follow me close,' Richard whispered, and led the King up a lane to a bridge while the miller pursued them, shouting 'Rogues! Rogues!' They then saw that he was accompanied by a troop of soldiers.

They jumped off the bridge, crossed the stream, and ran on till they reached a hedge. It was so dark that Charles had to follow Richard 'by the noise and rattling of his leathern breeches'. As they crashed into the hedge the King said, 'Leap, and lie still to hear if anybody follow us,' and they lay there for nearly half an hour. Then they walked on to Madeley;

Richard said, 'There is an honest gentleman, one Mr Wolfe, where Your Majesty may be with great safety, for he has hiding-holes for priests.' 'I will not go in,' said the King as they approached Madeley House, 'until I know whether he will receive so dangerous a guest as me. Ask him only whether he will receive an English gentleman, a person of quality, till the next day' – and retired underneath a tree while Richard knocked up Mr Wolfe and told him that a Royalist fugitive was in need of shelter. 'It is so dangerous an undertaking to harbour anyone,' said that gentleman, 'that I will not venture my neck for any man – unless it be the King himself.' 'It is the King.' 'Then,' said Wolfe, 'I will venture all I have in the world to secure him.' When Richard told Charles what had passed, he was 'a little troubled'. He thought Richard had been indiscreet, and should have asked his leave before giving away his identity. He made no comment and entered the house by the back door, to be greeted by an elderly gentleman, who dauntingly began, 'I am very sorry to see Your Majesty here, because there are two companies of militia foot in the town, who keep a guard at the ferry and examine everyone that comes that way. I dare not put you into any of the hiding-holes, because they have been discovered. Therefore Your Majesty has no other way of security but to go into my barn and there lie behind my corn and hay.' He then gave Richard and Charles some cold meat, which they took with them to the barn. Here they spent the night and all the next day.

Towards the evening of September 5th Mr Wolfe, accompanied by his son, came to the King with some food and they discussed his crossing the river. 'Do not venture upon it,' said his host. 'Strict guards are kept all along the Severn for preventing anybody's escaping into Wales.' So Charles reverted to his first plan of going to London via Boscobel. After Mrs Wolfe had stained the King's face and hands with walnut juice, he and Richard began their return journey.

As they crept up to the mill the King said, 'How deep is the river here?' 'It is a scurvy river, not easy to be passed in all places – and I cannot swim,' was the reply. 'I will undertake to help you over,' said Charles, and finding the water within his depth, gave Richard a hand. The two dripping figures trudged on, arriving at Boscobel at eleven o'clock, where they were received by William Penderel and the Giffards. By this time the King's feet were so blistered that he was 'scarce able to stand or go'. Mrs Giffard washed and dressed them, and gave him some cheese and a posset of skim milk and small beer. At this point Colonel Careless, another Catholic and one of the last Royalists to leave Worcester, arrived to take refuge, and Charles asked his advice. 'It would be very dangerous,' said Careless, 'for Your Majesty to stay in this house or to go into the wood. There is but one way to pass the next day, and that is, to get up into a great oak, in a pretty plain place, where we can see round about us – for the enemy will certainly search the wood.'

While preparations were being made for Charles and Careless to hide themselves in the oak they received a message from Lord Wilmot who, escorted by John Penderel, had found a safer hiding-place in a priest's hole at Moseley Hall, the residence of a Mr Whitgreave. When John Penderel returned to Boscobel to find the King in greater danger, he went back to Moseley Hall. Here he saw Mr Whitgreave and his nephews' tutor, Father Huddleston, walking in the garden. 'We are all undone,' he told them, 'the King has been forced to come back to Boscobel, and we know not how to dispose of him – ' going on to explain that the Roundheads were expected at any hour. It was then arranged that the King should be brought to Moseley Hall as soon as it was safe for him to leave Boscobel.

In the early morning of September 6th the King and Careless, carrying bread, ale, cheese and two cushions, climbed a ladder into the pollarded oak; it stood about a hundred yards from Boscobel House in a clearing between it and Whiteladies. Its boughs, says Charles, 'being grown out again, very bushy and thick, could not be seen through,' and so made a not too uncomfortable resting-place. 'I humbly desire Your Majesty,' said Careless, 'to seat yourself as easily as you can and rest your head on my lap.' Charles, who had been on the move for forty-eight hours, fell asleep at once. He woke to eat and drink – and saw a number of soldiers coming in and out of the wood on the other side of the clearing. Presently they came so near that he could hear them cursing him for giving them all this trouble. 'If we take him,' one said, 'he will see how we shall use him.'

In the evening Charles and Careless came down and sat in the summer-house over a bottle of wine. They were joined by Humphrey Penderel, who had just returned from an alarming interview with Captain Broadway of the Parliamentary army, at Shifnal. Broadway, apparently aware that Charles might be in the neighbourhood of Whiteladies, told Humphrey of the £1,000 offered for his capture, adding, 'I doubt not that in a day or two we shall have him delivered into our hands. If you are found to have hid him, you shall suffer death for it.' He then asked Humphrey if he knew anything of the King or of the house. Humphrey lost his head, but tried to reply as one ill-informed. 'I believe he has been there,' he said, 'but he has not stayed, as there are three families in that house, and all of them at odds with one another.'

Charles's face fell as Humphrey finished his story. Half the sum offered for his capture would enrich the whole Penderel family for life; and this brother, now beginning to apologize for his clumsiness, might be tempted. 'If it were a hundred thousand,' put in Careless, 'it would be to no purpose. I engage my soul for their truth,' and Humphrey, 'with many urgent asseverations', promised that they would all be faithful.

In fact, there was nothing for it but to go on trusting the Penderels, their Catholic neighbours and anyone else they chose to involve. As the number of conspirators increased, amounting finally to some forty persons, Charles grew more uneasy, especially as his own precautions to hide his identity were not always successful and the strain of his flight made further demands on his endurance. Yet he never showed his distrust or allowed his helpers to feel that he was unco-operative; he yielded to them whenever there was a choice of plan, whether he approved of it or not. Once only, his courage failed and he became desperate; this moment was now approaching. Charles himself omitted it in all but one of his own versions of his adventures.

Charles and Careless now entered Boscobel House, William and Joan Penderel's home, where there was an undiscovered priest's hole. After a supper of roast chicken, the King curled up on a pallet bed in a slit between two walls. The next day, September 7th, was Sunday; therefore the Roundhead army, although still surrounding them and on the watch, would not be searching the woods or the houses. Asked what he would like for breakfast, Charles suggested mutton. William and Joan ('My Dame Joan', as the King called her) had no sheep of their own; 'but,' said William, 'I will make bold at this time.' He and Careless killed a neighbour's ewe, skinned it and cut off a hindquarter, which they brought to the King. Roasting would take far too long, said Charles; so he sliced off collops in the Scots fashion ('I am a master cook,' he told them) which Careless fried. The King then sat in the summer-house, within easy access of the priest's hole, reading the Bible – presumably the Douai version. At some point there was an alarm, and he returned to his hiding-place. When he came out his nose began to bleed – an omen of violent death, which terrified his hosts. The King reassured them; it often happened, he said. Presently they saw him walking up and down the passage, 'at his devotions'.

As soon as it was dark Charles and Careless began their journey – they dared not risk being seen on horseback – to Moseley Hall. It then became clear that good Mrs Giffard's care for His Majesty's feet had been ill contrived. She had dried his heavy countryman's shoes until they cracked and stuffed the cracks with rolls of paper. Soon his blisters were bleeding and raw. He must rest before he fainted from the pain. Careless knew of 'a poor cottage', whose Catholic owner would help him; having introduced the King as a runaway Cavalier, he took him into the barn.

The cottager told them that they should separate. Careless was too well known to the Roundheads to be a safe escort; so the Colonel decided to leave Charles, to whom he promised to send 'a good honest man' to conduct him to Moseley Hall.

The exhausted King slept heavily. In the morning his host brought him a hunk of bread and a bowl of buttermilk. It was all they had, he said, their daily fare. 'If I procure better,' he went on in his slow way, 'people might think I have some one with me. I would get you some meat – but if you can bear this hard diet, you shall have enough.' 'It is the best food I have eaten,' Charles assured him. As the man was leaving, he added, 'I would have your company as much as you can give it me.' But his host was busy, and he spent the ensuing hours alone.

Careless, suddenly afraid to entrust the King to anyone else, now reappeared. Charles then changed shirts with his host – whose 'noggen' or canvas garment was so coarse that it galled his shoulders – and was given some shoes that seemed easier than the cracked pair. He and Careless had gone but a few miles, climbing hedges and wading through ditches, when the wounds from the blisters began to bleed again. Charles threw away his shoes; first his stockings and then his feet were cut and torn by thorns and stones. He collapsed in agony.

Careless tried to rouse him. 'I would rather be taken,' was all Charles would say. 'We have but a little further to go,' urged the Colonel. Charles 'cast himself down', and refused to move. 'Till morning,' he pleaded, 'then I may shift with less torment.' Careless was adamant. He dragged the King to his feet, and sometimes coaxing him, sometimes assuring him that they were nearly there, helped him along.

Yet it was not possible to proceed without help and inconspicuously. Once more Careless entrusted Charles to a cottager, borrowed a horse and rode back to Boscobel, where he found a mount to carry the King, and they left the cottage. When they reached Boscobel he said farewell to Charles and, after some wandering, escaped to France.*

The five Penderel brothers and Francis Yates, carrying bill-hooks and staves, rode from Boscobel to Moseley Hall on either side of Charles, who had the mill horse, led by Humphrey. Still bruised, and in some pain from

* As this portion of the narrative of Charles's flight appears only in Clarendon's *History*, it has been discredited, partly because it confuses the accepted dates of his travels. The Chancellor, who was incapable of invention, may have unwittingly enlarged its length; there can be no doubt of its authenticity.

the rubbing of his shirt, the King endured fresh pangs whenever the horse pecked or stumbled. 'Have a care, or it will fall,' he said at last. Humphrey, its owner, reassured him. 'That now fortunate horse,' he said, 'has carried many a heavier weight in his time – six strikes of corn.' As His Majesty looked rather blank at this local expression, Humphrey went on, 'He now has a better price on his back – the price of three kingdoms – and would not shame his master.' So at last Charles reached Moseley Hall, and what appeared to be comparative safety.

As he and Yates dismounted the Penderels turned their horses. The King called them back and held out his hand. 'My troubles make me forget myself,' he said. 'I thank you all. If ever I come into my kingdom, I will remember you.'

When that moment came, and the Penderels were ushered into the presence-chamber at Whitehall, Charles, for perhaps the twentieth time, recounted their adventures. The brothers were enraptured. His Majesty's courtiers made no attempt to conceal their yawns.

II

At eleven o'clock on the night of September 8th Mr Whitgreave was waiting to receive the King and his escort. When the tallest of the seven riders dismounted, passed him without a word and went into the house, he assumed that the worst had happened; that unkempt, limping figure, supported by a stick, his face dark beneath 'a very greasy, old, grey, steeple-crowned hat', could not be His Majesty. He hurried after the Penderels and brought them into the buttery.

Charles went upstairs to Lord Wilmot's room, where a light was burning. That nobleman – now only remembered as the father of the drunken and brilliant Rochester – seems to have been the one person he absolutely trusted and most needed, in spite of their disagreements in Scotland.

As the King sank into the nearest chair Wilmot ran towards him, knelt and clasped his knees. Neither spoke; Charles bent down and kissed his friend's cheek. Then he said, 'What is become of Buckingham, Cleveland and the others?' Wilmot shook his head. 'I hope they are in safety,' was all he could say.

For a few moments they remained alone. Then Wilmot called Father Huddleston and bade him fetch Mr Whitgreave. When they came in Charles and Wilmot were standing by the cupboard, their backs towards the door. By this time Whitgreave knew, and Huddleston did not, that the dirty, unshaven, crop-haired young fellow in the threadbare coat, sweaty leathern doublet and darned green hose was the King. Lord Wilmot turned and said, 'This gentleman under disguise is your master, and mine, and the master of us all, to whom we all owe our duty and allegiance.'

Whitgreave fell on his knees. The King gave him his hand to kiss. He managed to say, 'I have received such a character of your loyalty and readiness to assist me and my friends that I will never be unmindful of you or yours.' Father Huddleston was presented and Charles went on, 'Where is that private place my lord tells me of?' Whitgreave showed him the priest's hole. Charles glanced at it and mechanically remarking, 'It is the best place I ever was in,' returned to the chair by the fireside, suddenly speechless and unable to move. Huddleston and Whitgreave knelt and gently drew off his shoes and stockings; they exclaimed in horror as His Majesty's feet, 'most sadly galled', were seen to be plastered with gravel: pieces of paper had been stuck between the toes. 'I was advised to,' said Charles, as they began to wash and dress his wounds. 'His Majesty's shirt will dis-ease him much, and hinder his rest,' Huddleston whispered to Wilmot. 'Would he be pleased to change it?' Wilmot gave assent and the priest, who had a store of new linen shirts, fetched one and slipped off the other; it was still stiff and soaked with rain. Then Charles's nose began bleeding again; he pulled out of his pocket 'a handkerchief suitable to the rest of his apparel, both coarse and dirty'. This too the priest exchanged for one of his own, carefully secreting the discarded linen as precious relics. (In the years to come the blood-stained handkerchief effected many cures for the King's Evil.) He then observed that Charles was clasping his thorn-stick – 'crooked three or four several ways' – and when he suggested putting it aside the King shook his head, as if he were still under compulsion to keep going.

By this time Mr Whitgreave had brought up a tray of sherry and biscuits which he set before his guest. Charles ate and drank while the three friends stood watching him. Then he looked up, smiled and said, 'I am now ready for another march – and if it shall please God once more to place me at the head of but eight or ten thousand good men, of one mind, and resolved to fight, I shall not doubt to drive these rogues out of my kingdoms.'

After this they expected that he would want to sleep. Charles was too tired to relax; he sat on, talking of his experiences and of his and Wilmot's next move, till dawn. Then once more he had to fit his long legs into a bed too short for them, in the almost airless priest's hole.

Next morning Mr Whitgreave's mother, a very old lady, was waiting to kiss his hand. Having saluted her with his usual grace, Charles breakfasted in a little room above the porch, whence he could look out over the road. When Mrs Whitgreave brought up his dinner he insisted on her sitting down with him, while her son and Huddleston waited on them both. Meanwhile, all the servants but the Catholic kitchen-maid had been sent out to work on the estate; she was told that their master was sheltering a Worcester fugitive. The other inmates of Moseley Hall, Mr Whitgreave's nephews, and their friend, little Sir John Preston, were also ordered out of doors, and began to play at sentries – a game greatly enhanced by their being told to look out for Roundheads – till it was time for supper. As they all sat down Sir John said, 'Eat hard, boys, for we have been on the life-guard and hard duty this day' – a remark 'more truly spoken,' says Mr Whitgreave, 'than he was aware.'

All that night Charles remained in the priest's hole, while Huddleston kept watch indoors and Whitgreave walked about outside. Meanwhile Wilmot had arranged with a neighbouring squire, Colonel Lane, that Charles should be disguised as a groom and accompany his sister on her journey to Bristol, whence he would be able to find transport overseas.

In the morning Charles, entering his host's study, looked out and saw a straggling party of Royalists, some of whom he knew, making for the back door, 'some for provisions and others for plasters for their wounds'. As if the sight had released all his pent-up misery, he poured out the whole wretched story – the Scots' treacherous usage, the fruitless march to Worcester, the fatal siege. Suddenly he asked, 'How are this country affected? Who is against me?' Without waiting for an answer, he went on, 'How do Roman Catholics live under the present usurped government?' 'They are persecuted,' Whitgreave replied, 'on account both of their religion and of their loyalty. Yet Your Majesty shall see that they do not neglect the duties of their Church – ' and he led Charles into the chapel, 'a little, neat but decent' sanctum.

As he gazed at the altar and its ornaments Charles was reminded of some childhood incident – a grievance connected, presumably, with the disputes between his mother and his father's Anglican courtiers. 'I had an altar, crucifix and silver candlesticks of my own,' he said, 'till Lord Holland brake them. Which – ' he added abruptly, 'he hath now paid for.' They returned to the study and the King, glancing at the books, picked up Father Huddleston's manuscript of his *Short and Plain Way to the Christian Faith*. He read it through; then he said, 'I have not seen anything more plain and clear upon this subject. The arguments here drawn from succession are so conclusive, I do not see how they can be denied.' He turned to a Catholic manual – Turberville's *Catechism*. 'That is a pretty book,' he said (Did he know it? Whitgreave wondered). 'I will take it with me – ' and went back to the parlour to rest.

Wilmot then came in and said, 'If it should so fall out that the rebels have intelligence of your harbouring any of the King's party, and should therefore put you to any torture for confession, be sure you discover me first, which may haply in such case satisfy them, and preserve the King – ' and went out.

As Whitgreave, deeply moved, continued to watch from the study window, he saw a man he knew approach the back door. A few seconds later the kitchen-maid burst in, crying, 'Soldiers! Soldiers are coming!' Whitgreave rushed to the parlour; Charles had heard the alarm and was already in his hiding-place. His host walked out into the village street to meet the Roundheads. 'You are come from Worcester fight!' cried one, and the whole troop set upon him, 'ready to pull me in pieces'.

The villagers intervened. 'He was not there – he has been very ill a great while – ' they insisted. So Whitgreave was released and the troop went away, to search Boscobel House, Hobbal Grange and Whiteladies from floor to ceiling. He then returned to reassure the King. For a long time Charles remained silent and gloomy. He cheered up a little when Mrs Whitgreave joined them and told him – 'for his diversion' – that one of the villagers was saying that His Majesty had defeated his enemies at Warrington Bridge, and that 'there were three kings come to his assistance'. The King smiled rather sadly. 'Surely they are the three kings of Cologne come down from Heaven,' he said, 'for I can imagine none else.'

Indeed, it seemed as if the net was closing round him. While the Roundheads were threatening the inhabitants of Boscobel with death and torture, the ports were being watched, and the proclamation for his discovery had been issued from Westminster and was already placarded or read out by the criers all over the country. 'Take notice of Charles Stuart to be a tall man above two yards high, his hair a deep brown near to black, and has been cut off... Expect him under disguise.' In the midst of their anxiety Charles's hosts paused to comment on the horrid phrasing. Charles Stuart – what 'frontless insolence to His Sacred Majesty!' And the reward was a 'vile price for so inestimable a jewel!'

Meanwhile, in the village of Moseley a sinister individual known as Southall the priest-catcher was talking to the smith. 'Can you tell me where the King is? You shall have £1,000 for your pains if you discover him.' So it was arranged that at midnight Colonel Lane should come over to take him to Bentley Hall, where Lord Wilmot was already established.

On the evening of his departure Charles saw Father Huddleston alone,

After some further talk about the betrayal of his plans at Worcester, he said, 'I know you are a priest [the tutor habitually dressed as a layman]. You need not fear to own it to me.' 'Your Majesty,' Huddleston replied, 'is, in some sort, in the same condition with me now – liable to dangers and perils; but I hope God, that brought you hither, will preserve you.' 'If it please God to restore me,' said Charles, 'you shall never need more privacies. Both you and all of your persuasion shall have as much liberty as any of my subjects.'

They were now joined by Mr Whitgreave with news of Colonel Lane's arrival. Charles sent for Mrs Whitgreave who, as if she were seeing off one of her great-nephews, gave him a parcel of home-made sweets and another of almonds and raisins. Although the slightest delay was dangerous, Charles ate some then and there, praised the old lady's cookery, kissed and thanked her. Turning to the men, he went on, 'I am very sensible of the dangers you may incur if it is discovered to the rebels – ' and gave them the address of a London merchant who would shelter and finance them in case of need.

They knelt to kiss his hand. 'All the service I can now do Your Majesty,' said Whitgreave, 'is to pray heartily to Almighty God for your safety and preservation.' 'I will never be unmindful of you,' Charles replied as they went down to the orchard where Colonel Lane was waiting. 'Humbly and thankfully,' said Whitgreave, 'I deliver my great charge into your hands.' As the King mounted Father Huddleston, suddenly aware that the weather had become very cold and that His Majesty was thinly clad, took off his cloak and begged him to put it on. The priest was distressed that he had no gloves; but Charles refused to wear any. Once more they knelt to kiss his hand. As he rode away into the darkness they crossed themselves and prayed; both were in tears.

III

The Lanes, who were Anglicans, but noted for their friendly attitude towards their Catholic neighbours, consisted of old Mr and Mrs Lane, their son the Colonel and his sister Jane, a young lady of 'very good wit and discretion'. She was also handsome and elegant, but somewhat lacking in the allure afterwards attributed to her by those who would have romanticized her relationship with Charles. Her cousin, Mrs Norton, was about to lie in at her house near Bristol, and Jane had a permit to travel there with a single manservant, in order to look after her. Mr and Mrs Petre, Colonel Lane's other sister and her husband, Mr Lassels a Royalist officer, and Lord Wilmot were to be of the party. Neither the Petres nor the Colonel's parents were told who Charles was; they believed him to be Jane's new groom.

On the morning of September 11th Colonel Lane woke the King very early and helped him to dress in a respectable suit of grey cloth, neat boots and a cloak. They expected to reach Bristol in some four or five days, but were to set out from Bentley Hall as if on a hawking expedition, with spaniels, falcons and Colonel Lane as their escort for the first two or three miles.

Mr and Mrs Lane were in the courtyard to see them off. As Charles came out of the stable leading the horse he and Jane were to ride, Colonel said, 'Will, thou must give my sister thy hand.' In his hurry the King did so from the wrong side. Old Mrs Lane burst out laughing and exclaimed, 'What a goodly horseman my daughter has to ride before her!'

Some two hours later Charles's horse cast a shoe, and he took it to the nearest forge. As he stood holding it he said to the smith, 'What news?' 'None that I know of,' was the reply, 'since the good news of the beating of the rogue Scots.' 'Are none of the English taken that joined with them?' Charles inquired. 'I did not hear that that rogue Charles Stuart was taken – some of the others, but not Charles Stuart,' said the smith. 'If that rogue were taken,' said the King, 'he deserves to be hanged more than all the rest, for bringing in the Scots.' 'You speak like an honest man!' the other exclaimed, and so they parted.

Within four miles of Stratford-on-Avon they saw, some distance away, a troop of Roundheads baiting their horses. 'For my part,' said Mr Petre, 'I will not go by them, for I have been once or twice beaten by the Parliament rogues, and I will not venture again.' Charles whispered to Jane, 'Let us go on, lest they see us turn.' She and her brother-in-law argued the matter, but he would not be moved, and they took another route, only to find the Roundhead troop in the town. The Petres then left Charles's party, who proceeded to Long Marston, where they slept at the house of a kinsman of the Lanes. Here the King, who had been sent to the kitchen, was told to wind up the jack on which the joint was turning. He obeyed, but unhandily, upon which the cook, over-heated and fussed, cried, 'What countryman are you, that you know not how to wind up a jack?' 'I am a poor tenant's son, of Colonel Lane in Staffordshire,' Charles meekly replied. 'We seldom have roast meat, but when we have, we don't use a jack –' and the angry woman subsided.

Next morning they parted from Lord Wilmot, who was to meet them at the Nortons with a passport for the King in the name of William

Jackson; this he hoped to obtain from a Royalist magistrate. That evening Charles, Jane and Mr Lassels reached Cirencester, where they spent the night. Next day they arrived at Abbotsleigh, the Nortons' residence, three miles from Bristol.

Here Jane Lane summoned the butler, Pope, whom Charles recognized as a former servant of one of his gentlemen and a trooper in the late King's army. 'Take care of William Jackson,' said Jane, 'for he has been lately sick of an ague and is not quite recovered. A chamber must be provided for him,' she went on, 'and a good fire made, for he is not fit to go below stairs.' As they sat down to supper she sent Pope to Charles with the first course, a dish of porridge.

Pope had no sooner served the King, who was in bed, than he began to stare. Then he knelt, and, the tears pouring down his face, exclaimed, 'I am glad to see Your Majesty!' 'What do you mean?' said Charles, forcing a laugh. 'I was falconer to Sir Thomas Jermyn,' replied Pope. 'I know well enough to whom I speak.' 'Do not speak of what you know – not so much as to your master, although I know him to be a very honest man,' said the King.

Meanwhile the party in the parlour had been joined by the Reverend Mr Gorges, formerly a doctor, who, seeing Mistress Lane so careful of her servant's diet, began to question her. 'How long has his ague been gone? Has he been purged since it left him?' When they had finished their meal he good-naturedly offered to go and see the poor fellow, and went upstairs before Jane could stop him. At the sight of a stranger, Charles withdrew as far as he could from the light of the candle. Gorges took this for shyness, sat down, felt his pulse and asked him a number of questions, to which Charles replied that sleep was what he most needed. 'You will do well,' said the good parson, and bustled down to reassure Mrs Lane and tell her what to do if Will's ague returned.

Next morning Charles met Mr Gorges in the passage. 'What have you heard of the King and the battle?' asked the clergyman. As Charles hesitated, he said, 'I am afraid you are a Roundhead – but I will try what metal you are made of – ' and taking him to the buttery, told him to drink His Majesty's health, or be censured. 'I was never a man of that stamp,' said Charles, draining his glass. He then fell into talk with the other servants over their ale and bread and butter, one of whom, 'a bragging fellow', proceeded to describe his experiences at Worcester. Charles, thinking that by his dress he must be a Roundhead, asked, 'How come you to give so good an account of that battle?' 'I was in King's regiment,' was the answer. 'Colonel King?' 'Nay – *the* King's regiment – Colonel

Broughton's company.' 'Have you seen the King?' Charles pursued. 'Twenty times,' the soldier replied. Charles, who was beginning to enjoy himself, could not resist asking, 'What kind of man is he then?' The fellow exactly described His Majesty's clothes and his horse, adding, 'He is at least three fingers taller than you.' 'Upon which,' says Charles, 'I made what haste I could out of the buttery.'

He was then joined by Pope, who looked at him 'very earnestly', but said nothing and went away. Charles, remembering to take off his hat as he passed Mrs Norton in the passage, walked out into the fields and returned to find Mr Lassels looking rather anxious. 'What shall we do?' he burst out, 'I am afraid Pope knows you, for he says very positively that it is you, though I have denied it.' 'Is he a very honest man or no?' asked the King. 'I know him to be so honest a fellow that I would trust him with my life,' Lassels replied. Charles then sent for Pope and said, 'I will trust you, as an old acquaintance.' 'What does Your Majesty intend to do?' asked the butler, adding that he had better leave Abbotsleigh as soon as possible. 'For though my master and mistress are good people,' he explained, 'yet there are at this time one or two rogues in it – and I think I can be useful to you in anything you can command me.' 'I design to get a ship at Bristol,' said the King. 'Therefore go this very day to see if there are any for Spain or France – ' adding that he expected Lord Wilmot with his passport at any moment.

Pope thought this very dangerous – too many people in the neighbourhood who could not be trusted knew his lordship – went out to meet Wilmot and brought him in by the back way. They arrived with bad news; there would be no ships sailing from Bristol to the Continent for a month or more. It was therefore decided that Charles and Jane Lane should make their way to Trent in Somerset, to the house of Francis Wyndham, the King's old nurse's brother-in-law.

Charles and his companions remained at Abbotsleigh from the 13th to the 16th of September, during which time the King, having recovered from his supposed ague, was no longer allowed a room to himself, but given a truckle bed in Mr Lassels's chamber. As soon as everything was quiet Lassels changed beds with him. Charles spent the day below stairs; once he was asked to join the servants in a game of fives, but had to refuse.

Before Lord Wilmot preceded the others to Trent, Charles insisted that he disguise himself. Wilmot shook his head. 'I should look frightfully in it,' was all he would say – and the King had to yield.

Then Mrs Norton's labour began. She was delivered of a dead child and became so ill that it appeared impossible for her cousin to leave her. Yet the King must be moving on, and Jane Lane would not let him do so without her protection, for it had become clear that the only safe way for him to travel was as the servant behind whom she rode pillion. What was to be done?

Charles suggested that Jane should receive a counterfeit message from her mother saying that her father was very ill, and she must come home at once. The letter was delivered at supper, and the young lady played her part so well that it was possible for her and the King to leave for Trent early the next morning.

Having spent the night at Castle Cary, Charles, Lassels and Jane entered the grounds of Trent House. Sir Francis and Lady Wyndham were walking in the fields when they perceived 'a lady riding behind a pale and meanly dressed young man', who called out, 'Frank, Frank! How dost thou do?' and was joyfully received.

Here Charles, having taken leave of Jane and Lassels, remained till September 22nd, while the Wyndhams made plans for his escort to the coast. He spent most of his time in Lady Wyndham's rooms (where there was a priest's hole, the legacy of his hostess's Catholic parents) and found the days very long. Hearing the bells ring and seeing a crowd making a bonfire in the churchyard, he sent down the maid, who knew him, to find out what was happening. She returned to say, 'There is a rogue of a trooper come out of Cromwell's army that is telling the people he hath killed Your Majesty, and that that is your buff coat he has on.' Charles, realizing that the villagers were what he thought of as fanatics, said merely, 'Alas, poor people!' and turned away from the window.

By this time Sir Francis Wyndham had arranged with a neighbour, Captain Ellesdon, who traded at Lyme Regis, to put Charles on board the next ship to France. Ellesdon, hearing that a vessel, owned by Stephen Limbry, was leaving from Charmouth for St Malo on the night of the 23rd, went to interview him. 'A more convenient place,' says Ellesdon, '... could hardly be found, it lying upon the shore, a quarter of a mile from any house, and from any horse or footpath.' He offered Limbry £60 to transport a friend of his who had had 'a finger in the pie' at Worcester, upon which Limbry refused to risk his neck. Ellesdon increased the offer, and it was settled that Charles should wait for Limbry at the inn at Charmouth. Wyndham then sent his confidential valet, Peters, to the hostess, to engage rooms for 'a worthy nobleman, deeply in love with an orphaned maid, who ... was as much in love with him. But,' Peters explained, 'her guardian resisting the marriage, he has resolved to steal her away by night. Will you for some hours entertain them in your house?' He concluded his story with a tip, and asked the landlady to drink with him. 'Touched with compassion for the young lady', the woman promised to help her.

On the afternoon of the 22nd Charles set off from Trent, with Mistress Julian Coningsby, a Wyndham cousin, riding pillion behind him. They went first to Captain Ellesdon's house, where Charles was told that he would board the ship as Wilmot's servant, while that nobleman posed as a merchant flying from his creditors. After praising Ellesdon for his ingenuity, the King gave him a gold piece. As the number of his debtors increased, his assurances became more cautious. 'I have nothing else to bestow on you at present,' he said, 'but if ever it shall please God to restore me to my kingdoms, I will readily grant you whatsoever favour you may, in reason, petition me for.' Captain Ellesdon pierced the coin so that he could hang it round his neck, thereafter leaving it to his descendants.

On the evening of the 22nd Charles, Wilmot, Mistress Coningsby, Wyndham and Peters, escorted by Captain Ellesdon, reached the inn at Charmouth, where Ellesdon left them to wait for Limbry, who was expected soon after midnight. As the hours passed and he did not arrive, Wyndham and Peters, fearing that he had turned informer, went out to look for him. There, in the Charmouth Roads, was the ship. Limbry was nowhere to be seen.

For this disaster Mrs Limbry was responsible. Seeing her husband make ready to sail without warning, she suspected that he might be about to break the law. When he admitted it she locked him in his bedroom till the tide changed. 'If you do but stir out of doors,' she told him, 'I will inform against you,' and their two daughters took her side. Eventually Limbry persuaded her to let him go to the watchers on the shore to explain his absence. She would not trust him out of her sight; so Wyndham and Peters, on their way back to the inn, saw him walking along, followed by the three women. They pretended not to know him, and returned to find Charles in greater danger than at any time since his flight began.

September 23rd was the 'solemn fast day' ordained by Parliament for anti-Royalist propaganda. In Charmouth church Mr Westley, a Puritan ex-weaver, was preaching on these lines. He concluded his address with, 'Charles Stuart is somewhere in this [district]. You will merit from God Almighty if you will find him out,' going on to remind his congregation of the more immediate reward for so doing. At the same moment the local smith, who had been re-shoeing Wilmot's and Charles's mounts, said to the innkeeper, 'One of those horses has travelled far, for his shoes have been made in four several counties.' The landlord reported this to the parson, who, coming with an officer to question the suspected persons, found that they had just left. One of them, apparently the groom, had made himself very agreeable to the landlady, much to the amusement of the other guests. Westley said to her, 'Why, how now, Margaret? You are a maid of honour now.' 'What mean you by that, Mr Parson?' 'Why, Charles Stuart lay last night at your house, and kissed you at his departure – so that now you can't but be a maid of honour.' 'You are a scurvy-conditioned man, to go about to bring me and my house into trouble,' she exclaimed, 'but if I thought it was the King, as you say it was, I would think the better of my lips all the days of my life. And so, Mr Parson, get you out of my house, or I'll get those shall kick you out.'

The enraged clergyman then called upon the smith and desired him to report to the magistrates and obtain a warrant for the King's arrest. The smith would have none of it. 'I shall make myself ridiculous to all the county by such an undertaking,' he said. So Westley, hearing that the travellers had left for Bridport, pursued them alone.

While the villagers were in church Wilmot and Charles had decided to return to Trent – but how? Every road was alive with Roundhead soldiers and Parliamentary officials. It was then agreed that Wilmot and Peters should make inquiries about another ship and meet the King and Wyndham at Bridport, in the event of their being able to sail from there.

Late in the afternoon, Charles, Julian Coningsby and Wyndham came into Bridport to find it full of Cromwell's red-coats, of whom some fifteen hundred were embarking for Jersey. Wyndham's resources had failed him. 'What shall we do?' he exclaimed. 'We must go impudently into the best inn in the town,' Charles replied, 'and take a chamber there. It is the only thing to be done, because otherwise we shall miss my Lord Wilmot in case we go anywhere else, and that will be very inconvenient, both to him and to me.'

In the courtyard of the George, now packed with troops, the King dismounted and taking the horses, went 'blundering in amongst them', as one determined to get the best accommodation. Pushing and shoving, he led the horses into the stable, while the angry soldiers cursed him for his rough ways. Sustaining the part of the insolent groom, Charles shouted to the ostler for oats, with the result that the man helped him to unsaddle and feed the horses. Suddenly he looked at Charles. 'Sure, sir,' he said, 'I know your face?' To this 'no very pleasant question', Charles replied, 'Where have you lived – always here, or no?' 'I am but newly come hither,' was the answer, 'I was born in Exeter, and have been ostler at an inn there, hard by one Mr Potter's, a merchant.' Charles, who had stayed at that house, said genially, 'Friend, certainly you have seen me there at Mr Potter's, for I served him a good while – above a year.' 'Oh!' exclaimed the other, 'then I remember you a boy there. Let us drink a pot of beer together.' 'I must wait on my master,' said the King, 'and get his dinner ready for him. But he is going to London, and will return about three weeks hence, when he will lie here. Then I will not fail to drink a pot with you.'

While Charles was waiting on Wyndham and Julian Coningsby, Lord Wilmot, having failed to find a ship, went to another inn. The young lady, who was keeping watch, saw Peters in the courtyard of the George and hurried out to him. They then arranged that Charles, herself and Wyndham should depart by the London road and meet Wilmot at Broadwindsor, where they would stay the night at the single inn.

Soon after they set off Parson Westley reached the George, to find that the man he now knew to be the King had just left – for Dorchester, he was told. There he searched all the inns and ale-houses, with no result. He had passed Charles on the Broadwindsor road.

When Wilmot arrived at Broadwindsor he recognized the landlord of the inn as an old servant of his own. Much relieved, he and the King settled down for the night. An hour later, they were woken by the noise of a troop of some forty Roundheads, demanding billets. Now they were trapped. Their horses were exhausted; and they dared not draw attention to themselves by leaving the inn on foot. So they stayed where they were, prepared for the worst.

IV

From their rooms at the top of the house the King and his party listened to the voices of the soldiers and the clatter of accoutrements, expecting at any moment to be turned out and discovered. Suddenly these sounds were interspersed by a woman's screams. After a considerable interval, during which the screams increased, they heard a baby crying and the entry of another group of men. Some time passed before they learnt that one of the camp-followers, falling into labour in the kitchen, had given birth to a child, which the soldiers summoned the parish to maintain. The local authorities, already annoyed at being called out of their beds, refused to be responsible for the offspring of a Roundhead doxy, and a furious argument ensued between them and the Cromwellian officers, which lasted until it was time for the troop to embark from Lyme Regis. Just before dawn the inn was empty and the roads were comparatively deserted, with the result that Peters, who had gone in search of another ship, was able to go upstairs and report the failure of his mission. After some discussion Sir Francis Wyndham advised Charles to return to Trent House, while Wilmot went to Salisbury in order to get in touch with Royalists who would provide more certain transport overseas.

On the evening of September 24th Charles reached Trent House, where he remained till October 6th. He found the twelve days' inactivity extremely taxing, for the Wyndhams dared not let him come down to meals or walk in the grounds; his only diversions were those of cooking his own food and piercing holes in coins, which he later distributed as souvenirs. On September 27th Lord Wilmot returned, having failed to find a ship at Southampton.

On the 28th, a Sunday, the Wyndhams were warned that Wilmot had been watched, that they were suspected of harbouring Royalist fugitives and that the house was to be searched. This danger was averted by Wilmot accompanying his hosts to church and worshipping according to Presbyterian rites. The local authorities, believing that they had all been converted, left them alone. Next day Wilmot went to try for a ship off the Sussex coast.

The next alarm was the arrival of a troop of Roundhead horse at Sherborne, reported by Lady Wyndham to Charles with great agitation, 'at which,' she says, 'he laughed most heartily, as if he had not been in the least concerned.' A few days later they heard from the Philips of Montacute that they could guarantee a ship for His Majesty from Southampton. This promise failed to materialize.

On October 6th Wilmot returned with news of a ship from Shoreham, and Charles, still in the guise of Julian Coningsby's groom, moved to Hele House near Amesbury, the seat of the widowed Mrs Hyde, whose husband had been a cousin of the Chancellor's. The King, Wilmot and Julian stopped to dine at Mere, where the host, mistrusting Charles's 'sad-coloured' suit and black hat, greeted him with the Cavalier countersign: 'Are you a friend to Caesar?' 'Yes.' 'Then,' said the innkeeper, 'here's a health to King Charles!' and pledged the company in his best wine.

On the night of October 6th Charles, having parted from Mistress Julian and Wyndham, reached Hele House, escorted by Colonel Robert Philips, who was now in charge of his escape, and who introduced him as a fugitive Cavalier. At supper, observing that Mrs Hyde looked at him 'a little earnestly', drank to him and helped him to two larks when the other guests were given one, Charles told her who he was as soon as they were alone. She replied that although she had only seen him once, in his boyhood, she had recognized him immediately. It was then decided that until they received news of a ship the King should remain where he was, but appear to depart the next morning, returning to Hele House after dark. He and Robert Philips spent the day at Stonehenge, where the King gave the lie to the old superstition that the stones could not be counted twice alike.

On October 13th news came that Colonel Gunter, a Sussex landowner, had hired a ship at Shoreham. At two o'clock in the morning he and Lord Wilmot met Charles and Philips at Stonehenge, and they rode all day till they came to Broad-Halfpenny in Hampshire. It was now dark and their horses were exhausted. Charles asked Gunter, 'Canst thou get me a lodging hereabouts?' and Gunter took him to Hambledon House, owned by his sister and brother-in-law, Mr and Mrs Symons.

As they came to the back door Charles pushed Philips ahead, whispering, 'Thou lookest most like a gentleman now.' Mrs Symons, who believed that her brother was with a party of friends, welcomed them with ale, wine and biscuits. After sitting in the parlour for a little while, they went in to supper. They were half-way through the meal when Mr Symons came in; it then became plain, says Charles, 'that he had been playing the good fellow at an ale-house', for he was in a semi-facetious, semi-belligerent mood.

Glancing round at the company, Symons stared at the King's shabby clothes and cropped hair. Rather unsteadily, he drew up a stool and began, 'This is brave! A man can no sooner be out of the way, but his house must be taken up with I know not whom.' Perceiving his brother-in-law, he went on, '*You* are welcome,' adding boozily, 'and as your friends, so are they all.'

There was a pause. Then Symons got up and started walking round the table. 'These are all Hydes now,' he declared. As he came to Charles he thrust his face into the King's and proclaimed, 'Here is a Roundhead!' Turning to Gunter, he went on, 'I never knew you keep Roundheads' company before.' 'It is no matter,' Gunter replied. 'He is my friend, and I will assure you, no dangerous man.' Symons then collapsed in the chair next to Charles and took his hand. 'Brother Roundhead,' he said, 'for his sake thou art welcome – ' getting up a moment later to whisper to his brother-in-law, 'Is he not some Roundhead rogue's son? He looks very suspiciously.' 'I would trust my life in his hands,' Gunter replied, and Symons returned to the King. 'Brother Roundhead,' he urged, 'drink a good glass of beer with me.'

As Charles complied his host began a long and confused discourse, during which he insisted on filling up his new friend's glass, sometimes with ale and sometimes with brandy. The King drank as little as he could; when Symons saw that he was holding back, he burst into an oath. Charles held up his hand. 'O, dear brother,' he implored, in the Puritan whine, 'that is a 'scape! Swear not, I beseech you.' Symons immediately sank into gloom. Presently he lurched over to Gunter. 'I wonder how thou couldst judge so right,' he said in a loud whisper. 'He is a Roundhead indeed – and if we could get him to bed, the house were our own, and we could be merry.' Thankfully, Gunter rose and conducted the King and Wilmot to their rooms.

Next morning, with a parcel of neats' tongues and some bread, they set off for Shoreham. At Beeding, in a narrow lane, they ran straight into a troop of some forty Roundhead horse, who pushed them aside 'so rudely', says Colonel Gunter, that they were nearly thrown, with the result that Wilmot refused to let the King stop there as arranged. He and Charles separated from Gunter, agreeing to meet at Brighton.

In the late afternoon Gunter reached the single inn, ordered some wine and was half-way upstairs, when he heard the King say to Lord Wilmot, 'Here, Mr Barlow – I drink to you.' And so, he says, 'We became one company again.'

Barlow ... the name meant nothing to Gunter. Until now, Wilmot had called himself Colonel Reymes. Had some sentimental impulse made Charles give him Lucy's pseudonym? At Trent and Hele he had had plenty of time to think of her, and of their son.

At supper they were joined by Francis Mansell, the merchant who had chartered the ship, and her master, Tattersall. As they all sat down Tattersall looked hard at Charles. When the meal was over he took Mansell aside and said, 'You have not dealt fairly with me. That is the King, I very well know him to be so.' As Mansell denied it, he went on, 'Be not troubled at it, for I think I do God and my country good service in preserving the King, and by the grace of God I will venture my life and all for him, and set him safely on shore, if I can, in France.' Mansell reported this conversation to Charles, who, remembering how Limbry had failed him, decided to keep Tattersall drinking with them till it was time to leave for Shoreham. So they were very merry together. Gunter was much impressed by Charles's gaiety and courage. A deeply religious man, he came to the conclusion that His Sacred Majesty was sustained by 'a heavenly host ... which to us was invisible'.

When the innkeeper came to clear away Charles was alone, standing with his back to the fire, one hand hanging over a chair. The host seized the brown, weather-beaten fingers and kissed them. 'God bless you, wheresoever you go!' he said, adding, 'I do not doubt, before I die, but to be a lord, and my wife a lady.' Charles laughed and joined the others in the next room. Gunter, who had overheard the innkeeper's remark, began to apologize, with 'earnest protestation' of his own innocence. 'Peace, peace, Colonel,' interrupted the King. 'The fellow knows me and I him. He was one that belonged to the back stairs, to my father. I hope he is an honest fellow.'

All this time the wind had been contrary. Now Charles opened the casement and, leaning out, said, 'It has turned,' and they prepared to leave. Tattersall then said that he must be insured – he had already received £60 – or he would not sail. 'Two hundred pounds is my valuation,' he announced. Gunter agreed to this. Tattersall went on, 'I must have your bond.' Gunter lost his temper. 'There are other boats besides yours – ' he said, and was leaving the room, when the King said to Tattersall, 'He saith right. A gentleman's word, especially before witnesses, is as good as his bond.' Tattersall then left for Shoreham. Charles, Wilmot and Gunter followed him, to find the tide gone out and the vessel lying dry. They said goodbye to Gunter and entered by means of a ladder. Charles went to the cabin and lay down to rest. Suddenly Tattersall burst in, kissed his hand and said, 'I know Your Majesty very well – ' and assured him of his loyalty.

The crew, believing themselves bound for Poole Harbour (they were carrying coal), were not told that there were passengers on board till they stood off the Isle of Wight. Tattersall then asked the King if he would persuade them to sail to France. 'Upon which,' says Charles, 'I went to the men ... and told them that we were two merchants that ... were a little in debt ... and were afraid of being arrested in England.' 'If you will persuade the master,' he went on, 'to give us a trip over to Dieppe ... you will oblige us very much,' and gave them a pound. The seamen agreed and Charles returned to the cabin, where Tattersall was awaiting him. They were then joined by one of the sailors, who was smoking a pipe. He sat down next to Charles and, staring at this rather odd-looking young merchant, puffed the fumes in his face. 'Begone, and do not trouble the gentleman with your smoke!' Tattersall exclaimed. Sulkily remarking, 'A cat may look at a king,' the man obeyed.

When they came within sight of the Normandy coast, they were approached by a vessel which Charles thought was an Ostend privateer. He said to Wilmot, 'Let us go ashore in a little cock-boat, for fear they may plunder us and carry us back to England.' As they were leaving the ship, Charles turned to Tattersall. 'Stay with us,' he said, 'and share my fortune.' 'I wish Your Majesty all prosperity and happiness,' the master replied, 'but I will choose rather to return to my wife and children.'

At five in the morning of October 15th Charles and Wilmot landed at Fécamp, just as Colonel Gunter was halted by a party of Roundhead horse, 'come to search for a tall black man, six foot two inches high'.

CHAPTER FIVE

THIRD COURTSHIP OF
LA GRANDE MADEMOISELLE

I

NEWS of the King's defeat at Worcester reached the Royalists in France and the Low Countries within a few days; they heard nothing of Charles himself for seven weeks. Henrietta Maria, plunged into despair by the death of Princess Elizabeth and the solitary imprisonment of the Duke of Gloucester, was now roused to agony for Charles. She concluded that he must be dead or a prisoner; escape would have been impossible.[1] A letter from a Royalist captive describing his 'undaunted courage and steadiness of mind' ended, 'what became of His Majesty ... I know not,' while another wrote that 'God covered his head and wonderfully preserved his sacred person' during the battle, but said nothing of his whereabouts.

On the day that Charles and Wilmot landed at Fécamp news came that Lord Derby had been captured and condemned to death; his execution was preceded by that of Francis Yates, whose refusal to give information saved the King's life at the cost of his own.

Charles and Wilmot had just enough money to ride to Rouen and take rooms at the best inn in the town. Here, says the King, 'they made difficulty to receive us, taking us, by our clothes, to be some thieves, or persons that had been doing some very ill thing'.[2] He therefore sent a message to two English merchants, Mr Sambourn and Mr Parker, asking for clothes and money. On their way to the inn Sambourn and Parker met Charles's old tutor, Dr Earle, who got there before them and said to the first serving-man he saw, 'Where is the King?' The shabby young fellow smiled and held out his hand. Dr Earle burst into tears.[3]

Sambourn and Parker produced money and suits but no underlinen. Charles and Wilmot paid their bill and removed to the house of another English merchant, while the innkeeper and his wife, unable to believe that they had not been harbouring criminals, searched their rooms. Sambourn and Parker divided Charles's old clothes between them, 'to be kept as holy relics'.[4]

On October 20th Buckingham arrived in Rotterdam and went to see Sir Edward Hyde. His Majesty was secure, he said; 'but whether in France, Flanders or Holland, he cannot or will not tell,' wrote the exasperated Chancellor. At about the same time Henrietta Maria received Charles's letter; with Monsieur, the Duke of York and a number of English courtiers, she set off to meet him. Charles and Wilmot left Rouen and spent the night at Fleury. On the 31st the King was reunited with his French and English relatives just outside Paris. They were accompanied by the Venetian ambassador, who was hardly able to contain his amusement at the sight of the King's appearance. He arrived, Morosini reported, with only two attendants, one gentleman and one valet; as if this were not degraded enough, his dress was 'more calculated to cause laughter than respect'.[5]

When he reached the Louvre, Charles, who had not been able to change his shirt since leaving England, borrowed another from Jermyn. He then asked his mother for some money to buy one. She replied that she had not a sou, and that, if he had meals with her and his brother and sister, he would have to pay for them. Cardinal de Retz, who had supported her in the past and did not wish to do so again, was horrified; he appealed to Gaston d'Orléans to help his nephew. Monsieur replied, 'I can offer him nothing, because a little would not become me, and a great deal would entail too much.' De Retz then borrowed 1,500 pistoles from a friend and gave them to Lord Taaffe, an Irish nobleman, to give to Charles. Taaffe, who had met the King on his way from Rouen, was attending him, for Wilmot had retired to cheap lodgings (a pistole a week) in Paris, so that Taaffe became the King's chamberlain, equerry, cup-bearer and, at times, valet.[6] Their situation was an odd one. During Charles's absence Taaffe had become Lucy Walter's lover and she bore him a daughter. Both were living at the Louvre, much to Henrietta Maria's indignation. But she could not afford to pay Lucy to leave; Taaffe was keeping her and her children; and the Queen Regent and Cardinal Mazarin, both preoccupied by the Fronde Revolution, ignored her complaints of the infamous Mrs Barlow's impertinences.[7] Charles's behaviour was characteristic. He had done with Lucy, but was perfectly willing that she and Taaffe should remain under the same roof as himself, as long as he did not have to pay for her and could keep in touch with their two-year-old son. Already the idea was in his mind of removing the child from the mother as soon as he could afford to do so. Lucy's plan, in so far as it can be guessed at (for her motives were obscure when they were not discreditable), was to win back Charles; in this she was to be partially successful.

Henrietta Maria's rapture at seeing him safe and well and the general rejoicing for his escape kept up Charles's spirits for a day or two; and pride urged him to appear cheerful and optimistic. Then he fell into a depression from which there was little to rouse him. All he had done – the betrayal of his religion, of his father's memory and of his best supporters, all the humiliation and misery – had been for nothing. The troubles in France had so delayed his mother's pension that she was desperate; and anxiety and grief had destroyed such remnants of tact and common sense as she had left. Within a few days of their reunion she was telling Charles what he should do next, not when they were alone, but in circumstances which made it impossible for him to silence her or walk out of the room. She and York listened sympathetically to the recital of his disasters; but when he spoke of the treachery, ineptitude and cowardice of the Scots, she announced that in a combination of Scottish and continental forces lay his only hope of restoration. 'It was rumoured,' said Gaston d'Orléans, on one of these occasions, 'that you were going back there.' 'I had rather have been hanged,' Charles replied, and sank into a silence nothing could break.[8]

His financial situation was such that he could not borrow a hundred pistoles. The apartments he shared with his family were so shabbily furnished that few people visited them, once the amusement of hearing about his adventures was over. Only when the English Royalists were criticized did he rouse himself to speak with passionate gratitude of what they had done for him and what he owed them.[9] This bored his French audiences; those from whom he tried to borrow money did not hesitate to make it clear that he was an unwelcome guest – with the result that Henrietta Maria began, for the third time, to try to arrange his marriage with La Grande Mademoiselle. She combined this scheme with a renewal of her attacks on his faith. When Charles went to the room in which his chaplain, Dr Cosin, read prayers, he found the door locked; Cosin told him that Her Majesty had hidden the key and stopped his allowance.[10] At the King's protests Henrietta Maria promised to pay the chaplain as soon as she could manage it – she could not, at the moment, afford a fire in her rooms, and Princess Henrietta Anne had but one chemise – and the Sunday after Charles's arrival the services began again. Dr Cosin indicated his disapproval of the Queen Mother's actions by his text: 'And Jacob vowed a vow, saying, If God will be with me and keep me in this way that I go, and will give me bread to eat and raiment to put on, so that I come again to my father's house in peace, then shall the Lord be my God.'[11]

Mademoiselle, who was well aware of her aunt's intentions, did not go to meet Charles with the rest of his family, because she had a rash on her face. On the following evening she decided that she must welcome him (after all, the Queen Mother would expect it) no matter how she looked. So without even troubling to have her hair dressed, she appeared in Henrietta Maria's apartments, and was greeted in some agitation. 'You will find my son quite ridiculous,' the poor Queen began. 'When he was escaping his hair was cut short, and his clothes look very odd.'

As she spoke Charles appeared. Mademoiselle was agreeably surprised. 'I found him looking very well and much improved,' she says, 'in spite of his short hair and long whiskers.' (Evidently Charles had not bothered to shave.) Better still, he now spoke excellent French. When she asked about his adventures, he described them at length, and she became absorbed, although she was rather muddled by the uncouth nomenclature of the English towns. 'He got into a boat at London in order to get to a port, where he embarked,' she noted, 'and the captain of the ship recognized him. So he arrived at Dieppe.'[12] (This confusion and Charles's later additions to his story resulted in the belief that he had spent several weeks in London disguised as a washerwoman.)

When Mademoiselle got up to go Charles asked if he might have the honour of escorting her back to the Tuileries. As they walked down the long gallery which then connected the two palaces, his conversation took on a more personal tone. After describing the miserable life he had led in Scotland and remarking that he had been *furieusement ennuyé*, he went on, 'But the loss of the battle was less terrible to me than that of losing hope of returning to France – where I have been so charmed by those about whom I feel tenderly.' Mademoiselle made no reply, and the King continued, 'Shall we not soon be dancing together?' – rather shyly, as if he were afraid of a rebuff. She made an encouraging answer, and he pursued, 'I dare not tell you all that I feel for you. I would rather you thought me indifferent to my misfortunes than weary you by talking of them. I cannot tell anyone else how happy I am to be in France again, and how I long to dance – with you.'

On this strain of gallantry they parted. Mademoiselle was considerably affected, all the more so because, half-way through his narration, Charles's French had failed him; clearly, he was so afraid of offending her that he hardly knew what he was saying; she began to think seriously of this *amant craintif et timide*. As for dancing – she was not sure. Finally she decided that she would wait till her face regained its normal appearance.

Although the rash continued, she found it impossible to refuse to receive Charles. 'Will you not be so obliging,' he asked on his next visit, 'as to send for your musicians? I hear that you have an excellent hand of violinists.' Mademoiselle consented, and as soon as the fiddlers struck up, she and the King took the floor. He danced as well as ever: better, indeed. She forgot all about her rash and his occasional lapses into bad French. Undoubtedly, he was immensely improved; and his misfortunes had given him quite a romantic air.[13] This was enhanced when he bought, or borrowed, a wig, which he wore until his hair had grown to a more becoming length.

In fact, Charles had made up his mind. He must have a great deal of money, immediately. Whatever his feelings of boredom, derision (or perhaps even contempt), he pressed on with the courtship hitherto so negligently pursued. Meanwhile, those who had not seen him during his eighteen months' absence were much struck by what they felt to be the loss of his youthful looks, and the severity of his expression. 'Until he was [over] twenty years old, the figure of his face,' says one, 'was very lovely; but he is ... grown leaner, and now the majesty of his countenance supplies the lines of beauty,' adding that having been very reserved, His Majesty had become rather too free – 'his misfortunes forcing him to communicate himself to all sorts of people ... It is possible,' this loyal observer continues, 'that, in the heats of his youth, he *may* have surrendered to the powerful charms of beauty.'[14]

Poor Mademoiselle, with her rash and her riches! She took to her bed, trying all the cures she could think of, in vain. During the winter of 1651 her timid lover plucked up enough courage to visit her every other day. Soon most of the European Courts were under the impression that he would marry his heiress and become a Catholic within the next few months.

Meanwhile Mademoiselle was increasingly taken with Charles, whose manners she found 'the best in the world, gentle, gallant and polite'.[15] She now formed the habit of giving little parties, which lasted from five to nine o'clock and were frequented by a number of pretty young women. One evening Henrietta Maria, Charles and York appeared unexpectedly – by a strange coincidence, in time for supper. 'And though,' says their hostess, 'I knew my table was quite as good as theirs, I was sorry not to have provided something better.' After supper they played games and danced. Charles then managed to talk privately with Mademoiselle and to increase the warmth of his approach, of which she made a careful analysis. No one had ever fallen in love with her: but she thought she knew what the signs were. While treating her with the greatest deference, Charles did not cease to look at her, and sought her out whenever she gave him the slightest opportunity. Still she was waiting to hear the 'sweet things' he had failed to say two years before. Then came a moment of doubt. Charles said what she *believed* to be sweet things: as she was not quite certain in what these should consist, she consulted some of her other guests as to whether they were the genuine article – and was reassured. (Neither Mademoiselle nor any of her contemporaries has recorded this aspect of Charles's courtship; the text of those long-desired *douceurs* has not survived.) She was the more impressed because, when he was talking to her, his French – 'the language of love' – so improved that one could hardly believe he was English, although in his conversation with others his accent deteriorated.[16]

Charles's progress with Mademoiselle inspired Henrietta Maria to plan an equally profitable alliance for the Duke of York, still the handsomest and best loved of all her children. At eighteen, York made a better impression than Charles at the same age. He seemed more self-confident, partly because his innate stupidity made him invulnerable to snubs; and what one observer described as his 'childish' way of talking and behaving was considered rather attractive than otherwise.[17] Simple, forthright and slow, York was not without spirit and feeling: and his family loyalty was unshakable. He believed whatever he was told and submitted, not only willingly but eagerly, to being organized, thus becoming the prey of anyone who chose to use him. So when his mother announced that she was planning his marriage to an Orléans cousin, Mademoiselle de Longueville, a plain, dumpy heiress, he replied that he would have chosen her even without her fortune. (Throughout a long life of unremitting venery James preferred plain women, perhaps because pretty ones alarmed him.)

Just as Charles's spirits seemed to improve, news came of Jersey's capitulation to the Parliamentary forces. The loss of this last outpost – of the only place where he had been a king in more than name – was the final blow. Charles supported it in grim silence, and made no comment when York said, 'I glory that it held out for two days,'[18] although he found the boy's tactless exuberance almost as taxing as his mother's interference. This was now shown by her sending Charles's former secretary, Long, to Hyde, who was in Antwerp, with instructions not to join his master, for reasons of economy. At the same time Charles, uninformed by his mother of Long's mission, sent Henry Seymour to summon the Chancellor to Paris.[19] Hyde's quandary was solved by his own lack of funds and a severe attack of gout. He therefore put off his reunion with the King till Christmas, contenting himself with a letter of congratulation on his escape which ended with the inevitable lecture. 'God, by subjecting Your Majesty to these dangers, hath instructed you in much knowledge which could not have been purchased but at that price; your own fate, and that of your three kingdoms, depends now on your own virtue.'[20] By virtue, Hyde understood integrity; and he did not like what he heard of Charles's marriage plans; he disliked still more the rumours of his frequenting the beautiful Duchesse de Châtillon, and of that other 'young lady', who had procured a lodging at the Louvre without the Queen Mother's consent. He remained helpless, interchanging pious and melancholy reflections on the late disaster with Ormonde, who was similarly tied in Caen. 'He that for our sins hath covered us with this confusion,' wrote the Marquess, 'is able in a moment to bring greater things … to pass.'[21]

The Louvrian Royalists did not much concern themselves with the possibility of divine help; they were frankly jubilant at the Scots' defeat. It were better His Majesty should not be restored at all than by the Presbyterians. They described Worcester as a 'miscarriage', which would lead to his coming over to their party and relegating Nicholas, Ormonde and Hyde. Charles gave nothing away. All his endeavours seemed set on capturing Mademoiselle.

II

Naturally there was much conjecture about Mademoiselle's reception of the English King's advances, and very soon her friends were taking sides. The Princess Palatine (daughter-in-law of Elizabeth of Bohemia) was all for the marriage, and urged it on Mademoiselle. They were discussing it after Mass in the Tuileries gardens, when Mademoiselle de Choisy joined them and said, 'Mademoiselle ought not to see the King of England so often, it does not look well.' 'That is ridiculous,' the Princess replied. 'She must do as she likes.' Mademoiselle continued to see Charles – and then came a change.[22]

She could no longer shut her eyes to his interest in that lovely and alluring widow, Madame de Châtillon, who now, it was plain, encouraged his advances. 'She thought she might lose him,' says Mademoiselle acidly, 'not realizing that his feelings for me … were based on making a profitable marriage.' How soon Mademoiselle came to this conclusion is not clear; having done so, she did not entirely eliminate the idea of marrying Charles, but began to think how she herself would profit by such an alliance. Meanwhile Charles, apparently under the impression that all was well, continued to court her. He might have had more success if Henrietta Maria, becoming impatient, had not tried to force the issue. 'My son and I,' she told her niece, 'cannot speak of this to Monsieur without your approval. If my son had been more fortunate, he would have done so without asking you, as he believes that you favour him. But as it is a question of his circumstances, he relies on your kindness to speak to Monsieur.' Mademoiselle replied, 'I am sufficiently contented with my lot not to wish to marry. As I have all the wealth and position I need, I might not desire it. But I must consider, and I would like time to think it over.' 'I will give you eight days,' said Henrietta Maria, adding, 'Pray remember, that if you do marry my son, you will still have control of your fortune.' She then rather disingenuously explained that Charles and his entourage would continue to live on their French pensions and such moneys as they received from England. 'You will be more of a queen than you are now,' she concluded, 'and the happiest person in the world, because of the love my son has for you.' As Mademoiselle appeared unresponsive, she went on, 'The German princes have promised to help him. He has a great following in England, and when they see him married to you, that will encourage them. What with that and all the other support, he will soon be restored.'

Mademoiselle made no reply. A week later Charles said to her, 'The Queen my mother longs to see you.' Again she said nothing, and he dropped the subject. Henrietta Maria's next attack was cruder. She began to speak of her niece's secret hope of marrying Louis XIV. (Mademoiselle's eleven years' seniority was not, in her own mind, a disadvantage.) 'Naturally,' she said, 'you would rather be Queen of France than of England. But promise me that if that scheme does not succeed, ours will be brought about.' 'I do not know what you mean,' said Mademoiselle. 'I have not heard it spoken of. But ask Monsieur about it, if you like.' To Henrietta Maria's inquiries, Gaston d'Orléans replied, 'My daughter is at the disposal of the state – and of the King of France.' Mademoiselle was thankful that her position had been made clear, for she was now quite sure that she did not want to marry Charles – at least, not while England was in its present state.

Charles chose to interpret his uncle's attitude differently. He called on Mademoiselle and, drawing her aside, began, 'I am rejoiced at the kind answer Monsieur gave the Queen my mother. Now I can speak to you of my hopes. Hitherto, I have had to leave that to her.' 'And then,' Mademoiselle goes on, 'he said many wonderful things to me.' Having made, as he thought, some effect, Charles continued, 'Now I shall long more than ever to enter into my kingdoms, since I shall share them with you.' 'If you do not enter them soon, you are not likely to regain them,' said Mademoiselle sharply. 'What! Would you wish me to leave you as soon as we are married?' said Charles. Mademoiselle decided to speak out. 'Yes!' she exclaimed. 'Because, if that were so, I should be much more interested in your fortunes than I am now. It pains me to see you dancing the *tricotet* and amusing yourself, when you ought to be there, either risking your head or putting a crown on it. You are not worthy of a crown if you do not want to seize it at the point of the sword, and at the risk of your life – ' and she turned away.[23]

Charles did not trouble to point out that this was exactly what he had done, not once but several times, at the battle of Worcester, to no effect, and that he had come as near to being beheaded as any subject in his dominions. To such as Mademoiselle he never spoke of his exploits except derisively, or to entertain; and not even to Hyde did he describe his efforts to rally his army at the point of the sword which had broken in his hand. Mademoiselle's ideas of chivalry, her obvious but unspoken resentment at his frequentation of the Duchesse de Châtillon, were to him part of his tedious progress towards prosperity. Neither was in love with the other; their marriage, if it did take place, would be like other state marriages; but he was perfectly prepared to go through the motions of gallantry, and continued to do so. He had been too often and too deeply humiliated in matters which really affected him, to be in the least concerned by the rebuffs of this absurd creature. So when she again succumbed to her rash, he visited her regularly. He was equally well prepared for the next attack, which was on the religious issue. Among his French backers were the Duchesse d'Aiguillon and the Comtesse de Fiesque. How delightful it would be, they told Mademoiselle, if she converted him. 'I have the greatest regard for the King of England,' said Madame de Fiesque. 'Make him a Catholic – I beg you to speak to him of it.' When Mademoiselle did so, Charles replied, 'I would do anything for you – but if I am to sacrifice both my conscience and my well-being for your sake, then you must commit yourself to what I have so often spoken to you about.' Mademoiselle did not much like this calling of her bluff, and ignored Madame d'Aiguillon's passionate demands that she should accept Charles on condition that he did what she asked. 'You ought to do it – you are responsible for his soul,' the Duchesse declared.

Still Mademoiselle could not make up her mind. Finally, at one of her theatrical parties, she found herself so confused as to avoid Charles. He reproached her, presumably in the strain of gallantry she had once enjoyed. She replied coldly – and his visits ceased.

Then Jermyn took a hand. He was preceded by M. Goulas, her father's secretary, who told her, 'You will be wretched if you marry the King of England. Rich though you are, you have not enough to pay for the war he must fight – and when he has taken all you have and has not regained his kingdom, you will die of starvation. He might be killed – and then you will be the most miserable of queens, dependent on Monsieur, instead of being able to help him.' Goulas went on to speak of the bad impression made by Charles's pursuit of her fortune. 'It prevents other princes considering you as a possible wife,' he concluded, and went away.

Jermyn now entered and said, 'I believe the matter is settled? M. Goulas is a good advocate.' By this time, Mademoiselle had made up her mind. 'The King of England does me too much honour,' she replied, 'but as he is not in a very good position, I would rather he did not visit me so often. It causes talk, and that is not pleasant.' Jermyn was amazed; surely Mademoiselle was not thinking of refusing his master? He continued to plead; Mademoiselle was firm, and for three weeks Charles did not come near her. Somehow, this did not please her either; but she told herself that of course he must suffer more, as his life was a dull one. She was considerably shaken when Mademoiselle d'Épernon told her she had been wrong to discourage him, adding, 'The King of England visits me often, and we play forfeits – he enjoys that. He seems to get on very well without you.' 'I do not believe you,' said Mademoiselle – but she did not care for the picture thus created. Then she was told that M. de Fiesque was saying that she had fallen desperately in love with the English King: that she pined for him. She became enraged – perhaps all the more because Charles never came to her little parties now.[24] During the rest of that winter they met formally and seldom. In fact, he was considering another approach, which he discussed with Hyde soon after the Chancellor's arrival.

Sir Edward's gout was so severe that he was unable to have more than one long talk with the King, who poured out the story of his sufferings. In that first interview Charles made no attempt to bring out the lighter side of his experiences; he could only speak of his misery and despair. The torture he endured from his lacerated feet had been so great that he longed to die. 'I thought,' he said, 'that I was paying too high a price for my life.' He added that his deepest debt was to the Catholics; without their organization and courage, he must have perished; and presently Wilmot's account emphasized this aspect of their ordeals.[25] Charles did not tell the Chancellor that he had written to the Pope asking for £5,000 as the price of his apostasy and the support of his Catholic subjects – perhaps because Innocent X had rather drily replied that he could lend him nothing, as he did not consider this to be a case of genuine conversion.[26]

A few days later Hyde was better, and he and Ormonde together raised the subject of Charles's marriage to Mademoiselle. They pointed out the obvious disadvantages – her three years' seniority, and the effect his alliance with a Catholic would have on the English Royalists, adding that until he was restored it was pointless to think of any marriage. 'Set your heart on the recovery of England,' urged the Chancellor. 'My heart is set upon nothing else,' replied Charles. 'If I have inclination to this marriage, it is because I believe it will facilitate the other. I look on her fortune as a stock that will be at my disposal, by sale whereof I may raise a good army. If the lady does consent, she will affect nothing that does not advance the recovery of my dominions – which she will quickly understand any unreasonable concessions in religion will never do.'[27]

Hyde and Ormonde were much disturbed by this characteristically specious reasoning: yet Charles did nothing to prevent his mother's and Jermyn's pursuit of the heiress. In other respects he and Henrietta Maria were at odds. Charles told the Chancellor how she had insisted on his paying her for his board, from the very first night of his arrival. Hyde, who had failed to obtain anything from the Spanish (that 'proud, wretched, miserable, senseless people'), could only sympathize and find cheap lodgings for himself in Paris. Old Lord Cottington had died in Madrid; now Ormonde took his place in the Chancellor's affections. They hired rooms together at a pistole a week, and had to 'walk the streets on foot, which was no honourable custom' for persons of their rank in that city.[28]

At Charles's next meeting with Hyde the question of Henrietta Maria's quarrel with Nicholas arose. 'The Queen is in the wrong,' said Charles emphatically. 'If Nicholas were here, I should compose all that well enough.'[29] He then promised the Chancellor that he would abandon the idea of marrying Mademoiselle; still he did not stop the Queen's and Jermyn's manoeuvres: nor did he interfere in their plan of marrying York to Mademoiselle de Longueville, although Hyde told him (perhaps at too much length) that nothing but trouble would come of such alliances. Then Hyde tried to make his peace with the Queen Mother, who resented his coming to Paris and the renewal of his influence over her son. Hyde said bluntly, 'The King should not be entirely governed by Your Majesty,' adding that she expected too much and was being unreasonable. Henrietta Maria received this reproof meekly; she needed the Chancellor's help in getting rid of Lucy. Finally Hyde persuaded Charles to send her away (at whose cost, is not clear) and the young lady withdrew to Holland, where she told the English Royalists that Hyde's spitefulness had caused the breach between her and the King.[30] Meanwhile she tried to keep in touch with him through Dr Cosin, who was persuaded, and told Charles, that she had reformed. Early in 1652 she parted company with Taaffe, perhaps because she counted on regaining her hold over Charles. In this she was not wholly deceived.

On Christmas Day 1651 Charles, York and the English Royalists went publicly to Holy Communion in their chapel at the Louvre, thus strengthening Hyde's insistence that there was no truth in the rumours of his master's conversion. The King and his brother went up to the altar first, by themselves, while Wilmot and Lord Byron held the towel which covered the rails.[31] A few hours later Jane Lane and her brother, who had escaped from England in disguise, were received by Charles, York, Henrietta Maria and the seven-year-old Princess Henrietta Anne. 'Welcome, my life!' Charles exclaimed as he took Jane in his arms. She and Colonel Lane remained in Paris, living from hand to mouth, as did all the other Royalists except Jermyn.[32]

Then suddenly £10,000 arrived from the Emperor of Russia and the King of Poland. This sum was immediately seized by Henrietta Maria in payment of the debts contracted during Charles's absence. At about the same time the long-delayed help from Spain materialized. It consisted of thirty boxes of chocolate, entrusted to Hyde for Charles's personal consumption.[33]

NOTES

1 Montpensier, vol. I, p. 319.
2 Hughes, p. 144; Fea, *The Flight of the King*, p. 13.
3 Hughes, ibid.
4 Ibid.
5 *Cal. S. P. Ven.*, vol. XXVIII, p. 202.
6 Cardinal de Retz, *Mémoires*, p. 373.
7 Clarendon, p. 989.
8 *Cal. D. S. P.*, Nov. 1st, 1651.
9 Ibid.
10 Carte, *A General History of England*, vol. IV, p. 653.
11 Evelyn, p. 311.
12 Montpensier, vol. I, pp. 319–29.
13 Ibid.
14 Sir Samuel Tuke, *A Character of Charles II*, p. 4.
15 Montpensier, ibid.
16 Ibid.
17 *Cal. D. S. P.*, ibid.
18 Ibid.
19 Clarendon, p. 772.
20 *Cal. Clar. S. P.*, vol. II, p. 110.
21 *Nicholas Papers*, vol. I, p. 276.
22 Montpensier, ibid.
23 Ibid.
24 Ibid.
25 Clarendon, p. 773.
26 Gardiner, *Commonwealth*, vol. II, p. 158.
27 Clarendon, pp. 775–84.
28 Ibid.
29 Op. cit., p. 989.
30 Fea, *King Monmouth*, p. 7.
31 Evelyn, p. 312.
32 F. Eglesfield, *Monarchy Revived*, p. 22.
33 *Cal. Clar. S. P.*, vol. II, p. 114.

CHAPTER SIX

DIPLOMACY AND FINANCE

I

CHARLES and his Court remained in or near Paris from October 1651 until July 1654. Although his circumstances were deplorable and his prospects worse than at any time since the exile, the King enjoyed certain amenities. One was his relationship with Madame de Châtillon, another his popularity with the younger French courtiers of both sexes, which resulted in his being paid for by those who desired his company; thus he could hunt, play tennis and billiards and go to parties where dancing, concerts, a good table and the performance of plays by professionals were provided.

So Charles made it his business to be the perfect guest; his wit developed, his adventures gained in the telling and he was looked on as an asset – until he tried to borrow money. Very soon he learned to confine this side of his activities to his political correspondence, which now became very extensive. Yet Hyde deplored his master's inability to apply himself. It does not seem to have occurred to the Chancellor that a penniless exile in his twenty-second year would naturally seek pleasure when and where he could find it, and that to keep regular hours for interviews and letter-writing had not been part of the King's training. At this time, if there was work to be done, Charles did it, and thoroughly. A letter of some seven pages to Goring, now Earl of Norwich and his agent in the Low Countries, shows an industry and grasp of detail which Hyde himself might not have achieved at the same age.

This letter, written in February 1652 (and later seized by a Cromwellian spy), consisted of fourteen numbered items. The Irish Royalists, the English Navy, the Dutch interests and the King's plans for contact with the Emperors of Germany and Austria and a number of Electoral Princes – all were succinctly treated, as was the minor issue of his sister Mary's quarrels with her mother-in-law about precedence, money and the upbringing of the infant William of Orange. While refusing to interfere personally in these disputes, Charles advised Mary to adopt a more conciliatory attitude towards the Princess Dowager, but assured her that he would support 'the least title of her right', and added that he hoped she would 'revolve her passions so ... as ... to come to a good understanding'.[1]

It was perhaps easier to compose such epistles as these than to deal with the recriminations which followed Henrietta Maria's seizure of the Russo-Polish loan. How was it, Hyde repeatedly asked, that he, Wilmot, Ormonde and the other Royalists were often unable to afford a meal or a fire, and that His Majesty could not borrow twenty pistoles (although he was expected to provide for the Duke of York and his entourage) when Jermyn 'kept an excellent table for those who courted him', and Dr Goffe had managed to collect £800?[2] Charles tolerated Jermyn's hold over Henrietta Maria (it was rumoured that they had been, or were about to be, secretly married) and recognized the partial justice of her claim to the £10,000; for he knew that she spent next to nothing on herself and the Princess Henrietta Anne, and that she was bent on paying the debts which had accumulated since her flight from England in 1644; only so could she maintain his dignity and her own reputation. Hyde refused to admit the virtue of the Queen Mother's intentions. Meanwhile, she and Charles seem to have agreed that their only hope lay in the payment of their French pensions, now long overdue. Here again, the outlook was depressing. The recrudescence of the civil war – this stage was known as the Second Fronde – had resulted in the flight from Paris, and thus from the government, of Louis XIV, Anne of Austria and Cardinal Mazarin. So there was no one left to authorize the payment of this debt.

The effect on Charles of his experiences in the final period of the Fronde was deep and lasting; his memories of it obsessed him in much the same way as did those of his adventures after the battle of Worcester, in spite of the fact that his share in this useless struggle was that of a spectator, and that he was at no time in any real danger. What chiefly impressed him was the futility of the whole affair. When he said that 'government [is] a much safer and easier thing where the authority is believed infallible and submission of the people implicit',[3] he was thinking not only of his own country, but of France, where it produced a stricter dictatorship which in its turn was followed by monarchical absolutism.

The nature of the Fronde is symbolized by its being called after the Parisian street-arabs' favourite game – that of collecting into a gang in order to stone the passers-by and then running away. In 1649, when a section of the French nobility rose in an attempt to destroy Mazarin's regime, it was claimed that this was their version of the English Civil War. The comparison was absurd. In France, no principles and no constructive policies emerged, and no pattern was discernible. The Frondeurs took arms, revolted, changed sides, disappeared, came back, rallied their forces, deserted, changed sides again, betrayed one another – and were ignominiously defeated by Mazarin and the Queen Regent after four years in which the French people were the principal victims. Slaughter, famine and disease so increased the misery of their lives that two years before the war came to an end they would have subscribed to any tyranny which brought them peace. Charles, its victim in a different sense, shared this point of view. He did not care who won, as long as he got his pension, and with it some hope of regaining his kingdom.

In the first weeks of 1652 this hope was so remote that he decided to make one more attempt to marry La Grande Mademoiselle, who with her vacillating and treacherous father was about to ally herself with the Prince de Condé and the other rebellious nobles. Presumably Charles did not know of the mischief made between them; he might have cleared it up by a judicious application of *douceurs*, if Mademoiselle had not been told of Jermyn's remarks about the disposal of her fortune. Once the marriage contract was signed, he announced to a group of courtiers, 'we shall cut down her household and sell her properties'.

This proposed attack on what she cared for most in the world appalled and terrified Mademoiselle. She decided that, having definitely refused Charles, she must now prevent the Duke of York from marrying Mademoiselle de Longueville, and set about it in her usual downright fashion. She received Charles and his mother together, and told them, 'This marriage will not benefit you. Fifty thousand crowns is not enough to support the Duke of York.' A few days later Jermyn told Charles and Henrietta Maria that there was now no hope of Mademoiselle marrying His Majesty. Charles took the news philosophically; Henrietta Maria visited Mademoiselle and overwhelmed her with the bitterest reproaches. This scene was interrupted by Charles, who indicated his indifference to Mademoiselle's rebuff by accepting the chair with arms offered him, according to custom, by his hostess. Hitherto, he had courteously waved aside this tribute to his rank, and seated himself opposite her, on a stool. Now – there he was, beside her, on a level! She maintained her poise and Charles his sardonic impassivity, until the time came for him to leave. Then her resentment burst forth, and she decided to have nothing more to do with him. 'He thought he was causing me great humiliation,' was her final comment, 'but he did nothing of the kind.' A few weeks later she left Paris, in armour, *à la Jeanne d'Arc*, to defend Orléans against the Royalist troops, while the Prince de Condé, having allied himself with the Spaniards, entered Paris on behalf of the Frondeurs.[4]

By the middle of April most of northern France was in a state of war. The Duke of York, passionately anxious to prove himself, begged his mother and brother to let him fight for the French Royalists against the Spanish and the Frondeurs. He had been urged to volunteer – and thus to involve the English Royalists against their potential allies – by his friend and ruler, Sir John Berkeley. This nobleman, who had disgraced himself in the Civil War, was now planning to better his fortunes by setting up the Duke against the King and Hyde, and once more splitting Charles's Council. 'It will be to your honour,' he said to the Duke, 'to put yourself into action.' Having renewed the Queen Mother's plan for marrying York to Mademoiselle de Longueville, Berkeley then suggested that Mazarin, recently returned from abroad, should be consulted about the military issue. The Cardinal gave his approval, subject to Charles's permission.[5]

Although Mazarin had said, 'The Duke is now of an age to try his *métier*,' Charles, Henrietta Maria and Hyde agreed that York ought not to risk his life. The young man would have borne the disappointment without complaint (his loyalty to Charles and his sense of the proprieties forbade grumbling) if Berkeley had not told him that Hyde alone was responsible for this decision. As York believed everything Berkeley chose to tell him, his bitterness against the Chancellor so disrupted the Council that a new one was formed. To please his mother, Charles elected Jermyn; he then mollified Hyde by choosing Ormonde, and made up to Wilmot for refusing him an earldom by giving him a place.

By this time Berkeley had persuaded Henrietta Maria that he ought to be given the post made vacant by Cottington's death, that of Master of the King's Wards, at this time merely honorary; before the exile it had been extremely lucrative. When the Queen put forward Berkeley's application Charles said, 'He has no manner of pretence, and is not fit for it.' Berkeley then approached Hyde, on the grounds that Charles I had promised him the post. 'Do not ask the King for it,' said Hyde; but Berkeley, who knew that Charles was in the next room, went in to him and said indignantly, 'Will not Your Majesty make good the promise your father made?' After some hedging, Charles said 'I cannot,' and the enraged nobleman left him to abuse the Chancellor.[6]

This scene was followed by the first meeting of the new Council, which took place at eight in the morning and was presided over by Charles, York, Henrietta Maria and Hyde. When the question of the Duke's military service was raised Charles asked everyone to express their views, beginning with York, who correctly replied, 'I ask nothing but what becomes me.' Henrietta Maria and the lords remained silent. Charles then turned to Hyde, who said, 'I cannot deliver my opinion until I hear what others think.' Urged to open the debate, he spoke, at enormous length, against York's joining the French army, but concluded, 'His Highness ought now to make his own decisions.'

It then became clear that all the lords were backing York, who jubilantly prepared to leave. Before he did so Berkeley made a final attempt to arrange his marriage with Mademoiselle de Longueville ('You will do His Majesty great service by it,' he told the Duke), but York would not act without his mother's and brother's approval. Henrietta Maria and Hyde agreed that York should not be married before Charles, and the Duke joined Turenne, on whose staff he remained for four years.[7]

His service with the French Royalists was cleverly exploited by Jermyn, who went to interview Anne of Austria and Louis XIV at St Germain to beg for an allowance. The fourteen-year-old Louis, who had now attained his majority, was anxious to help – generous gestures appealed to him – and ordered the Treasury to give Charles 6,000 livres a month. As this amounted to nearly £6,000 a year, his Court should have become not only solvent but comfortably off; the debts were such that the first instalment was immediately swallowed up. Charles himself received nothing, and continued to be poorly dressed and unable to pay his entourage.[8]

Meanwhile Buckingham, who had been unable to afford the journey to Paris, was causing trouble at the Hague, where he was paying great attention to Mary of Orange; he proposed marriage to her without asking Charles's permission. Very properly, she refused him; but she liked his company, and he remained in the Netherlands, where he set in hand various schemes for Charles's restoration. When news reached Henrietta Maria of Villiers's advances to the Princess, she exclaimed, 'If I thought it were possible for my daughter to have so base a thought, I would tear her to pieces with my own hands,'[9] and was reassured by Hyde. 'The King abhors it and will take no notice of it,' he told Nicholas, adding, rather too optimistically, that His Majesty had never been taken in by Buckingham who, although 'accounted a wit', had no influence.

A few weeks later, when it was rumoured that Villiers was 'making his composition [with Parliament] ... at a high price',[10] he wrote to Charles to say that he had established contact with the great Leveller, John Lilburne, formerly a fanatical anti-Royalist and now, although exiled and broken, one of Cromwell's most dangerous enemies.

In some ways Lilburne represented all that was best in English politics;

but his ideas were so much in advance of his age as to make him a permanently persecuted rebel. His refusal to compromise or to hold his tongue about the injustices of the Government eventually destroyed his power over the army, and now, after a series of cruel punishments, his health was giving way. Although his spirit was high and his aims combined such vision and common sense as amounted to genius, he was strangely credulous. His ideas of government – which were what would now be called democratic and which, with some modifications, have nearly all been put into practice – were accepted with enthusiasm by Buckingham, who began to see himself as a demagogic leader in a reformed England. After several secret meetings in taverns Buckingham put forward Lilburne's scheme for a restoration, believing, quite mistakenly, that it would appeal to the bulk of the English people. Lilburne said that he could easily make Charles King of England, on condition that Parliament had control of the armed forces and all the fortifications. Charles, who never diverged from his view that 'a king who might be checked, or have his ministers called to account by Parliament is but a king in name',[11] mentally relegated both Lilburne and Buckingham. Not all his Councillors agreed with him, and furious quarrels ensued between those who were disgusted by Lilburne's absurd impertinence and those who thought that he might be used. Then, suddenly, Charles's amazing patience gave way. His 'singular and exemplary moderation' yielded to violence; when papers of which he did not approve were submitted for his signature, he threw them on the ground and marched out of the room.[12] Only with his Bablon, the exquisite de Châtillon, could he find happiness. He was in love with her; and presently Hyde was told – not by Charles himself – that he was thinking of marrying her, and perhaps even settling down in France.

Madame de Châtillon was much taken with the exiled King, and not unwilling to support him financially; but her first consideration was, naturally, precedence. If she married him, would she be given a chair with arms and allowed to walk out of the room before La Grande Mademoiselle and the two Queens? As soon as she gathered that this promotion was doubtful, she continued to entertain Charles on a romantic, *amour courtois* basis. When she became his mistress is uncertain: their relationship lasted for several years. When she heard how the King of England was consoling himself, Mademoiselle refused to believe a word of the story. True, he had sunk very low; but he could not possibly be in love with, or wish to marry, Madame de Châtillon, rich and beautiful though she was, for she had not a drop of royal blood in her veins.[13]

In April 1652 Louis XIV asked Charles to mediate between the French Royalists and the Frondeurs. He could not refuse: but his intervention had no effect, except to make him very unpopular with the French people. So it became clear that to remain in France was inadvisable. Charles wanted to join Mary of Orange: but he could not raise enough money for the journey. Nicholas reported that the Dutch would not help him unless he became a Presbyterian, and seemed on the point of advising him to do so. 'I wish,' he wrote to Hyde, 'that he had some confidant among these States.'[14]

Any suggestion that Charles should abandon his faith threw the Chancellor into a frenzy. 'All men of honour and worth will fall from him,' he told Nicholas, adding that 'all lovers of monarchy' (he meant the anti-Louvrian party, headed by himself and Ormonde) could at least rejoice in His Majesty's dismissal of Hobbes, 'that father of atheists... [who] would have done his best to poison the King's Court'.

This triumph was momentary. Having promised the Chancellor that he would not make Will Crofts, a 'vain and vicious' young man, his gentleman of the bedchamber, the King gave him the position a few days later. 'If I had known ... that he would suffer himself to be prevailed upon ... I would have left his service ... He is following out the worst and weakest policies of his father,' Hyde lamented.[15]

Suddenly Charles remembered the crown jewels of Scotland, which had been deposited at Dunottar Castle. He wrote to the Governor, a Royalist, to send them, and received no answer.[16] Then the Governor of Paris told him that he and Henrietta Maria must leave the Louvre for the Palais Cardinal, as the larger palace was to be made ready for Louis XIV. This move cost Charles £100, which he borrowed from Mary of Orange; his clothes were more disreputable than ever, his servants unpaid, and he was reduced to one meal a day.[17] Now it seemed as if he must placate the Dutch, and Jermyn suggested that he might give the impression of being sympathetic to some form of dissent by going to the Huguenot services at Charenton. Henrietta Maria agreed, on the grounds that this would begin the break with the Church of England and facilitate Charles's conversion to her faith. 'Your only hope,' she told him, 'is with the Catholic powers.' 'It is a thing that ought, in policy and discretion, to be done,' Jermyn went on. 'I will never go to Charenton,' said Charles, and spoke with violent bitterness of his treatment by the Scots Covenanters. As Jermyn continued to plead Hyde joined them, and, 'with equal passion', implored His

Majesty not to listen to the Lord Treasurer. Charles endured their diatribes 'with patience and attention', but when Hyde said that he should have nothing to do with the Scots, he replied, 'If I reject them, I can no longer consider Scotland as my kingdom. Whom then can I trust?' and pointed out that the Scottish Royalists were still able to rise. He added that he meant to employ one of the most redoubtable of these, General Middleton, who, having been wounded and captured at Worcester, had now escaped from the Tower and was in Paris. 'Middleton,' he told Hyde, 'is a man of honour and ingenuity. Deal cheerfully with him,' he went on, as the Chancellor looked disapproving. A few weeks later Middleton left for the Highlands.[18]

Then at last the King's hopes rose. War was declared between England and Holland. After a brief conference with Ormonde and Hyde, Charles offered his services to the Dutch through Boreel, their ambassador in Paris. Some representatives of the States General wanted to accept them; but after a long debate his offer was rejected on the grounds that his share in their victories would restore the powers of the Orange-Nassaus, as represented by the Princess Mary and her infant son.[19] So once more Charles was condemned to inactivity, shut up in the Palais Cardinal, while Frondeurs and monarchists fought in and round the city. Again Louis XIV asked him to intervene, and he went to the rendezvous, where 'he found both armies drawn up ... within cannon shot of each other'.[20] This time his efforts were successful, and the rival generals – Turenne and the Duke of Lorraine, who had temporarily allied himself with the Frondeurs – signed a treaty. But war continued inside Paris – by this time Mademoiselle was defending the Bastille against the monarchists – and Charles was blamed. The mob stormed the Louvre and the Palais Cardinal. The King with his mother and little sister left for St Germain, escorted by Royalist troops, while the furious people stoned their coach. Charles rode beside it, his hand on the door, his pistol cocked. He and his family reached St Germain in pouring rain at midnight on July 13th, where they remained for two months. Here they were joined by Cardinal Mazarin (who gave a party for Charles and Louis XIV), Sagredo, the newly appointed Venetian ambassador, and a Cromwellian spy.[21]

At such gatherings as those given by Mazarin Charles's height and grace of bearing must have drawn attention to the shabbiness of his clothes, quite apart from the fact that he was surrounded by persons whose silks and velvets were encrusted with jewels and that he was waited on by glittering lackeys, dragonfly pages and gorgeous major-domos. He had developed, and continued to sustain, an apparent indifference to this bitter contrast, and seemed so unashamed of his status as a pensioner and a poor relation that he gave the effect of caring for nothing but amusement. Even those who worked with him every day would recall, long after the exile, that 'he never seemed to lay anything to heart ... and seemed to be as serene under the loss of a crown as the greatest philosopher'.[22]

As is often the case with those who conceal their deeper feelings from their intimates, Charles sometimes spoke freely of them to acquaintances. Sagredo, after several conversations about the 'intolerable' behaviour of the King's drunken and insolent representative in Venice, was impressed against his will by Charles's resolution. 'He will never shrink from any enterprise, however hazardous ... ' he told the Senate, 'but will display the courage ... he has always shown.'[23] And the spy whose reports from France reached the Protector through another in Breda, who in his turn conveyed them to a third agent in Coney Court, Gray's Inn ('if a loose board be taken up under the window, there will be found the instructions'),[23] saw Charles Stuart more clearly than did his family, his tosspot companions or the older Cavaliers. 'All those will be on ticklish terms if they think to use this young man as they did his father,' he concluded, 'for though in appearance he is gentle, familiar and easy, yet he will not be gourmanded [overcome] and governed by violent humours from others.'[25]

Historical retrospection completes and lights up Charles's development during his twenty-second and twenty-third years. He had not yet become entirely cynical, cold-hearted or embittered; nor had he quite reached the stage when he most easily forgot his troubles in the pleasures of the alcove. (Were they always pleasures? Like most Don Juans, he came to dislike and despise women long before they ceased to pine for him.) At this time he was infatuated with de Châtillon, and perhaps her lover; he was trying to placate Lucy Walter, to whom he sent forty pistoles in August 1652 in reply to some unrecorded threat or plea; but his main energies, concealed beneath what his contemporaries described as 'an easy and affable exterior',[26] were bent on his restoration. In this resolve he did not waver, although he was now beginning to perfect the elaborately deceitful technique so much deplored by Hyde.

In fact, Hyde's influence was far more detrimental than that of Charles's most dissipated and irresponsible hangers-on. The Chancellor's sarcasms, his criticisms, his insistence that he himself was not, and never could be, in the wrong (why did others persecute and misunderstand him?), his determination to force the King into the mould of a high-minded, High Church, incorruptible ruler, drove Charles, who was really fond of him, into a series of petty evasions and broken promises. The King's constant use of the word 'cheerfully' in his interviews with the man he most relied on, explains his attitude. If, in addition to all the disappointments and degradations, Charles was met by frowns, disapproval and censure, then there was nothing for it but escape, however momentary. If Hyde, Ormonde and Nicholas had been able to laugh at misfortune once in a while – the Chancellor did so in his letters but never in his conversation – their young master might have come a little nearer to their impossible ideal of a king. As it was, when more bad news came, only Charles affected the indifference which was his best defence. He shrank from and was probably embarrassed by Hyde's solemnities, his pious adjurations and, above all, his memories of His late martyred Majesty's golden age – that halcyon time, which Van Dyck's ecstatic and reverent vision has recorded for our wondering delight; when, according to the Chancellor's talk with Charles (his *History* is brilliantly realistic), no one lied or cheated or fornicated or got tipsy – until those evil rogues took it into their heads to rebel against the sacred person of the Lord's Anointed.

It was not in Charles II's nature to snub, or reprove, or even interrupt his best, most loving and most faithful servant. Gratitude, respect and pity forbade an explosion which might have improved their relationship. The King slid away – to hunt, to dance, to make love – rather than endure that ceaselessly lecturing voice, the sight of that flushed, pouting, unhappy face and the stout, awkward body. As the months went by and the outlook became blacker, and the complications – financial, political, religious – multiplied, the King began to resort more often to distractions with those who shared his tastes, but who were as unaware as was Hyde of what His Majesty was thinking while he lounged and laughed and drank and made himself so agreeable. In Paris, the young and pretty women, the elegant and wealthy nobles, did not care whether he regained his crown or not, so long as he was gallant and gay, and showed proper concern for the newest dances, songs and fashions. Charles's situation is best summed up by the Cavalier drinking song,

> Come, pass about the bowl to me,
> A health to our distressèd King,
> Though we're in hold, let cups go free –
> Birds in a cage may freely sing.[27]

Charles could always sing – he had to, often, for his supper. Sometimes that was all that remained to him.

NOTES

1 *Cal. D. S. P.*, Feb. 15th, 1652.
2 Clarendon, pp. 775–84.
3 Burnet, *History*, vol. I, p. 183.
4 Montpensier, vol. I, pp. 331–3.
5 Clarendon, ibid.
6 Ibid.
7 Ibid.
8 *Cal. Clar. S. P.*, vol. III, p. 51.
9 *Nicholas Papers*, vol. I, p. 284.
10 Ibid.
11 Burnet, ibid.
12 *Fairfax Correspondence*, vol. II, p. 127.
13 Montpensier, ibid.
14 *Nicholas Papers*, vol. I, p. 277.
15 Op. cit., pp. 295, 299, 304.
16 *Cal. Clar. S. P.*, vol. III, pp. 56, 61.
17 Op. cit., p. 73.
18 Clarendon, ibid.
19 Ibid.
20 Ibid.
21 *Cal. S. P. Ven.*, vol. XXVIII, p. 261.
22 Burnet, *History*, vol. II, p. 478.
23 *Cal. S. P. Ven.*, vol. XXVIII, pp. 250, 268.
24 *Portland MSS* (H.M.C.), vol. I, p. 581.
25 Gardiner, *Commonwealth*, vol. III, p. 84.
26 Tuke, p. 4.
27 M. Pickel, *Charles I as Patron of Poetry and Drama*, p. 90.

CHAPTER SEVEN

DETERIORATION AND DISPUTE

I

SHORTLY after Charles and Henrietta Maria returned to Paris Cardinal de Retz told the King that the inefficiency of his Council was harming his reputation in all the Courts of Europe. As the Cardinal was one of the few persons who had been kind to him since his escape, Charles took the warning seriously enough to consult with Hyde. 'I am exceedingly troubled,' he said. 'I will speak an hour with you on the subject, if you will give me time,' the Chancellor replied, and proceeded to do so.[1]

No reform was effected, partly because Henrietta Maria's attitude made this impossible. The obvious solution was to send for Nicholas from the Hague; then he, Ormonde and Hyde could have formed an incorruptible and hard-working trio. As the Queen Mother's dislike of Nicholas was only equalled by her jealousy of Hyde, Nicholas's arrival would have increased the disputes between himself and the Louvrian party, thus making further trouble for Charles and the Chancellor; and neither they nor Nicholas could afford to pay for his journey or his keep in Paris. Nicholas was deeply hurt by this rejection – as the King's principal Secretary of State, his place was on the Council – but he complained only of his poverty to Hyde, who replied that his own 'beggary [was] extreme, unheard of and intolerable'. During the bitter winter of 1652 the Chancellor had to borrow money, to fetch his letters from the post and to buy ink and paper. Very soon, he would not be able to do that; his landlady was ruined, and his room was so cold that sometimes he could not hold a pen.[2] The more fortunate Ormonde, who was very popular with the French nobility, economized by staying with a friend outside Paris. When he left, he had but ten pistoles with which to tip the valets. His host called for his horse and pursued him in order to return the money, saying indignantly, 'You are treating my house as an inn, I can very well pay for my servants myself.'[3]

The financial situation was now so desperate that Charles suggested selling the Scilly Islands to the Dutch. This offer did not interest them; they said they would help him if he attacked England by sea, but that plan fell through for lack of funds. Again the King was reduced to an aimless inactivity, which was made more painful by Mazarin's sending an ambassador to Cromwell. Charles, for once making no secret of his distress, tried, without success, to persuade Mazarin not to embark on what promised to be an alliance.[4]

So his circumstances appeared in a worse state than ever before. Yet the reports from England made it clear that dissatisfaction with the Cromwellian regime was widespread and the King's return much desired. (This information came from some letters of the Parliamentary spy in Breda, which were seized by Charles's agents.) Still, no rising could be organized, much less carried out, without money; and now Cromwell's power was such that few countries cared to support Charles openly or on a large scale. The usual policy was to encourage him just enough to curb Cromwell, while making tentative advances to the English Parliament. These cat-and-mouse tactics so dispirited Charles that he decided to leave France; once more, penury bound him to the treadmill of the Palais Cardinal.

He now confided in de Retz, who said, 'Has Your Majesty made any attempt to draw assistance from the Pope? Do you think anything may be drawn that way to your advantage?' '*You* are better able to judge,' said the King with some bitterness, 'whether the Pope is liable to do anything for a man of my faith.' 'I have no thought of speaking of Your Majesty's faith,' said de Retz, smiling. 'It becomes me, as a Cardinal, to wish Your Majesty a Catholic for the saving of your soul – but I must declare, that if you do change your religion, you will never be restored to your kingdoms. If Your Majesty will give me leave, and trust to my discretion, I will write in such a manner to some of my friends in my own name.' 'I will leave it to your own wisdom,' said Charles. De Retz then asked for detailed information about the King's circumstances, and it was agreed that Charles and Hyde should produce a statement in the form of a letter, upon which the Cardinal would base his campaign on the King's behalf.[5]

Shortly after receiving this document de Retz went to see Anne of Austria at the Louvre and was arrested, on the grounds that his activities during the Fronde had shown him to be a traitor to the state. All his papers were seized, and Charles's letter was handed over to the Queen, who showed it to his mother. When Henrietta Maria saw that he had asked Innocent X for help without consulting her, she became enraged; this was another example of Hyde's interference in what should have been her responsibility. She and her sister-in-law commented mockingly and, it seems, indiscreetly, on Charles's mistakes in French. Henrietta Maria then rated him for his secretiveness. When he evaded her, she produced his letter to de Retz.

Charles was very angry. He went at once to his aunt and told her that she had behaved with discourtesy and disrespect. She had no right either to read or to pass on his private correspondence, or, he added, to encourage his mother's enmity to the Chancellor.

Anne of Austria was completely taken aback and rather alarmed. She had never seen her easy-going nephew in this mood. During the next few weeks she was considerate and kind; but both she and Henrietta Maria were still in alliance against Hyde (was not he responsible for Charles's heresy?) and neither would receive him. When Henrietta Maria declared that all her disputes with Charles were engendered by Hyde, Anne of Austria exclaimed indignantly, 'How should any man dare to interpose himself between mother and son?'

Soon after Queen Anne made up her quarrel with her nephew, she and Louis XIV issued invitations for a party, at which a masque was to be performed. Charles said, 'I like this very well,' and persuaded Hyde, rather against his will, to accompany himself and Ormonde to the Louvre.

When he entered, Charles took care that Hyde and Ormonde should sit in the chairs reserved for the most privileged courtiers, just behind those of the royal party. Anne of Austria was displeased; she had not meant the Chancellor to be included in her invitation to her nephew's entourage. She turned to Charles, and said coldly and distinctly, 'Who is that fat man sitting next to the Marquess of Ormonde?' 'Oh,' Charles replied, very loudly indeed, 'that is the naughty man, who does all the mischief, and sets me against my mother.'

Anne of Austria, completely silenced, grew very red. Hyde's round face was empurpled. All the courtiers, French and English, were in fits of laughter. Suddenly Queen Anne – 'a very worthy lady,' says Hyde kindly – saw the absurdity of the situation, and joined in the laugh. Thereafter her attitude towards the Chancellor was reserved but not discourteous, much to his relief.[6] While desiring to be on good terms with everyone, Hyde continued to offend and upset persons of whose conduct he did not approve: and how could he approve of those who did not share his views?

In February 1653 Charles made another effort to ally himself with the Dutch against his enemies by asking them for the command of a ship in order to 'engage my own person ... and either by God's blessing prevail ... or perish in the attempt'. When his offer was ignored, he suggested selling them the Orkneys; this letter was not answered, and in an outburst of wounded pride the King told Sagredo that he would have nothing more to do with the States General. 'If I join them,' he said, 'they might sell me, as the Scots did my father.'[7]

Then came better news. The Scots proclaimed Charles in Edinburgh and other cities; the ghost of the martyred King appeared in Whitehall, and Cromwell's coach was stoned by the Londoners. The Protector retaliated by asking Mazarin not to 'harbour' Charles Stuart, and the Cardinal suggested to the King that he would be wise to leave – why did he not go to one of the German principalities? Charles replied that he would go if his expenses were paid, and nothing more was said. In fact, Mazarin preferred to keep him in France, as a weapon against Cromwell.

The English government's difficulties were now further complicated by an increase of Royalist feeling concentrated on the twelve-year-old Duke of Gloucester. Mr Harry, as everyone called him (he was not allowed his title), was reported to be intelligent, serious and adaptable; he might be a better candidate for the throne than the King, who was suspected of apostasy. Cromwell therefore decided to get rid of Gloucester, and with his tutor, Mr Lovell, he was dispatched to Holland, £500 being provided for his maintenance.[8]

This news threw his mother into a frenzy of longing for the son she had not seen since his third year. Mary of Orange was equally anxious to keep him with her; and in this she was supported by Charles and all the Council. To pay for Henry and his tutor would be another problem; and they realized that as soon as he and his mother were reunited she would begin to convert him– indeed, she and Anne of Austria were planning to make him a cardinal. 'Thus,' their confessors pointed out, 'Henry IX will rebuild what Henry VIII has destroyed.' Hyde wrote to Nicholas in great anxiety – the Duke must stay in Holland. Nicholas replied, 'Would you believe it? The Presbyterians, as well as the Catholics, have designs on that sweet Duke!'[9]

Henrietta Maria then went to Charles and solemnly gave him her word that she would not proselytize Gloucester – if she could but see him! The King hesitated, prevaricated, and seemed to give his consent; then he wrote to his sister, telling her to keep Gloucester and Lovell at the Hague, adding that the tutor could be relied on to prevent any attempts made on the boy's faith. The Duke remained with his sister from the beginning of March to the end of May 1653, while his mother continued to plead for him to join her. Charles exercised his usual patience; sometimes it wore rather thin, and then he took refuge in what Hyde condemned as 'pleasure'. To a friend in England the King wrote, 'Take heed of melancholique, I keep myself from it as well as I can, and so must you.'[10] Charles practised this remedy so consistently as to evoke a gloomy report from Hyde, who complained to Nicholas that on Fridays (post day) His Majesty was seldom to be found; his excuses were most ingenious. 'That day of late hath been spent otherwise – *by accident*,' the Chancellor remarked.

Hyde's resentment increased when he found that he had to deal with Sir Edward Walker, Garter King-at-Arms, who was living at the Hague. Sir Edward, having several times risked his life in the Royalist cause, endured hardship and discomfort without complaint; for he was a dedicated man, in the sense that his function as an expert on heraldry and ceremonial absorbed him to the exclusion of everything else. For some time he had been inactive owing to the King's preoccupation with international politics, a subject Sir Edward regarded as an appendage to two vital and pressing issues: the design for the Duke of Gloucester's arms, and the bestowal of the Garter on him, the Prince of Orange and the Elector of Brandenburg.

As soon as he obtained Charles's permission to proceed with these highly complicated and urgent matters, Sir Edward embarked on an immense series of letters, with which the King would have nothing to do. 'He is a very foolish fellow – I have no mind to be troubled with him,' said His Majesty in his casual yet authoritative manner, and so the Chancellor, who described Walker as a correspondent 'not to be endured',[11] had first to answer his proposals for His Royal Highness's heraldic device, passed on by Nicholas.

As Sir Edward got into his stride, he rejected the customs of Edward III, Edward IV and Henry VIII as not sufficiently distinctive for the young Duke. Labels argent, labels ermine, roses gules, dragons, antelopes, greyhounds, bulls and white harts crowded into the picture (could His Majesty immediately study and approve these suggestions?), only to be superseded by the intoxicating prospect of the *written* investment of the Elector. This honour had not, in Sir Edward's experience, been bestowed by correspondence. Still, there were quantities of precedents, and he submitted a selection. 'May it not induce the Elector,' he wrote, 'to place a higher value on His Majesty's favour, if this letter be fairly written in parchment and have the Great Seal by a silk label affixed? ... Would not His Majesty's letter be more properly written in Latin than in French? I desire as speedy and positive directions as may be.'[12]

His next letter, one of enormous length, contained the text of the speech he was going to make when investing William of Orange, then in his third year, and an outline of the ceremonial entailed. When Hyde answered these inquiries briefly, Sir Edward pursued him with long and involved accusations of neglect. He was slighted: nobody heeded him. To exist on one meal a day in the humblest tavern – to be shabby, cold and in debt – did not trouble the poor gentleman in the least: but that His Majesty and the Chancellor should not immerse themselves in essentials – medieval symbolism for Brandenburg, tactful references to Anglo-Dutch ties for the little Prince – was not to be borne. (A few months later, when Charles sent Lord Craven a Garter costing only six pistoles, of which even Hyde was ashamed, Sir Edward was not told; his loyalty might have been shaken by the disgrace.)

When these demands had been satisfied, it became clear that something more must be done for Lord Wilmot, who was given the earldom of Rochester and sent on a mission to Ratisbon, where he did not acquit himself very well. He took to drinking, and shortly after his arrival formed the habit of thrusting all letters, unopened, into his pocket, where they remained – as he did in Ratisbon, for there was no money to pay for his removal.

By the beginning of April 1653 Henrietta Maria's demands for Gloucester had become so pathetically insistent that Charles gave in, merely stipulating that he should come to her (she and the Princess Henrietta Anne were now living in the convent she had founded at Chaillot) for a short visit, and then return to the Hague. Gloucester arrived on May 23rd, was met just outside Paris by his mother and brother and installed at St Germain.

Hyde's conventional tribute of 'a prince of extraordinary hopes' is an inadequate summing-up of a boy not yet thirteen, whose experiences as a prisoner of state had helped to develop an emotional, deeply religious temperament, much like his mother's. Gloucester's life had been sad and bewildering, gradually forcing him into a brooding, sometimes agonized inarticulacy; he wanted above all else to be loved, petted and indulged. At the same time he was haunted by, yet given up to, the memory of his and his sister Elizabeth's interview with their father, the day before his execution.

Charles I, taking the eight-year-old prince between his knees, had begun, 'Sweetheart, now will they cut off thy father's head.' As the boy stared up at him blankly, he repeated, 'Mark, child, what I say – they will cut off thy father's head.' He instructed Gloucester never, no matter what pressure was used, to allow himself to be crowned before either of his brothers, or to desert his religion. 'I will be torn in pieces first,' said Henry with a sob. The King gave more detailed instructions to the Princess Elizabeth, which she promised to write down.[13] A few months later both children were placed in the care of the Countess of Leicester, and in 1650 removed to Carisbrooke Castle, where they heard that the new King had apostasized by signing the Covenant, and that he had sold himself to their father's enemies. To the Princess, already consumptive, this was the final blow; she cried every day, and Henry watched her die of what his attendants told him was grief for their brother's sin.

And now, after two years alone with his tutor, he and that brother were reunited. He was put in the care of his Catholic mother and became the companion of his Catholic sister, aunt and cousins, in a Catholic country, where the religion for which his father had died was practised in an atmosphere of dispute and disapproval. Then Henry realized that he was not, as he had thought, on a visit; there was no money to send him back to Holland: he must stay where he was. (It was the first time he had ever thought about money: Parliament and his guardians had paid for everything.) By this time he had fallen under the spell of Charles's genial, sympathetic kindness and listened, enthralled, to the tale of his adventures. Then he met his brother York again, now on leave and already a gallant and distinguished officer – and the younger boy could imagine no more desirable career. He pitied and reverenced his mother, whose good humour and gaiety revived in his company, and was much taken with his frail, lively little sister. He wanted to please everyone, even the less approachable aunt and cousins, with whom he conversed in his halting, schoolboy French; for they were all very kind to him, and there were so many treats – hunting, games, parties and dancing.

Presently he began to understand that he was a very important person, not only because he was a Stuart prince, but because he was a member of the Church of which his brother was the head. Hitherto, as his letters make clear, it had not occurred to Gloucester that this was, in his mother's view, a tragedy: nor that his father's last commands, both to her and to himself, might be flouted – had she not given her word that she would not attempt to convert him? As Gloucester absorbed these ideas, Charles's attention was turned to two new crises – one financial, the other political – and his brother's problems were set aside.

II

Just before Gloucester reached Paris Prince Rupert returned from his three years' voyage in search of prizes. The King, who had been expecting great things from these piratical ventures, wrote affectionately to his 'dearest cousin' (he seems to have counted on paying all his debts through

Rupert's services) and asked him to come to France as soon as possible.[14] The Prince, broken in health after a series of disasters, warned Charles that he might be disappointed, and when they met explained that all the treasure he had acquired must be set against his own losses. This set-back was very serious, not only for practical reasons, but because Charles's faith in Rupert's efficiency was destroyed. Eventually he asked his cousin to give him a rough account of his expenditure, which the Prince was unable to do; when pressed, he became very angry, assuming that his integrity was impugned. This miserable quarrel lasted for many months, partly through Hyde's tactlessness (*he* would have kept records, and His Majesty should insist on a statement of some kind), with the result that at one point Charles told his mother, 'Rupert shall never more have my trust nor my company,' and the Queen and Jermyn used the Prince's failure against the Chancellor.[15]

Once more, Charles resigned himself to remaining in France. His circumstances were so straitened (he owed Henrietta Maria for all his food and thus had to endure her reproaches) that he plunged into any distraction that offered, neglected his work and ignored the gossip caused by his recklessness. Cromwell's Paris agent reported him as 'so absorbed in pleasures, especially women, that the whole town rings of them'.[16] This conscientious worker provided first-hand evidence by doing 'as the wicked would have me, for which my head ... paid for it since'. He accompanied the King and his party on a number of expeditions, and obtained a copy of an obscene drinking-song, but was completely won over by Charles, whom he described as 'a goodly young man. God forgive me, I drunk his health a dozen times that cursèd night ... I was good-natured and pot-valiant.'[17] Meanwhile, Hyde was writing to Nicholas, 'When anything is to be done by the King's own hand, we must sometimes be content to wait, he being brought unwillingly to the work, which vexes me exceedingly ... I would have [him] do his business himself and be governed by nobody ... He hath more judgement and understanding than many, and that is the only thing that breaks my heart, that he makes no use of it.' When Hyde lectured Charles, His Majesty was so glibly reassuring that the Chancellor cheered up. 'I am confident,' he told Nicholas, 'that he will outlive all these scandals and give the world evidence of another temper of mind.' But the very next day he had to speak about the King's indiscretion – why did he 'discourse all his affairs' to his gentlemen of the bedchamber?[18]

In August 1653 Charles developed a high fever and became so ill that he was let blood five times in as many days. His magnificent constitution survived both the illness and the remedy, and a fortnight later he was sitting up in his room (but unable to answer letters) and then visited the Queen at Chaillot. When Hyde said something about his going to church, Charles pointed out that a boil on his cheek made this impossible.[19]

By the beginning of September he had entirely recovered, but was sunk in deeper gloom than at any time since his escape; so it was arranged that he should go to Chantilly for a change. Hyde and his suite went with him; one of these was Lord Gerard, who had distinguished himself in the Civil War, and was now on the Council; he and Lord Herbert, recently appointed Keeper of the Great Seal, were deeply resentful of the King's reliance on Hyde and determined to get rid of him. The Chancellor, unaware of their enmity, so played into their hands that they were able to plan an attack on him.

While Charles was at Chantilly he and some of his gentlemen made up a party 'to see a dog set a partridge'.[20] Hyde drove out with them; his gout prevented his walking, and he remained in the coach with Lord Gerard, while the others set out across the fields. After some talk about the blackness of the situation, the Chancellor said, 'I think His Majesty is not active enough, nor does think of his business – and I, who am known to have credit with him, ought to advise him to be active, for his honour and his interest, otherwise his friends will fall from him.' He added that the King ought to leave France, 'where everybody is weary of him', and went on, 'He is indisposed to business, and takes too much delight in pleasures, and does not love to take pains, for which I am heartily sorry, but I cannot help it.' Gerard agreed, and then said, 'His Majesty ought to go to every Court in Christendom, and should have gone to Ratisbon himself, instead of sending Wilmot.' The Chancellor replied tolerantly, 'The King is given to pleasure like other young men,' adding, 'If he stay in Paris, he will be undone – you know how indisposed and inactive he is.' Gerard, delighted at being presented with all this ammunition, took up a loyal attitude. 'You ought not to asperse your master in that manner,' he remarked, and the unsuspecting Hyde (had he not made these same criticisms to the King himself?) said no more. Gerard and Herbert then got into touch with Robert Long, whom the King had dismissed from his place when he was in Scotland. Long, who was anxious to co-operate and thus regain his secretaryship, called on Massonet, formerly the King's writing-master, to provide the required evidence. Both men were in Paris; with Gerard and Herbert, they then concocted their case, independently of the other Councillors.

Those who wasted time and energy in trying to get rid of Hyde were moved not only by jealousy and spite, but by the conviction that he was responsible for the failure of the Royalist cause, through his refusal to persuade the King to go over either to the Catholic or the Presbyterian interest. It was partly Hyde's fault that they blamed him; he made no secret of his contempt for their opinions, and never consulted them. The future Earl of Clarendon, that historian of genius, was then a civil servant of the upper middle class, who had never seen active service; his arrogance and his disdain of flattery and compromise outraged the exiled nobles, who were accustomed to be treated by such persons with reverence, if not with servility. With the exception of Ormonde, a man of some intellectual power, the lords surrounding Charles saw very little further than the points of their swords; and while they were using these at the risk of their lives and fortunes, Hyde had been sitting at his desk giving orders and generally asserting himself. Some of them might have recognized his worth if he had shown the faintest comprehension of their point of view, or tried to share their tastes. He did neither; he merely made them feel inadequate, uninstructed and – what most enraged them – estranged from the King, who seemed, they thought, to make the Chancellor's decisions his own. Hyde made matters worse by his perpetual reminders of his power over Charles ('I, who am known to have credit with him') and this, combined with his capacity to bore and irritate, drove the haughty patricians into a frenzy which the King might have soothed if he had troubled to do so. But Charles's *laisser-faire* method was one of his defences against despair. As the Royalist situation deteriorated and general agreement or concerted action became impossible, Cromwell perceived that he had been provided with a powerful weapon.

So Gerard and Herbert persuaded themselves that by getting up a case against an innocent man they were doing their master a service. When the general Council, presided over by Charles, Rupert, York, Gloucester and Henrietta Maria, met in January 1654, the conspirators were sure of success.

Henrietta Maria gave them their opportunity by suggesting that Long should be reinstated as Charles's secretary. Long then rose and told the Council that Hyde was a Parliamentary spy. Asked to substantiate this accusation, he replied that M. Massonet had obtained the necessary information from a maid in the Protector's household. There was a pause – and then a burst of laughter all round the table.[21]

Hyde got up and asked that Massonet should be called. The old writing-master's story was so muddled and ridiculous that Jermyn, aware that Hyde's position was now being strengthened, said it should be ignored.

Herbert objected, 'While the evidence is heard, the Chancellor should not be present.' Then Charles broke in with 'I see well the design. It is so false and wicked a charge that if I have no other exception against Mr Long than this foul and foolish accusation, it is cause enough never to trust him.' As Hyde moved to leave, he went on, 'Sit in your place. I am sorry I am not in a condition to do more than declare you innocent.' Turning to the Clerk of the Council, he told him to make out an order declaring the Chancellor's innocence, which he signed. Then he said, 'I wonder that such trash should come from some of those persons – ' his dark glance fell on Herbert and Gerard. 'The accusation is a groundless and malicious calumny.'

Herbert announced, 'I am very much troubled. I will ask my Lord Gerard to repeat his story, that the scandal may be brought to light.' Hyde said, 'I ask Your Majesty to let Lord Gerard tell all.' At a sign from the King, Gerard then repeated his conversation with the Chancellor at Chantilly.

Hyde, finding himself 'a little out of countenance', said, 'I have made reflections of this kind, I will admit it. I will retire while His Majesty makes his decision.' 'I forbid it,' said Charles. Herbert exclaimed, 'These words amount to an offence of a high nature. They are words of great malice and iniquity.' 'The accusation is a groundless calumny,' Charles repeated, adding more calmly, 'I do really believe that the Chancellor has used these very words, because he has often said that – and much more – ' with a smile – 'to myself, which I have never taken ill.' He went on, with the winning frankness which sometimes made him irresistible, 'I believe I myself am in fault, and do not delight enough in my business. I am very well satisfied in the Chancellor's affection, and take nothing ill that he hath said.' He then desired the clerk to enter that statement in the records, and announced that the meeting was at an end.[22]

Although Charles showed energy and common sense in dealing with such situations as these, they did not always foster those qualities, but created a tendency to boredom, which grew on him as he matured, so that, by the time he was thirty, this weakness amounted to a disease. As he was neither a heavy drinker nor interested in the arts, nor a great reader, his most effectual panacea became that of sexual adventure – if drifting from one woman to another can be so described. Charles was not temperamentally ardent; he swam, danced, hunted and played games far more strenuously than he made love; the frenzied pursuit of the sex was, as he would have said himself, something he had no mind to be troubled with, partly because his mistresses were so easily captured. Now, in his twenty-fourth year, he might have conquered ennui if he had not been pestered with a quantity of minor worries.

The white ink his agents used for their secret dispatches did not respond to treatment; Buckingham appeared at the Palais Cardinal bursting with schemes about the Levellers; Sir William Davenant and Sir John Denham joined the exiled Court and had to be encouraged to write poetry and plays, however tediously, as they had no political skill; a warning came that one of the Councillors was in Cromwell's pay; York was always talking about his military ambitions, and insisted on going to Mass when he came on leave.[23] And the wild indiscretion of other newly arrived Royalists called for firm but tactful treatment which the King found extremely irksome. These young men would approach him publicly, offering to murder Cromwell – 'which plan,' says Hyde, 'he civilly discountenanced' – or implored him, 'Will Your Majesty command me *any* service into England?' 'Commend me to my friends there,' Charles would reply, 'and command them that they shall be quiet, and not engage themselves in any plots – which will prove ruinous to them, and not do me any good.'[24]

The most persistent of these heroes was Mr Wogan, 'a beautiful young person', according to the Chancellor, who, leaving England after Charles I's execution, came to Paris with Ormonde at the age of seventeen, and asked the King's leave to join Middleton in Scotland. Charles became so weary of his importunities that he passed him on to Hyde, who refused him the necessary papers, upon which Wogan burst into the ever-ready tears of his day, accused Long of treachery and challenged him to a duel, got round the King, forced his commission from the Chancellor, joined Middleton and was fatally wounded just before the failure of the Scottish rising.[25]

Then Henrietta Maria, who had been very much put out by the inefficacy of Gerard's and Herbert's attack on Hyde, began another campaign, and so influenced everyone against him that Charles was warned of two movements, one Catholic and one Presbyterian, to discredit the Chancellor. The King destroyed these by remarking, as he and the Queen Mother sat down to dinner, 'And when will the two petitions be brought against the Chancellor of the Exchequer?' – with the result that everyone but Henrietta Maria burst out laughing and her scheme collapsed. Thereafter her anger so increased that she refused to speak to or look at Hyde, and he ceased to wait on her, although they were now lodged in the same palace.

He did not realize that she had never forgiven him for his criticisms of three and a half years before; these, made in his usual lecturing style, were still as bitterly resented as what she considered his share in her estrangement from Charles, with whom she now quarrelled openly and violently about policy, money and his manner of life. By the spring of 1654 they were no longer on speaking terms, and the King had to communicate with her through Jermyn, to whom he wrote, 'I cannot accuse myself of having used the Queen as ill as she says I have ... I cannot promise to follow any advice she may give ... and to give up my liberty upon sometimes impossible and always unreasonable conditions. I will always defer to her judgement ... and no misconstruction ... shall ever lessen my duty and affection.'[26]

Charles was trying to convey that he would listen to his mother as patiently and amiably as he did to Hyde, and then go his own way. So it was that Henrietta Maria was not consulted about his dealings with a highly organized and widespread movement for his restoration called the Sealed Knot, whose emissaries he first received in April. Certain powerful nobles, among them the Earls of Southampton and Hertford, were in control, and their agents at home and abroad were efficient and industrious. This organization was so extensive that as soon as one group defaulted or was discovered another took its place. Part of it – what might now be described as a sub-committee – was occupied with the murder of the Protector, a plan Charles would not discuss or, officially, approve. He seems to have made this clear when he interviewed the first contingent of Sealed Knot agents at six in the morning in the Tuileries gardens and in his bedchamber at the Palais Cardinal that same evening. When he wrote to them about their recruiting campaign, his instructions were that all 'gaudy titles' were to be avoided, and only those of Governor and Eldest Colonel used; in this way he planned to attract those anti-Royalist Parliamentarians who were now working against the dictatorship of the army.[27]

It then became obvious that Charles's supporters in England could do nothing for him while he remained in France. Fortunately, this realization coincided with Mazarin's resolve to let him go in order to placate Cromwell. Hertford and Southampton sent the King £3,000, and the Cardinal promised to pay his debts in Paris and the expenses of his journey to Germany, where the Elector of Cologne eventually agreed to receive him.[28] Indeed, Cromwell was now so powerful and his continental spy system so organized that English travellers dared not visit the Palais Cardinal under their own names. In the first week of July young John Reresby, then on the grand tour, went to watch the King, York and Prince Rupert playing billiards; 'but was incognito, it being a crime sufficient the waiting upon His Majesty to cause the sequestration of my estate, had it been known.'[29]

A few days later Charles was making his final preparations and the selection of his suite. He decided not to take Herbert, as his post was honorary; the Lord Keeper protested with tears that he would be thereby humiliated, and Charles, to Hyde's disgust, gave in. Gloucester then implored his brother to let him come too.

Charles hesitated. He was not in a position to support the boy – to whom he had become as devoted as to the ten-year-old Princess Henrietta Anne – and his tutor seemed conscientious and trustworthy. While he was trying to make up his mind, his mother came to him and said, 'Harry has not learnt the ways of courts. To carry him away from all these advantages to live in Germany would be to use him ill.' For the last time Charles asked her, 'with great respect and quietness', to promise that she would not try to convert Gloucester. 'It is not in my thought,' Henrietta Maria replied, 'that any such attempt should be made.'[30] Charles did not trust her; but his circumstances enforced him to agree to what appeared the most sensible plan.

He then asked her to make up her quarrel with Hyde and to receive him courteously before they left. She consented, the Chancellor came to her private gallery and before she could speak, began, 'I hope Your Majesty will let me know the grounds of the displeasure you have against me.' In a loud, furious voice, the Queen replied, 'I have allowed you to see me and to kiss my hand to comply with the King's desires. Otherwise, you have no reason to expect to be welcome to me. Your disrespect to me is notorious to all men. You never come where I am, though you lodge under the same roof.'

She continued this harangue for some time. As soon as she paused for breath, the Chancellor said in his harshest, most satirical tone, 'Your Majesty has only mentioned my punishment and nothing of my fault. How great soever my infirmities are, in defect of understanding or of good manners, I have never yet been in Bedlam. I am not such a fool as to provoke the wife of my dead master.' By this time, the Queen, bursting with indignation, was ready with her next speech. Hyde ignored her attempts to interrupt him, and continued his lecture, which did not, he noted, 'seem to satisfy Her Majesty ... Carelessly,' he goes on, she gave him her hand to kiss and swept out of the gallery, leaving him to reflect that he had done all and more that could be expected of him.[31]

On July 18th, 1654, Charles left Paris with a small train and a little pocket-money, the gift of Cardinal Mazarin. He was seen off by the Venetian ambassador and all his relatives. Henrietta Maria cried bitterly, and even the cool-headed Sagredo was strangely moved. 'He has the sympathy of all France,' he told the Senate.[32]

Henrietta Maria might have dried her tears if she had known that Charles, who was on his way to meet Mary of Orange at Spa, spent his last nights on French soil at Merlou, the Duchesse de Châtillon's country place. Hyde accepted the situation without comment – until, a few days later, he was told that the King and Madame de Châtillon had been secretly married.[33]

NOTES

1 *Cal. Clar. S. P.*, vol. III, p. 107.
2 Op. cit., p. 120.
3 Carte, *Ormonde*, vol. II, p. 159.
4 *Cal. S. P. Ven.*, vol. XXVIII, pp. 299, 317.
5 Clarendon, pp. 804–14.
6 Ibid.
7 *Cal. Clar. S. P.*, vol. III, p. 141.
8 Op. cit., p. 150.
9 Ibid.
10 Ibid.
11 Op. cit., vol. II, p. 183.
12 *Cal. D. S. P.*, March 19th, 1653.
13 Sir Thomas Herbert, *Memoirs of the two last years of the Reign of Charles I*, p. 49.
14 B. E. G. Warburton, *Memoirs of Prince Rupert and the Cavaliers*, vol. III, p. 418.
15 Clarendon, ibid.
16 *Cal. Clar. S. P.*, vol. II, p. 218.
17 *Thurloe State Papers*, vol. I, p. 471.
18 *Cal. Clar. S. P.*, vol. III, p. 170–1.
19 Ibid.
20 Clarendon, ibid.
21 Ibid.
22 Ibid.; *Nicholas Papers*, vol. II, p. 37; *Cal. Clar. S. P.*, vol. II, p. 285; *Cal. D. S. P.*, Jan. 4th, 1654.
23 *Thurloe State Papers*, vol. I, pp. 263, 319, 592, 622.
24 Clarendon, p. 798.
25 Op. cit., p. 804.
26 *Cal. Clar. S. P.*, vol. II, p. 348.
27 Op. cit., p. 386.
28 Clarendon, pp. 813–15.
29 Sir John Reresby, *Memoirs*, p. 7.
30 *Thurloe State Papers*, vol. II, p. 180.
31 Clarendon, ibid.
32 *Cal. S. P. Ven.*, vol. XXIX, p. 227.
33 Clarendon, p. 815.

PART FOUR

◆◆◆◆◆

The Black Boy

(AUGUST 1654–MAY 1660)

> Se tu segui tua stella,
> Non puoi fallire al glorioso porto.
>
> .　.　.　.　.　.　.
>
> La tua fortuna tanto onor ti serba,
> Che l'una parte e l'altra avranno fame
> Di te . . .
>
> Inferno

CHAPTER ONE

SPA, AIX AND COLOGNE

I

THE young man who rode out of Paris with a modest train of gentlemen and servants and his few pieces of plate and luggage in a cart was beginning to look like the Charles II Lely painted at the Restoration – the Charles II of the history books – except that he wore his own hair, 'of a shining black, not frizzled, but so naturally curling into great rings' as to be 'a very comely ornament'.[1] To those who had been with him throughout the exile, his melancholy aspect – 'rather grave than severe' – was not perhaps apparent; but anyone who saw him for the first time since 1651 would have been struck by the harshness, the forbidding contempt of his expression, emphasized by the haggard lines reaching from the corners of his full mouth to the long lean jaw. This formidably withdrawn impression was lessened when the King spoke; his voice and manner were friendly and gentle. When he smiled, the effect was not so agreeable; there was a cool mockery, a cynical, gibing awareness in His Majesty's acceptance of pleasantry or compliments that sometimes made those who sought his favour uneasy – was he laughing at them, or at some private jest of his own?

In fact, the gallant, open-hearted, enthusiastic youth had become a reckless, disillusioned, embittered adventurer, whose brilliant glance, careless yet acute, saw beneath courtesies and flattery, and turned away from what it saw. The lover of Lucy Walter, the pupil of Argyll, the dependant of Louis XIV and Cardinal Mazarin, the outcast no continental power seemed to want, had now 'a very ill opinion of both men and women, and did not think that there was either sincerity or chastity in the world' – a view from which he never diverged.[2]

This metamorphosis may be partially traced back to the experiences of the child of ten who blurted out to his father his fear of disinheritance, and who, a year later, went to plead for Strafford's life and was rejected by that father's Parliament. He had come a long way, on a stony road, since then; and those who worked and prayed for him in England would have been distressed and bewildered if they had grasped the extent of his disbelief, his opportunism and his ironic acceptance of treachery and greed.

For now, in the kingdom he had lost and seemed unlikely to regain, a legend was being created – the legend of a 'tall, black man above two yards high', pursued, persecuted, threatened, condemned to execution, in vain. In the four years that elapsed between Charles's flight from Worcester and his departure from Paris the stories of the King in the oak tree, the spirited, ready-witted fugitive who had fooled the Roundheads, mimicked their pomposity and laughed at their stiffness ('I did not much like his starched moustachios' was his comment on a Cromwellian captain) had become part of a wonderful saga – the saga of the Black Boy so loved and longed for, that hero of adventure and romance. Now those whispered anecdotes were the basis of a dream, one in which His Sacred Majesty would triumph through the bravery and resource of the humblest of his subjects – farmers, squires' daughters, sailors, innkeepers, peasants, even children – had he not taken little Nan Penderel on his knee, and asked a poor cottager to keep him company?

It was perhaps as well that those who secretly enlarged upon and delighted in the dignified simplicity, the patient endurance of the exiled King whom the Scots had betrayed and Cromwell would have hounded to his death, did not know of his cold resolve never again to go through that ignominy and suffering; and that they were unaware of his lying, intriguing, offering to barter his faith for a few hundred pounds, trying to sell the Orkneys or the Scillies to one national enemy and angling for the payment of his debts from another – and then forgetting his troubles in the arms of his Bablon, who could be relied on not to take him too seriously.

As a son and a brother, the less sophisticated Royalists would have approved of Charles. Even the glum and underpaid individual whose duty it was to follow and report on him was impressed by his patience with the 'mad and peevish' Queen Mother, whose 'poor subsistence [was] dearer to her than that of her eldest son', and who had 'nothing of the kindness of a mother'.[3] And although this morose critic could not but despise the King's dancing with his little sister in ballets at the Louvre, he did note his love for her and his brothers, his concern for Gloucester's isolation, his care that York should be happily employed and not irked by jealousy of himself.

The party – now slightly diminished – who dreaded Charles's return did not wholly consist of politicians and soldiers. Shortly before he left Paris, a Bristol felt-maker, resting under a hedge, was approached by two gentlemen, one of whom told him, 'I will acquaint you of very good news – certain Jesuits have taken an oath on the Sacrament to kill the Lord Protector, which means that Charles II's party would strike in,' and the other added, 'It would do well, if it could be effected.'⁴ The horrified tradesman who reported this talk to the Privy Council was one of many who saw in Charles Stuart the son of the Man of Blood, the destroyer of the Word, the anti-Christ. The persons who accosted him were almost certainly Government agents instructed to spread panic at the thought of a restoration; for to mention Catholic plots was to conjure up the spectres of Guy Fawkes, the Spanish Armada and the Protestant martyrs of Queen Mary's reign.

Charles was perfectly aware of the varied prejudices and terrors he had to overcome, and that the most delicate of his problems was the religious issue. This last consideration complicated his relations with Madame de Châtillon, who had not yet definitely refused to become his wife. And now their situation became like that of a couple in a fashionable romance, for the lady was pursued by two more aspirants, the 'wild and vicious' Will Crofts, and George Digby, who had recently been fighting with the French Royalists against the Frondeurs, and who was as exuberantly headstrong as when he planned to kidnap Charles in Jersey.⁵

Both young men were in love with the Duchesse. She would have neither of them. They then, says Hyde, 'lamented to each other their mutual infelicity ... and boldly proposed to her marriage with the King',⁶ with the result that Charles offered again in the belief that she would accept him. She did not vouchsafe a definite answer – he was an agreeable *prétendant* – and Digby told Hyde his plan, enlarging on the benefits of such a marriage. 'You have great presumption for interposing in an affair of so delicate a nature,' said the Chancellor, 'as might prove the ruin of the King.' 'I will leave it to His Majesty's own inclination,' promised Digby; but when he and Crofts joined their master at Merlou, they 'made their last effort' to persuade the Duchesse to accept him. By this time Charles had begun to see the disadvantages of being tied, and did not renew his proposal. He and his hostess seem to have parted on friendly terms.

When Charles and his suite entered Flanders, then Spanish territory, their first stop was Cambrai. Here they found the gates closed against them, and had to wait some six or seven hours before they were opened. At last the Governor, having apologized for the delay (he had been told that Turenne was about to attack), came to offer Charles his house. When it became clear that this was all the attention the King was to receive, and that the Spanish nobility were not going to wait on him, he moved on to Mons, where he was joined by a number of English Royalists, who reported an increasing and general dissatisfaction with the Government. The jails were full – Cromwell had arrested five hundred suspected persons that summer – the taxes appalling, and the rules and regulations more tyrannical than ever, in spite of the fact that peace had been signed with the Dutch in April. Best of all, the split in the army was widening. In fact, the usurping regime would not last – when could they expect His Majesty?

Charles held a conference with those returning to England – most of them were young men bursting with wild schemes – and said, 'Live quietly, without making any desperate or unreasonable attempt, or giving advantage to those who watch you, to put you into prison and ruin your wives and families.' He warned them that the discipline and organization of the army was firmer than they believed, and went on, 'I will be ready to venture my own person with you in any well formed and reasonable undertaking – so, with patience, attend God's own time for such an opportunity. And in the meantime, I will sit still in such convenient place as I shall find willing to receive me, of which I can yet make no judgement.' He and Hyde then discussed with the leaders of this group the hope of a further 'schism' in the army, adding that their best hope lay in Cromwell's death.[7] They emphasized the fact that Charles had neither signed nor had anything to do with a proclamation issued from Paris in May, describing the Protector as 'a certain mechanic fellow' whom anyone had His Majesty's 'free leave' to kill, for a reward of £500.

Charles then moved on to Namur, leaving it by water for Liège. After a six-hour journey he reached Spa, to be joined by Mary of Orange the next day. The brother and sister, who had not seen one another for four years, embraced with tears of joy. 'Her tender love and zeal to His Majesty,' remarked a contemporary, 'deserves to be written in brass with the point of a diamond.'[8]

Shortly after this reunion – while the King and his sister were settling in at Spa, where they intended to spend some months – Henry Bennet, later Arlington of the Cabal and at this time one of Charles's agents in the Low Countries, told an anonymous correspondent that His Majesty was writing every week to Will Crofts (from whom he had just parted at Merlou) and that the King, through Crofts, was again in touch with an extremely shady individual whom he employed as a go-between in his most private and personal affairs, those he concealed from Hyde and the Council. This man, Daniel O'Neile, was one of the persons Charles used to deal with Lucy Walter.

Bennet's letter – so worded as to compromise neither Charles nor himself – goes on to say that His Majesty's correspondence with Crofts 'may be a great corrupter of the King's judgement, when he shall be brought to the point of determining where he shall live'. (At this moment Charles's destination was uncertain.) He adds that Mrs Barlow has come to Liège, and continues, 'Take Daniel O'Neile to task and ask ... whether there be any progress made towards that ... I have suspected.'

This letter might conceivably indicate that Lucy was pursuing Charles and that he was thinking of a reconciliation. The King, who for the first time since his exile was in funds, still wanted to remove little James, now in his sixth year, from his mother; later it turned out that the boy's education was being shockingly neglected, and perhaps Charles was already aware of this. O'Neile knew how to manage Lucy, and Charles was to use him and Crofts for that purpose more than once. Finally, Bennet's mention of her being at Liège, where, at this time, Charles spent only a few hours, might be linked up with the baseless report of his having been married to her there in an inn, with the innkeeper and his wife as witnesses. Whatever advances Lucy made – if she did make any – were fruitless. She did not reappear in Charles's life until three months after his departure from the Low Countries.

The King was so rejoiced to be out of France and with his sister that he would make no plans. Many friends, among them Henry Bennet, were now able to join him and the Princess Royal; they were fêted by the citizens and 'as merry', Cromwell's agent sourly reported, 'as if they had the three kingdoms.'⁹ Yet Charles was still worried about his brothers. York's lack of perception and Gloucester's inexperience might get them into trouble in his absence; and their situation had been further complicated by the arrival of Colonel Bamfield, who because he had helped York to escape was completely trusted by him, but whom the King knew to be a Parliamentary spy. Now Bamfield was trying to persuade York to go to Scotland. Charles wrote to him 'not to employ Bamfield in anything', and to consult himself before taking action. He sent Bennet with this letter, in which he enclosed a note 'for my brother Harry', reminding the little Duke that he had been allowed to remain with his mother on condition that he stuck to his faith, spoke with no one about religion and attended morning and evening prayers under Dr Cosin. 'You must attend your book and exercises diligently,' Charles went on, 'and set some time apart every day to spend at your book with your tutor, to whom you must always show kindness and regard.'¹⁰

Such advice came rather oddly from the man whom Cromwell's spies reported as given up to debauchery and whom Hyde was not able to pin down on post days. But Charles had already observed the effects of freedom, luxury and gaiety on the thirteen-year-old Henry, who was much admired at the French Court 'for the comeliness and gracefulness of his person, and the vivacity and vigour of his wit and understanding'.[11] Queen Anne was eager to spoil him, the correct young King treated him with carefully regulated graciousness, and he had made a special friend of Louis's younger brother, Philippe d'Anjou, who was exactly his own age. Although they had not much in common – Anjou, a peculiarly precocious child, was chiefly interested in fashions – the two boys hunted and played tennis and billiards together, an arrangement of which Gloucester's tutor could not but approve.

Charles did not mean to send for Gloucester, unless it turned out that Bennet's reports made it necessary; for when Wilmot arrived from Ratisbon with no more than the promise of support from the confederation of German princes and a comparatively small sum in hand, the King realized that he must still economize. Hyde took charge of his household, which now numbered some eighty persons; his servants were paid their arrears of wages and well fed and housed, with the result that for the first time in years there were no complaints and everything was managed 'with good husbandry' by the complacent Chancellor.

Then smallpox broke out in Spa, one of the Princess's ladies caught it and died, and Charles decided to move on to Aix-la-Chapelle, a free city governed by magistrates who hastened to wait on him and his sister. Here Nicholas joined them and was made the King's private secretary.

Charles and Mary found Aix even more enjoyable than Spa. She could take the waters, nasty though they were – the smell from the pump-room and bathing establishment was appalling – and as her expenses were paid by the States General, she took over her brother's. He lived with her and boarded out his servants. As soon as they were installed expenses rose – 'no reasonable lodgings', the Parliament spy reported, 'to be had under half a crown a night' – but they received many presents in kind, including wine, from the city fathers, whose hope it was to convert their guests to the Catholic faith. To this end they organized a sight-seeing tour for the royal party, beginning with a visit to the Cathedral, where their greatest treasures, Charlemagne's iron crown and his sword, together with his right hand and skull, were kept and shown to privileged persons.

The canons received Charles and Mary, and they attended vespers, for which special music had been composed, sitting in the choir on chairs covered with black velvet. They were then taken to see the relics, which they were allowed to handle. The Princess kissed the Emperor's skull and his hand; Charles, more circumspect, or perhaps more fastidious, kissed the blade of his sword and measured it against his own.[12]

Hunting and hawking parties were then organized, at one of which the King was entertained by the Landgrave Van Hussa who, it was said, was about to marry Queen Christina of Sweden. This amused Charles, whose name had already been linked with that of the unattractive and eccentric lady. Their sport was poor: after ranging the countryside from seven till four, they returned with two brace of partridge and a hare. That night Mary and Charles feasted the Landgrave and, according to the spy, 'were extreme merry' when Charles toasted Queen Christina to her supposed suitor. The party went on till the small hours, with singing, drinking and dancing; the agent was worn out by the time it was over. There was some jesting about the Swedish Queen's marrying Charles – 'the poor good King of England', as she called him – 'but this,' added Cromwell's correspondent, 'I do not believe.'[13]

The after-effects of these gaieties were not so happy. Wilmot and Lord Newburgh fell out and challenged one another; Charles heard of the quarrel in time to prevent them fighting, which he did in his sternest manner. A few nights later he was woken by angry voices and the crash of overturned furniture in the next room, then occupied by Lord Wentworth and Major Boswell, both drunk and 'knocking one another', according to the agent, whose rest – was he employed as a secretary? – was also disturbed. He then complained that he could not afford to keep up with these fine gentlemen. 'Of all the monies you sent me being but £20,' he wrote, 'I disbursed the most part for myself in equipage to follow R.C. [Charles's code name] to wherever he goes; and in case he moves ... I shall be straitened ... therefore ... I pray you furnish me with monies.'[14]

Shortly after his arrival in Aix Charles received another party of Royalists from England, who assured him that the disputes in the army could bring one or other side over to his cause. 'How shall we behave ourselves upon such a contingency?' their leader asked. 'Do not flatter yourselves with vain imaginations,' the King replied, 'nor give easy credit to factions and divisions.'[15] When news came from Scotland of another Royalist rising Charles called a Council and announced that he might go to the Highlands that year. 'I would rather die sword in hand,' he said, 'than live in such contemptible calamities as I am likely to be pressed with hereafter,' and told the Scots emissary, Sir James Turner, to assure the Presbyterians of his support. He and Hyde then saw Turner privately; when the Chancellor and Sir James disagreed about where the rising should begin, Hyde asked, 'Will you not go where the King thinks fit to send you?' 'At the King's command I would go to Japan,' Turner replied. 'Japan would be out of your way,' put in Charles dryly. 'It could not,' Turner declared, 'if Your Majesty sent me there –' and retired, rather disappointed with Charles's lack of enthusiasm.[16]

Then, apparently through Turner, Hyde was told that the Royalists were criticizing the King for his refusal to move without proper support and more definite news from the Highlands. His Majesty seemed, they thought, to be resigning himself to idleness and exile. In these grumblings the Chancellor perceived an opportunity for the prevention of 'pleasure'. As soon as he and the King were alone, he began, 'It is Your Majesty's misfortune to be thought by many not to be active enough towards your own redemption, and to love your ease too much.' He then embarked on an immense lecture, which ended with the proposal that Charles should at once leave for Scotland. 'Very calmly' the King replied, 'It is impossible for me to lie there with security or health. If sickness does not destroy me, which I have reason to expect from the severe accommodation there –' (Did he know that Hyde knew he had not had a day's illness in Scotland?) – 'I should in a short time be betrayed and given up.' He then told Hyde how Leslie had warned him that the Scots troops would not fight, and went on, 'However, if my friends will advise me to that expedition, I will transport myself into the Highlands, though I know very well what will come of it – and they will be sorry for it.'[17]

The Chancellor was silenced; he had to admit himself in the wrong when news came that George Monk, the most remarkable of the Cromwellian generals, had routed Middleton with the help of the Scots themselves, who had offered to sell him Middleton's plans.

II

Hyde would never have admitted that Charles, at the age of twenty-four, knew more of the political situation than he did. While the King's first-hand experience of Scottish affairs had to be accepted, his judgment of the continental powers was discounted by the Chancellor, who preferred to think of his master as an amateur being trained by himself. Hyde's devotion to Charles and Charles's tolerant affection for Hyde made it possible for them to spend several hours together every day without quarrelling. This helped to delude the Chancellor, who never took in the complexity of Charles's character. The King's apparent laziness and frivolity deceived him, as it did most, if not all, of his intimates. Hyde thought that Charles, although extremely intelligent, was sometimes careless and foolish; he did not realize that when the King was amusing himself with a set of worthless tosspots, he was often inwardly withdrawn, summing them up as mercilessly as, and far more acutely than, Hyde did himself. Paradoxically, it was the King's enemy who saw beneath the surface gaiety of the man he looked on as the embodiment of evil. When Cromwell's agent accompanied Charles and his sister to a cloister where the Canonesses feasted them, and to the meadows where they danced till dusk, 'as merry as could be', he added, 'but for all his dancing, I think he has a heavy heart.' [18] Hyde, writing many years after the autumn of 1654, describes his master as being in excellent spirits throughout his stay at Spa and Aix; his only regret was that Charles did not seek relaxation as his father would have, in the arts, nor in books, as he himself did. And neither Hyde nor the spy perceived the cause or the nature of what one described as debauchery and the other, more generously, as pleasure, with the result that then and long after his death Charles's reputation was partially falsified. He would have preferred it to be so, for he was always secretive and often devious.

Closer analysis of Charles's fame as a debauchee during the exile shows that he fell slightly below the standard of his day. Occasionally he got drunk (oddly enough, quite respectable and hard-working young men are still apt to succumb in this manner) and quite often he spent the night with a woman – and this also is not unknown. Yet these pursuits never dulled his understanding or diminished his energies. However late he stayed up (or did not stay up) he was out of bed and actively employed early next morning; and this was partly accounted for by his liking to see others make fools of themselves while he remained cynically aloof and outwardly genial. He seemed to be drinking glass for glass; and he frequented women without the least regard for appearances. When Cromwell's agent reported his behaviour as being the talk of Paris, he was unconsciously describing one of the conventions of the time, which set discretion above conduct. No one in Charles's circle, not even Hyde, objected to his relationship with Madame de Châtillon. (The Chancellor admired her immensely, and stayed with the King at her house.) But when Charles made no attempt to conceal his casual and fleeting rencontres with unknown, and possibly low-born, females, he was censured, not so much for the practice as for the manner of it; the fact that secrecy entailed expenses he could not meet was not considered.

When Charles was reduced to eating his meals in taverns because his mother's charges were more than he could afford, he sometimes combined this necessity with the luxury – it cost very little more – of sexual intercourse. Then, and for several centuries, this combination, natural enough in a vigorous and enforcedly aimless young man, came under the heading of 'vice' and 'dissipation'. Unless they amused or excited him, women bored Charles; and he was easily bored, easily amused and, until middle life, easily excited. In his leisure hours indoors he preferred talking to theologians, scientists, philosophers and inventors. When one who knew him after the Restoration said that he was 'apter to be persuaded into debauchery for the satisfaction of others',[19] he might have been describing him in his twenties. Indeed, one of Charles's less agreeable characteristics was this cool and ironic detachment. While his companions drank themselves under the table, hiccuped out insults and obscenities and staggered to relieve themselves in the nearest corner, the King's dark glance dwelt on them from a distance of which he alone knew the extent; and when he laughed and called for another bottle, pledging them as one of themselves, they never guessed that he was being entertained by the spectacle of their degradation.

In his sister's company the King behaved correctly, although the citizens of Aix were rather pained to see him going about on foot – he refused Mary's offer of a coach – with some five or six of his gentlemen. Every morning the Princess went to bathe and take the waters; a few hours later Charles would be seen, in black, with white silk stockings and his Garter star, striding through the streets to fetch her. In the afternoon he and Mary received callers; in the evenings they danced, and when the Princess and her ladies retired the King sat on drinking with those of his courtiers who had not slipped away to the taverns, as the guests of the intelligencer, who says, 'it cost me some £5 ... for thereby I have engrossed familiarity with them, which will give me occasion to know their designs.' In fact, these were known only to Charles, and he gave nothing away.[20]

This pleasant time was concluded by Mary having to go back to Holland. She decided to do so via Cologne, and Charles, who did not like 'the ill smell' of the baths, accompanied her, with the intention of staying in that city if he were made welcome. 'And so the poor King and his train live, feeding on hopes,' reported the agent, when he and they set off on October 8th, via St Juliers, where Charles was received with a salute of guns, reaching Cologne in the afternoon of the next day.[21]

Hyde and Ormonde were a little anxious about the King's reception, for the subjects of the Elector were fervent Catholics, while their wine trade chiefly depended on the English Government. But the brother and sister were warmly greeted and tactfully installed in the house of a

Protestant widow, 'very fair and curious, full of decent rooms and pleasure gardens'. On the day after their arrival Charles and Ormonde explored the city incognito, with two servants; then they went hunting and shot two and half brace of hares. Next day Charles and the Princess were entertained by the Jesuit fathers at their college, whose pupils made speeches in Latin and gave them presents. When they were shown into the refectory, 'there stood prepared to receive him seven boys richly habited, holding in their hands seven shields, with the letters *Carolus* written on them ... and in an instant, turning them, the word *Colonia* appeared. And then they all sung *Colonia Her Welcomes*, bowing their knees to the ground.' After more speeches and music, the King and his sister, 'standing, ate grapes and fruit, and drank two glasses of wine'. By this time the spy was exhausted and very hungry; he made a dash for the buffet, but was outstripped by the English courtiers, who finished up everything.[22]

Cologne, a medieval city of some beauty, had many amenities. The hunting was indifferent and the climate harsh; but there were wooded ramparts from which to look out over the Rhine towards the forests, local wines and rich meals – all free. The magistrates at once waited on Charles; the Elector, who lived at Bonn, five miles away, and never entered his capital, ignored him. 'A melancholy and peevish man', according to Hyde, he made ill health the excuse for discourtesy.[23]

Cologne was full of monasteries and nunneries, and many Protestants had been turned away; but the inhabitants, Hyde noted, were so 'civil and conversible', that they insisted on paying Charles's debts in Aix, and gave him and his sister comfortable lodgings. Thus encouraged, he sent for some of the other exiles, and wrote politely to the neighbouring princes, reminding them that his promised allowances had not arrived. The Duke of Neuburg, whose Court was at Düsseldorf, a day's journey by water from Cologne, sent a handsome sum and suggested that Charles and Mary should visit him. They wanted to accept: but the situation had many problems.

The Duke had not sent what Hyde describes as 'a solemn invitation', which meant that Charles might be received incognito. This would never do; it could result in the other potentates withdrawing their respective allowances, for they attached immense importance to protocol and ceremony. At last the difficulties were whittled down to two points: would the Duke be allowed to kiss the Princess on the cheek, and would she and Charles address him as 'Highness' in return? Eventually it was agreed that this interchange should be the basis of an official visit.[24]

In the afternoon of October 16th Charles and Mary reached Düsseldorf to find the Neuburgs and their Court waiting to receive them on the bank of the river. Kisses from the Duke and Duchess were accompanied by the careful repetition of 'Altesse' from the guests, and the party drove away in twelve coaches to the castle, 'a princely house', and were taken to their rooms. They then attended vespers in the chapel and went into supper, a long, heavy and elaborate meal (there were twenty-two tables, each of which had sixty-eight dishes) served to vocal and instrumental music of a very high order. When the pages knelt before the King with the gold ewer, the Duke 'took the lavation', offering him the towel, which Charles, according to custom, politely set aside. His host 'could not well have done more', reported the informer, impressed in spite of himself by this thoughtful attention. A vast quantity of wine accompanied the implacable succession of courses, but there was no drunkenness and the conversation remained solemn and formal. The Duchess, a very plain lady who spoke no French, 'was rather a spectator of the feast than a part of it'. 'She confirms me,' said Charles to the Chancellor as soon as they were alone, 'in my aversion from ever marrying a German.' To the Duke he said, 'I give you my word that within ten or twelve days I will visit you again, and spend some time with you in sports.'[25]

On his return to Cologne Charles decided to stay there for three months. With a heavy heart, Mary now prepared to leave. Her last few days were spent walking, dancing, hunting and visiting the English residents, where she and Charles were 'nobly feasted', and received the Papal Nuncio, 'a proper and grave man', from whom the King unsuccessfully tried to borrow money. He was becoming an expert professional beggar. The Nuncio was one of the few able to withstand his graceful importunities.

When Mary left for the Hague Charles went with her via Düsseldorf (where they were once more superbly entertained) and so to Xanten. Here they parted. Mary cried bitterly, and Charles's grief moved even the Cromwellian agent to pity; all the way back to Cologne the King remained silent and melancholy. Then, soon after he had settled in for what promised to be a not too unpleasant winter – 'drinking and wenching' – he heard very bad news, the worst indeed since his return to the Continent. Letters arrived from Paris telling him that the Duke of Gloucester was about to be received into the Catholic Church.

NOTES

1 Tuke, p. 4.
2 Burnet, *History*, vol. I, p. 183.
3 *Thurloe S. P.*, vol. II, p. 147.
4 Op. cit., p. 178.
5 Clarendon, pp. 814–21.
6 Ibid.
7 Ibid.
8 *Ormonde MSS* (H.M.C.), new series, vol. I, p. 303.
9 *Thurloe S. P.*, vol. II, p. 488.
10 *Cal. Clar. S. P.*, vol. II, p. 382.
11 Clarendon, p. 812.
12 *Thurloe S. P.*, vol. II, p. 567.
13 Ibid.
14 Op. cit., p. 586.
15 Clarendon, pp. 814–21.
16 Sir James Turner, p. 114.
17 Clarendon, ibid.
18 *Thurloe S. P.*, vol. II, p. 614.
19 Duke of Buckingham and Normanby, *Character of Charles II*, p. 4.
20 *Thurloe S. P.*, vol. II, p. 556.
21 Op. cit., p. 646.
22 Op. cit., pp. 646, 662.
23 Clarendon, ibid.
24 Ibid.
25 Ibid.; *Thurloe S. P.*, vol. II, p. 694.

CHAPTER TWO

THE ORDEAL OF
THE DUKE OF GLOUCESTER

I

AFTER January 1649 Gloucester's moral obligations became rather
complicated. If his father had been a private person, his absolute
obedience would have been automatically transferred to his mother.
As it was, his duty divided itself between her and his elder brother, who
was now God's representative and the head of Church and state. If
Gloucester did not obey his mother, he was breaking the second com-
mandment and thus endangering his soul. This was not the only danger.
If he abjured the faith in which he had been baptized, he would be eter-
nally damned; and such a fate was then visualized in concrete terms. In
the seventeenth century, and for approximately the next two hundred
and fifty years, Hell was known to be a place of ceaseless physical torment
and mental despair; its modern equivalent would perhaps be a combination of a lunatic asylum and a concentration camp, in which the inmates
lived as did the Struldbrugs, in a state of deathless misery.

Gloucester's adherence to his religion was not assailed till his fourteenth
year. As the prisoner of the English Parliament, he remained spiritually
unmolested; and though he knew that his mother, as a Papist, was due for
damnation, this knowledge had probably sunk below the surface. When
they met again, he saw her at her best; the reports of his behaviour show
that he not only loved and honoured her, but would have liked to protect
and help her, if he had been able to do so.

Gloucester's solitude and separation from his family had intensified his
powers of thought and feeling. He was responsive, intelligent, and something of a hero-worshipper. In Charles II he found the perfect hero: a
brother who loved, encouraged and understood him, and who treated
him as a responsible adult. To sit in Council and listen to Charles dealing
with factions, jealousy and intrigue; to hear, over and over again, the
thrilling recital of his escape; to observe and envy his skill at games, dancing and outdoor sports; to realize, if only in part, his difficulties and his
talents – all this created in Gloucester an adoration of the brother whose

subject and servant he was. When Charles left him in Paris, he was in great grief, but loyally submissive, and more anxious than ever to look after his mother and do battle for the Royalist cause. Unfortunately, he could not prove himself in Scotland or on a secret mission to England; the next best thing was to fight for his mother's country, against the Spaniards. This, to his rapture, he was allowed to do. He was given a commission and, in charge of his brother York, joined Turenne's staff at the siege of Arras in September 1654. The great General spoke kindly to him, and made no objection to his being under fire. With York, Buckingham, Lord Gerard and Sir Charles Berkeley, all experienced and gallant officers, the eager boy became a soldier and felt himself a man. What his share amounted to is summed up in Jermyn's report of the siege to Charles. 'Little Mr Harry,' he wrote, 'now and then, did his part well.'[1] A fortnight later, when Gloucester and York were back in Paris, Nicholas was told that the junior Duke had become 'unsupportable to all persons'.[2]

Military glory had gone to Gloucester's head; and this, allied to the attentions paid him by the younger French courtiers, who treated him as one of themselves, praised his looks and took him away from his lessons to drinking and gambling parties, made him quite odious. His tutor could do nothing with him; even his mother did not always command his respect and obedience; and Charles's instructions about minding his book were hastily read and soon forgotten.

In this problem, her immediate responsibility, Henrietta Maria saw the chance to convert Gloucester, although she may not have been aware of her own disingenuousness. He must be disciplined and go on with his neglected education: and Paris was not the place for that. In England he would have been sent to a country palace with tutors, chaplains and a carefully selected group of companions of his own age. In France the equivalent was to place him at Pontoise, an abbey just outside Paris, of which Walter Montagu, formerly a courtier of Charles I, later a convert and now Henrietta Maria's confessor, was the head. This arrangement appeared eminently suitable, especially because Mr Lovell, a conscientious but not very forceful character, who was no longer able to cope with his pupil, accompanied him there. Gloucester had outgrown him; a change of direction was essential: yet Charles's orders that Lovell should not leave him were obeyed.

Gloucester was not deeply disturbed by this decision, although no doubt he found life at Pontoise rather dull; for he was not naturally studious, and it could not have been agreeable to return to schoolboy status after the excitements of active service. The Abbé Montagu was kind and tactful. Gloucester went on with his lessons; and at first nothing, or almost nothing, was said about his faith, although he could not, of course, perform his religious duties. Believing his stay at Pontoise to be temporary – for Charles had promised to send for him as soon as he could afford it – this did not worry him. Mr Lovell, who had forbidden him to play games till he made better progress with his studies, was superseded by Montagu, who encouraged him in all outdoor pursuits, and he was very happy.[3]

Meanwhile, the room in the Louvre which had been set aside for Dr Cosin's celebration of Anglican rites was again closed by Queen Anne's orders. Hearing of this, Lovell became very agitated, but did not report to Charles till the second week in October, when he was summoned to Paris by Henrietta Maria, who said, 'It is my intention – by all fair means – to submit my son to my Church.' Lovell, prepared for this, replied, 'I am under Your Majesty's power – only in the case of religion, I have an obligation on me to speak what I believe to be the truth, therefore while I have the honour to serve that sweet Prince, I shall not be able to say otherwise to him,' adding that if this were an offence, he would not rebel against Her Majesty's sentence. In her kindest manner Henrietta Maria assured him that she would consider before taking further steps. Lovell said, 'I am bound to signify to the King of Your Majesty's discourse,' and offered to show her anything he wrote. She made no objection to this, and Lovell returned to Pontoise and told Gloucester what had passed. The Duke was deeply distressed. 'Ask the Queen not to make me disobey my father and brother,' he said, and assured the tutor that he would be faithful. That same day Montagu told Lovell that he would shortly be dismissed.

A week later the Queen sent for Lovell again and said angrily, 'You are in a plot to steal away the Duke from me.' Lovell denied this, but added that he must stand out against the boy's conversion. Then Gloucester was summoned. Henrietta Maria began, 'You are to be instructed in my religion.' The Duke replied, 'Your Majesty remembers the commands my father left me, and the instructions I received from the King.' Henrietta Maria did not choose to answer this. She said, 'You are to remain in Paris. It is not fit that Mr Lovell should be with you. I do not intend to send him away, but to absent him for a little while. I shall allow him a pension.' She then wrote at length to the King, explaining that she was acting for Gloucester's good and for Charles's service, 'which always holds the first place in my thoughts'. She was not going to use force in saving her son's soul, or fail in her promises to her husband. By the same post, Jermyn told Charles that Gloucester's conversion was in the balance, and that he himself had nothing to do with the Queen's intentions.

All these letters, including one from Gloucester asking for his instructions, reached Charles on or about November 10th. He was in an agony; reserve and self-control were utterly destroyed. Hyde, who had never seen him in such a state, was as much concerned for him as for Gloucester. To Henrietta Maria Charles wrote, 'I am so troubled by this that I cannot say all that I would ... If you proceed in this I cannot believe that you either believe or wish my return to England ... Nothing I can ever say or do will make my Protestant subjects believe but that this is done with my consent – and all that I say or do is only a grimace. Remember the last words of my dead father, who charged my brother upon his blessing never to change his religion ... ' He then rated Jermyn for his negligence and added that he was sending Ormonde to fetch Gloucester away. To the Duke himself he sent the celebrated letter of protest and warning which unconsciously reveals his own attitude towards all religious belief.

Dear Brother, I have received yours without a date, in which you mention that Mr Montagu has endeavoured to pervert you in your religion. I do not doubt but that you remember very well the commands I left with you ... and am confident you will observe them. Yet the letters that come from Paris say that it is the Queen's purpose to do all she can to change your religion, which, if you hearken to her or to anybody else in that matter, you must never think to see England or me again; and whatsoever mischief shall fall on me or my affairs from this time, I must lay all on you, as being the cause of it. Therefore consider well what it is, not only to be the cause of ruining a brother that loves you well, but also of your King and country. Do not let them persuade you either by false or fair promises; for the first they neither dare nor will use; and for the second, as soon as they have perverted you, they will have their end, and will care no more for you. I am also informed that there is a purport to put you in the Jesuits' College, which I command you upon the same grounds never to consent unto. And whensoever anybody shall go to dispute with you in religion, do not answer them at all ... If you do not consider what I say to you, remember the last words of your dead father ... Which, if you do not observe, this shall be the last time you shall ever hear from, dear Brother, your most affectionate Brother,

CHARLES R.[4]

275

Four years earlier, the writer of this letter had professed himself convinced by Father Huddleston's *Short and Plain Way to the Christian Faith*. Now he announced that the members of that faith, having 'perverted' his brother, would abandon him. Yet this change of front is less remarkable than the King's total disregard of spiritual values. Religion is here treated as the appendage to politics. The only moral issues raised are those of Gloucester's promise to his father and his duty as a subject. Although it would have been pointless, in such a crisis, to discuss dogma with a boy of the Duke's calibre, the single-minded practicality of Charles's instructions, dashed off at white heat, show the high price he put on religion being a trump card in a game of which he had now grasped all the complications. Whatever the beliefs of the man whose death-bed conversion is one of the most famous in history, they were subordinated, then and always, to material issues. Charles's appeal was magnificently phrased; he did not know that it was superfluous. Nothing could shake Gloucester's piety, which was immovably based on the faith the King himself had already betrayed.

Some days before this letter was written Gloucester was put to the test by Montagu, who praised his dutifulness to Charles and pointed out that he could best serve him by becoming a Catholic.[5] 'I should thereby but hurt the King,' said the Duke. 'That need not be,' Montagu smoothly replied, and gave him a brief explanation of his brother's dependence on the Catholic powers, adding that Gloucester himself would benefit by being made a Cardinal. The little Duke burst out furiously with his only argument: the Queen's promises to his father and brother, and his own oath to the dead King. Before Montagu could reply, he asked why he had been left without advice – where were Mr Lovell and Dr Cosin? – and haughtily added that he should not be attended by only two grooms and his page, Mr Griffiths. Montagu then lost his temper, told Gloucester that he was to go back to Paris, to be received by Louis XIV – and that he looked disgracefully untidy and must get his hair cut before appearing at the Louvre.[6]

On his arrival in Paris Gloucester and Henrietta Maria resumed their arguments. At last she said sharply, 'There is nothing left for you to rise but by your book and the Church. If you do not become a Catholic, your brother will never succeed. Also, the Queen of France will give you benefices which will maintain you in great splendour.' 'I will never change my religion,' Gloucester repeated, 'I beseech Your Majesty not to press me further.' They then left for the Louvre, where the Duke was received 'with great civility' by Louis XIV, Anne of Austria and Cardinal

Mazarin. There was no talk of religion till Queen Anne said to Henrietta Maria, 'Is the Duke absolutely turned?' 'Not yet,' was the answer, upon which both Queens refused to speak to or look at him.[7]

Meanwhile, Lovell was told by Montagu that he would be wise to leave France. The tutor went to ask Henrietta Maria if she commanded him to do so. She replied, 'I thought you would be best away while I have the Duke otherwise instructed.' 'I must follow my duty,' Lovell expostulated. 'I expect your obedience,' said the Queen. 'May I continue as I am until I hear from His Majesty?' pleaded the tutor. 'That will be too long to wait,' was the answer. 'And should the King send any directions contrary to my will and pleasure, you cannot expect to be allowed to follow them.' Once more, Lovell referred to the King's instructions. 'One promise was made only against force,' she replied, 'the other on the condition that it should be to the Duke's good that you should be gone.'[8]

All this time no word came from Cologne. Gloucester wrote asking for advice and support from Mary of Orange, and from York, who was once more at the front. These letters seem not to have reached them. Lovell's and Charles's did, a few days later. Meanwhile Dr Cosin was appealing to Lord Hatton, whom Charles had told to keep an eye on the Duke, with the result that Hatton was able to provide Gloucester with a written argument defending his faith. This threw the boy into greater confusion; theology was beyond him. Griffiths then read the paper and made a précis of it, which his master learnt by heart.[9]

A few days later, when Gloucester had returned to Pontoise, Lovell and Montagu came in to him together, and a fierce dispute ensued. By now Gloucester realized that his tutor was too frightened of Henrietta Maria to be of any use. As soon as they were alone, he said, 'They have brought me to ruin – I am left without any assistance.' 'Appear submissive, but remain constant,' was all Lovell could think of to say. Gloucester suggested that when he next saw his mother he should show her the instructions left him by the King. When he did so, she told him that he had misunderstood them.

So the battle raged till November 20th, when Ormonde arrived and went at once to Henrietta Maria at the Palais Royal. Two days later York, at Charles's desire ('I conjure you ... to hinder these practices'), came on leave and was told by his mother that she would allow him to see Gloucester only on condition that religion was not discussed.[10]

Shortly before Ormonde's arrival Hyde's and Charles's letters to Gloucester, Henrietta Maria, Lovell and Jermyn reached them, and their replies were being received at Cologne. This immense correspondence shows the most persecuted figure to be Gloucester's tutor. Poor Mr Lovell, hurrying from Pontoise to Paris and back again, in agony for his charge and his livelihood, and beaten down by the Queen Mother's rages, was now subjected to the King's cold censure and Hyde's blighting criticisms. In his agitation, Charles blamed Lovell for not removing Gloucester the moment Henrietta Maria's crusade began, regardless of the fact that she held the purse-strings, and that the only way Lovell could keep in touch with his pupil was through partial submission to her. When Hyde rated Lovell for 'giving up the game' and Gloucester reproached him for his weakness, the miserable man begged to be allowed to leave, and finally fell back on the excuse of ill health; and indeed what he went through might have affected the strongest constitution. A dynasty and a kingdom were at stake; by this time, all Europe was watching the fight for Gloucester's soul. The English Government was jubilant; most of the exiled Protestants, Mary of Orange among them, expected defeat: while those Catholics who were, so to speak, inside the barrier, considered that the Queen of England was once more making a fool of herself and had not a chance of success. 'I admire the madness of the scheme,' remarked the elegant Duc de Vendôme; indeed, the French nobility found themselves spectators of the best entertainment they had seen for years.

The hand-writing of the protagonists, most of whose letters are now in the Bodleian, is curiously indicative of their respective temperaments. Charles's hurried, rather shaky yet legible script contrasts with his mother's vast, sloping, blotted characters. Gloucester's schoolboy scrawl, starting at the top of the page and ending in a corner, shows him toiling to explain and forcing back his tears. 'Whatsoever ... anyone may say against Your Majesty, I will never believe them or disobey you ... Your Majesty's most affectionate and most humble and most obedient brother, subject and servant, Henry.' Charles's penultimate warning to his mother is a masterpiece of respect, firmness and common sense.

> Madame, I cannot forbear renewing my humble suit to Your Majesty concerning my brother Harry ... See the unrecoverable mischief it will be to me, nay, I may say ... to Your Majesty and all Catholics ... Your Majesty will think that reasonable which I so much

insist upon and resolve ... Therefore I humbly beseech Your Majesty not to press ... upon him until he knows my pleasure. Your Majesty's most humble and most obedient son and servant, CHARLES R.[11]

This letter reached Henrietta Maria just as arrangements had been completed to put Gloucester in the Jesuits' College, thus making it clear to the world that he was about to be received into her Church. At this point Sir George Ratcliffe, a friend of Lord Hatton's, managed to see the Duke alone and, assuming that he had given in, warned him that by English law anyone so educated was, technically, a criminal. Henry said, 'My father bid me to be neither Papist nor Puritan,' and burst into complaints of his brother. 'If he had taken me with him, I had not been in this trouble.'[12] Ratcliffe was followed by Anne of Austria, who gently begged her nephew not to dramatize the situation and upset his mother. 'Why not go to the Jesuit College on condition that religion is not discussed? If you do not, you will cause a division in the royal family, and complete all their misfortunes.' Gloucester replied, 'The King's commands are positive against my going to the Jesuits' College, as against changing my religion – and therefore my going thither will of itself make this division.'[13]

Jermyn also tried to make light of the whole affair. When the struggle was at its height, he sent Charles a chatty, gossiping screed. The Duke of Gloucester was very well, the Princess Henrietta Anne had been poorly but was better, Louis XIV was 'after a great stag', etc. etc. Meanwhile Lovell was able to report that His Highness's behaviour had been 'so pretty' that he needed no one's help. This was far from being the case; but Gloucester received support with Charles's next letter. 'I am so overjoyed at your handsome carriage in this business that I cannot say enough to thank you for it ... Be steady and stout ... Follow what my Lord of Ormonde shall advise, and hearken to no one who shall say anything to the contrary.'[14]

When the Duke heard that Ormonde had talked to his mother, his spirits rose; then once more he was plunged into misery by the substitution of the Abbé Montagu for Mr Lovell as his tutor. Now, but for the faithful Griffiths, he was alone at Pontoise. Why did not Ormonde come to him? He waited in despair.

James Butler, twelfth Earl and first Marquess of Ormonde (he received his dukedom in 1661), was an astute, high-principled and selfless patrician, who had lost his whole fortune – nearly a million pounds – in the Royalist cause. Everyone liked and respected him: but he could be formidable; and later on he put Henrietta Maria in her place. When she said that if she had been trusted, Charles would have now been in England, Ormonde replied, 'If it had not been for Your Majesty, he would never have been out of England.' She dreaded seeing him; when she did so, on the evening of November 21st, Jermyn was with her.

Ormonde gave her Charles's letters and repeated his protests and arguments. The Queen heard him without interrupting. Then she said, 'It lies upon my conscience to reform my son of his errors. As to the danger to the King, that has been put into his head by others.' Ormonde replied, 'Your Majesty would be loath to answer for some of the designs the Roman Catholics might have,' and asked her why she had broken her promises to Charles. 'They extended only to using no violence,' said the Queen. (She was perfectly sincere, for she had neither flogged, starved nor imprisoned her youngest son.) 'The discharging Mr Lovell,' replied Ormonde gravely, 'the sending the Duke to the country where none can have free conference with him, and the purpose of sending him to the Jesuits cannot but be held as a very austere compulsion.' Henrietta Maria then tried to make out that Lovell's dismissal was partly his own wish. 'Lovell absolutely denies his consent,' said Ormonde. 'My Lord Jermyn,' the Queen insisted, 'told me that Mr Lovell's departure could not injure the King.' Jermyn, who had decided to change sides, contradicted her. 'Allez – allez! Vous êtes un impertinent!' screamed the exasperated lady, and turning to Ormonde said that she would think over what he suggested. 'You need not go to Pontoise,' she went on hastily. 'The Duke will return tomorrow or the day after.'[15]

Ormonde ignored this hint, and early the next morning reached Pontoise to find Gloucester in deep depression but resolute and calm. On the 23rd they returned together to Paris, and Gloucester was reinstalled in his rooms at the Palais Royal. He was then implored by Anne of Austria to remember that he was 'a child of France', which he stoutly denied.[16]

On the morning of the 28th Henrietta Maria sent for him and embraced and coaxed him. Of course he could join the King if he liked. 'But for love of me,' she said, 'enter the Jesuits' College and listen to the Abbé Montagu.' She then left him to think over what she had said till the evening, when Henry confronted her with his final refusal, formally phrased. 'I am extremely afflicted,' he said, 'to be unable to obey both my mother and brother. But the King's commands are more suitable to my inclination and duty.' Henrietta Maria cried, 'I will not own you as my son! I will see your face no more! Leave me, leave my lodgings – you shall have nothing! My lord of Ormonde shall provide for you.'[17]

Gloucester burst into tears and rushed away to York's apartments. James, having tried, unsuccessfully, to plead with the Queen, did his best to comfort Henry. When Montagu and Ormonde came in to them next morning, the elder brother was silent and embarrassed. Seeing that Gloucester remained firm, Montagu said, 'Then Her Majesty will see your face no more.' 'At least let me have her parting blessing,' the young Duke sobbed out, and Montagu, who was very fond of him, suggested that he should waylay her as she went to Mass at Chaillot.

On November 29th, York and Gloucester, followed by Montagu, waited outside the chapel. As the Queen's coach came by, Gloucester knelt in the road, holding out his hands. She swept on, without a word or a look. Montagu came up and asked what had happened. The tears streaming down his face, Gloucester replied, 'What I may thank you for, sir. And what my mother said to me, I now say to you – I will see your face no more.' 'Where you are going, Sir?' 'To church!' replied the Duke, and with his brother went to morning service in Sir Richard Browne's chapel.[18]

When Gloucester returned to his rooms he found that the sheets had been stripped from his bed, his horses turned out of the stable and no food provided. In a last attempt at reconciliation, he went to the Queen's apartments. The ten-year-old Henrietta Anne was there alone. She had been told that her brother had committed a great sin and was forbidden to speak to him. The servant was so taken aback when Gloucester appeared, that he announced him as 'a gentleman', and withdrew. The poor little Princess cried, 'O God, my brother – O me, my mother! What shall I do?' As she stood there sobbing, Gloucester turned away in silence and went to find Ormonde, who had been asking Henrietta Maria if he might remove the Duke from the palace. 'I will take no more care for him,' she replied. 'Have I Your Majesty's leave to go with him to the King?' Ormonde asked. 'You may have my leave for nothing – but I will not hinder you from doing what you please,' said the Queen. Meanwhile, as a final assault, Philippe d'Anjou, attended by his Governor, was pointing out to Gloucester the evils of heresy. After a heated argument the two boys parted in anger.[19]

On November 30th Ormonde and Gloucester went to Sir Richard Hatton's house, where they stayed till the Marquess raised the money for their journey to Cologne. He sold his last and most treasured possession, the diamond George given him by Charles I. Even so, he was not able to collect the necessary funds for Gloucester to travel as became his rank – Ormonde was very strict in such matters – till December 18th, when they left for Antwerp. Here the Duke, worn out, fell ill and they were detained for some weeks.

The Catholic point of view was summed up by the Venetian ambassador. 'The princes of the House of Stuart,' he informed the Senate, 'having been expelled from the kingdoms of this world, will now submit to banishment from the kingdom of Heaven.'[20] In England, the effect of Gloucester's victory was a blow to the Government, driven home by a member of the Commons rising in the House to demand the King's return. Nicholas set about publicizing the story as a proof of Charles's integrity; but he thought that Henrietta Maria's behaviour – 'though I am one she hates' – and above all, her refusal to give Gloucester her blessing, should be glossed over. When Mary of Orange wrote to Charles to say that she thought he had been too severe with the Duke, he replied that all further discussion of 'this unhappy business' must cease. Mr Lovell accompanied Gloucester to Holland. No one trusted him. Presently he was accused, quite unjustly, of having become a Parliamentary spy.

Henrietta Maria's resolve that her youngest son should see her face no more was confirmed. He never went back to Paris. He died of smallpox in September 1660, six weeks before her return to England.

NOTES

1 *Cal. Clar. S. P.*, vol. II, p. 392.
2 *Nicholas Papers*, vol. II, p. 91.
3 *Cal. Clar. S. P.*, vol. II, pp. 403–21.
4 Ibid.
5 *Nicholas Papers*, vol. II, p. 119.
6 Ibid.
7 Ibid.
8 *Cal. Clar. S. P.*, vol. II, pp. 403–35.
9 Carte, *Ormonde*, vol. II, p. 162.
10 *Cal. Clar. S. P.*, ibid.
11 Ibid.
12 Ibid.
13 *Nicholas Papers*, vol. II, p. 113.
14 *Cal. Clar. S. P.*, ibid.
15 Ibid.
16 Ibid.
17 Somers, vol. VI (2nd collection), p. 323.
18 *Cal. Clar. S. P.*, ibid.
19 Ibid.
20 *Cal. S. P. Ven.*, vol. XXIX, pp. 282–3.

————◆•◆•◆————

CHAPTER THREE

SPIES AND PLOTS

I

THE politician who advertises his religious beliefs without complete conviction of their validity is sometimes more to be pitied than the devotee whose adherence to his faith entails perils and sacrifices. As soon as it was known that Gloucester had refused to be converted, the German Catholic powers on whom Charles now most relied showed that they were disappointed, and that they would have helped him if his brother had become a member of their Church.[1] So, once more, the King was made to feel that his efforts had been wasted and to wonder if he would have done better to let his mother send Gloucester to the Jesuits' College, thus giving Europe the impression that he himself was in favour of the Duke's conversion. No one in Charles's immediate circle doubted that he had acted rightly; but his much deplored 'aversion to all sorts of strictness in religion' was enhanced by the disapproval of the Catholics and the comparative indifference of the Anglicans, when they heard the story of Gloucester's resistance.

Although Charles's own convictions remained, as he intended, hidden till the moment of his death, there is some evidence that several years before the Restoration he had come to prefer the old faith to that in which he had been baptized. Halifax and the Duchess of Portsmouth, both good judges of character, who knew him intimately during the last ten years of his life, stated categorically that he became a Catholic – though it is unlikely that he was formally received into that Church – during the 1650s.[2] Some less reliable witnesses – Burnet, Henrietta Maria and James II – shared this view. (James's belief in his brother's conversion was conclusively established in 1668, when Charles told him, with tears, not only that he was himself a secret Catholic, but that he desired his brother's advice on how best to restore the old faith throughout his dominions.) The Bishop's final judgment – 'he seemed to have no sense of religion' – is perhaps the best guide to Charles's state of mind when he realized that his support of Gloucester had been of no practical use, and might in fact have weakened his own position. He appears to have received little or no praise from the English Royalists for his behaviour in this crisis, perhaps because they took Gloucester's firmness for granted. And this so-called victory raised two new problems: the disposal of the little Duke and the appeasement of the infuriated Queen Mother. Charles could not afford to keep Gloucester; nor could he ask his Catholic hosts to support him. Henrietta Maria refused to answer his and Gloucester's letters; she returned the Duke's unopened. So Charles fell back on Mary of Orange. That devoted sister agreed to receive Gloucester and to arbitrate with the Queen. As soon as he recovered, the Duke, accompanied by Mr Lovell, joined her at Teylingen.

By this time, Gloucester had been told, and of course believed, that he was a hero and a martyr, with the result that he became as rude and over-bearing as when he was being made much of in Paris. He wrote facetiously to Nicholas and Hyde, whom he promised to join 'in all sports', urging the Chancellor not to be lazy.[3] When Ormonde's restraining influence was removed by his return to Cologne, and one of Charles's gentlemen, a rather undesirable character called Nicholas Armorer, escorted Henry to the Hague, the young Duke became still more out of hand. He annoyed the functionaries of the States General by his arrogance; they particularly objected to his habit of mounting his horse at the foot of the staircase instead of in the courtyard.[4] Mary could have put an end to this boyish swaggering; but in her eyes her brothers could do no wrong, and she ignored the Stadtholders' request that Gloucester should be sent away.

Another reason for Henry's bad manners may have been his impatience to join Charles, who was now resigned to spending a dull and icy winter in Cologne. It was impossible to keep warm indoors; so every day the King and his gentlemen walked round the city ramparts or rode in the fields; here etiquette was preserved for the public view by the courtiers going bare-headed. Sometimes they hunted, leaving with the first light and returning at dusk; but sport was always poor. Yet Charles remained cheerful. He 'composed', Hyde noted, 'his mind to his fortune; and ... prescribed so many hours in the day to his retirement in his closet; which he employed both in reading and studying the French and Italian languages.'[5]

Meanwhile, he was criticized for refusing to subscribe to impractical schemes for invasion, the murder of Cromwell and a secret journey into England. 'I hope,' he wrote to one disappointed Royalist, 'my friends will think I am now too old and have had too much experience of things and of persons to be grossly imposed upon ... I hope we shall shortly see a turn and ... that I shall live to bid you welcome at Whitehall.'[6] Henry

Bennet's request to spend Christmas at Cologne was answered in His Majesty's most genial manner. 'Harry, you may easily believe that my approbation for your coming hither would not be very hard to get, if you had no other business here than to give me an account of how Arras was relieved, or who danced best in the masque at Paris ... One of the greatest alterations you will find here is that my Lord Taaffe is become one of the best dancers in the country ... I have nothing to add ... but to tell you that I am still a good Bablon.'[7]

Charles, Bennet and Taaffe were making the best of such diversions as these, when Lucy Walter appeared with little James and Sir Henry de Vic, the King's representative in Brussels. Their relationship had caused some talk ('I am sorry for poor Sir Henry,' remarked Elizabeth of Bohemia[8]) with the result that this rather simple gentleman was bent on marrying the fascinating Mrs Barlow. So they had come to Cologne for Charles's permission. This was refused, de Vic was reprimanded for having left his post without leave, and he, Lucy and the child returned to Brussels. In January 1655 Charles consulted with Hyde and Ormonde, and it was agreed that Lucy must, somehow, be pensioned; for she had parted from de Vic, and was now in sole charge of the six-year-old James, for whom his father was, as ever, much concerned. Charles then sent Lucy a written promise of £400 a year, 'at four several payments ... from three months to three months ... with assurances to better the same, when it shall please God to restore us to our kingdom'.[9] A few months after she received the first instalment Lucy and her children came under the protection of a married man, Colonel Thomas Howard, brother of the Earl of Suffolk and Master of the Horse to Mary of Orange. So, presumably, Charles tried to forget the mother of his son. He could have threatened to stop her annuity if she became a nuisance; he could have handed her over to Sir Henry de Vic and saved himself £400 a year. That he did neither seems to show that she still had a hold over him.

Shortly after dealing with Lucy Charles received a message from the Duke of Neuburg announcing the death of Innocent X and the accession of Alexander VII, 'of which,' the envoy told him, 'Your Majesty has great cause to be glad'. As the new pontiff seemed even less likely to finance him than the old, Charles made no reply. Next day Neuburg, after thanking him for the gift of a horse, said, 'Alexander VII will do you greater service,' going on to explain that for many years the new Pope, a Chigi, had been planning to restore the English monarchy. 'I will promote it,' the Duke continued, 'having some influence with His Holiness.' He suggested sending a Jesuit emissary to Rome on Charles's behalf. The King listened in silence; then he said, 'I will commit it to your wisdom to do those offices with the new Pope which you think fit. I will do anything it is fit for me to do.' Neuburg replied that Charles must first promise to suspend the anti-Catholic laws.

It was the old story. 'If it shall be in my power,' said Charles patiently, 'it shall never be in my will, to execute those severe laws. But it is not in my power absolutely to repeal them – and it would be less in my power, if I declare that I have a purpose to do it. Therefore, that must be left to time.' A few weeks later he received 'general good wishes' from the new pontiff without even the promise of support. All Charles could do was to renew his vague assurances of toleration, adding, 'If the Pope will supply the King only with money, it will enable him speedily to put himself in a good posture.' There was no answer to this letter.[10]

By this time, Charles's financial situation had so deteriorated that he was forced to send to London for some of the money which was being held against the next Royalist rising. In the first week of January the reply came. There was no money left, and no hope of any. 'Yours of the 3rd,' the King wrote, ' ... brought me the most melancholic news ... I have yet received. I am so unable to bear this condition of life much longer, that if there be not a probable hope ... I resolve ... to serve against the Portugals in the Indies, or to serve the Venetians against the Turks, rather than lead this idle life.'[11] Later that day, when the French invasion of Naples was being discussed, the King burst out, 'It were better for Mazarin to give me that army! I will do more service with them in England than Guise should in Italy. But God grant that Mazarin may be as good as his word in what else he promised.'

In moments of black despair judgment is lost. When the Royalists whom Charles had instructed to take no risks wrote to tell him that a new rising had been planned, and that they were fully armed and prepared, he hesitated. To their next message – 'We only desire Your Majesty to appoint the day' – he gave a non-committal answer. He said to Hyde, 'I know very well they will be deceived. There is too much division and lack of trust.' He was then informed that a general rebellion would begin on April 18th. All he had to do was to wait in some port whence he could embark as soon as Parliament capitulated.[12]

Charles's pessimism gave way; even Hyde thought that he should obey the summons. Wilmot was sent on ahead, to say that His Majesty would sail from Flushing. In the second week of February Charles and Ormonde, with a single groom, left Cologne very early in the morning for the island of Middleburg, where they were concealed in the house of Sir

Gelyn Quirensen, a Dutchman knighted by the King soon after his accession.

Charles and Ormonde were not counting on victory; but the prospects seemed excellent. Neither of them knew – and nor did the Chancellor, though he chose to be wise after the event – that all their correspondence, both with England and the Continent, was being copied and passed on to Cromwell's Secretary of State. A new agent – efficient, meticulous and perfectly disguised – had been installed in Cologne some months earlier. Already the Protector's secret service was looking out for the arrival of 'a young, tall, black man called Charles Stuart' in London.[13] ('If he is in London,' noted one disillusioned Royalist, 'he is doubtless in Bedlam, as a madman.'[14]) Meanwhile, some hundreds of Cavaliers were telling one another that the day of reckoning had come at last.

II

In the winter of 1654 there arrived at Cologne an intelligent, handsome and well dressed Catholic Cavalier called Henry Manning, whose credentials were of a high order. This 'very proper young gentleman', educated in the household of the Marquess of Worcester, had lost his father and had himself been wounded in the shoulder at the battle of Alresford. Among other letters of recommendation he brought one from Dr Earle, Charles's former tutor and chaplain. When the King told him that he could not afford to employ any more secretaries, Manning replied, 'I have sold the encumbered fortune my father left me. I have enough to maintain me, and resolve to spend it in waiting upon Your Majesty, till Your Majesty can raise an army – in which I hope to have an opportunity to avenge my father's blood.' Further questioned, he was able to show that he knew, and was in touch with, most of the leading Royalists in England. Another asset was his acquisition of the Parliamentary *Diurnal*, or news-sheet, which was circulated in Europe but difficult to obtain in Cologne. A friend in Antwerp, Manning said, sent it to him every week.[15]

Manning was first introduced into Charles's circle by Wilmot who, hearing his qualifications, declared that he had been sent from Heaven. During the weeks that elapsed between his arrival at Cologne and Charles's secret departure to Middleburg he proved himself invaluable and came up to all his patron's expectations. Hyde, who never got on with Wilmot (he disapproved of his drunkenness and had been disgusted by his inefficiency during the mission to Ratisbon), took against Manning, not so much for himself as because he was Wilmot's protégé. This upset the young secretary, who begged Wilmot to speak for him to the Chancellor, and hinted that he had something of great moment to tell Hyde and the King. When they received him, Manning produced a 'token' from the Earl of Pembroke. This was a classical waxen head, which seems to have been copied from an item in Pembroke's collection, and to have been recognized by Charles. Manning then said that if His Majesty and the Chancellor would accept this object as being the proof of his connection with Pembroke, he was empowered to offer the King £3,000 on the Earl's behalf. Charles was delighted. Hyde had a feeling, which he could not then verify, that Pembroke had been ruined in the Civil War, and was not in a position either to lend or give such a sum. While he was trying to find out about Pembroke's finances, Manning became one of the King's inner circle and went everywhere with him.[16]

Manning's contact with Cromwell's Secretary of State was effected through a Parliamentary agent in Antwerp, from whom he received his salary and instructions, and who sent on his letters to London. This channel of communication was so well organized that for eleven months – from January to November – Manning was able to send off long and detailed reports two or three times a week. Early in 1655 his information led to the imprisonment and execution of a number of Royalists, whose rising had been planned for February.

As an agent, Manning was well worth what he earned, but for two weaknesses; he was inclined to over-rate his own abilities, and fancied himself as a writer. His descriptions of Charles's life in Cologne and elsewhere were sometimes interlarded with irrelevant discourses, most of which were commonplace generalizations about life. During the summer and autumn of 1655 these gave way to invention. Fearing, perhaps, that his employers might find his information humdrum and thus valueless, he supplemented it with fictitious accounts of dramatic scenes in Council, or in the King's bedchamber. This habit grew on him. His first efforts had been accurate and succinct.[17]

When Manning realized that the King had left Cologne for an unknown destination, he was very much disturbed. Then, through Colonel Herbert Price, one of Wilmot's friends, he found out where Charles was going, and got Wilmot's leave to follow him there before Wilmot himself left for England. With Price, he shadowed the King and watched the Quirensens' house. The result was not very satisfactory. Charles remained indoors during the day, only venturing out at twilight to walk alone, or with Ormonde, along the canals and by the seashore. Manning, aware that his sudden appearance might arouse the King's distrust, told Price – who had no idea that he was a Parliamentary spy – to approach Charles on one of these walks, find out what his plans were and offer him their joint services. When Price did so, the King was displeased and taken aback. 'I charge you,' he said, 'make no discovery, but remove out of the island, lest your being seen here raise suspicion.' 'May I bring Manning to speak with Your Majesty – as an honest man?' Price asked. Charles refused, Price went away and Manning remained, taking care that the King should think he had gone back to Cologne.[18]

It was much more difficult for Manning to convey his reports to Antwerp from Middleburg than from Cologne, and they were not of great value. But he did possess, and had already given, full information of the Royalist rising planned for April 18th. He could not find out what Charles's next move would be, because the King did not know it himself; he and Manning both waited, therefore, for news from England. The only thing Manning did not observe was that a young lady, a niece of Lord Cottington's, joined Charles in his hiding-place with her parents. 'Though but little more than a girl,' said Ormonde, '[she] makes the King's confinement more supportable.'[19]

As the weeks went by and Charles received no summons from Wilmot or anyone else, he began to realize that his whereabouts, and therefore the Royalist plans, must be known to Parliament. He could only wait, in fearful anxiety, miserably aware that he had made another fatal mistake.

Wilmot, travelling ahead of his master through Flanders, had fallen in with an old comrade, Sir Joseph Wagstaffe. They got drunk together, and then left for London. Here Wilmot assumed the disguise, a fair wig, which he had refused to wear during the flight from Worcester, and busied himself with the Royalist centres in the city and in the north, risking his life with the utmost coolness. He was energetic and efficient; but he could not get in touch with the King till all his efforts had proved fruitless.

At this point Parliament, alarmed by the spread of Royalist power and feeling, reorganized and increased their intelligence system, and instituted what might be described as terrorist methods. When a nobleman who had been working for the Government asked the Protector's leave to travel on the Continent, he was given it, on condition that he did not see Charles Stuart. On his return Cromwell sent for him and asked, 'Have you punctually obeyed my commands?' 'I have.' 'It's true,' said Oliver, 'that you did not see Charles Stuart – for to keep your word with me, you agreed to meet him in the dark, the candles being put out for that end.'[20] He then outlined their conversation, which seems to have taken place shortly after the King's departure from Middleburg, in the first week in April. Charles left the island when the Dutch began to ask where he was. Meanwhile Manning reported that the King had given out that he was about to embark from Ostend, in order to conceal his real movements.[21]

The Royalists were in arms against the Government in the north, south and west of England during the whole of March 1655. Lack of co-ordination and generalship helped to defeat them; but Manning was chiefly responsible for Parliament being prepared and thus able to dispose of one group after another. Indeed, it is arguable that his efforts prevented a third Civil War and the slaughter of thousands of English people. As it was, twenty Royalist leaders were executed and some hundreds sold as slaves to the Barbadoes.

The disaster was complete; and presently those who had escaped abroad or were still in hiding at home began to say that Charles – recently described by the Venetian ambassador as 'bold and hazardous, [with] more courage to brave danger than patience to suffer wrongs'[22] – was largely to blame for his followers' martyrdom. 'The King kept not the day appointed, but broke twice with them, which made them think they were fooled,' wrote one; and in Paris, Buckingham was saying that 'the failing of the King's designs [was] through his own default'.[23]

Charles did not attempt to defend himself from these perfectly unjust accusations. When he joined Hyde at Breda, and with him and Ormonde returned to Cologne, he was given up to horror and despair. Long afterwards, Hyde remembered the young man's 'agony' as the news came in of Cromwell's reprisals. 'His heart was almost broken,' he wrote;[24] and the fact that the King had authorized the rebellion after much consideration and against his better judgment was no consolation. Now his situation appeared quite hopeless; yet in these first weeks he seemed not to concern himself for that, but to be thinking only of his lost Cavaliers, those gallant gentlemen who had mounted the scaffold declaring that they asked nothing better than to die for King Charles.

His misfortunes were to continue for five more years. Yet never again was he able to feel rather for others than for himself. Remorse so ravaged him that he looked ten years older – 'withered', as one of the intelligencers put it; and he emerged from that misery, brief though it was, in a state of dull, hard indifference, turning away from sadness because it bored him. He could no longer feel love, or hate, or pity; the 'merciful nature' so admired by his companions[25] sprang from this same destruction of the spirit. Revenge was tedious and pointless, his 'cause' a mockery.

The only advantages worth struggling for were what his contemporaries lumped under the heading of 'ease and quiet'. On these points Charles's standards were very high.

He was now more than ever determined to enter his kingdom in order to enjoy absolute freedom from all irksome obligations; for that, he was prepared to work and intrigue and tell as many lies as seemed necessary. The cool determination, the unbroken front which his later correspondence reveals was the result of what Halifax described, many years afterwards, as 'deadness rather than severity'.[26] Charles now looked on stupidity, corruption, treachery, intolerance and conceit as the basis of all human endeavour. Those who, like Hyde, Ormonde and Nicholas, were faithful and laborious had their value because they saved him trouble; and the fact that they and a number of others could not be bought was very convenient. As for his family, the younger they were, the fonder he was of them. At this time, his son and Gloucester came highest in Charles's affections; his attachment to the sister whom their correspondence has made famous as 'my dearest Minette', had not then been formed.

Unless he was alone with Hyde, Charles concealed his moods of depression; it was his policy to appear undefeated and, when surrounded by his younger courtiers, to be all things to all men. The result was that, worthless and trivial though most of them were, they became increasingly devoted to him, partly because he had no use for formality, disliked flattery and was sure enough of his own dignity to be able to dispense with reverential treatment. Then and always, Charles was one of those who enhance gaiety by making others feel witty. Just after his return to Cologne, Taaffe was writing to Ormonde from the Hague of his longing to rejoin their master. 'May I never drink wine,' he says, 'if I had rather not live at six sous a day with him than to have all the pleasures of this world without seeing him ...' adding, 'We shall want you for a dancer, and the King for a toper.'[27]

There was no question of Charles appearing at his sister's Court as a toper, or in any other guise. The States General had forbidden her to receive him in a letter so insolently phrased that she refused to answer it. They now insisted on her getting rid of Gloucester; to his delight, the young Duke joined his brother, in lodgings vacated by Ormonde so that he should be suitably housed. In the same week, May 25th, Henry Bennet wrote from Paris suggesting that Charles and he should meet at Spa, to which the King replied that he could not afford the journey (all his plate had just been stolen), adding, 'Pray send me some of Dupré's opiat, and water for the teeth' – and, a fortnight later, 'Do not forget to send me the *Gazette Burlesque* every week.'[28]

Charles and Gloucester were now studying Italian together. In reply to a letter asking for some books in that language, Mary of Orange concluded a long, gossiping, affectionate screed with the casual messages which were to cause so much misunderstanding about the King's relations with Lucy. 'Your wife is resolving whether she will write or no; therefore I am to say nothing to you from her; but will keep open my letter as long as the post will permit, to expect what good nature will work, which I find now does not at all; for 'tis now eleven of the clock, and no letter comes.' A month later she says, 'Your wife desires me to present her humble duty to you, which is all she can say. I tell her 'tis because she thinks of another husband, and does not follow your example of being as constant a wife as you are a husband; 'tis a frailty that they say is given to the sex; therefore you will pardon her, I hope.' In a third, much shorter letter, Mary speaks not only of 'your wife' but of 'your mother', whose messages she conveys. As Henrietta Maria was then in Paris, the second lady falls into the same category as the first; she becomes one of a circle among whom nicknames are interchanged.[29]

There is no evidence that Mary – a great stickler for etiquette and something of a prude – ever received Lucy, whose reputation was by this time notorious. 'Wife,' then sometimes the equivalent of 'sweetheart' or 'loved one', should therefore be regarded as part of a private joke between the brother and sister – Mary's teasing remark about Charles's 'constancy' is proof of this – concerning somebody who had taken his fancy. His sister's letters cannot be used to clear Lucy's name; for she was now the public mistress of Colonel Howard who, as Mary's Master of the Horse, would never have ventured to bring her to the Princess's Court.

III

Charles had now acquired the attitude of mind of those who, living on credit and charity, contemplate payment of their debts from far off and without conviction. In June 1655 he had enough ready money to afford meals in taverns for ten more days, and he owed his servants three months' board wages; such jewels as remained to him were in pawn, and although a considerable sum was due to him from the German princes, it was already promised to a number of creditors. This did not prevent him ordering, through Bennet, several suits of summer clothes ('very thin and light') from his Paris tailor, a new sword, and some horses from an agent in the

Low Countries. To buy all these items in Cologne would mean being pressed to pay for them; as it was, he could rely on his friends to guarantee, however unscrupulously, his good faith. At the same time, he was planning to entertain his sister Mary and her entourage, which entailed his moving into a larger house. 'How they will all live, God knows,' wrote Manning on June 2nd; a fortnight later he reported that 'this little Court lives still in some splendour ... I wonder by what means.'[30]

These plans were subordinated to more serious endeavours. When Charles's efforts to raise an army in Sweden were abandoned, he began to reconsider the advances of the Republicans, urged on by Buckingham. The Duke wrote that General Sir Thomas Fairfax, whose daughter he was planning to marry, might join in a rising. Once more, the question of Cromwell's murder was raised, but, 'Charles Stuart will not have it done,' wrote Manning in some surprise. A group of Royalists then left the Continent in order to kill the Protector without telling Charles, and were arrested. Again the King was told that he had but to appear in England for 50,000 men to rise. At a Council meeting, he was about to discuss his consent, when Ormonde and O'Neile knelt and begged him not to take the risk. Hyde remained silent and doubtful; Nicholas thought he might succeed. Charles said that he did not trust these advances, adding, 'But I will go, rather than be thought a coward.' To Hyde and Manning he said gloomily, 'They will crown Cromwell.'[31]

By the end of June all hope of another rebellion had faded, and the King was again placating the Catholic princes by taking Gloucester to compline for the feast of St Anthony of Padua, with the result that on July 8th the moneys due to him arrived. 'Very jocund', at being in funds, Charles saw the Duke of Neuburg alone for two hours, presumably in order to discuss Mazarin's letter, in which the Cardinal had offered him the hand of one of his nieces; this scheme was abandoned.

On July 5th Charles wrote to Bennet about his Paris commissions. 'My clothes are at last come, and I like them very well, all but the sword, which is the worst I ever saw; I suspect very much that it was you that made the choice, therefore you have no other way ... but to make choice of a better, and if you go to the shop where I bought mine when I came out of Paris, you can hardly be mistaken.' A fortnight later he wrote, 'Pray get me pricked down as many new corants and sarabands and other little dances as you can, and bring them with you, for I have got a small fiddler that does not play ill.' All these preparations were for Mary, whom he was impatient to see. 'You must not expect,' he told Bennet, 'to hear from me very often as long as my sister is here ... Indeed, Cologne is not a little altered, for from having very little company, and some of those worse than none, we have now as good a time as can be, and pass our time as well as people can do that have no more money, for we dance and play [cards] as if we had taken the Plate fleet.'³²

In this cheerful mood, Charles made up his quarrel with Prince Rupert, whom he sent to raise money from the German Protestant principalities, beginning with Heidelberg. The King was once more in touch with the Scots Royalists, who visited him in August with a number of impracticable suggestions. They wanted York to come to Scotland, Hyde to be dismissed from the Council and were proposing to hire out their troops for foreign service. 'I doubt not,' Charles wrote to Lord Leven, 'you have [not] ... the least ill purpose ... but I look on all designs of that nature as most prejudicial to my service.'³³ The King then received a Jesuit agent from Rome, to whom he complained of the Holy Father's lack of response to his promises of toleration for Catholics. ('The returns are not such as I expected.') This agent, Father Talbot, described by Hyde as 'the foolish Father', was corresponding with the exiled anti-Cromwellian Presbyterians, who, though willing to support Charles, were disgusted by his courtiers. 'The Cavaliers,' one of them told Talbot, 'are a generation that God cannot prosper; but for their swearing, drinking and whoring – and little secrecy – Cromwell had been down before.'

When Charles set off to join Mary at Aix, he was preceded by Manning, who took the opportunity to call on his fellow-agent in Antwerp. Here he made his first miscalculation. It did not occur to him that the King also had competent intelligencers, many of whom worked for nothing, or paid others to work for them out of their own money. In Antwerp, Goring's spies were well organized, and on the watch, if not very discreet. Manning came across a party of them in a book-shop, where he overheard them abusing Cromwell. He fell into talk with them, and they drank together; they then suggested that he should act as their messenger into England. This alarmed Manning, and he left for Aix to wait for the King.³⁴

Accompanied by Ormonde, Gloucester and a number of attendants, Charles and Mary left Aix for Frankfort, where the annual fair was in progress – 'a strange journey,' complained Nicholas, who was now in charge of the King's finances, 'but young princes think of nothing but pleasure.'³⁵ Here they were joined by Christina of Sweden, who since her abdication had become more peculiar than ever. She dressed as a man, changed her clothes three or four times a day, was very dirty and grimaced when she spoke. Although she continued to praise and pity Charles ('If I had another crown, I would give it you,' she told him) she did nothing for him.[36] Together she and the Stuarts went to a Lutheran service, to a party given by the Bishop of Mainz, and to the opera, where an awkward situation arose. The guest of honour was Charles's cousin, Charles-Louis, eldest son of Elizabeth of Bohemia, who had taken the Parliamentary side in the Civil War, thus cutting himself off from his brothers and his English relatives. He and the King had not met since that day in 1642, when Charles I had taken them to spend the afternoon with Mr Ferrar at Little Gidding. Now Charles-Louis wanted to entertain his cousin, but as a poor relation – in other words, he would not give him or the Princess precedence. The King would not meet him, and retaliated with a cool nod when he and Charles-Louis came face to face at the fair. Charles and his sister spent some time at Heidelberg, where the citizens gave them a present of wine; a few days later a 'stinking' haunch of venison arrived from Prince Rupert which had to be thrown away.[37] They then left for Brussels, where they parted, no doubt thankfully, from Queen Christina, and together returned to Cologne at the end of October, bringing with them rumours of the Protector's death. 'If Cromwell be not dead,' wrote Ormonde to Hyde, 'see there be a good piece of beef – if he be, chickens will serve.'[38] Charles was in high spirits – 'very well pleased with ... as pleasant a journey as ever I saw' – and in great hopes of benefit from England's breach with Spain.

In the King's absence the long-delayed information about Manning's connection with Pembroke had arrived. 'A loose person, of no reputation', and almost penniless, the Earl was totally uninterested in the Royalist cause. 'I doubt Manning has made that part of the story to make himself the more welcome,' said Hyde, as soon as he and the King were alone. 'Use all the means you can to discover the truth,' Charles replied. Hyde did so, and was reassured. Manning was above suspicion. He saw the King most days, and attended all the Council meetings, but remained self-effacing, discreet and conscientious. Everybody liked him, and even the Chancellor had to admit that, although he had been over-optimistic about Pembroke, that was the fault of his youth. His frank, simple manner was particularly pleasing, his piety and industry set his contemporaries a fine example, and his behaviour contrasted admirably with that of the gentlemen of the bedchamber who, in the King's presence, sometimes 'hit and struck one another', till they were forcibly separated by the older Cavaliers.[39]

The Princess of Orange, who remained in Cologne till the second week of November, was also taken in; her chief concern in leaving her brother was her inability to help him. So far, she had failed to reconcile him and Henrietta Maria; she was not allowed to receive Gloucester: and she had no money to spare. Just before she departed news came that Mazarin had decided to discontinue Charles's pension, in view of his rumoured alliance with the Spanish. In the same week the King's financial difficulties were increased by the well-meant but foolish gift of a pack of hounds – fourteen couple – from England, followed by another of horses.[40] How to keep the creatures was a fearful problem; and no one would buy them. By the time they were disposed of, they had incurred another large debt. Momentary relief came with a loan of £2,000 from an anonymous Royalist, and Charles wrote to Bennet, 'I think I may say it, to a Bablonist, that I hope to see you ... before many months',[41] but a few days later his debts had swallowed up the loan, and he was glibly writing to a ruined adherent of his 'grief and compassion', and of his inability to help. While the English Royalists remained 'passionately attached' to Charles and openly drank his health, their efforts to get rid of Cromwell always ended in imprisonment and sometimes in torture. Now his murder was spoken of as 'the most deserving and glorious action'. Even Nicholas considered it worthy of 'a very honourable reward ... on earth, as in heaven'.[42] Then all other considerations gave way to a letter from Goring.

That nobleman had been informed by a Spanish friend recently returned to Antwerp from England, that all the King's plans and those of his correspondents were known to the Protector through an agent in that city. 'The mischief,' Goring added, 'proceeds from some persons near Your Majesty.' Further inquiries showed that, of all his servants, Manning alone heard regularly from a merchant in Antwerp. In the last week of November Mr Jamott, 'a dextrous, faithful and vigilant' courtier, was sent there to find out what he could. On December 4th he returned with several large packets of letters from Manning to Thurloe, Cromwell's Secretary of State, which showed that that hard-working and popular young man had been responsible for the deaths of some dozens of Royalists and the imprisonment and exile of hundreds more.[43]

In a long and secret discussion Charles, Hyde, Ormonde and Nicholas made their plans. The spy must be caught in the act of treachery, and with the proofs of it on his person. A supper-party was arranged for the night of Sunday, December 5th.

Those courtiers who knew nothing of Manning's real activities must have been somewhat taken aback when they realized that Nicholas and Hyde, that elderly and abstemious pair, were about to take part in a 'roistering' evening, instead of leaving them to drink with His Majesty.

The result was that Manning, whose sobriety had so impressed his seniors, felt free to enjoy himself with his contemporaries, and soon reached the hilarious stage. As they continued to pledge him, he was carried from gaiety to somnolence, and fell asleep in his chair. His keys were then taken from his pocket, and the party continued.[44]

When Manning came to himself he got up and staggered to his room. A few minutes later two gentlemen who were in the secret and had remained sober, walked in to find him at his desk, surrounded by letters, ciphers and dispatches. As he tried to tear up the letter on which he was engaged, he was seized, bound, and locked in a room guarded by four of the King's footmen. Next morning the contents of his trunks and desk were examined, and this fresh evidence, together with that already brought from Antwerp, was placed before Nicholas, Ormonde and Hyde, who made a précis of it for the King. The case against Manning was then prepared, great care being taken that it should be conducted according to law and the prisoner given a full and fair hearing. Meanwhile his treachery was made known to the local magistrates, who agreed to imprison him in the city jail. From there he was escorted to an improvised court, in which the principal examiners were Nicholas and Hyde, supported by Charles and Ormonde. Nicholas's son John acted as clerk. In accordance with contemporary custom, the prisoner, although allowed to speak freely and at length and to submit his defence in writing as and when he desired, had no legal adviser. During the next fortnight, for some seven or eight hours a day, he confronted his accusers. He spent most of the night writing long, confused, hysterical letters of remorse and self-exculpation, interlarded with cringing pleas for mercy.[45]

The sensation caused throughout Europe by the Manning case made a fair trial essential. The vast mass of incriminating evidence must be so handled as to publicize the King's justice and thus deprive the English Parliament of all weapons against him. Although there could be but one end to the drama, the process of an ultra-scrupulous hearing was meticulously gone through in order to show that Manning was being given every chance to prove his innocence.

He, of course, could only reiterate that he had been engaged in double-crossing his employers, from whom he had received the enormous salary of £1,200 a year.[46] He declared that he was, and always had been, a Royalist; he 'boiled to avenge his father's blood' and the sequestration of his estate. In proof of this he was able to show that a number of his reports had been invented.

His prosecutors had to admit the truth of this statement, and for a few days it was thought that Manning would escape the supreme penalty. The Cologne magistrates, while refusing to have anything to do with the trial, were keeping a strict watch on it, in the event of the King and his advisers breaking their laws,[47] with the result that the questions put by Nicholas and Hyde (with interventions from Charles and Ormonde) covered every detail of Manning's movements and correspondence for the last eleven months. As they drew the net closer the wretched creature took refuge in muddled and self-contradictory denials. A few examples illustrate the whole.

Q. How did you come to know of His Majesty's purpose to go into Zeeland? You were there as soon as he.

A. I did not know of the King's going to Zeeland or being there, till I came to Middleburg, and saw Sir John Mennes and others there, which gave me suspicion of it, and afterwards I saw His Majesty, as I remember, about Rammekins in a waggon, but I know not whether it were before I spake with Colonel Price or not.

Q. What advertisement have you given of any persons in Kent and what grounds had you for those advertisements?

A. I have often named ... Mr West, Jones, Weeks, Tanner, Draper and some other names, which I cannot remember ... There were no such men in truth, but only names invented by me to amuse [impress] those in England, and to make them believe that I was industrious.

Q. How do you know that the King sent letters to Mr Barton at the Peacock, near Temple Bar, and from whom had you the advice?

A. I knew not that the King sent any letters to Mr Barton ... but ... I did it to amuse Mr Haley with that intelligence.

Manning's other replies abound in such phrases as 'I know nothing', 'I was in drink', 'I do not remember the particulars', 'I wanted money.' These interchanges were supplemented by his written statements which, signed by himself and endorsed by Nicholas, were read aloud in his absence.

I take God to witness, I intended to have served His Majesty ... Having not done it, I most heartily crave my Saviour's forgiveness and my sovereign's most gracious and favourable clemency ... I ... humbly submit myself at His Majesty's feet, to deal with me as he shall think most meet ... My heart hath never run astray from the resolution of dying as willingly in His Majesty's cause as my father before me, although my actions for these months last past have not been suitable.[48]

From the point of view of the English Parliament, Manning was expendable. Another agent, John Adams, had been installed in Rotterdam and was now sending Thurloe reports of the trial. Adams described how, in the first week of December, the Cavaliers had burst into his room with 'the joyful news' of Manning's arrest,[49] while the doomed man, abandoning his defence, begged for mercy on any terms – counter-espionage, retirement into a monastery or a prison – in return for his miserable life. 'I am now in the flower of my age, and have days enough to expiate ... this pernicious crime ... My life shall ever be a pledge to you for it.' At the same time he continued to protest his innocence. 'I never had to do with the rebels' ... 'Those letters that were taken in my trunk were the last that ever should have been written into England.'[50]

His final appearance before his judges was formal – if that can be called so in which the prisoner, half-crazed with terror, sobs out wild denials of accusations already admitted. With merciless propriety, the Council continued to address him as 'Mr Manning' and to record his frenzied replies; yet they themselves were in a quandary. It was all very well to find Manning guilty and to condemn him to execution; but they could not even make the charge in a country where they had no jurisdiction. For several days their appeals to the magistrates of Cologne were received evasively or in silence. 'Nevertheless,' Adams wrote, 'I do not think he can escape alive out of their hands.'[51]

Charles and his advisers were determined not to commit murder. 'All other affairs,' according to Adams, were 'laid aside', while they persisted in their endeavours to follow the form, at least, of legal procedure. When they were allowed to condemn Manning to death, they received another set-back. The Elector of Cologne would not permit him to be executed in his dominions. What was to be done?

Eventually it was decided to put the whole case before a neighbouring potentate, the Duke of Brandenburg, who, after some consideration, gave his verbal consent to a private execution within his territory. It was not a very satisfactory arrangement: but it must suffice; and on December 14th Manning was told to prepare for death on the following morning. He dashed off a last appeal for 'pity, charity and mercy ... from ... a dying man ... Sir, I pray, speak with His Majesty this night, if it be intended so soon.' When the door of his cell did open, it was to admit a Jesuit priest.[52]

At dawn the next morning, Sir James Hamilton and Major Nicholas Armorer came to fetch him, and took him out to the courtyard of the prison, where horses were waiting. He was told to mount, and the three, who had spent so many gay evenings together, rode out of the city. That ride lasted two hours.

They then entered a wood, and Manning was told to dismount ... That same afternoon, a Dutch traveller on his way to Cologne came upon the body of a well-dressed young man lying beneath a tree, shot through the heart. This discovery was duly reported to the authorities.

So Manning's penultimate desire, that he might be allowed to die for His Majesty, was fulfilled. Charles scribbled his epitaph in a gossiping letter to Henry Bennet. He had been too busy to write before, because 'I have ... spent the time examining and discoursing of one of the greatest villains that ever was,' presently adding, 'Bespeak six pair of shoes of my Paris shoemaker, such as he sent me last ... Three must be black, and the other coloured ... Remember to bespeak my sword ... '53

NOTES

1 *Thurloe S. P.*, vol. III, p. 44.
2 Marquess of Halifax, *A Character of King Charles the Second*, p. 7.
3 *Clar. MSS*, vol. LXIX, fol. 190.
4 Scott, *The Travels of the King*, p. 50.
5 Clarendon, p. 820.
6 *Thurloe S. P.*, vol. I, p. 668.
7 *Miscellanea Aulica*, pp. 109–10.
8 Steinmann, pp. 180–216.
9 Ellis, series 2, vol. III, p. 352.
10 *Thurloe S. P.*, vol. III, p. 100.
11 Clarendon, pp. 820–30.
12 Ibid.
13 Ibid.
14 *Nicholas Papers*, vol. II, p. 241.
15 Clarendon, ibid.
16 Ibid.
17 Ibid.
18 Ibid.
19 *Cal. Clar. S. P.*, vol. III, p. 26.
20 Welwood, p. 111.
21 *Thurloe, S. P.*, vol. III, p. 358.
22 *Cal. S. P. Ven.*, vol. XXX, p. 30.
23 *Nicholas Papers*, vol. III, p. 41.
24 Clarendon, ibid.
25 Bulstrode, p. 222.
26 Halifax, *Character of King Charles the Second*, p. 50.
27 H.M.C. Report 3, vol. III, p. 569.
28 *Misc. Aulica*, p. 114.
29 *Thurloe S. P.*, vol. I, Addenda.
30 Op. cit., vol. III, p. 533.
31 Ibid.
32 *Misc. Aulica*, pp. 116, 120.

33 *Thurloe S. P.*, vol. II, p. 692.
34 Op. cit., vol. III, p. 721.
35 *Nicholas Papers*, vol. III, p. 60.
36 *Thurloe S. P.*, vol. IV, p. 61.
37 *Cal. Clar. S. P.*, vol. II, p. 59.
38 Ibid.
39 Clarendon, pp. 821–30.
40 *Thurloe S. P.*, vol. II, p. 206.
41 *Misc. Aulica*, p. 123.
42 *Nicholas Papers*, vol. III, pp. 265, 270.
43 *Cal. S. P. Ven.*, vol. XXX, pp. 168–9.
44 Ibid.
45 *Nicholas Papers*, vol. III, pp. 149–203.
46 *Thurloe S. P.*, vol. IV, pp. 290–1.
47 *Hastings MSS* (H.M.C.), vol. IV, p. 94.
48 *Nicholas Papers*, vol. III, pp. 155–72.
49 *Thurloe S. P.*, vol. III, p. 290.
50 *Nicholas Papers*, vol. III, p. 196.
51 *Thurloe S. P.*, vol. III, p. 291.
52 *Nicholas Papers*, vol. III, p. 198.
53 *Misc. Aulica*, pp. 124, 127.

CHAPTER FOUR

THE SPANISH ALLIANCE

I

'THE King of Spain is fierce and yet trembles within himself for the English fleet,' wrote Cromwell's Paris agent in the last week of 1655. 'There is only the poor King of Scots who lies lurking behind the hangings, having no part to act upon the theatre of the world,'[1] while in a London tavern Christopher Emerson was heard to say that the Lord Protector was 'a rogue and a rascal and a bloodsucker, and that his throat should be cut and his head cleft'.[2]

Cromwell was also afraid, not only of the dangers illustrated by such remarks as Emerson's, but of Spain using Charles as a means to encourage and implement them. He had introduced military rule in England, and was about to fight two wars, one against Royalism, and one against Spain, whose representatives in the Netherlands were the Archduke Leopold, General Fuensaldaña and Don Alonzo de Cardeñas, formerly ambassador in London.

The belief that Spain preferred England to be a republic because it weakened her was illusory. The Spanish were ready to work for Charles's restoration so that he might support them against France as soon as he was in a position to do so; and they seem to have been under the impression that the Cromwellian regime was tottering. They therefore offered the King a residence and an income in the Spanish Netherlands through Father Talbot who, in December 1655, set forth their terms. These were Charles's abandonment of the French, his conversion to Catholicism, marriage with one of the Infantas and, rather incongruously, his affiliation with the English Republicans whose disgust with Cromwell was only equalled by their horror of Popery.

Charles was certain that he could handle this situation. It called for his now highly developed technique of 'managing all things ... with ... craft and dissimulation', and so twisting the strands of Royalist support, Republican revolt and Franco-Spanish enmity into a rope with which to hang Cromwell and his dictatorship together. He was not so foolish as to underrate Oliver's power; but he did not grasp the extent of the divisions in Spanish policy, which resulted in their taking away with one hand what they had given with the other. He knew that there could be no question of his openly becoming a Catholic; but a secret (and of course genuine) conversion might be hinted at and talked about while he pinned down Spanish support and collected an army. Meanwhile, he must give the impression of being eagerly courted by the Spanish and advancing towards them in a hesitant and cautious manner. To their first offers he replied that he would leave Cologne only on condition that they establish him and his Court in Dunkirk, as being the nearest port for England. They refused and offered him Bruges, which he rejected. He then agreed to meet their representatives, but not at once.[3] This produced an enthusiastic letter from Father Talbot, suggesting His Majesty's immediate conversion and private talks in Antwerp as a preliminary to his being received by Leopold, Fuensaldaña and Cardeñas in Brussels. 'Tell the King,' Fuensaldaña had said, 'that he shall find among us secrecy, honour and fair dealing ... If he will do what we desire, we will live and die together. Let him make no capitulations, for that will be suspicious. The more he trusts the King of Spain and the Pope, the better it is.' His Holiness, Talbot added, would then help to finance Charles – 'and before six months, the business shall be done'.[4]

Disillusioned though he was, the King did not entirely discount these promises. Some months earlier, he had written to Bennet, 'I cannot hinder myself from building castles in the air,'[5] and paradoxically, these castles now seemed to be materializing in Spain. Charles shared Hyde's contempt for Father Talbot, but was ready to make use of him, in spite of the Chancellor's disapproval. Healthy and attractive young men are naturally resilient; and at twenty-five, Charles's spirits rose at the mere thought of some new activity. Further encouraged by the Princess Mary's promise of some money, he sent Daniel O'Neile to the Hague to collect it in January 1656.

This mission, concealed from Hyde, was to be combined with bribing Lucy to hand over the seven-year-old James, whom his father intended to place with some nobleman to be educated as became his station. Then and always, Charles was a family man; he not only acknowledged, but made himself responsible for, all his children; and he was more than ever concerned for James, who had inherited his mother's beauty and his father's sweet temper. Charles and O'Neile believed that Lucy would part with the boy if it were made worth her while.

In the first week of February, O'Neile got in touch with Lucy through another Royalist. He did not approach her himself, because Charles wished their negotiations to be kept secret. O'Neile was assured that Mrs Barlow 'would obey all His Majesty's commands'. A few days later she said that the King had promised 'he would not have her son from her'.[6]

Very much disconcerted by this volte-face, which he knew to be based on a lie, O'Neile made inquiries as to Lucy's manner of life – and was appalled. It was that of a common prostitute, in spite of the fact that she was being kept by Colonel Howard. Worse still, she was advertising her connection with Charles; she declared that she was his wife, while continuing her relations, not only with Howard, but with a number of other men. 'I am much troubled,' wrote O'Neile, 'to see the prejudice her being here does Your Majesty; for every idle action of hers brings Your Majesty upon the stage.'

O'Neile then went to see Lucy. She told him that Charles had treated her very badly, and taken no care of her or of their son. A few days later, O'Neile, neither a credulous nor a soft-hearted man, was convinced of the beautiful Mrs Barlow's wrongs and wrote to Charles, begging him to help her, in a letter which has not survived, but of which the content is made plain by his next communication.

After some further consideration, O'Neile interviewed Anne Hill who, although still in Lucy's service, was threatening to blackmail her. She said that Lucy had tried to murder her by 'threading a bodkin into her ear while she was asleep'. She added that Lucy had brought on two miscarriages 'by physic', which she had obtained from Dr Russell. (Nothing else is known of this physician.) O'Neile, thinking that this might be an invention, found and interviewed the midwife who had attended Lucy; she bore out the maid's charges, as she did 'the infamous manner of Mrs Barlow's living with Mr Howard'.

O'Neile decided to avert the scandal by bribing Anne Hill to hold her tongue; she agreed to do so for two hundred guilders. By this time, his visits to Lucy had been discovered, with the result that two Dutch ministers, Heenvliet and Neerwick, called on him to say, 'Only ... the consideration of Your Majesty has held [them] not to have her banished this town for an infamous person by sound of drum ... I am not less ashamed,' O'Neile continued, 'to have so much importuned Your Majesty as to have believed her worthy of your care ... It would be well, if Your Majesty would own that child [evidently Lucy had told him that Charles had not done so] and to send her your positive command to deliver him unto whom Your Majesty will appoint.'[7]

At their next interview O'Neile put forward his master's terms. Lucy replied that she did not intend to part with James. It then became clear to

O'Neile that she was so well provided for (she was still receiving £400 a year from Charles) as to be able to use the child in order to bleed the father. 'The only way,' he explained, 'is to necessitate her, if Your Majesty can think her worthy of your care.' Defeated, he left the Hague, without making any further attempt to rescue James, to whom, in fact, his mother was devoted, although her love did not entail the slightest concern for his upbringing or education. He was still illiterate, and living in what might be described as a one-woman brothel. For the moment, Charles could do nothing more; he turned his attention to his dealings with his Spanish allies, while continuing Lucy's allowance.

These negotiations were momentarily halted by the Spaniards' assumption that Charles would inaugurate their joint campaign by 'allowing' Gloucester to become a Catholic. (Henrietta Maria was partly responsible for the general belief that the Duke had been on the point of conversion when Charles recalled him to heresy for political reasons.) Talbot told the King that nothing could be agreed on until his and Gloucester's conversions were accomplished, upon which Goring wrote to Hyde in deep distress – could it be true that His Majesty was about to betray his faith? 'I could say much more to you upon this subject,' he went on, adding that he had hoped to come to Cologne, but could not afford the journey; and now his only pair of shoes was past cobbling, and his coats were so threadbare that he dared not venture out of doors.[8] The Chancellor replied reassuringly; by this time he had resigned himself to Charles's crooked policy, while continuing to deny the rumours of his apostasy.

In February Mary of Orange, who was about to visit Henrietta Maria, complained to Charles of her mother-in-law's interference; when he intervened, the Princess Dowager replied that she had been much offended by his not addressing her as '*ma cousine*' in his last letter.[9] As soon as this breach was healed Charles sent Ormonde to Brussels to announce his arrival. On March 8th he himself left Cologne with two servants and a dozen horse, arriving at Louvain on the 11th. He reached Brussels on the 14th, and was at once asked to leave that city. The Spaniards, annoyed by his precipitate and informal approach, desired him to await their summons in Vilvorde, 'a little, vile dorp', some miles away. Here Fuensaldaña and Cardeñas saw him privately. As Spain and England were now in a state of war, they were afraid of officially committing themselves to the Royalists, and they were disappointed that neither Charles nor his brother had yet been converted. Charles placated them by hinting that he might be able to supply them with Irish troops, of whom a number were serving under Turenne. He said, 'I would remove to Brussels, or to some place in Flanders, that it may be notorious that I am in alliance with His Catholic Majesty. And then you will quickly find what influence I have upon the Irish in France.' The Spaniards refused, on the grounds that Philip IV could not, at the moment, give Charles the honours due to him. 'Will not Your Majesty remove to Bruges,' one suggested, 'and remain there incognito? You will find all respect from the inhabitants of that city.' Charles agreed, on condition that they signed a treaty with him, which they promised to do. Meanwhile, he was once more being shadowed by Cromwellian agents, who bribed the Flemish clerks to give them details of his talks with their Spanish masters.[10] 'Charles Stuart,' Thurloe reported, 'is come into Flanders, and speaks much of the prizes he will take when he makes war against us.' A month later his spies told him that the King had 'declared himself in private to be a Roman Catholic'.

At Vilvorde Charles was recognized – people stopped to stare at him when he went out walking – so he remained indoors during the day in the house provided for him by the Spanish Government. Here he was joined by Bennet and Wilmot, with whom he played cards and worked at his languages. To Ormonde, who was still in Brussels, he wrote for a Spanish Testament and a religious work in Italian, adding, 'I hope for as good news tomorrow as the wine and mutton were to-day, and that you will have better luck at piquet than I have with Harry Bennet at crib-bage.'[11] On April 8th he returned to Brussels for a final conference with Cardeñas, who found 'more in him than in any of his Council', and was much taken with his manner and appearance.[12] On the 12th the treaty was signed, in which the Spaniards promised Charles 4,000 foot and 2,000 horse in return for the West Indian Islands taken from them by Cromwell. In a separate and secret treaty Charles renewed his promise of toleration for Catholics. Next day he attended Mass with the Archduke Leopold, and then retired to Bruges, where one of Hyde's most characteristic letters was awaiting him. 'The eyes of all men,' wrote the Chancellor, 'are on Your Majesty, whose nature they do not yet know ... You will find more ease from one day's frank declaring of your purposes, than of reservations, leading people to believe what, in truth, you absolutely ... abhor.'[13] Hyde went on to describe his own difficulties. Gloucester was impatient to join his brother; and the Cologne tradesmen were sending in bills and threatening letters.

Charles ignored the lecture, and instructed the Chancellor to organize his Court as if 'we were there in person'. He was sending them their wages and writing to Gloucester to explain 'why I have not nor yet cannot send for him'. The King was now staying with old Viscount Tara, 'with trouble to the lord, and no great conveniency to myself', and there was no house available for Gloucester.[14] When Hyde asked leave to join his wife and children at Breda (he had not seen them for over a year) Charles refused, on the grounds that he must remain with the little Duke. 'This is a hard chapter,' he added, 'and I must ask my lady's pardon for it ... I shall have a great care of my papers,' he went on, 'I would you had given me the same caution for my keys, for I lost them on Good Friday, seeing the procession.' William Chiffinch (brother of Charles's famous page of the back stairs), whose wife was the King's laundress, was sent to Bruges with a number of His Majesty's books and papers. 'Pray take order,' Charles wrote, 'that all my books be put up carefully.' Hyde answered with a list of further problems – Gloucester was constantly 'importuning' him to be sent to Bruges, and Mrs Chiffinch had insisted on accompanying her husband; but what really alarmed him was the news that Buckingham had joined His Majesty; Charles's reputation would suffer thereby.[15]

By the end of April Charles had collected enough money to send for Gloucester and Hyde to come to Bruges. 'I ask your wife's pardon for it,' he wrote, 'that it is most necessary for you to make as much haste as your gouty feet will give you leave ... If it had not been for the consideration of my lady, I had not permitted you to play the truant so long. I would you were *beshit* for not letting me have a copy of your book of [ciphers].'[16] Now Charles himself was once more in financial difficulties. The Spaniards had insisted on his refusing his French pension, recently resumed by Mazarin, although theirs was not yet forthcoming.

The King said nothing of the arrest of a Parliamentary spy, who had been paid £2,000 to kill him, nor that this person had committed suicide in prison.[17] It may have been that he was too busy to think of anything but his plan of meeting Lucy at Antwerp in order to persuade her to part with their son. He went there with Wilmot and Ormonde, apparently intending to bring back James to Bruges the same day.

II

Shortly after Charles left Cologne, Lucy Walter, still calling herself Mrs Barlow, had decided to leave the Dutch Netherlands for those of Spain, presumably in order not to be drummed out of the Hague. This entailed her parting from Colonel Howard; it seems to have been understood that he should follow her as soon as he was free to do so. In Antwerp she, young James ('Master Jacky', as Anne Hill called him) and Taaffe's six-year-old daughter were joined by Lucy's two brothers, Justus and John.

At about this time, John offered his services to Nicholas as a spy; they were accepted, and under the name of Mr Hall he travelled to and from England, and appears to have given satisfaction. He was in fact a Cromwellian agent, and one of his duties was to report on his sister's dealings with the King. As the 'debauched' lover of a whore and the father of her son, Charles's reputation would, it was hoped, be so blackened as to make him unacceptable to the majority of Royalists.

After the Manning case Charles's Council had re-doubled their precautions, and it was much more difficult for Cromwell's agents to obtain information. John Walter's Royalist connections protected him, and he continued to work for Parliament without being suspected by Nicholas until the late summer of 1656. Neither Lucy nor Justus seems to have guessed what he did or how it was that he had plenty of money.

They had all been living in Antwerp for some weeks when Charles and his companions arrived. Lucy was wearing a pearl necklace, afterwards valued by one of the brothers at £1,500.[18] It was probably worth a good deal less; in any case, her funds were such that she still had it several months after she parted from Charles.

By this time, the parents of the future Duke of Monmouth had been estranged for four and a half years. Charles's attitude was then that of a man who, trying to behave fairly, as the terms of his settlement show, yet feels hostility and resentment towards the neglectful guardian of a much-loved son. And now that son, although still as seductively beautiful as his mother, was beginning to look like his father's family; his miniature, painted a few weeks after Charles came to Antwerp, shows him as all Stuart; then and later, he rather resembled his uncle York than the King, for his colouring was fair and his eyes a greyish-blue.

Charles was more anxious than ever about his education and his future. In an age when most upper-class English children were reading and writing, not only in their own tongue but in French and Latin, before they were six, it was deplorable that this intelligent seven-year-old had been taught nothing at all. That he was healthy and well cared for in a material sense was the sole consolation.

What passed between the King and his former mistress, what persuasion he used to get hold of the boy, is not recorded. Charles and Lucy remained in the house at Antwerp, 'a night and a day together', according to Justus.[19] Then the King returned to Bruges – without his son.

This was one of the bitterest of Charles's failures. Henceforth his attitude towards Lucy was one of fierce and relentless enmity. He did not care what became of her. He was determined to remove the child, at any cost to himself, and without scruple or compassion. For the moment, having spent all he could spare, he was helpless, and this presently turned his anger into something like hatred, the cold, enduring hatred of the easy-going man who has been tried beyond his capacity. The Antwerp visit resulted in his treating Lucy with extreme harshness.

From the desultory and denigrating records of those who had to do with her Lucy herself emerges as a shadowy figure, save in one respect – her power over men. The Sidneys, Charles, Taaffe, de Vic, Colonel Howard and many more – all grew as tired of her as she did of them, and were perhaps sickened by her; but while they were with her, they did what she wanted. That fact, her portrait – the portrait of a voluptuous siren, whose beauty verges on decay – and half a dozen contemptuous or disgusted references to her manner of life, hardly constitute a character; and any further description falls into the negative. She was the kind of woman whom her own sex dislikes or dismisses: whom respectable men resent: who bewilders or bores those she does not fascinate; yet who manages, if only for a time, to get her own way. She terrified Anne Hill; but the girl remained in her service after that attempt, if attempt it was, to murder her. For a little while she persuaded the wary and hard-bitten O'Neile (how? In a day and a night?) that she had been ill treated; and was to cajole other emissaries by the same tactics. None of the men she lived with had wealth or ease; yet she, desiring both, obtained them, however precariously. The first recorded judgment of her – Robert Sidney's 'Let who's have her, she's already sped' – made when she was eighteen, sounds like the refrain in a ballad or a rhymed romance; and her brief and baleful career much resembles those of the doomed sorceresses – Morgan le Fay, the Lady Maisry, La Belle Dame Sans Merci – who appear only to destroy, and triumph only to sink back into the depths from whence they came.

If Lucy Walter had any influence, it was detrimental, in Charles's case, at least. She brought out the merciless, brutal streak in his character; his tendency never to forget, and eventually to revenge, an injury is perfectly exemplified by his treatment of his Welsh 'lady of pleasure'.

When he returned to Bruges Charles's disappointment and frustration were enhanced by the problem of Gloucester's debts, which had, some-how, to be paid. In Paris and Cologne the young Duke had been attended by four gentlemen, a tutor, a laundress, three footmen, two grooms, dancing, fencing and riding masters, Spanish and Italian teachers – and a mysterious Captain Straghan, whose duties are unspecified.[20] No sooner had Gloucester been installed than the King received a long letter from his cousin Lord d'Aubigny, imploring him to become a Catholic, which stirred him to reply in his most forthright and reasonable vein. For once Charles neither hedged nor protested. Patiently, he assured d'Aubigny of his belief in his good will and pointed out the folly of his plan. 'I would never persecute the Catholics ... but am willing to indulge them.' The person recommending his apostasy, he went on, 'is very much mistaken in the temper of England ... of which I may be reasonably thought to understand somewhat ... by having opportunity for many weeks during my last being there, to discover the humours of the people ... myself being unknown amongst them'. He concluded by saying that his refusal to change his faith was 'a matter of principle, as well as of policy'.[21]

By the middle of June Charles's Court was established in Bruges, he had raised three regiments of English, Irish and Scottish troops and was waiting for a summons from Spain. The recall of the Irish from France enraged Mazarin and caused a breach between the King and York, who commanded them. The Duke was so appalled at the thought of fighting against Turenne that for the first time in his life he refused to obey his brother and remained where he was. Henrietta Maria took York's side and was reported to 'care little' when, a fortnight later, she realized that Charles's hopes had sunk lower than at any time since the exile.[22] 'He is in a poor condition,' wrote Cromwell's spy. '... Almost everybody doth forsake him ... He will be only a charge to Spain, and will do no great harm to the Lord Protector.'[23] Indeed Charles was now so desperate for allies that he told Nicholas he would be willing to receive Sir Edmund Ludlow, one of the regicides, simply because he had become 'an irreconcilable enemy' to Cromwell.[24]

While the King was consoling himself with Catherine Pegge, by whom he had a son in 1657 (this boy was then known as Don Carlos and created Earl of Plymouth some years after the Restoration), there came further news of Lucy. Escorted by Colonel Howard and Justus Walter, she and her two children crossed to England. On June 19th they were all lodging above a barber's shop in the Strand, where Lucy gave out that she was the widow of a Dutch sea-captain. Cromwell's agents had followed her (they reported her as living 'in a costly and high manner'[25]) and presently she, Howard, Justus and Anne Hill were arrested and examined by the Privy Council. Lucy declared that she had not seen the King for two years, that their son was dead and that both her children were by her Dutch husband. Howard said he had met her for the first time on board ship and that he had not seen Charles for eighteen months. Justus cleared himself by producing his pass for Italy. Anne Hill's evidence contradicted Lucy's and Howard's statements, with the result that Lucy was sent to the Tower, while the Protector made up his mind as to how best to use all these stories, 'the Lady Lucy Walter's' lies and the papers found on her.

On July 1st he wrote out an order for her release, and the *Mercurius Politicus* published Charles's letter promising her an allowance, together with her confession that her son was by him. 'And it is generally believed,' the announcement added, 'the boy being very like him. By this,' the journalist went on, 'see ... what a pious, charitable prince ... and how well he disposeth of the collections and contributions they make for him here towards the maintenance of his concubines and the royal issue. Order is taken forthwith to send away his lady of pleasure and the young heir and set them on shore in Flanders, which is no ordinary courtesy.'[26]

So Lucy returned to plague Charles. By the middle of August she had parted from Howard (he appears to have deserted her) and both she and the King were in Brussels. Although there is no record of their meeting, this alarmed Hyde, who did not think that his master could resist her wiles. 'There is much talk,' he wrote to Ormonde, 'of a certain lady ... and I assure you, very shrewd discourses of it, which will quickly get into England. I pray you, let her go to some other place.' When Lucy refused to move, Ormonde replied disconsolately, 'She has her son and heir with her, to make up the cry.'[26] Before Charles left Brussels he arranged for Lucy and her children to be established in the house of a loyal but not very intelligent Royalist agent, Sir Arthur Slingsby, whom he secretly instructed to get his son out of her hands as soon as it could be managed, and as quietly as possible.

The King's even temper had been roused by this further trial. He quarrelled with one of his Scottish officers, called him a villain, and dashed his name from the list of those to be sent into Spain. When the frightened Colonel asked, 'What have I done?' Charles accused him of treachery and refused to listen to his defence.[28] Then at last, the Spanish allowance came in, and the King, whose clothes had become unpresentable, wrote to Henry Bennet for two beaver hats, another sword ('for my lord Bristol's ... I do by no means like it, therefore do not bespeak mine of that fashion') and a 'small' fiddler. Then once more his plans for an invasion were intercepted and a number of English Royalists imprisoned and tortured, so that he was forced to seek allies elsewhere. On September 24th he sent out instructions to his representatives in Germany, Holland and Poland, with no result. Four days later York arrived, sullen and unwilling, with Sir John Berkeley (whom Charles had ordered to stay in Paris) and a number of English Royalists. Their spirits rose when they heard that the famous astrologer, Lilly, had foretold His Majesty's restoration in 1657.

Lilly was always right – had he not prophesied the execution of the late King? With Charles, they celebrated this news by 'whoring, swearing and drinking', according to the intelligencer, who reported that Charles was now paying his troops at the absurd rate of sixpence a day. This person was told by a Jesuit that the King had been received into the Catholic Church, and that the Spanish were preparing another invasion. A few weeks later Charles left for Ghent, 'something sad' and 'a little pensive', to interview some Irish Royalists. By the beginning of October 8,000 men were waiting to invade from Ireland. This alarmed Parliament, until they were informed by General Monk that the men were mutinying for their pay and that there was no chance of its forthcoming. By November their numbers had sunk to 800. Meanwhile, Charles had returned to Brussels, to interview the new viceroy, King Philip's bastard son, Don Juan.[29]

When the usual compliments had been interchanged and Don Juan had congratulated the King on his assembly of Scottish troops, he added, 'I doubt that the Scots will be loyal, as they failed you before – ' and said something about Argyll and Lorne being on friendly terms with Parliament. 'These doubts being removed,' he concluded, 'I shall have no further scruple.'

'They will perish,' Charles assured him, 'before they make any address [advances] to the English. I and my brothers will all go with them. I know how to gain Argyll – their friends are my friends. Argyll is a wise man, and will not stand alone in my way. And to tell the truth,' continued His Majesty, with the frank simplicity which so became him, 'I have more hope of him than of any other – and except for Cromwell himself, he carries mortal hatred at Lambert and Monk, and all the rest of their officers. If I have once the opportunity, it will soon be seen what part his shall be.' The cautious Spaniard politely hinted that he would like proof of this optimistic view. 'It is true,' Charles admitted, with the same engaging openness, 'that the ministers of Scotland have ever stood in my father's way – but that which hath lost them to my father hath gained them to me. My father trusted always to his cause,' he went on, 'never daring to make the leading men of the ministers for him. I have done this. They durst do nothing without my consent.'

Don Juan, completely won over by this adroit mixture of truth and falsehood, replied genially, 'I am glad to hear that, and shall think the better of all the rest, if that be so. I will give a full account to His Majesty of Spain.' He raised the question of a Franco-Spanish agreement, adding that once that was made, it would be a simple matter to proceed with Charles's restoration. Further compliments were interchanged. Then

Charles, who had begun to realize that this new ally might be as slippery as himself, turned to his gentleman-in-waiting, and said, presumably in Spanish, 'You are witness, and I have trusted you to advertise to my friends what you have heard.' This courtier's name was Ramsay. He might conceivably be identified with the agent who reported Charles's talk with Don Juan to Cromwell's Secretary of State.[30]

Charles's precautions were those of a defenceless man. He was now paying his Irish troops 'out of the little money remaining for his bread', and the governor of Ostend referred to him as 'the King of I cannot tell what', when asked for a pass by one of his representatives.[31] In December he was joined by Mary of Orange, whom the Spaniards ignored, perhaps because they had been offended by the Scottish soldiers' impious plundering of a church in Bruges, and shocked at the indecent spectacle of kilted Highlanders in their streets and on their waterways.

The King was so delighted to be with his sister that he remained cheerful, in spite of the fact that she was now taking Henrietta Maria's side against him, although not, it seems, in a disagreeable manner. She brought him some money, and taught him and his courtiers the latest dances. The difficulty was to find good 'fiddle-de-dees', as the King called them; those he had knew no difference, he complained, between 'a hymn and a coranto'. On Sundays he took Mary to see a travelling company of French players, to the horror of Cromwell's agent. 'Their most solemn day of acting,' he reported, 'is on the Lord's day. I think I may truly say that greater abominations were never practised than at Charles Stuart's Court. Fornication, drunkenness and adultery are esteemed no sin amongst them.'[32]

Charles appears to have said nothing to Mary about the bad news from London, which reached him a few days after her arrival. The Royalist merchants were ruined, and could send him nothing. She went with him on his next visit to Don Juan, whom he asked for more money and 'some respect' from the Spanish authorities, but she took no part in his disputes with the Duke of York. James had agreed to give up his French pension and join the Spanish forces, but, having made this sacrifice, he would not comply with Don Juan's next demand, which was that he and all his staff should take an oath of loyalty to Philip IV. Charles might have managed to prevent a quarrel, if George Digby, now Earl of Bristol, who had left the French army to work for him in the Low Countries, had not intervened in his most exuberant and tactless manner. When Digby told the Spaniards that James ought to command one of their armies, they required the Duke's oath in return, upon which Digby persuaded the King to enforce it. York, hearing of these arrangements through a third person, came to Digby and asked him, 'What truth is there in this?' Digby, enraged at being put in the wrong, replied, 'Whoever hath informed Your Highness of this is a traitor to His Majesty, and a villain,' and went on to abuse York's informant at the top of his voice. The King, over-hearing this altercation from the next room, came in and asked his brother who had told him about the Spaniards' insistence on the oath. The Duke replied, 'I hope Your Majesty will pardon me if I do not name him. After what hath been said by my lord Bristol, it is almost as much as to accuse him of high treason,' angrily adding that the whole imbroglio amounted to an attack on his 'best friend', Sir John Berkeley. Digby then apologized. 'My zeal for His Majesty's service,' he explained, 'is my excuse.'[33]

Digby's much advertised zeal was as badly timed as had been his efforts to marry Charles to Madame de Châtillon. He infuriated Hyde by his insulting and facetious letters, and made his own arrangements with the Spaniards. Don Juan and Cardeñas were won over by his fluent Spanish, his flatteries and his assurances that Charles would do all they required. In the last weeks of 1656 Digby, having wrung some useful concessions from Don Juan and Cardeñas, so misled them that they began to treat Charles rather as a paid servant than as an equal and an ally. They informed Hyde that the regiment of which His Majesty was the Colonel must not be employed until officers and men had taken the oath to the Spanish King. Charles at once wrote to Cardeñas,

> I have seen your letter to the Chancellor and am so full of indignation at the affront ... that I have scarce patience to write this letter. I send this bearer ... expressly to let you know that before I will suffer this affront to be put upon my regiment – which was never yet offered to any private Colonel whatsoever – I will break the regiment a thousand times over. I command you to tell Don Juan this from me, and that, according to the usage I receive in this particular, so I shall judge what I am to expect from him in the rest of my affairs. Let me have without delay a positive answer of what I may trust to; for I cannot, nor will not, any longer, be at the charges and trouble I am at.[34]

There was no answer to this letter. A few days later, Don Juan received Charles as if nothing had happened. Their meeting was informal ('only two chairs', according to the intelligencer) and the King came away with the loan of 40,000 guilders, the promise of more and the assurance that he would be treated with royal honours by the local magistrates. His troops

were then placed in better quarters, and their wages – supplemented by a
loaf of bread for each man – paid every Saturday.[35]

NOTES

1 *Thurloe S. P.*, vol. IV, p. 301.
2 Op. cit., p. 55.
3 *Cal. S. P. Ven.*, vol. XXX, p. 153.
4 *Cal. Clar. S. P.*, vol. II, pp. 75–7.
5 *Misc. Aulica*, p. 113.
6 *Thurloe S. P.*, vol. I, pp. 683–4.
7 Ibid.
8 *Cal. Clar. S. P.*, vol. III, pp. 75–7.
9 *Cal. D. S. P.*, Feb. 8th, 1656.
10 *Thurloe S. P.*, vol. IV, p. 592.
11 *Cal. Clar. S. P.*, vol. III, p. 162.
12 *Thurloe S. P.*, vol. IV, p. 677.
13 *Cal. Clar. S. P.*, vol. III, p. 113.
14 *Nicholas Papers*, vol. III, p. 275.
15 *Cal. Clar. S. P.*, ibid.
16 Ibid.
17 Steinmann, pp. 80–116.
18 Ibid.
19 *Cal. Clar. S. P.*, vol. IV, p. 198.
20 *Thurloe S. P.*, vol. I, p. 740.
21 Op. cit., vol. V, p. 184.
22 Op. cit., p. 141.
23 *Nicholas Papers*, vol. III, p. 149.
24 *Thurloe S. P.*, vol. I, p. 683.
25 Ellis, series 2, vol. III, p. 352.
26 *Thurloe S. P.*, vol. V, p. 160.
27 Op. cit., p. 301.
28 *Misc. Aulica*, p. 127.
29 *Thurloe S. P.*, vol. V, pp. 84, 119, 301, 315, 431, 447, 473, 479, 521.
30 *Misc. Aulica*, ibid.
31 *Thurloe S. P.*, vol. V, p. 645.
32 Ibid.
33 Clarke, vol. I, p. 285.
34 *Thurloe S. P.*, vol. V, p. 104.
35 Ibid.

CHAPTER FIVE

STRANGE ALLIES

I

I N the 1650s the provincial cities of the Spanish Netherlands – Ghent, Bruges, Antwerp and Damme – although still prosperous and in a fair state of preservation, looked like picturesque memorials. Design, architecture and atmosphere reflected the forgotten splendours of the Middle Ages: so that the spectacle of persons walking about in jack-boots, ruffles, lace berthas, satin cloaks, plumed hats and roquelaures must have appeared anachronistic and incongruous, especially when contrasted with the dress of the poorer classes, which had changed very little in two hundred years.

Then as now, the beauties within and without the cathedrals, town halls, fortresses and palaces of these commercial centres appealed specific-ally to sight-seers, antiquaries and historians; those with money, leisure and aesthetic taste were happy to wander along the alleys of the Béguinage, or the cobbled squares of the Marchés au Beurre and du Vendredi, and to explore the crypts and ambulatories of the Holy Blood, Our Lady and St James; they could commission local artists to copy their favourite Memlings and Van Eycks; they could spend their days in ecstatic con-templation of Gothic and Burgundian glories, and their nights eating and drinking in the palaces of Spanish grandees or in comfortable inns run by respectfully genial hosts.

But to those exiled in such places, without money, interest in the arts, or friends: to those forced to sponge and hint and angle for a meal or a bed: to those with prices on their heads and darkened reputations: to undesirables, refugees, suspects – the sombre peace, the back-water orderli-ness of these damp, enclosed, low-lying, intensely respectable market towns were at the same time enervating and destructive; to get away from them became a passionate desire: and while in them to be distracted, no matter how, a necessity.

Here, during the last three years of Charles's exile, Spanish reserve, Spanish *laisser-faire*, Spanish penury, Spanish obsession with the past, above all, Spanish gloom, created a background of corrosive melancholy.

Nothing ever happened, or was accomplished. Procrastination, inertia, silence (accompanied, always, by a cold and terrible dignity, an undeviating adherence to an iron yet meaningless etiquette) prevailed in the private mansions of the nobles, in embassies, official residences, and civic buildings. The response of governors, clerks, guards and secretaries was as sluggish as the waters of the canals encircling their shuttered and chilly habitations. The depression, the sense of futility, of moving like an automaton in an endless dream of lost hopes, were perdurable, all-embracing – and enhanced by a climate in which mist, fog and rain seemed to dominate, only lifting to reveal fresh moisture on walls and pavements and to emphasize the feeling of having been soaked, mercilessly, to the bone.

Charles was more fortunate than many of his followers, in that his business with the Dons made it necessary for him to be on the move, although always in the same territory. From Bruges, where he held his Court from the autumn of 1656 until the spring of 1657, he travelled to Ghent, Antwerp and Brussels; yet from his point of view all these cities were much alike. If he arrived secretly and put up at an inn, he could afford only the poorest fare; if he came as the guest of the governor, he was at once surrounded by a horde of exiles, who either claimed his bounty or pestered him with crazy schemes for Cromwell's murder and his immediate restoration. He could not afford to ignore or snub them; and to give them money or encouragement was equally impossible. Nor could he avoid these persons; wherever he was, they found him out; every week their numbers increased, while many of those calling themselves Anabaptists or Independents were in fact eccentrics, religious maniacs and visionaries, whose royalism was merely a symptom of what would now be diagnosed as mental disturbance.

These wild-eyed, ranting creatures carried arms, and were just as likely to stab or pistol their newly elected leader as the rulers who had cast them out. The most original and, in a sense, the most appealing, was a Mr Walter Gostelowe, whose mission was revealed to him through a mystical experience after his first conversation with Charles in Bruges.[1]

Gostelowe had followed Charles and his brothers for some weeks before he was able to speak to them. Their meeting probably took place in what is now known as the Gruute Huus, a rambling, fortified palace in the centre of the city, which, recently restored, still contains several mementoes of Charles's residence; notably a marble bas-relief of himself, a portrait of Gloucester and two daubed conversation pieces of the three Stuart brothers with their Spanish hosts.

Here Gostelowe pursued Charles, and presently was allowed to watch him at his devotions. He was immensely impressed, not only by His Majesty's worshipping twice a day, but by the 'harmony and good affection' existing between him and the two Dukes. (At this time, Charles and York were on very bad terms, and Gloucester was, as ever, something of a handful.) And then, 'the last Tuesday in every month, if not oftener,' was 'set apart for a day of humiliation' – what could be more admirable? – with 'psalms and suitable prayers ... The Almighty,' Gostelowe concluded, 'will not leave [the King] without a blessing, which blessing will ever go along with him and them, for the subduing of all his enemies – and, I doubt not,' he added cautiously, 'for his corruptions also.' (For of course it would be foolish to discount His Majesty's occasional lapses.) However – 'I see through him,' he declared. 'There is grace in His Majesty's heart. I see him ripe for tears at his devotions, which he performs ... with the best intentions; but those godly sorrows ... are the distics [signs] of once vile and unwarrantable affections.' (Evidently Mrs Barlow's arrest had had some repercussions.)

At last the moment came when Gostelowe was given audience by Charles and York. As he was recently from England, and had visited the Protector's Court, he was listened to patiently enough. ('God,' he reported, 'disposed His Majesty to hear me to the full.') As soon as Gostelowe allowed him to speak, the King said, 'I do not at all doubt that God will restore me to my right of inheritance.' On this point Gostelowe was able to provide first-hand news. 'God will plague them that hate you, and scatter their dust before the wind,' he replied. York then asked him, 'How does the Protector?' (For some weeks the rumour that Oliver's health was failing had sustained the more credulous Royalists.) 'How does he look? Is he, as I have heard, much more of a gentleman than formerly?' Gostelowe replied favourably, and the Duke pursued, 'Is he in good health? And likely to continue so?' Once more, Gostelowe gave a good report of the Protector's constitution and manners, and York turned solemnly to the attendant gentlemen. 'Well,' he said, 'this I observed, when so many of their army, Fairfax also, came to see me.' (Presumably he was referring to the Parliamentarian occupation of Oxford in 1646.) 'None kneeled down when they kissed my hand, but he.'

Much gratified – for he retained great admiration for the Protector – Gostelowe then informed the sardonically impassive King that he had already written to Cromwell about His Majesty's virtues and, as soon as the spirit guided him, would do so again. He seems to have assured Charles and 'the so valiant ... beloved and heroical Duke of York' that he had the business in hand, and that their troubles would shortly be over. A few nights later he received the expected demonstration.

It began with 'the stars falling from heaven and carried away before me with a most mighty, strong and sudden wind; so continued they ... for some very considerable time, in the end they melted as they fell. The vision ended ... I besought God the meaning of it. And then did I see a most serene sky, the most sublime heavens, the clearest stars ... altogether a new heaven, as if they had received a most glorious change.'

This of course meant that God was giving instruction, through Goste-lowe, to the Protector, to restore His Majesty, and 'for ever carry away the corrupt powers, unwarrantable rule and misgovernment of the wicked'. Not only so. 'The vision demonstrates to me, and I will demon-strate it to you,' the seer informed Cromwell, 'that your power shall be taken from you, if you resign it not the sooner into his hands, whom God hath in His mercy resolved it on (for his viceroy on earth) Charles Stuart, Charles the Greater, Charles the Good.'

Next day Gostelowe had another vision, about the Jews, 'and the parts out of Christendom'. It was not relevant to his mission, and he dismissed, or rather pigeon-holed it, for the time being. He then described his im-pressions of Charles's Court, of which he thought highly (they all seemed so serious, and yet so agreeable), and his chat with the King. And how 'pleasingly' His Royal Highness of York had asked after the Protector – who, in fact, need not be distressed. God was very merciful. He had told Gostelowe that Cromwell, although a usurper, was 'highly blessed, yea, even in the company of kings and princes,' in spite of the fact that 'the multitude ... certainly hated you ... Well, Sir, I leave your lordship to God's direction ... that, making your little finger heavier than our late King's loins ... your government may ... obey their King ... Strip and denude them of what they have so unwarrantably stolen from others ... As I shall answer to God Almighty,' Gostelowe went on, 'I am deputed for this work ... No man alive hath ever dictated a word of this letter to me, or seen it before I gave it to the post ... I know I shall live to see that day when you shall bow before your King – and then, I hope, possess him of his militia.' Finally, the writer assured the Protector of his own and the Almighty's favour, warned him against fanatics (he had been rather weak with these) and promised him Charles's patronage. 'I do this,' he con-cluded, 'to God's glory, my King's good and your happiness. I pray you for a Restoration.'

Gostelowe then made inquiries about the Protector's behaviour at prayers, and was told that Cromwell often wept when worshipping.

'These,' he maintained, 'are abominable ... and crocodile tears (both which God hates) if they proceed not from a heart desirous to subdue every corruption' – as, for instance, His Majesty's did. When he discussed his letter to Cromwell with his friends in Bruges, one said, 'He will never submit to your King, nor ever be so mad as to trust him.' 'He which truly fears God,' Gostelowe replied, 'cannot be afraid of himself or man. God hath given us a King for His viceroy – like Jesus.'

No one else seemed to see the likeness. To Gostelowe it was obvious. He settled down to wait for the answer to his letter; this he sent through a friend, who in January 1657 was arrested, as being a member of a gang organized by Miles Syndercombe to murder Cromwell. Syndercombe and his fellow-conspirators were hanged a few days later. And so good Mr Gostelowe disappears from the history of the exile.[2]

II

The discovery of the Syndercombe plot exasperated the Republicans who, if they had been able or willing to ally themselves with the other rebels and exiles, might have enforced a restoration and started another civil war. They were now headed by Colonel Sexby, an energetic and determined man, author of the famous pamphlet, *Killing No Murder*; this described the Protector's assassination as a patriotic duty, and was smuggled into England in large quantities. Sexby seems to have been under the impression that Charles would agree to some form of constitutional monarchy rather than remain the pensioner of the Spaniards. The King's tactics were what they had always been. Sexby's party must be used and then, if necessary, discarded. Meanwhile Sexby was ready to ally himself, temporarily, with the Catholics in order to defeat Cromwell. As a diplomat, Charles was infinitely more skilled and unscrupulous than Sexby, whose republican principles pinned him down to trivialities. He told Father Talbot that he could not meet the King if he had to kneel to him. Through Hyde, Charles replied that the Colonel would be 'very graciously' received, adding, 'If he do not wish to kiss my hand – which may appear another form of idolatry – he will not be expected to kneel.'[3]

In January 1657 matters had so far advanced that Sexby attended a Council meeting headed by Charles, Hyde, Digby and Don Juan. The Cromwellian agents were instructed to seize him if he attempted to cross into England, but he remained in the Spanish Netherlands for the usual reason – lack of money – and his rising did not materialize. Charles therefore decided to turn to another group of rebels, most of whom were

Anabaptists. Their leader, 'a young gentleman of honourable extraction and great parts', brought with him two immense addresses, one of which described the sufferings of His Majesty's subjects ('How does England sit solitary! How is she become a widow!... Thus do we fly, like partridges hunted') while the other set forth their terms of agreement.[4]

These were so extreme as to be immediately rejected by Hyde. They included a return to Charles I's Isle of Wight Treaty, through which Presbyterianism would become the national religion for three years. The bearer of these suggestions burst out laughing when the Chancellor stated the impossibility of his conditions. Of course they were impossible; many of his followers were extravagant and mad. 'But if Your Majesty will encourage them,' he went on, 'they can be made to moderate their demands.' When he left, Charles said to Hyde, 'I believe these distempers might be of use to me,' and told him to arrange another meeting with this group.[5] He then turned to the composition of his dispute with the Duke of York.

James resembled his father in that, mistrusting the majority, he became dependent on the few; of these, a single person would then rise and dominate him to the exclusion of all others. At this time Sir John Berkeley so influenced him that he was described as his Governor by the other Cavaliers. Charles could not accept Berkeley, partly because the Spanish objected to him on the grounds that he was pro-French and thus, they told the King, 'disaffected' to their cause. Also Digby, who had subjugated Don Juan by hinting that he might become a Catholic and by his interest in astrology, had warned him that Berkeley was a bad influence, which may have been the case, in another sense; he and his nephew, Charles Berkeley, were always telling York that he was unjustly treated by His Majesty who, they said, wanted to 'mortify' him out of jealousy.[6]

Not unnaturally, York felt injured. Out of loyalty to his brother, he had left the French service, where he was happy, successful and well paid; as if it were not enough to have sacrificed his career, he was required to dismiss his closest friend – and not even by the King himself, but by Digby, who seemed to be controlling the Royalist party. At the same time Jermyn, of whom the Duke now had a very high opinion, wrote to him from Paris begging him not to accept a command in the Spanish forces and reproaching him for his desertion of Turenne.[7]

The result of all these attacks was that in the first week in January York went to Charles and complained that the Council treated him disrespectfully and that decisions were made without his knowledge, adding that he would not dismiss Berkeley simply to gratify Digby's prejudices.

It was an unfortunate moment to choose for a scene. A few hours earlier Charles had heard that a quantity of expensive armaments had been ship-wrecked. The loss was crushing – it removed all hope of invasion for months to come – and for once he gave way, shutting himself up and seeing no one. Just before York broke in upon him Ormonde, whom he was sending to Brussels, came to him for money. He had not a penny and neither had the King. Charles then pawned his George, the last of his treasures, his father's gift. No sooner had Ormonde left, than Hyde began to grumble about what he called that nobleman's 'gadding', on an un-necessary mission. Poor York's irruption was the last straw. 'High words' were exchanged and, with Berkeley, York left Bruges in a rage.[8]

Charles emerged from his closet to be told that his courtiers were gambling, that the tradesmen had not been paid for three weeks, that his Spanish allowance had not arrived, that his latest appeal to the Scots Royalists had met with no response and that York had gone to Holland without his leave. Digby then came to complain of his companions' be-haviour – 'it is a scandal and a shame' – and of Father Talbot's inefficiency. Through a third person Charles heard that Digby was also complaining of his 'want of steadiness' and thus making mischief between him and the Spanish.

A few days later Charles pulled himself together and sent York a firm but tactful summons. Berkeley might still remain in his service, but for the present he had better stay in Holland. A Royalist agent then arrived from Kent, with whom the King 'talked alone almost every day'. She was a friend of his cousin's wife, the Duchess of Richmond, who had sent him a little money.[9] The lady and the cash doubtless combined to cheer him up and to receive the now apologetic York 'very kindly'. With him, Gloucester and the Princess Mary Charles had intended to go to Brussels for another conference with Don Juan, whose astrologers assured him that the King was on the point of being restored. 'This is the time' was the purport of their visions.

Charles found that he could not afford so long a journey, and instead took his brothers and sister by boat to Damme, a medieval port on the Sluys canal, some three miles from Bruges. The authorities had instructed the garrison to honour His Majesty with a volley, as soon as he and his party arrived. They were on their way to the Town Hall when Charles, looking all about him and walking very fast, as his custom was, saw that one of the sentries, 'a poor lame boy', was aiming straight at them, instead of firing in the air. Calling out, 'He will be amongst you, my masters!' the King dodged just in time, but two of his courtiers were peppered, to the horror of their hosts.[10] Charles made light of the matter, and having seen his sister off (she had been away for a year, and was anxious about the four-year-old William) returned to Bruges the next day. In England it was said that the accident had been part of a plot to murder him.

Such a scheme was being put in hand by a group in London, who believed that Cromwell was about to restore the dynasty on his own terms. They planned to invite Charles and his brothers to come over for a secret conference with the Protector and to kill them as they landed. Another party, so Hyde was informed, had been promised £2,000 apiece to dispatch the King in Flanders.[11]

Charles discounted both stories, and refused to take any precautions. In London the rumour that Cromwell, whose health really was failing, had considered sending for him and marrying him to his daughter Frances, was supported by those believing that both the girl and her mother were eager for the match. At last Lord Broghill, an ex-Royalist in the Protector's confidence, said to him, 'I have been told that you are in treaty with the King, who is to be restored and to marry your daughter.' Cromwell made no reply, and Broghill pursued, 'I see no better expedient. You may bring him in on what terms you please, and retain the same authority with less trouble.' The Protector answered rather strangely. 'The King will never forgive me his father's blood,' he said. 'You are one of many that are concerned in that,' Broghill replied, 'but you would be alone in the merit of restoring him.' There was a pause. Then Cromwell said gloomily, 'He is so debauched he will undo us all,' and changed the subject, leaving Broghill under the impression that he had been thinking of some such plan.[12]

Anxiety for the future of the Commonwealth was expressed by Parliament offering Oliver the crown in March 1657. His refusal disappointed the English Royalists. 'It would have brought about his ruin,' said one, adding that the army was going to ask Charles to come over. By this time the King had persuaded Don Juan to let him move to Brussels, where he and a Court of some seventy persons were established in April, leaving Hyde in Bruges.

Soon after his arrival, Charles was told that Digby had attended Mass in St Gudule. 'What hath brought you over to the Church of Rome?' he inquired. 'I am writing a book in favour of the Reformation, so please Your Majesty,' was the characteristic reply. 'Pray, my lord,' said Charles rather wearily, 'then write one in favour of Popery.' 'My lord of Bristol will never stick to any religion,' he wrote to Hyde.[13] Meanwhile, that versatile nobleman was telling everyone that His Majesty should publicly acknowledge his Catholicism, as it was already known. Henry Bennet shared this view. Hyde did not; the King was careless, that was all – and increasingly indifferent to the impression he made. He sadly agreed with Ormonde's opinion that His Majesty's 'immoderate delight in empty, effeminate and vulgar conversation has become an irresistible part of his nature'.[14]

When Ormonde made this judgment he did not realize that Charles (who inclined towards clever men and stupid women), while unable to choose his own company, was in a state of black depression. He concealed his gloom from everyone but Bennet, to whom he confessed, 'If this winter pass without any attempt on my part, I shall take very little pleasure in living till the next.' So far, the Spanish alliance had brought him nothing but disappointment, isolation, and worse penury than he had yet endured. During the spring and summer of 1657 his circumstances so deteriorated that he decided to join King Philip's armies and risk, or even court, death in battle rather than remain inactive and degraded.

Apart from the older Cavaliers and a few of his gentlemen, Charles was still surrounded by persons he either despised or mistrusted. Although Cromwell's intelligencers now found it very difficult to obtain any detailed information, they were able to report that 'Charles Stuart's business hath received some damps of late', and that his new allies were doing nothing for him. Yet the situation in England was such that on March 31st Parliament once more declared him 'incapable of government' or of any 'right, title or dignity', and set spies on their own agents, one of whom wrote to Charles that he was ready to bring His Majesty Cromwell's 'head in a bag', if given the opportunity.[15]

In the same month, what looked like an increase of Spanish favour followed the acquisition of St Ghislain, a fortified town held by Irish troops in French pay. Digby persuaded the officers to submit to Don Juan's forces, with the result that Charles was invited to a series of celebrations and called on by the grandees. He and Don Juan went to a dance, played tennis and fives together, visited a nunnery and were feasted in Ghent. Charles took the opportunity to borrow money from his patron, and from the Marquess of Caracena, but had to spend most of it on mourning for himself and his Court when the Emperor Ferdinand VII died a few weeks later. Meanwhile, his unpaid troops were begging their bread and beginning to desert. In May Charles volunteered for active service in the Spanish campaign.[16]

For some time no answer was forthcoming. Then his offer was refused, on the grounds that if he were killed King Philip would be deprived of his principal weapon against Cromwell. The Spanish had given York a command; Gloucester was too young to be of use. Once more, the King turned to the Republicans – Sexby assured him of success – and allowed the optimistic Colonel to leave for England, where he was arrested and put in the Tower before he could get in touch with any of his supporters. The King then renewed the offer of his services to Don Juan, who replied with polite evasions. By June Charles was so desperate that he planned to slip away and join the army on his own, only to find that he could not afford the journey. Hyde managed to send him £100 (the Chancellor himself was so deeply in debt that he could not afford a new pair of spectacles),[17] but this was seized by the King's creditors, and again he was unemployed and reduced to consorting with 'vulgar and empty' persons. 'Don Juan's scurvy usage,' he wrote to Hyde, ' ... puts me beyond my patience. If I were with him, I would swear two or three round oaths. I am so vexed with the delay that I ... give all men that have ... to do with money, to the devil.'[18]

The Chancellor replied with a lecture. His Majesty made a great mistake in asking for so little money; when he borrowed, he should never put the figure below £50. Also, his desire for action should be restrained. 'Nothing,' he wrote to Ormonde, 'will do the King so much good as being sometimes alone, and recollecting himself.'[19]

In June, Charles's Spanish pension was once more overdue. When he asked for it, he was told that he must wait, perhaps indefinitely. ('The Lord have mercy on us!' exclaimed Nicholas, who had been hoping to placate the Brussels tradesmen.[20]) Still the King had to control his rage and appear at Government receptions, in spite of the fact that his worn clothes drew attention to his status, while the magnificent Dons received him with the minimum of courtesy. Then the Newcastles invited him to Antwerp, where, owing to the Earl's semi-professional practice of *manège*, they were living quite comfortably. The meals were delicious. 'I perceive,' said Charles, on his first evening, 'that your lordship's credit can procure better meat than mine.' Although he was always hungry these days, he needed very little to cheer him. When Newcastle suggested a shooting match, he was delighted. 'What, my lord,' he said, 'have you invited me to play the rook with me?'[21]

Charles returned to Brussels via Bruges. Here he found more appeals for money from the English Royalists, and disturbing news of Lucy Walter, who was once again causing a scandal. She was now the mistress of a young Welsh cousin. When Colonel Howard appeared, this youth was set on by Lucy to challenge him. Howard refused to fight over a prostitute. Mrs Barlow's protector then stabbed him, and escaped into a neighbouring church. Although dangerously wounded, Howard survived.[22] In a letter to Digby, Hyde made a joke of the incident, to which Digby replied, 'You may be merry concerning Mrs Barlow, but I assure you I cannot.' The Chancellor then went on to Brussels with Charles, who insisted that he should stay in order to share a feast provided by an anonymous supporter. 'A venison pasty,' said His Majesty, '[is] an affair of importance.'

Charles then entered into rather an acrimonious correspondence with Mary of Orange about her patronage of Lord and Lady Balcarres, whom he suspected of intriguing against him with Mazarin and thus further annoying the Spanish. Mary thought his request that Lady Balcarres should be dismissed from her service 'unreasonable', and they were still estranged when Charles asked her to lend him £1,500, which he promised to repay before Christmas. 'I never was more unwilling [to borrow] than now,' he wrote. 'This is only between you and me, and I do not desire it should be known to anybody else.'[23] Mary sent him a jewel to pawn, some of his bills were paid and fresh plans for an invasion set in hand.

Then at last, for no ostensible reason, Don Juan gave Charles leave to join the army, and in October he left for Dunkirk. There he heard that Buckingham, who had been in England for some months, was married to the only child and heiress of Sir Thomas Fairfax, thus regaining his estates, which Parliament had given Fairfax for his services in the Civil War. This widened the split between the Protector and his old comrade, but in no way furthered the Duke's much advertised scheme for Cromwell's murder. 'If I cannot oblige the Protector,' he had told one of Thurloe's agents, 'I will venture hard to destroy him.'[24]

Charles accepted Buckingham's desertion philosophically, the more easily because he was now being actively employed. He took part in the siege of Mardyk and, with Ormonde, whose horse was shot under him, charged the fortifications during a night attack. This recklessness so impressed the Parliamentary commander that he ordered his soldiers not to fire on the King when they saw him walking on the sands, sent him a present of wine and approached him privately with the offer of his services.[25] When Hyde wrote imploring Charles not to take such risk ('I am not one of those who think you are likely to recover your kingdom without being in danger of your life, but let it be when the adventure is of use')[26] the King took no notice.

So the death he may have been seeking eluded him. Two months later he returned to Bruges. There he found letters from Sir Arthur Slingsby who had chosen this moment to try to imprison Lucy and kidnap her son

Brussels was in an uproar. The authorities were very angry with Slingsby, and with the King, whom they blamed for 'all the noise and scandal'. What did His Majesty intend to do? The matter must be dealt with immediately – at his expense.[27]

NOTES

1 *Thurloe S. P.*, vol. V, pp. 673–5.
2 Ibid.
3 *Cal. Clar. S. P.*, vol. II, p. 205.
4 Clarendon, pp. 852–8.
5 Ibid.
6 Clarke, vol. I, p. 285.
7 Ibid.
8 *Thurloe S. P.*, vol. VI, pp. 52–3.
9 Op. cit., pp. 235–6.
10 *Cal. Clar. S. P.*, vol. III, p. 252.
11 *Cal. D. S. P.*, March 5th, 1657.
12 Burnet, *History*, vol. I, p. 127.
13 D. Townshend, *George Digby, Earl of Bristol*, p. 181.
14 *Cal. Clar. S. P.*, vol. III, p. 351.
15 *Cal. D. S. P.*, Feb. 1657.
16 Op. cit., April 12th, 1657.
17 *Cal. Clar. S. P.*, vol. III, p. 352.
18 Op. cit., p. 306.
19 Ibid.
20 Ibid.
21 Newcastle, p. 102.
22 *Thurloe S. P.*, vol. VI, p. 363.
23 Op. cit., pp. 363, 378.
24 Op. cit., p. 363.
25 Clarke, vol. I., p. 327.
26 *Cal. Clar. S. P.*, vol. III, p. 351.
27 Op. cit., p. 383.

CHAPTER SIX

THE LAST OF LUCY WALTER

I

I T was characteristic of Lucy that eight men were involved in her final disputes with Charles, and of her story that all but two of them joined in hounding her down and separating her from her son. The scandal caused by her cousin's attempt to murder Thomas Howard in August 1657 resulted in Sir Arthur Slingsby renewing his efforts to remove the boy and get rid of her. This he did in the first week of December.

His methods were so crude and inefficient that she defeated him, to the dismay of Alonzo de Cardeñas who, as Governor of Brussels, was forced to intervene, partly on her behalf. In his report to Charles Cardeñas described how Slingsby, who by this time was very short of money, had Lucy arrested for debt. When the officers arrived she caught up the eight-year-old James (he was tall and heavy for his age) and, clasping him to her, rushed out into the street. Here she began to cry and scream for help. The neighbours gathered round her, and made an indignant, indeed a belligerent audience, so that Slingsby and the constables were overawed. The people, said Cardeñas, were 'scandalized' by Sir Arthur's violence and brutality to a defenceless woman. When it became clear that the whole street was ready to fly to her rescue, Slingsby was forced to abandon his scheme. Lucy then seems to have announced that she would not stay in his house a moment longer, and it was arranged that she and the boy should go to that of another Royalist, Lord Castlehaven.

When Slingsby reported the matter to Cardeñas, the Spaniard gave Lucy permission to remain with Castlehaven, if Charles approved. While he was waiting to hear from the King, Lucy's account of Slingsby's behaviour so wrought upon Castlehaven and his friends that Sir Arthur's 'barbarous, abominable and unnatural behaviour' became the talk of Brussels, and Charles was blamed. Cardeñas's secretary, Egidio Mottet, was instructed by him to deal with the situation. 'I am ashamed,' Mottet wrote to Charles, 'of Slingsby's treatment of Mrs Barlow.'

When Mottet approached Slingsby, Sir Arthur replied that he was acting under Charles's orders. Luckily for the King, Ormonde was representing him in Brussels, and when he was appealed to, told Mottet that unless His Majesty was given some money to bribe Mrs Barlow, nothing could be done, adding that Slingsby's action had contradicted the King's commands. 'Slingsby,' he said, 'was to get the child out of the mother's hands in a quiet way – if he could – but never with that noise and scandal.'

Charles replied that James must be removed from Lucy and put in charge of someone of whom he approved. 'If Mottet can effect this,' wrote Ormonde, 'it will be an obligation to the King and a great charity to the child and to the mother herself, if she shall now at length retire to such a way of life as may redeem in some measure the reproach of her past ways; if she consent not to this, she will add to her former follies a most unnatural one in reference to her child, since neither of them will any further be cared for or owned by the King, who will take any good office done to her as an injury to him. It ought to be considered whether she should not be compelled to be good to herself, or at least be restrained from ruining her innocent child by making a property of him to support herself in these wild and disgraceful courses she hath taken.' 'If I cannot have the child disposed of, according to my direction,' added the King, 'I will free myself the best I may from any further trouble or scandal.'

It then became clear that Lucy, besides ignoring the King's calling her bluff, had so worked upon Castlehaven and one of his friends, a Mr Berkeley, that they were on their way to Bruges to plead for her with Charles.

By this time, the citizens of Brussels were abusing Charles for his harshness. They would not believe Cardeñas when he explained that the King had had nothing to do with Slingsby's treatment of Lucy. Cardeñas was then rebuked by Don Juan for allowing the outbreak, and the Council of Brabant issued a formal complaint against Slingsby's 'interruption of justice'. Cardeñas offered Lucy and the child accommodation until she and the King came to an agreement. She said, 'I will be content to leave him to be bred and instructed as the King shall appoint, provided that I live in Brussels in the house of the person whom the King shall choose with my consent for the care of the child – and that I have a pension.' (Presumably Cardeñas did not know that she was already receiving this money.) She added that she would not accept Slingsby as her son's guardian, and suggested that Castlehaven should be given the post.

This enraged Slingsby, who wrote to Charles saying that he had been ruined by having to keep Mrs Barlow, and that he had used violence in order to obtain the money she owed him. He added that he would bring an action against Mottet and Cardeñas, and therefore against the Viceroy, unless he was paid, thus making it obvious that Lucy had been living at her usual rate, regardless of the consequences to the child. Slingsby then called on Daniel O'Neile to support him. When O'Neile appeared, Lucy added his name to the list of her enemies. The reason for this was that O'Neile knew about her secret weapons against the King – 'certain letters and papers – which,' he explained, 'she must be forced to give up.' 'If the King does not give me satisfaction,' said Lucy, 'I will post up all his letters to me.'

That one of these papers was the supposed marriage certificate is un-likely. It had not been found on Lucy when she was arrested and sent to the Tower by Cromwell, who would certainly have published it. It may be that it was among other papers entrusted to Colonel Howard, of which he was still in possession, and that her cousin's attack on him was part of an attempt to get hold of them. Slingsby suggested that her trunks should be searched in Cardeñas's presence, and Lucy appears to have been forced to agree to this.

Edward Prodgers was then sent by Charles to Brussels to kidnap James. He persuaded Lucy to 'look for a paper', and while she was upstairs took the boy away. She followed them, and using the same tactics as with Slingsby, got her son back.

Mottet wrote to Ormonde that he was in the process of persuading Mrs Barlow to give up her child. 'It will be your ruin not to do so,' he told her. Still Lucy stood out – why should not she and James live with Lord Castlehaven? A Lieutenant Amand then appeared, whom Lucy seems to have persuaded to support her against the other agents. Meanwhile, Slingsby warned Charles that she might at any moment slip through their fingers, with the child and the papers. (He had some of these, but not all.) Cardeñas complained bitterly of being involved in this sordid affair, and Slingsby asked Charles to write him a grateful and placating letter.

The wrangle continued till the first week of January 1658. Then Lucy gave in and consented to let the King take charge of their son. By this time, he was again so short of money that he could not send anyone to take him to some place where Lucy would not be able to trace him. For the next two months she remained in Brussels, presumably under Castle-haven's protection, and in receipt of an increased pension from the King, part of which had been supplied by Cardeñas.[1]

In this, the penultimate stage of her battle with Charles, Lucy appears as her defenders would wish: a persecuted, courageous, deeply wronged heroine; and there is little doubt that she was brutally treated, not only by his agents, some of whom acted on their own initiative, but with his connivance. To tear a child of eight from his mother's arms and permanently separate them now seems an act of horrible cruelty; in the seventeenth century the correct and suitable upbringing of a king's son was considered more important than his mother's feelings. It occurred to none of Charles's most high-minded and domesticated followers, such as Ormonde and Hyde, to censure him for his actions, although they deplored the way in which his orders had been carried out. The fact that Lucy was 'making a property of her innocent child to support herself' was paramount; and indeed, however much she loved him, it is obvious that she loved money, and sexual indulgence, even more.

It is at this point that Lucy's case may be compared with that of Catherine Pegge, also a young woman of gentle birth. Having borne Charles a son, Catherine lived, like the other Royalists, on what he was able to give her, without drawing attention to herself and presumably doing her best for their child, as the question of his being removed from her never arose. At the Restoration she returned to England to collect a husband, a dowry and, eventually, a title for their son.

The essential difference between Catherine Pegge's situation and Lucy's lies hidden in the lost papers and letters which the Welshwoman threatened to 'post up' in Brussels. When Charles, at the age of eighteen, fell desperately in love with her, he may have been besotted enough to put some vague promise of marriage in writing; or have gone through such a ceremony as he did thirteen years later, with Louise de Kéroualle, when he had been Catherine of Braganza's husband for nine – that of a mock marriage, treated as a joke by all the participants, but which invested Mlle de Kéroualle, a very proper young lady, with the semi-respectable status of *maîtresse en titre*.[2] If the King did the same for Lucy, she would have been encouraged to say that she was his wife. This treatment, in whatever it consisted, combined with her temperament and habits to make an impossible situation for Charles, who reaped the harvest of his youthful folly for eight and a half years.

Of his fourteen surviving children Lucy's son was the one he loved best and for whom he did most, in spite of the fact that James inherited her violence, as was shown when, shortly after he reached manhood, he murdered an unarmed night-watchman and, later, formed a gang to beat up and slit the nose of a courtier who had spoken contemptuously of his father's mistresses. Neither these crimes nor his political disloyalties affected Charles, who, at the height of the young man's assaults on his power, merely told him to 'go to Hell', and sent him into exile, while continuing to finance him. Like Lucy, James was irresistible.

In 1658 however, Charles's position was such that Lucy's behaviour (not their former relationship nor the existence of their child) did him infinite harm. Most kings, whether exiled or not, had mistresses; such ladies were expected to conform to certain standards; and Lucy Walter outraged these throughout her short life. That she did so when Charles was dependent on the Spaniards was particularly unfortunate; for that nation's sense of dignity and decorum was then, as now, a by-word, and resulted in a suggestion that Hyde should compose a 'character' of his master publicizing his virtues. The Chancellor realized that this would only draw attention to the recent scandal, as did Ormonde, who was deploring His Majesty's inability to wait patiently in the *ville morte* of Bruges. This restlessness, he wrote to Hyde, was 'a greater danger to my hope of his recovery than the strength of his enemies. This, to any but you ... were too bold a lamentation ... But God bless him, and fit him for his work.'

What work? Charles might have replied. He remained inactive and penniless, while his brothers continued their military careers, and were well fed, paid and housed. Yet he was not discouraged; the reports from England showed increasing hatred of the regime, and once more rebellion was being planned on a large scale; one of the leaders was that Colonel Gunter who had helped the King in the last stages of his flight from Worcester. Charles and Hyde therefore issued a declaration, appealing to the English people to overthrow 'the most odious usurper and execrable murderer of my and your lawful sovereign', promising pardon to all but the regicides and a religious settlement 'according to the best reformed Churches'. They added that the soldiers would receive their arrears of pay and that those who had church lands would be allowed to keep them at slightly higher rents.[3] Cromwell replied by arresting a number of suspected persons; but preparations for a revolt continued.

At Charles's next conference with Don Juan a league with Hungary, Denmark and Poland was discussed, but nothing came of this scheme. At the end of January Ormonde went to London where he remained, at the risk of his life, till the first week in March. (His only disguise was a wig, which, when it rained, became parti-coloured.) The Royalist agents told him that if the Spanish promise of 6,000 foot and 2,000 horse materialized, they were certain of success. Yet again the pattern of failure was to be repeated. No effort could unite the anti-Cromwellian groups; and none of them was prepared to attack till the King appeared. Eventually his landing was arranged for March 15th.

While he waited for news from Ormonde Charles met Mary of Orange at Bruges, where he had to deal with a violent attack on Hyde and an outburst of quarrelling, in which three of his courtiers – Sir James Hamilton, Nicholas Armorer and Sir Marmaduke Darcy – were involved. 'I was in drink ... ' Hamilton admitted, 'and so mad drunk I threatened the Lord Chancellor with death.' He was now abject, and ready to submit to 'any punishment' in return for His Majesty's favour.[4]

Charles and Mary then moved on to Antwerp to stay with the Newcastles. It was perhaps as well that they were bound on a party of pleasure; for the last month their relations had not been happy, and neither would take the blame. When the Spanish forces moved into winter quarters York left them to stay with his sister, accompanied by Lord Jermyn's nephew, Harry Jermyn. A few weeks later Charles heard that the Princess was being courted by this rather undesirable young man, and that she favoured him, just as her mother favoured his uncle; the assumption was that she would either marry him secretly or become his mistress. In fact, Mary was then innocent of either intention; but the gossip caused Charles to recall Jermyn from the Hague, at which the Princess, with some reason, protested. 'Consider,' she wrote, 'what consequences your severity will bring upon me,' and pointed out that Jermyn's sudden departure would give rise to 'public discourse'. Charles, equally annoyed, refused to send Jermyn back, told Mary that he was acting in her interests and suggested that she and York should join him.[5] She obeyed, although resentfully; her devotion to Charles forbade her referring to Mrs Barlow, Catherine Pegge, or any other member of that 'vulgar and effeminate' society so much deplored by Ormonde and Hyde.

Naturally Mary subscribed to the view that men, whether married or single, were not expected to be chaste, and that a woman's reputation must be stainless; but she was deeply hurt by her brother's assumption that she had been indiscreet, if nothing more. She would not admit, or perhaps did not care, that since her arrival in Holland, sixteen years before, she had never made the faintest attempt to endear herself to the Dutch, who now seized the opportunity to malign her, and were increasingly irritated by her long absences from her son and her devotion to her brothers.

As she became more unpopular with, and estranged from, her husband's people, Mary's dependence on Charles's affection developed into an obsession, to the point indeed of taxing his patience. So far, her generosity and loyalty had never failed; the price she exacted was that he should be prepared to listen to all her grievances, and intervene in her endless disputes with her mother-in-law, or with the Stadtholders, whatever his own preoccupations. When she, York, Gloucester and the King met in Antwerp the surface relationships were smooth, and they were all ready to enjoy themselves.

Means for doing so had been lavishly planned. The proceedings opened with Charles holding a Chapter of the Garter, at which he invested his French ally, the Comte de Marchin. This enraptured Sir Edward Walker, who after an interval of seven years appeared in his glory as Garter King-at-Arms, and was handsomely tipped by de Marchin, now an English earl.[6]

A few days later the Newcastles gave a ball, in which the splendours of Charles I's golden age were partially re-created. Ecstatically Sir Edward Walker described how, when all the guests were placed,

> The King was brought in with loud music, and ... Major Mohun, that was the player, in a black satin robe and garland of bays, spake a speech in verse, of his Lordship's own poetry, wherein as much was said of compliment to His Majesty as the highest hyperbole could possibly express. After that they danced for two hours, and then my Lady Moore, dressed all in feathers, came in and sung a song of the same author's ... Then was the banquet brought in, in eight great chargers, each borne by two gentlemen ... Wines and other drinks ... being dispersed to all the company, they danced again for two hours more, and Major Mohun ... ended all with another speech by way of prophecy of His Majesty's establishment.

Next day, Charles was so injudicious as to warn Mary against the Jermyns; she replied with great bitterness, and they parted on bad terms.[7]

A few nights later the King was the guest of honour at another dance; then he returned to Brussels. In the midst of these festivities news came that Wilmot, who had been ill for some time, had died in Ghent. Of all the Cavaliers, Charles had loved him the best; he concealed his grief, which may have been obscured by his anxiety about Ormonde, from whom nothing had been heard.

II

In the first week of March Ormonde's report arrived. He advised Charles to invade the east coast without delay, but had found the situation 'sad in many particulars'.[8] In fact, the inability of one group to work with another was now increased by mistrust. When one of the leaders asked a Royalist agent what local support he could count on, he was told, 'You must be content to be ignorant of all but your own [district].'[9]

In the interval between Ormonde's departure from England and his momentary halt in Paris the Government had been warned, the harbours were blocked and the fleets ready. During the next three months the rounding up of the Royalists continued, and preparations for crushing punishments set in hand. The Spaniards then turned upon Charles; he was told that his negligence had enabled Cromwell's spies to prevent his restoration. Once more, he was 'in the greatest want', and 'no money, only fair promises' came from Don Juan.[10] When his pension did arrive, he had to pay Gloucester's debts; but there was enough left for him to send Thomas Ross, one of his most trustworthy courtiers, to remove his son from Lucy and take him to Antwerp. Soon Ross realized that Lucy was not going to keep her promise and that they must move on. 'He cannot be safe from his mother's intrigues where he is,' he wrote to Charles, adding, 'It is a pity so pretty a child should be in hands that have neglected to teach him to read or to tell twenty, though he has much wit and a great desire to learn.'[11]

For some months Ross concealed his charge, while Lucy appears to have pursued them in the intervals of defending herself from Colonel Howard, who brought an unsuccessful action against her for £500. She was then at the Hague. When Dr Floyd, one of Charles's chaplains, tried to have her drummed out of the city, she defeated him.[12] Charles kept in touch with her through his cup-bearer, William Erskine, who brought her money. Their son, now tutored by Ross, who had become devoted to him, was placed in the charge of Lord Crofts in his house near Paris, and he was known as Mr Crofts, passing as his guardian's nephew. Henrietta Maria then took charge of his religious education, and the future Protestant hero was received into the Catholic Church by Father Goffe, formerly an Anglican and another of Charles's chaplains. He never saw his mother again.[13]

Eventually she traced him as far as Paris, where she died, according to York, 'of a disease incident to her profession ... She was very handsome,' he added, writing some thirty years later, 'with little wit and some cunning.'[14] The man who sent Lucy's son to the block may have been prejudiced; but James II was essentially truthful – incapable, indeed, of invention. And so no more of Lucy Walter ...

As soon as his son was settled at Colombes Charles renewed his offer of joining the Spanish forces, and was again refused. When Gloucester came to him in Brussels with news that his sister Mary could no longer finance him, the King had to let the boy join his brother at the front, while he himself kept in touch with Don Juan, who ignored his warning that Parliament was about to attack Dunkirk. Charles then heard that several of Cromwell's agents were watching him, and that the trial of the Royalist leaders would take place in May. 'His Majesty's just cause,' wrote Giavarini, Venetian Resident in London, ' ... though abandoned by men, may one day have the protection of God.' During the course of the trial the treachery of one of Charles's best agents was revealed by this same sympathizer, who told the Senate that God 'had allowed a Judas ... among the twelve Apostles'.[15] In June the leaders of the revolt went to the block declaring their loyalty to King Charles, and healths were drunk to the Black Boy in secret. Then Charles was told that General Monk should be approached. 'I am confident,' a Royalist informer wrote to Hyde, 'that the person ... able alone to restore the King is Monk,' adding that the General was about to change sides because Cromwell had announced that his son Richard would succeed him. At once Charles wrote to Monk, promising him rewards and 'a title of honour ... upon the word of a King' – and received no reply. Monk's loyalty to his party appeared unshakable.[16]

When Dunkirk fell to the Franco-English forces Charles heard nothing from his brothers; for a time it was believed that both had been wounded and taken prisoner. As soon as he knew that they were safe, he went to Sevenbergen to meet Mary of Orange and to confer with his old ally, Cardinal de Retz, now also in exile, about his next move – should he leave for Frankfort to attend the Diet for the election of the new Emperor, or go to Madrid, in the hope of persuading Philip IV to include him in any treaty he might make with France? De Retz advised him to do neither, but to appeal to the Pope, through Cardinal Barbarini, to whom he himself wrote that 'the King of England possesses all the qualities of a great monarch – his word is ... absolutely inviolable'. Barbarini replied that he had Charles's interests 'passionately at heart' – and did nothing. Meanwhile, the Dutch asked Charles to leave their territory, and he returned to Brussels, to be followed by a reproachful letter from Mary about his insistence on her dismissal of Lord and Lady Balcarres. 'You left me,' she wrote, 'with much unkindness.' This was followed by a protest from Henrietta Maria, begging Charles not to persecute the Balcarres family. 'I cannot obey Your Majesty in this matter,' Charles replied, and to York, who also took his sister's side, he pointed out that Balcarres had sent 'mutinous and seditious' instructions to Scotland, and was disobeying all his orders. He told his mother not to interfere, adding, 'I must ... desire you to adjure my sister not to disobey me.'[17]

He was then told that Digby had become a Catholic, that Taaffe had killed another courtier in a duel and that de Vic was threatening Hyde. Having dismissed Digby and de Vic and banished Taaffe from his Court, Charles plunged into rather disreputable obscurity, journeying from one town to another in search of distraction, till he reached Hoogstraten, a little dorp lying exactly between the Dutch and Spanish Netherlands. Here he remained during the whole of August, and here he was pursued by a long lecture from Hyde about his fondness for undesirable company. Gossip about his habits had reached the Louvre, much distressing Louis XIV, who remarked that his cousin 'should rather with tears seek to appease the wrath of God than follow his amours'.[18] Charles ignored both diatribes and continued to amuse himself, in the intervals between playing tennis, hunting and hawking with Ormonde, Armorer, Sir Stephen Fox and a diminished Court. Then he received a letter from Dr Cosin, about the strange behaviour of Thomas Ross and Father Goffe. They were not only telling little James that his mother had been married to the King, but had suggested to Cosin that they should forge a marriage certificate in order to prove their pupil's legitimacy.[19]

Charles at once dismissed Ross; but the mischief was done, and by one of his most devoted and incorruptible servants, who, just before he and his charge found a home at Colombes, was writing to another Royalist, 'Upon my faith, I had rather go to plough than live as I do, were it not to serve that noble family.' When through his own stupidity Ross lost his position, he remained loyal, merely complaining, 'All is drawn again into the old channel, and I fear we shall all sink in it,' for he had no warm clothes, was half starved and could only console himself by 'cursing the dice at the tables'. Charles reinstated him as his son's tutor after the Restoration.

Goffe and Ross had combined in lying to their charge for separate and individual reasons. The priest wanted to present him as the Catholic heir to the English throne; and Ross was so captivated by his beauty and his winning ways that he seems to have promised him anything. There is another possibility. James was now in his tenth year and, although un-taught, extraordinarily – as it afterwards proved, fatally – receptive. Ever since he could remember he had heard his mother and her relations declare that she was married to the King, and that she had papers to prove it. So it may have been the boy's assurances which convinced the grown-ups. Twenty-two years afterwards, when James was Duke of Monmouth and

Buccleuch, and the question of his legitimacy became a major political issue, his striking the bar sinister from his arms was perhaps connected with his beautiful mother's assertions and his tutors' acceptance of them. His father's categorical denials that he had ever been married to Lucy Walter, and his announcement that he would sooner see their son hanged at Tyburn than legitimize him could not quite obscure the thrilling legend of childhood. Finally, the marriage certificate which Dr Cosin forbade Ross and Father Goffe to forge might already have been in existence and thus, at long last, have reached the Buccleuch archives to be discovered and burnt two and a half centuries later.

The immediate effect of Ross's folly was that Lord Crofts, then known as 'mad Will', became the paramount influence in his ward's life. As a duellist, a gambler and a rake, this nobleman was entirely unsuited to his position; the only serious-minded persons in the boy's new circle were his grandmother and her Catholic advisers. The contrast between existence at Colombes and that with Lucy and her lovers must have been bewildering, if not disruptive. It was not until long afterwards that James knew his mother had 'died miserably, without anything to bury her', at the age of twenty-eight.[20]

Shortly after dismissing Ross Charles secretly entered the forbidden territory of the Hague, for reasons known only to Ormonde, whose first biographer, Carte, recorded the incident fifty years later, as coming from the King himself. According to Carte, Charles reached the Hague at six o'clock in the evening with a single gentleman, and took a room in an obscure inn, where he waited while his attendant went to the Binnenhof to inform the Princess. Suddenly the door opened and 'an old, reverend-looking man, with a long grey beard and ordinary grey clothes' appeared. This person locked the door, removed his disguise and, falling on his knees, announced himself as George Downing, Parliamentary ambassador to the States General. 'I have come to seek pardon for past offences,' he said. He then told Charles that his arrival at the Hague was already known, and added that, although he had had to issue a warrant for His Majesty's arrest, he had so delayed matters as to ensure his escape.[21]

Downing's action sprang from the knowledge that the Protector was dying, and from his conviction that Richard Cromwell would not be able to sustain his father's power. He did not tell Charles that Oliver had but a few days to live, and the King would not have believed him if he had; for as soon as he returned to Hoogstraten he received an express from York, who was in Bruges, telling him of Cromwell's death. Knowing his brother's gullibility, Charles ignored this message.

In the evening of September 3rd, 1658, that formidable genius and empire-builder – or, as Elizabeth of Bohemia put it, 'that Beast, whom all the kings of the earth do worship' – expired, and his son was proclaimed Lord Protector. Three days later, Charles was playing tennis when Sir Stephen Fox walked into the *dedans*, fell on his knee and told him the news.[22] Next day the King left for Brussels.

The miracle had happened. Rejoicings burst out all over Europe. 'No man,' reported an ecstatic Royalist, 'is at leisure to buy or sell, the young fry dance in the streets at noon-day. "The Devil is dead", is the language at every turn; and the entertainment of the graver sort is only to contemplate the happy days approaching.'[23]

For the next few weeks, Charles was too much occupied and too constantly in demand to realize that he had now entered the grimmest and most despairing period of the exile.

NOTES

1 Fea, *King Monmouth*, p. 20; Steinmann, pp. 80–116; *Cal. Clar. S. P.*, vol. III, pp. 392–401.
2 Evelyn, p. 559.
3 *Cal. Clar. S. P.*, vol. III, pp. 407–8.
4 *Cal. D. S. P.*, Feb. 17th, 1658.
5 *Thurloe S. P.*, vol. I, pp. 662–3.
6 Scott, *The King in Exile*, p. 341.
7 Ibid.
8 Carte, *Original Letters*, vol. II, p. 118.
9 *Thurloe S. P.*, vol. VII, p. 78.
10 *Cal. D. S. P.*, March 3rd, 1658.
11 Op. cit., March 25th, 1658.
12 *Thurloe S. P.*, vol. I, p. 337.
13 D'Oyley, p. 28.
14 Steinmann, p. 116.
15 *Cal. S. P. Ven.*, vol. XXXI, p. 184.
16 *Cal. Clar. S. P.*, vol. III, p. 413.
17 Op. cit., vol. IV, pp. 52–63.
18 *Thurloe S. P.*, vol. VII, p. 325.
19 J. Macpherson, *Original Papers*, vol. I, pp. 75–6.
20 Evelyn, p. 816.
21 Carte, *Original Letters*, no. 130.
22 Airy, p. 46.
23 *Cal. Clar. S. P.*, vol. III, p. 412.

CHAPTER SEVEN

IN THE DEPTHS

I

THE fact that Oliver Cromwell was now 'the dead monster' made it necessary for the Royalists to work out another form of anti-Protectorate propaganda. It was no longer enough merely to fore-tell the downfall of an evil Government; for the new Protector's mildness and his civilian status threw a different light on the English scene. The Cavaliers did not grasp this aspect of the situation, partly because, during the nine years that elapsed between the execution of Charles I and Cromwell's death, they had fallen into the habit of circulating a number of horror stories based on the judicial murder of the man who, if he had been allowed to live, would eventually have destroyed all belief in, or devotion to, the mystique of monarchy. If the Roundheads had but known it, Charles I was their greatest asset.

As it was, Royalist pamphleteers, agents and historians had not ceased to recall the night of January 30th, 1649, when Cromwell, inspecting the body of the dead King in the palace of Whitehall, 'did with his fingers search the wound, as if he had still doubted of the effect of his hellish cruelty',[1] while Hyde recorded the Protector's cool comment on his sainted victim, as being of 'so admirable a constitution, that he would probably have lived as long as nature could subsist'.[2]

These stories, whether true or false, had enabled the Cavaliers to display their great enemy as a satanic fiend; not even the most ingenious could make anyone believe that Richard Cromwell reproduced his father's wickedness. It was left to the factions in his own party to give him a contemptuous nickname and to deprive him of his inheritance.

In these first days of hope and joy Charles kept his head, although it must have been difficult not to make a dash for England when he heard that the French regarded their contracts with that country as dissolved, that Monk and Fairfax were about to combine against Richard Cromwell and that Don Juan was sending him 17,000 florins.[3] His cunning and his sense of self-preservation, partially fostered by Hyde (in a crisis the King consulted no one else) and now fully developed through twelve and a half years of ruthless and unscrupulous diplomacy, saved him from disaster. After another flying visit to the Hague, he returned to Hoogstraten in order to proceed with a scheme on which he had been working since August – his marriage with Mary's sister-in-law, the twenty-one-year-old Princess Henriette Catherine of Orange.

This young lady was one of four sisters, two of whom were already married. She, her youngest sister and their mother, the formidable Princess Dowager Amalia, were living in the country palace of Turnhout, some four miles from Hoogstraten, when Charles first arrived there. It seems that Henriette was indulged by the Princess Dowager, who had contracted her in infancy to Prince William of East Friesland, but who allowed her, when he arrived as a bridegroom, to break off the engagement. (By this time Henriette had seen something of Charles and appears to have fallen in love with him.⁴)

Princess Amalia received Charles's first offer coolly, and said nothing of it to her daughter. When the Protector's death enabled him to renew it, he did so in a letter showing his awareness of his effect on Henriette, whom he referred to by her pet name, in the manner of a love-stricken suitor. After announcing that he would rather be restored to his kingdom through the help of the States General than by any other power, he went on, 'I beseech you to let me know whether the Princess Harriette be so far engaged that you cannot receive a proposition from me concerning her: and if she be not, that you would think of a way how, with all possible secrecy, I may convey my mind in that particular to you.'⁵ When Amalia showed this letter to Henriette, she swooned away, and had to be put to bed.⁶

Charles then returned to Ghent, where he was joined by his sister and a number of Cavaliers. He circulated between that city, Antwerp, Breda and Brussels for the next three weeks. On September 28th he heard that Monk had 'cheerfully proclaimed' the new Protector in Scotland, that all forces had taken the oath of loyalty and that the continental powers were prepared to treat with the English Parliament as before. 'The King's condition,' says Hyde, 'never appeared so hopeless, so desperate; for a more favourable conjuncture his friends could never expect than this, which blasted all their hopes.'⁷

Charles managed to preserve an unbroken front, and renewed his efforts to marry Princess Henriette Catherine, sending Ormonde to the Dowager with a formal offer for her hand. She temporized, and the King then visited her at the Hague, where she 'civilly declined' him as a son-in-law. Charles won her over, and during the first week of October was still being 'highly entertained' at her house.[8] She then told him that she could not give him her daughter without the consent of the States General. He replied by hinting that the Stadtholders were about to back him. He was so persuasive that Ormonde was allowed by the Dutch to marry his eldest son, Lord Thomas, to a Nassau cousin of the Princess's, Emilia van Beverwaert, with whom the boy had fallen in love; for they all believed that the King would bring off the marriage with Henriette. Emilia was rich enough for Lady Ormonde to 'divert' (convenient word) some of her dowry to her daughter Elizabeth, whom she had planned to marry to Lord Chesterfield. When it became clear that the King's fortunes were at their lowest ebb, and that he would not be allowed to collect his Dutch heiress, Lady Ormonde gave him what she could from the Beverwaert dowry, instead of using it for the match between her daughter and Chesterfield: a sacrifice typical of the Ormonde family. Meanwhile Princess Henriette was warned that Charles was living with a mistress, the Comtesse de Sainte-Croix. A month later she was removed from the King of England's dangerous fascination by being married, out of hand, to Prince William of Anhalt.[9]

Although this rebuff was not of great importance, its repercussions widened the breach between Charles and Mary. Detesting her mother-in-law, she took his attempt to ally himself with the Orange-Nassau family as a personal slight. Nothing could have been more unreasonable; yet Mary managed to persuade York and Gloucester that Charles had not only been disloyal to her in proposing to Henriette, but had thereby lowered the Stuart prestige. If the Dutch had allowed him to join her and his brothers at the Hague, he would have brought her round; as it was, the three persons on whose love and loyalty he most depended were now allied, with his mother, against him. And while they all lived comfortably together, Charles, ragged, hungry and ignored, wandered from one lodging to another. He sold his plate, pawned anything he could lay hands on, ate off wood and pewter and was again reduced to one meal a day. The Spanish had not paid his allowance for four months; having let his house in Brussels, he was homeless, became shockingly thin and so morose that one of his courtiers complained, 'he has not the least good nature left', while another added, 'If we continue longer as we are, we must perish.'[10]

Yet when Mrs Elliott, his old nurse's daughter, visited him, he managed, somehow, to entertain her suitably, although he could not pay for her journey to Bruges, and when she asked him for money, only gave her a hundred guilders. 'The King pretends poverty,' she remarked disgustedly, 'but I never in my life saw such bravery.'[11]

Meanwhile, Mary of Orange was complaining that Charles's refusal to let Harry Jermyn remain at the Hague had 'ruined her fame'. To one of her ladies she confessed that she had fallen in love with Jermyn and would have married him if Charles had not interfered. 'Hereafter,' she declared, 'I will never have anything to do with him ... I am no more his subject, nor will be. I am a free woman, and may marry whom I please.'[12]

In the last weeks of 1658 better news came from England. Richard Cromwell and the army had fallen out. 'The storm,' a Royalist informed Charles, 'after so great a calm, is now begun,' and advised His Majesty to be ready, although he admitted that his party did not want to move just yet. A more perspicacious agent, John Barwick, sent Charles a little money, and told him he must wait till the factions in the Government brought on a revolution; then he would be able to return on his own terms.[13] Barwick was the only correspondent who then held this view; it had occurred to no one else, nor did it immediately occur to Charles, that to take no action at all – to sink into what looked like the inertia of despair – would ensure a bloodless and triumphant restoration. Even Hyde still clung to the idea of invasion and conquest. No one, the King least of all, imagined that he could possibly be called for with little or no dispute by a vast majority.

By this time, Charles had become more cautious and more determined than any of his advisers. He desired action, and was not afraid of being killed. But there was one form of restoration he was never going to submit to – that by which he became a symbol of royalty, the helpless puppet of a party, as in Scotland. Rather than endure that mockery of kingship, or wear that paper crown, he would either wait indefinitely, or give up all hope of victory. In fact, he did not give up hope, in this, the blackest period of the exile.

His endurance now seems inexplicable. It might perhaps be accounted for by some hidden, atavistic instinct, one of the mainsprings of his whole existence. To one born to be a king – a Stuart king – misfortune may, at intervals, seem trivial, fleeting and irrelevant. It had appeared so to his great-grandmother when for eighteen years she not only thought of herself as Queen of England, but persisted in working for the achievement of that position against all warnings, and in the face of hideous danger. Her son's obsession with 'kingcraft' expressed a similar view of that sacred claim; and Charles I's refusal to give away his prerogative had strengthened his heir's belief in it.

The difference between Charles II's attitude towards kingship and that of his forbears sprang from his intellectual power, which grew with his growth, finally amounting almost to genius; yet it was so lightly worn as to deceive his acutest contemporaries. He was what we now call a realist; seeing his situation, he accepted it; and he knew that his kingdom would be an impoverished heritage. It did not matter. He had something better, something endemic and indestructible. Behind that steely brain, behind that cynical assessment of human folly, behind the wit and the amiability and the graceful, winning ways lay a dedicated, unshakable awareness of his own divinity, a divinity which had no connection with rites and ceremonies, or the trappings of royalty. For nearly half his life he had done without such fripperies, and could afford to despise them. In this moment – unanointed, deserted, penniless and disreputable – Charles Stuart was still morally undefeated, because his personality was sheltered and enclosed within the fortress of an impregnable regality.

II

Although preparations for Charles's arrival in England had reached the point of a professional embroiderer being engaged to work on his robes,[14] his situation was so dismal that in January 1659 he was considering an approach to Richard Cromwell. Both the King and Hyde thought that the dispute between the army, or 'Commonwealth men', and the Protector's party was serious enough for Richard to ally himself with the Royalists. When Charles empowered Lord Bellasis to open negotiations – 'I believe,' he wrote, 'that Richard Cromwell is not without some affection for me' – nothing happened.[15] Once more he was reduced to inactivity, begging and borrowing just enough to keep himself and his Court. The most convenient way of living would have been at the Hague; there he could have regained Mary's support (the breach between the brother and sister was beginning to cause comment) and made further overtures to the Dutch. This refuge was closed to him by George Downing, who had now decided to stick to his own party. He urged the States General not to receive Charles; and he reported his movements and schemes to Thurloe through one of the King's most trusted servants, Thomas Killigrew, who for several years had been a gentleman of the bedchamber.[16] Killigrew's information enabled the Government to keep down the Royalists in England, while his intimacy with Charles protected him from all suspicion; so much so that he remained in his service till after the Restoration.

When the unpaid Parliamentary troops began to mutiny, and all Royalists were told to remove twenty miles from London, the anti-Cromwellian Republicans rose to momentary strength. This enabled them to suggest to Charles that he should be restored on the same terms as in Scotland. 'Your Majesty's sweetness of disposition ... and temper will prevail,' he was told; but Charles was not to be trapped a second time.[17] He was perfectly indifferent to the increasing complaints of his slackness; these were partially the work of Buckingham, by whom the Republicans were still subjugated. The Duke, now living in great comfort with his father-in-law, and on his wife's money, retailed all the scandal he could rake up or invent about Charles. The King, he told his new allies, was not only a cheat but a coward. He had disgraced himself at the siege of Worcester; worst of all, he was a Papist. 'My ink is not black enough,' wrote one of the Royalists, 'to express the base and horrid language Buckingham doth belch out concerning our master.'

One of the results of this doldrum period was that those Cavaliers who had neither Charles's tenacity nor their seniors' steadiness ceased to maintain the faintest show of decorum. Hitherto, quarrelling and insobriety had been confined to taverns, private rooms and late hours. Now, just when Charles had collected enough money to ask York and Gloucester to visit him in Brussels and they were all playing tennis, Lord Newburgh staggered drunkenly into the gallery to watch the game with two other courtiers, Mr Stanley and Sir Marmaduke Darcy. Stanley, amused by Newburgh's stumbling movements, twitched at his hair and then hid himself behind Darcy. Newburgh shouted, 'Leave playing the fool, or I will knock you.' 'O pray, my lord,' Darcy interposed, 'be not so foolish as to give such language in the King's presence.' 'You are a whoreson son of a puppy,' replied Newburgh, shaking his fist, 'and if the King were not here, I would pull you by the ears, like a rogue and a rascal as you are.' 'Let us find a cudgel,' Stanley whispered to another of His Majesty's gentlemen, and they crept away.

They returned to find the game over and the King gone; York and Gloucester were talking, and Lord Newburgh was making water at the side of the court. Stanley came up behind him and hit him six or seven times. Newburgh turned and drew his sword. They were all struggling together when Gloucester, followed by York, rushed up, forced them apart and reported them to the King, who interviewed the culprits that evening. All he could do was to have them locked in their rooms, like naughty children, without food or drink. Next day the quarrel was made up, with shaking of hands, kisses and 'humble submission' to His Majesty.[18]

In such wearisome crises as these Charles's patience seldom failed. One who was with him at this time was amazed by his 'temperance of speech

... "You are an insolent fellow" was ... the hardest expression I ever heard him use,' he remembered long afterwards.[19] In fact, within a few weeks of his twenty-ninth birthday, the King had acquired the outlook and behaviour of middle age; already there were threads of grey in his hair, and he was never again to feel either the impetus or the sudden change from hope to despair which belongs to youth. In April, when the Protector's Parliament was dissolved and Richard Cromwell retired into private life, Charles's spirits seemed unaffected.

This was not the case with such persons as Newburgh and Stanley. When the confusion caused by the change of government and the restoration of the Rump Parliament slackened the watch on the ports, the Royalists travelled to and from the Continent in comparative safety. The result was disastrous. Little was hidden from them, and they hid nothing from their enemies. In vain Hyde and Nicholas urged secrecy, and assured those who complained that all was well. Most of the Royalist agents advised inaction. Then, in May, Lord Mordaunt, a Royalist who up to now had been working in England, stirred up the more cautious, and approached Charles with a new plan.

At a conference in Brussels Mordaunt, who had narrowly escaped death under the Protectorate, outlined the scheme of a rising which would cover the whole of England and Wales. This seemed no hare-brained plot, but a general movement, in which each leader was responsible for his own section while co-operating with the rest, and which Charles would open by landing at Lynn. 'Then I will venture my own person,' said the King, and it was arranged that he should embark from Calais in July.[20] Yet even as they talked the Royalist captains were quarrelling about precedence, and accusing Lord Mordaunt of playing for his own hand. With that nobleman's return to England in June Charles's situation reverted to its original state, although he was not immediately aware of this.

In July he was approached by a deserter from the Parliamentary camp – Samuel Morland, who was in a strong position as an anti-Parliament informer. For some years he had been working as Under-Secretary in Thurloe's Intelligence office, and thus knew which of Charles's staff were betraying him. He did not mention Killigrew (who seems to have been informing on a separate basis), but began by warning the King against Sir Richard Willis and Colonel Thomas Howard.

Charles dismissed Lucy's former protector as negligible. 'He knows no more than those that walk in the streets,' he said, but refused to believe in Willis's treachery, on the grounds that he had sheltered Ormonde on his last expedition to London and had worked for the Royalist cause to good effect. The matter was so serious and Morland so insistent, that a Council was called for the ex-Cromwellian to prove his case.

Morland began by saying that he himself had nothing to gain from slandering Willis. Having changed sides, he wished to ensure his own safety with the removal of all traitors, of whom Willis was the most dangerous. Charles said, 'Nothing can convince me of the infidelity of that gentleman, or make me withdraw my trust, but the evidence of his hand-writing, which is well known. He knows most of my friends,' he went on, 'and few men are more generally believed to be honest.'[21]

Morland agreed, and was presently able to produce the required evidence. Willis, then operating in London, was proved to have been in Thurloe's pay since 1656. Morland begged His Majesty to keep his name out of the business – 'Failing which,' he said, 'I am a dead man.'

Hyde and the King protested. They could not show up Willis without implicating Morland; no one would believe such a story. (Later evidence indicates that Morland had forged the letters and that Willis was innocent.[22]) As the agent hesitated, Charles took a sheet of paper on which he wrote out his promise that Morland should continue to be employed by him after the Restoration and receive the Garter. The turn-coat gave in.

A few days later Lord Mordaunt came again to Brussels, and told the King that the Royalists had become so 'wary and incredulous' that they might be discouraged. 'What do you think,' asked Charles, 'of Sir Richard Willis?' 'I complain principally of him,' Mordaunt replied, and explained that Sir Richard always advised against action. 'Have you any suspicion of his want of honesty?' Charles pursued. 'Though I do not take him to be my friend,' said Mordaunt, 'I would put my life in his hand tomorrow.' Charles then told him what he believed was the truth, without mentioning Morland. 'I charge you,' he went on, 'no further to communicate with that person, and to give your friends caution.'[23]

In the second week of July Charles left for Calais with Ormonde and two servants, while York waited for his summons at Boulogne. The rebellion began on a large scale. Then, after a struggle lasting some ten days, General Lambert routed the Royalist forces, and imprisoned those of their leaders who had not escaped. In England the general opinion was that Charles's cause had been irretrievably lost through his own fault. Why would His Majesty not trust his loving servants, Willis especially, whom all deemed 'a very fine gentleman ... extremely honest, and brave beyond expression'?[24] Once more John Barwick produced a few hundred pounds, and advised another approach to Monk, whose rivalry with

Lambert was further splitting the Government. On July 21st, 1659, Monk heard from the King as follows.

I cannot think that you wish me ill, nor have you reason to do so; and the good I expect from you will bring so great a benefit to your country and to yourself that I cannot think you will decline my interest ... If you once resolve to take my interest to heart, I will leave the way and manner of it entirely to your judgement, and will comply with the advice you shall give me ... It is in your power to make me as kind to you as you can desire, and to have me always your affectionate friend,   C.R.

There was no answer to this appeal. The whole situation had to be reconsidered.

NOTES

1 *Trial of Charles I* (ed. J. G. Muddiman), p. 155.
2 Clarendon, p. 698.
3 *Cal. Clar. S. P.*, vol. IV, pp. 73–9.
4 Carte, *Ormonde*, vol. I, pp. 161–3.
5 Carte, *Original Letters*, vol. II, p. 156.
6 Scott, *Travels of the King*, p. 369.
7 Clarendon, p. 864; *Thurloe S. P.*, vol. VII, p. 421.
8 Ibid.
9 Carte, *Ormonde*, ibid.
10 *Thurloe S. P.*, vol. VII, p. 113.
11 *Cal. Clar. S. P.*, vol. III, p. 337.
12 Ibid.
13 P. Barwick, *The Life of the Reverend D. John Barwick, D.D.*, p. 103.
14 Clarke, *James II*, vol. I, p. 55.
15 *Cal. Clar. S. P.*, vol. IV, p. 137.
16 *Thurloe S. P.*, vol. VII, p. 421.
17 *Cal. Clar. S. P.*, vol. III, p. 489.
18 *Bath MSS* (H.M.C.), vol. II, p. 130.
19 Tuke, p. 4.
20 Clarendon, pp. 868–78.
21 Scott, *Travels of the King*, p. 387.
22 W. Dampier, *The Restoration of Charles II*, p. 31.
23 Clarendon, ibid.
24 Barwick, ibid.

CHAPTER EIGHT

THE ENIGMA OF GENERAL MONK

I

FOR some years Charles had been in the position of a skilled card-sharper reduced to playing with a worn, greasy pack. Nearly all his agents were inefficient or false. Try as he might to keep an ace up his sleeve while sliding another knave on to the table, the tattered things stuck together one minute, slipped from his fingers the next, and generally showed him up as a clumsy cheat. And as he could not always conceal his employees' inefficiency, his 'good looks, kind words and fair promises ... charmed all who came near him, till they found how little they could depend [on them]'.¹ By now he was in any case perfectly indifferent to the disillusion of his allies on the Continent. Both he and they realized that he had been there too long. In England, although many were disappointed at his not appearing, sword in hand, to destroy the Commonwealth dragon, they still thought of him as the hero, and the victim, of Worcester fight, recklessly brave in action and stubbornly patient in misfortune.

The King himself remained dogged, persevering and cautious. He was not so eager, now, to throw his own life into the balance of war; if nothing else would serve, those of others must be sacrificed, while he gave himself up to his peculiar form of diplomacy, sponging on or winning over one distrustful potentate after another. When in August 1659 he heard that East Anglia and Kent had not risen and that only Cheshire and Lancashire were holding out, he moved to Rouen, in order to make his way to Brittany, so as to be ready to land in the west or in Wales. 'Upon the whole matter,' he wrote to Hyde, 'I am very cheerful; and though I am not altogether so plump as Mr Skinner [one of his nicknames for the Chancellor] I begin to grow sanguine.' This bolstering up of morale was followed by a rhyme in French about the daughter of an ivory-worker, seemingly designed to pain the recipient; it was in fact a code order to be passed on to an agent in Brussels.²

Charles then heard that de Marchin had collected and armed 10,000 men; all he needed was the transport promised by the Spaniards. Naturally

349

this did not materialize; by the time the King reached St Malo the rebellion was over, and Monk was busily hunting down Royalist nobles in Scotland.

After a brief conference with Ormonde, Charles decided to start two movements, one in Spain and one in France. Don Juan was now in Madrid; so he himself would go there in order to obtain some practical help from the King and his ministers, of whom Don Louis de Haro was the most powerful. As Spain and France were making a peace treaty, of which Louis XIV's marriage with the elder Infanta was the base, it was necessary for Charles to get in touch with Mazarin. He could only do this through his mother, whom he had not seen for five years, and who was still brooding resentfully over his rescue of Gloucester. From Brussels, where he returned secretly to confer with Hyde, go through his letters and make arrangements for his journey,[3] Charles wrote to Henrietta Maria in his blandest and most respectful manner, as if they were on the best of terms. She replied, '*Monsieur mon Fils*, although you show me no confidence, I continue to serve you –' and recommended his sending agents to Mazarin and Turenne. The King dispatched Ormonde to Colombes; he was then to ask the Cardinal for a pass into Spain, official recognition of Charles's presence at the peace meetings and a force of 1,000 foot and 500 horse, while York was to approach Turenne.[4]

Ormonde's interview with Henrietta Maria was successful. She agreed to do all she could for Charles with his French relatives and to meet him whenever it was convenient to himself, although she had been very much upset at his 'remonstrating' with his Palatine cousin, Princess Louise, for running away from the Hague and entering a Catholic convent in Antwerp. That Charles had done this because Elizabeth of Bohemia asked him to try and re-convert her daughter, further exacerbated Henrietta Maria, who was bitterly jealous of the King's attachment to his Protestant relations.

When Ormonde waited on Mazarin, whom he pursued to St Jean de Luz, he got a very different reception. According to his own account, the Cardinal interrupted the Marquess's stately opening with, 'I know that there is a King of England exiled from his kingdom. I know all his misfortunes, so it is useless to tell me any more. I can do nothing for him.' It would be most inadvisable, Mazarin added, for His Majesty to go to Madrid – and as for a pass, it was out of the question. Poor York was equally unfortunate in his overtures to Turenne.[5]

Apparently undaunted, Charles decided to leave for Madrid on his own, incognito, and without a pass, although he would have to go through French territory. Having returned to St Malo, he went to La Rochelle, whence he intended to proceed by sea. He had now re-engaged Digby as his private secretary (that nobleman's fluent Spanish and his knowledge of the country made him indispensable) while he sent Ormonde by another route to meet him at Fuenterrabia. His other companion was O'Neile, who was to take charge of the practical, and perhaps also of the private, side of the trip; for Charles, having been forced into a secret and roundabout route, had determined to enjoy himself.

So for three months – from the beginning of September till the end of November – the King was completely cut off from his Court and his agents; he did not write to Hyde, or to anyone else, for a fortnight. When he reached La Rochelle he stayed there a week, waiting, he said afterwards, for a favourable wind. Then he changed his mind and proceeded by public coach (this upset Nicholas and Hyde a good deal, when they heard about it) to Saragossa. From there, on October 15th, he wrote to the Chancellor in his most casual vein. 'You will wonder,' the letter began, 'to find me no further advanced... Contrary to all expectations, Don Louis is still at San Sebastian.' Charles went on to describe (fortunately not in detail) the 'pleasant accidents' of his journey, the excellent food and the comfortable inns. 'The only thing I find troublesome is the dust,' concluded His Majesty. '... God keep you, and send you to eat as good mutton as we have at every meal.'⁶

It was useless for Hyde and Nicholas to fume and protest. Charles was on holiday. All they could do was to write to Ormonde, now waiting in even greater anxiety at Fuenterrabia, urging him to stir up his master and recall him to his duties. His delay had in fact much offended the punctilious de Haro; and those Royalists who only knew that the King had disappeared were beginning to turn to the more serious York as their leader. Even Dr Fraser, Charles's devoted adherent since his childhood, had been seduced by York's supporters into casting doubts on the King's health, and hinting that his habits were such that he could not long survive. 'Reputation,' wrote Nicholas to Ormonde, '... is the interest of princes... and he has lost much of it by this unseasonable delay... My heart is full, and I impart to you my tender apprehension, leaving... you to make... use of it to the King's advantage.'⁷

Ormonde managed to placate de Haro, who had declared himself eager to help the English King, although the peace negotiations made it temporarily impossible for him to conduct Charles to Madrid or to present him to King Philip. On October 28th the meeting took place, and Charles was received 'with every possible mark of respect'. Don Louis, sallow, taciturn and invalidish, knelt in the dusty road to kiss his hand, and escorted him to his lodging in state to a salute of guns.[8] Here Charles was treated as a reigning sovereign, and visited daily by the grandees. In three days, his reception of these honours and his general behaviour had so entranced his hosts that his negligence was forgotten. They were ready to do anything for him – provided that the treaty with France was not endangered. 'He is the finest gentleman of the age,' de Haro announced, 'and of an obliging carriage.'[9]

In a country where but for his height and his lively, easy manners, Charles could have passed for a native, there was no need to play a part; he might have been born a Spaniard, people said; and for the first few days his high spirits were unforced. After months of discomfort and privation, he was comfortably housed, well fed and courteously welcomed Also, at the receptions in Fuenterrabia his shabby clothes were less noticeable than they would have been in the capital. When he tried to get down to business the atmosphere became rather chilly; for Mazarin was also in the city, and his first action had been to warn de Haro that there was no chance of His Majesty ('All I can do is pity his misfortunes') being restored, either then or later.[10] The Cardinal emphasized this statement by entertaining Lockhart, the Parliamentary ambassador, 'with the greatest pomp and splendour'.

When Charles was reduced to asking Mazarin for an audience, there was no result. Finally the Cardinal consented to meet Ormonde, 'in the road, as if by accident'. 'I can do nothing for His Majesty', was all he would say. Charles persisted, but Mazarin would not see him. 'I shall do great things,' said His Eminence in his most Machiavellian manner, 'but I cannot talk of England till the peace is signed.'[11] The King then suggested that he should marry the Cardinal's twelve-year-old niece, Hortense Mancini. Mazarin replied that he could not dispose of her while La Grande Mademoiselle remained single. (Thirteen years later Hortense ran away from her insane husband and became Charles's mistress. She remained in England till his death, having formed her own Court of fashionable Lesbians and impoverished intellectuals.)

Charles's hopes rose when King Philip suddenly announced that he would prefer Louis XIV to marry the younger Infanta, and the negotiations were held up. He took the opportunity to attend Mass in one of the private chapels, with Digby, who was begging him to make his conversion known. Immediately the news spread through the Netherlands that both Charles and York had apostasized, and once more Hyde and Nicholas had to assure the Royalists in England that this was a malicious slander, upon which Lord Mordaunt wrote to Ormonde, 'Your master is utterly ruined ... if this be true, though he never had a fairer game than at present.'[12] Ormonde replied, 'If they are Papists, I would rather see them restored as such, than not at all.' But he took the danger seriously enough to suggest to the Chancellor that an act should be drawn up 'whereby it may be made treason' to accuse His Majesty of abandoning his faith.

Meanwhile, Charles was pressing de Haro to let him come to Madrid. (His request for a command in the Spanish Netherlands had been refused.) His Majesty's bearing, reported O'Neile, who had been rather nervous, was very 'discreet' – perhaps the local ladies were either immured or un-attractive – and his 'dexterity and composedness' in dealing with the enigmatic grandees were admirable.[13] After some days of the usual evasions, Don Louis suddenly gave Charles all his pension – 7,000 gold pistoles. The King was beginning to think how best to fit out himself and his suite for their appearance in Madrid, when de Haro told him that the money was to pay for his journey back to Brussels.[14]

For a short time Charles gave way to black despair. Then he got a hope-ful letter from Hyde, begging him to return as quickly as possible, only pausing at Colombes in order to make it clear that he and Henrietta Maria were reunited. There was strange and exciting news from England. Monk's army had declared for the monarchy in Scotland, and the great General himself was about to approach the King.[15]

Charles left Fuenterrabia on November 8th. When he passed through St Jean de Luz he was asked by one of the Royalists who came to meet him whether it was true that he had become a Catholic. With a smile the King replied, 'My enemies are now put to hard shifts, and I take it for a good omen that they fight with such bulrushes.'[16]

While Charles was making his way towards the frontier ('I enjoyed the *varieties* of the journey,' he told Hyde[17]), he wrote to a Royalist agent in London suggesting that he should employ his old tactics by writing to both Lambert and Monk, in order to play off one General against an-other. 'You will be undone, they are enemies,' was the reply, and the King was wise enough to do nothing.[18] When he and his suite were approaching Bayonne, Ormonde received an extraordinary and, some thought, most heartening report from Lady Inchiquin's aunt, a con-nection of his own, who wrote to him from Utrecht in awe and wonder. It seemed that in London a three-day-old child had cried out, 'A King! A King! Bring me to the King!' When this utterance had been repeated several times, the infant was given some money and asked, 'What would you do with it?' 'I would give it to the King,' the phenomenon replied. 'I myself saw and heard this,' added Lady Inchiquin, and her aunt told Ormonde that it could only mean His Majesty's imminent triumph.[19]

At Blois Gaston d'Orléans and La Grande Mademoiselle offered Charles a grand reception. He declined, on the grounds that he must reach Colombes as quickly as possible. Just before he left, he heard that Parliament and the army had come to an agreement, but he remained 'cheerful and satisfied', so that people began to say that his Spanish visit must have been successful. On December 5th he reached Colombes.

As Henrietta Maria, in floods of happy tears, released him, Charles remembered to look round for the Princess Henrietta Anne, whom he had not seen since her eleventh year. He stooped to kiss her – and was undeceived by one of his courtiers.[20] That was not the Princess – and there came forward a frail, exquisite, elegant young lady, in whom Charles saw nothing of the little sister he had danced with and casually petted five years before. Henrietta Anne was not pretty in the accepted sense; her extreme thinness defied the mode, and one shoulder was higher than the other; but she moved and spoke as one accustomed to please and allure. And Charles was more than pleased with the delicate creature who gazed up at him with shy reverence and wondering curiosity; he was enchanted. She was perfect. He could not bear her out of his sight.

If Charles had spent a few months instead of a fortnight at Colombes, his relationship with his youngest sister might have assumed rather different proportions. In the short time they had together (he seems not to have taken much notice of her during his previous stay at the French Court) he had neither the time nor, certainly, the inclination to perceive the deficiencies concealed by her hero-worship of himself, her attractive exterior, and the gentleness and gaiety which endeared her to all her circle. As it was, their love for one another became devotion because he saw her at her best, before ill health and her disastrous marriage to Philippe d'Orléans destroyed much of her natural warmth, drove her into a frenzied search for admiration and thus into seeing herself as a politically minded, influential figure. Henrietta Anne was neither; and at fourteen it did not occur to her that she would become particularly important, in spite of the rumours – mostly fostered by her mother – that if the Spanish match fell through she might marry Louis XIV.

By the winter of 1659 Charles's relations with the rest of his family had ceased to bring him either happiness or moral support. He was fond of, and loyal to, all of them; but one by one they had failed him. York's stupidity, obstinacy and solemn tactlessness far outweighed his better qualities; Gloucester's arrogance, his ignorant support of such persons as Colonel Howard, and his selfish extravagance had made him a nuisance. Henrietta Maria's activities had always been as annoying as they were destructive; and the open-handed and adoring Mary of Orange had maddened Charles, first by dwelling on her grievances, and then by her insistence that he should idolize her as she had from time to time idolized him.

There remained, then, his French relatives, his Palatine cousins and their mother, and his eight-year-old nephew, William of Orange. With Anne of Austria and her sons he had never had much in common; he found Louis irritating, and despised Philippe. He had drifted apart from Rupert; Charles-Louis was a traitor, Maurice was dead, Sophia married and Louise a nun. He saw very little of the other brothers and sisters (there were eleven grown-up Palatine Stuarts in all) and though he corresponded affectionately with his Aunt Elizabeth, circumstances prevented their meeting. So it was that, of the Protestant group, Charles became especially attached to little William. At this time, he cared for children almost as much as he was to care for dogs a few months later; in his view, both species were preferable to grown-ups. They made no demands he could not satisfy, and – unlike his mistresses – could be dismissed without fuss or expense when they grew wearisome.

In William of Orange Charles found the assets and qualities he most preferred. The little Prince was pretty, exceptionally intelligent, well brought up, spirited and original. Brief and widely separated though their meetings were, the uncle would have delighted in mildly spoiling the nephew, if William's mother had not made Charles's affection for him into another grievance. When the King asked for the child's picture, she sent it; she wrote to him of 'Piccinino's' progress; but in the spring of 1658, when Charles's circumstances were unusually depressing, she had made a jealous scene about his interest in the boy. In reply to a letter from the King in which he seems to have pointed out that it was neither natural nor desirable for her to care more for himself than for her only child, she replied, 'You are so partially kind to him that I fear at last my desiring your kindness to him will turn to jealousy that he may take some from me. For I must assure you that I shall obey all your commands ... except that of loving him above all things in this world, as long as *you* are in it.'[21]

It was therefore inevitable that when this jaded exile discovered, as it were, the sister he now began to call Minette, his dried-up capacity for love should be re-created. Appearing to her as a semi-divine, semi-fraternal, romantically unfortunate being, whose legend had become a refrain in her life, Charles was also the central point of her religious day-dreams. His conversion – and so, if her hopes materialized, that of the country she thought of as her own, although she could neither speak its language nor understand its history – became part of a picture to which she could return when the original was absent.

This unfortunate Princess was accomplished, quick and a little pre-cocious. As is often the case with such persons, she developed so early as sometimes to give the impression of brilliance. Her intelligence was of the type now described as silly-clever.

This kind of mentality was especially appealing to Charles. For him, she remained an enchanting, nymph-like child, about whom he became so besotted as to entrust her, eleven years later, with the high explosive of the Dover Treaty. And so it followed that his dependence on her fostered the English hatred of all she stood for, as a Catholic and a natural-ized Frenchwoman – and, eventually, gave rise to mutterings and con-jectures about an incestuous relationship, of which she and Charles were of course completely innocent.[22] In the seventeenth century it was most unusual, to say the least, for a brother who was also a king to confide and keep in almost daily touch with a sister fourteen years his junior living in another country and married to a national enemy. Such a situation could only be explained, according to the hostile minority, by a perverted obsession. In the Princess's lifetime this view was not shared by her odious husband; but it is possible, now, to sympathize with his furious distrust and violent jealousy of Charles, as of all his wife's English connections.

The nearest of Charles's relations did not, on this occasion, disappoint him. When he parted from the Queen and Henrietta Anne, they returned to Chaillot, and he moved into Lord Crofts's house in order to see his son, with whose progress he seems to have been perfectly satisfied. He then finally sealed the breach with Henrietta Maria by giving Jermyn the earldom of St Albans. To Lady Fanshawe, whom he met after an interval of several years, he said, 'If it please God to restore me to my kingdoms, you and your husband shall partake of my happiness,' and they had a long conversation about English affairs.[23] Then Lord Mordaunt, who had reported the Royalist party to be 'in confusion and misery', suddenly appeared, and with him Charles left for Brussels on December 17th. Ten days later he arrived there at dusk, 'in very good health ... and humour', according to Hyde.[24]

This mood could not last. The Spanish had lost all interest in his cause; France and the States General had cast him out. York then accepted an admiralship from de Haro, only to be told that he could not go to sea until he changed his faith. Gloucester, now as penniless as Charles, spent his time on the tennis-court, and it was rumoured that he intended to earn his living as an instructor. 'If it had not been for the King's own steadiness,' says Hyde, ' ... men could have been more out of countenance than they were.'

Then, on December 29th, Monk wrote from Scotland, asking pardon for his share in the rebellion. He begged Charles to trust him, and added that as soon as he had His Majesty's permission, he would go to London to await his instructions. 'I trust you absolutely,' the King replied, 'I shall own you in everything you shall act for God's glory and the good of my people.'[25] A fortnight later Monk marched into Berwick. Charles then heard that the incalculable General had returned to his Parliamentary allegiance.

II

At fifty-one George Monk was at the height of his powers as a professional soldier. He had begun his career under Princess Amalia's husband, Frederick Henry of Orange, returning to fight for Charles I during the first half of the Civil War. After being captured and imprisoned he transferred to the Cromwellian forces, and when the Protector died he had become, with Lambert, one of the most influential men in England. His appearance and address were so uncouth – although of gentle birth, he spoke with a Devonshire accent – that he was relegated as a 'dull, heavy man' by those meeting him out of his own sphere.[26] His wife, whom he was supposed to have married bigamously and who had great influence on his policy, had been bred a milliner; she was known as 'dirty Bess', and had amassed a private fortune through the sale of commissions.[27]

Monk's ambition was controlled by astute realism, a calculating brain and a stolid taciturnity. With Oliver Cromwell's death he set about further strengthening his position; by the time Richard Cromwell retired into private life, he was personally impregnable, As he saw the position, the country seemed, on the whole, to desire Charles's restoration, while Parliament and the army were divided on many issues. For some time – roughly, from the beginning of December 1659 to the middle of March 1660 – some people believed that, out of all this confusion, Monk might seize the dictatorship of England and perhaps even enforce his own dynasty. He worked out and followed a day-to-day policy which was ostensibly inconsistent and which completely baffled Charles and Hyde; they felt themselves dependent on the General's whims and despaired of guessing his purposes, one of which was to secure a stable government.

On November 28th, 1659, Monk was appointed General of the nation's forces. During his march from Berwick to London he had ignored all demands for a free Parliament (which would have ensured a restoration) and, halting at St Albans, announced that a Commonwealth was the desire of his soul. A few weeks later, when someone said to him, 'I plainly see there is an utter impossibility of a settlement without bringing in the King,' he replied, 'May my right hand rot off if I have the least design for him.' He and Mrs Monk were then installed at Whitehall. (By this time Lambert had been cashiered and sent to the Tower, whence he eventually escaped to retire into private life.) On February 12th Monk and his family left Whitehall for St James's. A week later he made a speech in Parliament declaring his absolute loyalty to the Commonwealth and his hatred of Charles Stuart. A month after that, when a visitor asked his young son, 'Who are you for, a King, a Protector, or a free state?' the child replied, 'I am for the King, and so is my mother.'[28] Meanwhile Monk himself was receiving a number of Royalist agents, to one of whom he said, 'I will consider of a restoration,' adding that he must be guided by Parliament. To another he declared, 'I will spend the last drop of my blood rather than that the Stuarts should come into England.'[29] Parliament then rewarded him with £20,000, upon which, without committing himself in writing, as in December 1659, he appeared to have changed his allegiance again and to be acting for Charles while 'protesting' against him.

These tactical divagations brought Charles to the verge of despair. On the Continent, his cause was regarded as almost hopeless, but not quite; he was therefore promised help by Mazarin and de Haro in letters which he described to the Chancellor as 'specious pretences ... They are afraid of offending England,' he added.[30] His best prospect lay in Mordaunt's courage and ingenuity. That nobleman thought of everything and never wasted a moment. While Charles was in Spain he had set in hand a scheme for his marriage to Lambert's daughter Fatima, and when Lambert was eliminated he began to rally the City of London. The Lord Mayor was in favour of a restoration, but insisted on 3,000 armed men, 'for our shelter'. According to another agent, the Aldermen and Sheriffs were 'sneakers ... and obedient asses' to the Rump Parliament.[31]

As soon as Mordaunt left Brussels for London the apparently insuperable difficulty of sequestered property arose. Those who had acquired Church or Royalist lands during the Protectorate were now ready to declare for Charles as long as they were not deprived of these rewards; the original owners assumed that their stolen possessions would be restored with the monarchy. The King therefore 'reassured' his latest supporters in England, vaguely, yet in such a manner that they were convinced. Those who had not seen His Majesty since his boyhood prepared to trust him; while the Cavaliers were ready to risk anything rather than remain in exile.

By now, Mordaunt's position had become almost as trying as the King's. His party had divided itself into pro- and anti-Mordaunt factions. His enemies said he was arrogant and indiscreet – why should His Majesty owe his crown to this would-be dictator? Mordaunt received their censure philosophically. '*Il ne faut pas aller au bois qui a peur des feuilles*,' he wrote to Hyde, 'and provided I may be serviceable to my Prince, I have ... constancy enough to stand more shocks of envy and malice.'[32]

Meanwhile the optimists in Charles's party were adding up his debts to them and presenting their bills, although they must have known that he was living on the barest subsistence. One lady made a claim of £20,000 dating from 1651; and York chose this moment to announce that his attendants' salaries were long overdue and must be paid. Charles seems to have ignored the major claim, but he told York to cut down his staff. The Duke took offence, and once more the brothers were estranged, with the result that Charles consoled himself by corresponding with his youngest sister, and with the messenger responsible for delivering their letters, referring to her simply as Jeanneton, or, 'the best girl in the world'. The Princess's pleasure in their relationship was still faintly shadowed by timidity. After thanking Charles for 'the honour you do me in writing to me so often', she enlarged on 'the love and respect I bear Your Majesty', signed herself 'your very humble servant', and sent him a scapular. Charles replied in French, 'I will never fail in my love ... Jeanneton [and I] talk of you every day ... She sings very well, and has taught me ... a quantity of songs ... For the future, pray do not treat me with ... so many Majesties, for there should be nothing but love between us two.'[33] He may even have kept his promise to wear the scapular, although his doing so would have alarmed his Anglican followers.

This interchange took place at the beginning of February 1660. A fortnight later Mordaunt sent over a pair of agents, Mr and Mrs Palmer. The lady, formerly Barbara Villiers, was a cousin of Buckingham's, and of a sinister and exotic beauty. Soon after their arrival there was a rumour of a smallpox epidemic in Brussels. Hyde was talking of precautions, when Charles casually announced that Mrs Palmer had had the disease.[34] The Chancellor was amazed – of what interest could that person's immunity be to anyone but her husband?

NOTES

1 Burnet, *History*, vol. I, p. 83.
2 Townshend, pp. 191–3.
3 *Bath MSS*, vol. II, p. 135.
4 Carte, *Ormonde*, vol. I, pp. 187–91; *Original Letters*, vol. II, p. 186.
5 Carte, *Ormonde*, ibid.
6 *Cal. Clar. S. P.*, vol. IV, p. 400.
7 *Cal. D. S. P.*, Oct. 1659.
8 *Bath MSS*, vol. II, p. 139.
9 Welwood, p. 115.
10 *Cal. Clar. S. P.*, vol. IV, p. 420.
11 Ibid.
12 Op. cit., vol. III, p. 602.
13 Carte, *Original Letters*, vol. II, p. 278.
14 Clarendon, p. 878.
15 *Cal. D. S. P.*, ibid.
16 'Eyewitness', *The Royal Pilgrimage*, p. 3.
17 Clarendon, ibid.
18 *Cal. Clar. S. P.*, ibid.
19 Carte, *Original Letters*, vol. II, p. 186.
20 Scott, *The King in Exile*, p. 431.
21 *Thurloe S. P.*, vol. I, p. 644.
22 Burnet, *History*, vol. I, p. 551.
23 Fanshawe, p. 121.
24 Clarendon, ibid.
25 Somers (2nd Collection), vol. III, pp. 1–5.
26 Pepys, vol. I, p. 84.
27 Op. cit., pp. 52, 89.
28 Scott, *The King in Exile*, p. 456.
29 *Cal. Clar. S. P.*, vol. III, p. 697.
30 Clarendon, ibid.
31 *Cal. Clar. S. P.*, vol. IV, p. 512.
32 Op. cit., vol. III, p. 662.
33 J. Cartwright, *Madame*, pp. 52–3.
34 *Cal. Clar. S. P.*, vol. IV, p. 557.

——————◆◆◆◆◆——————

CHAPTER NINE

THE BEGINNING OF HOPE

I

ONK's insistence that the Moderate members excluded by Parliament should be readmitted resulted in the dissolution of the Rump on March 16th, 1660. This did not much reassure the Cavaliers, whose situation had not changed since the King's return to Brussels. His household remained in 'incredible and fearful want', while his creditors continued to threaten him. (In Flanders alone his debts amounted to £80,000.) Any hopes he might have had were now destroyed by the defeat of a Royalist rising in the west of England, the news that Richard Cromwell was to be restored and Monk's anti-monarchist speeches. In England, those who had worked with the General warned the exiles that he would do nothing for Charles. Samuel Pepys, who began his great Diary on New Year's Day, observed that everyone took this for granted,[1] and Nicholas began to say that His Majesty should have landed before Monk reached London. Now he had missed his chance of being restored without bloodshed, and must once more rely on the continental forces whose aid he had sought in vain for eleven years.

Two people were certain of Charles's immediate triumph. When the Venetian Resident saw the London crowds spearing and roasting rump-steaks in the streets and openly drinking the King's health, he assumed that the restoration would be effected in a few days, although he was rather pained by this coarse denigration of a national body. 'The name is appropriate, if obscene,' he observed, adding that this 'General Monch' might yet do His Majesty's business.[2] Sir John Hinton, who was working for Charles on his own, asked the great man to dinner. When the meal was over Monk drew his host into another room, shut the door and 'took a lusty glass of wine'. Then he said, 'Here's a health to my Black Boy!' and drank it down.[3]

Charles remained sceptical; and now more than at any time since the exile he needed all his coolness. At the beginning of January he was warned that the Spanish, who had not sent him his allowance since he left Fuenterrabia, were planning to arrest him as a pledge for Dunkirk and

Jamaica. The King ignored this danger. His behaviour was so 'mild and agreeable', according to Nicholas, that he was more than ever beloved by all who had to do with him.[4] Hyde's view was slightly sharper. 'He hath so true a judgement and so much good nature,' he wrote, 'that when the age of pleasure shall be over and the idleness of his exile, which makes him seek new diversions for want of other employment, he will shake off those entanglements.' Years later, a more sophisticated observer summed up the King's attitude towards 'entanglements' with cynical accuracy. 'His inclinations to love,' observed Halifax, 'were the effects of health and a good constitution, with as little admixture of the seraphic part as ever man had ... His [passions] stayed in the lower regions.' So it was, the Marquess concluded, that His Majesty, 'having no love, but some appetite, was incapable of jealousy'.[5]

It could not have been otherwise. Charles's conviction that human folly and greed were the rule, and virtue a freakish exception, detached him, mentally, from both sexes. So it was natural for him to be 'mild and agreeable' with persons he either tolerated or despised; for the same reason, he found no difficulty in courting Monk with the assiduity of a besotted admirer, and presenting himself to the City of London as a selfless patriot. 'I desire to recover my power,' he wrote to them, 'rather for the protection and benefit of good men than to satisfy any appetite of my own.' To the anxious Royalists he suavely announced, 'I am much pleased with Monk, though the man is less steady than I expected.'[6]

Thus Charles indicated that he too could play a waiting game. In the last week of February Monk appeared to be completing his plan of re-creating the Protectorate for himself; among those he favoured one of the most influential was Sir Edward Montagu, Pepys's cousin and patron, who was now appointed 'General at Sea',[7] and who was about to leave England with a fleet of fourteen frigates. 'I value my honour more than all that family,' the Admiral replied, when asked if he was a true Parliamentarian. He then told Pepys that if another Protectorate were established it could not last, adding, 'No, nor the King neither, unless he carry himself very soberly and well.'[8] The fear that Charles was about to become a Catholic and would subordinate England to France – which he engaged himself to do in the Dover Treaty ten years later – still prevailed, in spite of all his denials, and Nicholas's protestations that no one had suffered more for his faith than His Majesty, and that there was no question of his marrying either Hortense Mancini or Catherine of Braganza, recently put forward as a bride by the Portuguese ambassador in Paris. 'It is much to be feared,' said one of Pepys's Presbyterian friends, 'that the

King will come in, for all good men and good things will be discouraged.'[9]

Yet, as the diarist observed, the people wanted him back on almost any terms. To those who knew nothing of politics, he now represented stability and freedom; they made their wishes clear, and were unpunished. On March 14th a man with a paint-brush entered the Royal Exchange and, watched by an excited crowd, walked up to the plinth which had formerly supported the statue of Charles I and which was now inscribed *Exit Tyrannus*. This person obliterated the opprobrious words, painted over them 'Long Live King Charles II' and was wildly cheered by the people, who celebrated his demonstration with a bonfire.[10] Shortly afterwards Charles's picture was hung in the streets, and when a passer-by observed that it flattered him, he was set upon and beaten.

Still Monk continued to protest that he had 'no design for Charles Stuart', and would not openly countenance a restoration. His power was such that these declarations destroyed the optimism caused by his march to London. 'All the little remainder of [His Majesty's] hopes were extinguished,' says Hyde, 'and he had nothing left before his eyes but a perpetual exile, attended with all those discomforts whereof he had too long experience, and which ... would be improved with ... neglect ... A greater consternation of mind cannot be imagined than at that time covered the whole Court of the King'.[11]

Then came the reports of the people's enthusiasm. 'It might reasonably be true,' admitted the Chancellor, when he and Charles discussed the news that evening; and they went to bed in better spirits, in spite of the fact that they had received the account from a drunken Irishman, who delivered it 'with many pauses and hesitations'.[12] Next day Charles decided to tell his courtiers, who at once assumed that all their troubles were over. 'I thank God for this new dawning of hope,' was all the King would say.

So he continued to wait – and almost to starve. The Spanish ignored his request for his allowance, and every day he was besieged by Royalists from England, begging him to embark and to grant them places at Court. 'Have patience – make no attempt whatsoever,' he would say. 'It is not His Majesty's fault that there has been much waste of time,' said one agent when they criticized his inactivity. 'He is known to be venturesome above the ordinary.'[13] Then came another scare: would the King place himself in the hands of the Presbyterians? Charles reassured them. 'I will not buy my crown on conditions that would make me ashamed of wearing it,' he said.

It was now the middle of March – and still Monk remained silent. When publicly approached, he chewed tobacco, and gruffly enunciated platitudes about service and patriotism.

II

At no moment in the exile can suspense have been harder to endure than in the weeks which preceded Parliament's humble request for the return of His Sacred Majesty King Charles II. England was in a state of turmoil; and this meant that events followed one another too rapidly for the King and his advisers to keep up with them. The anti-monarchist rising caused by Lambert's escape from the Tower came to an end while the exiles were making up their minds to defeat; and a Royalist movement from the City was followed by Monk's recommending a form of Presbyterianism as the national religion before they could decide on the correct response to either demonstration. Mordaunt's letters and messages alternated between gloomy warnings and ecstatic encouragement. They dared not hope, yet their days of despair were shot through with visions of triumph; and all the time they were dogged by poverty and humiliation.

The effect on Charles was unexpected. He retained his calm: but it was that of a man frozen into apparent indifference, who speaks and acts as if wound up to produce the desired response of a public figure, the proto-type of a king in exile. Of his behaviour in private there is no record; and Hyde's silence on this point seems to indicate the reticence of a loyal but disappointed servant, who knows that his pupil has become his master, and that he can no longer be influenced. Now at last the Chancellor accepted Charles as he was; he continued to hope for his improvement, just as he continued to lecture him about it; but he realized that he himself would never be able to bring about that transformation. So, rather than criticize, or even assess, the King's development, he confines himself, in this stage of his *History*, to the record of events.

These were sufficiently dramatic. Culminating in the supreme and re-pellent irony of the Restoration, they show Charles at his best – and worst: as the product of fourteen years in situations of which the con-trasts resembled those of a torture chamber, and which might have de-formed or destroyed the characters of most men. The King not only survived but was strengthened by those changes from raging heat to icy cold, from shattering violence to enforced inertia.

On March 17th Monk began to move in the Royalist direction: but so deviously as to give the impression that he was extremely doubtful of success. He began by sending for his Devonshire agent and friend, Mr William Morris, whom he interviewed privately at St James's. He said – rather as if the idea had just struck him – 'I find most gentlemen of quality and interest inclined to call in the King – ' and went on to speak deprecatingly of the conditions discussed in Parliament. Morris, who at once grasped what was expected of him, replied that His Majesty was 'impatiently longed for' in the west. Monk, receiving this well-known fact as news, then sent for Sir John Grenvile, whose younger brother, a clergyman, had already approached him in Scotland on Charles's behalf, and whose record as a Cavalier was unspotted. Monk knew that Grenvile was in constant touch with Mordaunt, who was now openly negotiating the King's affairs, but he chose to behave as if there was no connection between the two men. When Grenvile appeared before him and Morris at St James's the General said, 'I conjure you to secrecy, upon peril of your life. I intend to send you to the King – but I am resolved not to give him anything in writing.' He then issued his instructions.[14]

Grenvile was commanded to tell Charles to write Monk a letter, in which, 'after many kind and gracious expressions', the King must draw attention to an enclosure directed to Parliament. In this second letter – with which, officially, Monk would have nothing to do – His Majesty was to outline terms for his restoration, on the basis of referring all conditions to the Houses. Finally, although Grenvile, accompanied by Mordaunt, would interview Charles in Brussels, no advances must be made from there, since it was hostile and Popish territory. As soon as Charles, Mordaunt and Grenvile had conferred, the King must leave for Breda and date his letters to Parliament from the Dutch Netherlands.

Grenvile took notes of all he was to do. Monk desired him to memorize them then and there, and to burn them in his presence, adding that his friend Mr Morris must be suitably rewarded for his share in the transaction. Grenvile obeyed and, with Mordaunt, left for Brussels.

On the morning of their departure Hyde received a letter from Bennet, who was now in Madrid. The Spanish, he said, ridiculed the idea of a restoration, and had relegated Charles as a failure, to be got rid of as soon as possible. On March 30th Grenvile and Mordaunt arrived. Grenvile had not seen the King since the summer of 1645; when he had delivered his message, Charles told him to rise; he said, in that rather disturbingly ironical manner, 'Little do they in England think that I am on such good terms with General Monk, for I myself could hardly have believed it till your arrival, which hath brought me such happy news – and with so great secrecy, too – from the General, of my restoration.' Grenvile said nothing, and the King continued, 'And without conditions, even beyond our expectation here, or the belief of our friends in England – excepting yourself, who was above all employed in it.'[15]

After some further talk, which was presumably given up to the homage and congratulations of his Court, Charles retired with Hyde, Ormonde and Nicholas to find out from Grenvile and Mordaunt what his immediate obligations were. Reward – that too familiar, still dreaded word – was uttered. Grenvile said, 'Have I exceeded Your Majesty's instructions?' The King replied in the formula which had become habitual. 'Whatever you have promised,' he said, 'shall be punctually performed.' 'I have propounded to the General,' said Grenvile, '£10,000 a year for ever, all which he has most modestly refused,' adding that Monk had also declined Parliament's offer of Hampton Court Palace as his private residence.[16]

Charles, concealing what must have been considerable relief, asked, 'What shall I do for him?' 'Wait,' suggested Grenvile, 'till he sees Your Majesty at Whitehall.' The King agreed; he promised Grenvile his earldom (Mordaunt's title was bestowed later) and the posts of Groom of the Stole and first Gentleman of the Bedchamber. They then discussed the King's Act of Indemnity, to be issued to all who had taken part against the monarchy – except, Charles put in, the regicides; and suddenly the King's tone changed from that of business-like debate to one of high and majestic authority. 'It is not consistent with my honour nor my conscience,' he said, 'that those who have condemned my father to be murdered should be comprehended in this act of pardon.' Returning to his usual manner, he added that this point also would be referred to Parliament. Mordaunt then left for Breda.[17]

Next day Charles called on the Marquess of Caracena, the Spanish minister responsible to Don Alonzo de Cardeñas, who was still Governor of Brussels. 'I intend,' he said airily, 'to go to Antwerp, and from thence to Breda, to spend two or three days with my sister the Princess of Orange.' Caracena, who knew that the Dukes of York and Gloucester were already there, and that the Dutch were afraid of receiving Charles, became suspicious, and seems to have objected. The King reassured him. 'There are some persons come from England,' he explained, 'who will not venture to come to Brussels, from whom I expect some information which might be beneficial to me.'

Caracena, afraid that the King might be abandoning their alliance and thus working against their war with England, began to talk about their agreement with the Republicans, which, he said, was nearing completion. It would be best, he added, that His Highness of York should leave at once for Spain to represent his brother. Charles was all amiability; York should leave immediately. Then he said, 'I desire that the forces you have promised for my service may be ready against my brother's return, to be embarked.' Caracena, knowing that these armies would never materialize, was silenced. He made some kind of promise; Charles said, 'I shall leave tomorrow morning,' and went out.

Nothing happened during the rest of that day, and both Hyde and Charles went to bed rather earlier than usual. In the middle of the night the Chancellor was woken by his secretary, who told him that William Galloway, Cardeñas's Irish page, was waiting to see him. 'I must speak with my Lord Chancellor,' he had said. 'It is a matter of the King's life.' Galloway was then admitted and, standing by the bed, trembling and white-faced, told Hyde that Cardeñas and Caracena had 'talked long alone together' immediately the King left Caracena's rooms. 'I overheard them saying something about sending a guard to attend the King,' he went on. 'About an hour after, they parted, and Cardeñas received a letter from Caracena. When Cardeñas went to bed, he laid it on his table. I looked at the paper when my master was in bed,' the young man added fearfully, 'and seeing what it is, I have brought it to you.'

The paper was an order that Charles should be attended by a guard – an unprecedented honour, remarked Hyde satirically – who would not permit him to leave the city. Hyde got the impression that the Spanish would not hesitate to use violence if Charles tried to escape them. He was too lame to get up and dress quickly, so he sent his secretary, with Galloway and the paper, to the King. Charles read it lying in bed; then he dismissed Galloway, who hurried home and replaced it on Cardeñas's table. Charles roused Grenvile, Armorer and Ormonde and told them to call their grooms. 'We must be gone by three o'clock,' he said. Just before that hour the eight riders stole out of the city, and galloped to the Dutch border. At eight thirty a Spanish officer and his troop came to the King's lodging. They left with long faces, 'to the no small mortification', Hyde triumphantly records, 'of the Spanish Government.' It was Charles's last escape from his enemies. He may have owed his life to the Irish page.

Charles took with him to Breda a collection of letters and documents of great length and elaboration, to the Lords and Commons, to the City of London and to Monk. When he, Mordaunt and Grenville had gone through these, the King said that if the General objected to any particular items, he must of course alter them. Grenvile asked for the Secretaryship of State for Mr Morris – he knew that Digby's becoming a Catholic had made this post available – adding, 'He is well qualified for it.' 'I am very glad,' replied the King, 'to gratify a person who has so much credit with the General.' Grenvile and Mordaunt then left for England with Charles's declarations, all of which were headed, 'From Our Court at Breda, April 14th, 1660, in the twelfth Year of Our Reign.' They reached London two days later – and again, silence fell.

It was as if Monk had never received the King's communications. These cloak-and-dagger tactics, while giving him the part of a national hero in the event of a restoration, had concealed all his activities on Charles's behalf. He would now be able to prove that he had done nothing for him; if Grenvile, Mordaunt and Morris gave evidence against him, he had merely to denounce them as malignant rebels, and reaffirm his loyalty to the Commonwealth. On the other hand if the Commonwealth ceased to exist, Monk was sure of a dukedom, the Garter, great wealth and the command of the forces. There remained his letter of December 29th, 1659. Presumably a copy of this was preserved so that his claim upon Charles's bounty was assured.

In the week that elapsed between Grenvile's arrival with the declarations and Parliament's first sitting, it became clear to the continental powers that the King of England was now worth some attention, and Caracena wrote asking him to come back to Brussels. Charles replied that business kept him in Breda, and that he was unlikely ever again to return to Spanish territory. He made the same answer to Mazarin's invitation, much to his mother's annoyance. Then he had to deal with another attempt to discredit Hyde, whom the younger Cavaliers were trying to deprive of a share in their master's victory, although even now it was not certain that that victory would be accomplished.

Meanwhile Hyde, now at Breda, would not let himself count on a restoration; but he could not help thinking about all the books he might be able to buy, in the intervals of dealing with the King's creditors who he observed, were less clamorous than formerly. (Byzantine history, for instance – there were so many splendid volumes on that subject for which he longed.) His chief preoccupation was that of restraining the younger Cavaliers, who swaggered about, boasting and gloating. Revenge! was their cry – they would make their enemies pay for all they had suffered.[1] When the Chancellor had crushed these dangerous outbursts he drew up a long paper of advice for the King to study while he waited for the news from England. Under eleven heads Hyde desired His Majesty to 'walk with wariness', to trust neither the Scots, the Irish, the Presbyterians nor the army, to appear friendly towards France and Spain, and to forbid his agents in those countries to behave as victors 'before it is time', adding rather gratuitously, that Charles should not consider himself bound by any promises he made.[19]

By this time Breda was crowded with Royalists from England, and the King's return seemed assured. Still Charles preserved his baffling impassivity. 'His face,' Halifax wrote long afterwards, 'was as little a blab as most men's; yet though it could not be called a prattling face, it would sometimes tell tales.' So it was that when Charles was told that Mr Roger Palmer had been commissioned to give him £1,000, but that he would expect a percentage, as he had a 'gay wife' and a small income, the King agreed without comment.[20] His opinion of the future Lady Castlemaine had nothing to do with the appetite she inspired.

A few days later he had to take into account the wishes of a very different and much more influential lady. Mrs Monk, Mordaunt wrote, must now be made much of; she had given out that she would like some personal tribute from His Majesty. She was already occupied with the refurbishing of his London palaces, and giving special attention to the linen. 'That is my old trade,' said Dirty Bess. 'I will save the King one half in laying out the other for the chambers, tables, etc.'[21] Charles prepared a suitable response. Still he could not send it; still he was corresponding in cipher, and followed by Parliamentary informers. To William Morris he wrote, 'Unless the devil be in it, you shall find the benefit of being faithful,' and, referring to Monk as 'the Gentleman', implored Grenvile to get an answer from that enigmatic potentate.[22]

Then there was the matter of his summer outfit; Minette should deal with it. He said nothing to her of Gaston d'Orléans's death, or of the talk about her marriage with Philippe, who had now succeeded to his uncle's title, but assured her that, 'I love you as much as possible ... Never fear that others ... shall get the advantage ... No one can share my love for you ... I have sent to Gentseau to make me some summer suits, and have told him to take the ribbons to you, for you to choose the trimming and the feathers ...'[23]

On May 1st Parliament met. When the new Speaker, Sir Harbottle Grimston, had taken his place, Sir John Grenvile was announced and admitted. He gave the King's letters to Grimston, who stood up. The members also rose and removed their hats. The declarations were then read aloud.

The King's first consideration was, naturally, the Protestant religion. 'We have given proof,' His Majesty declared, 'that neither the unkindness of those that hold it, nor the civilities of a contrary profession can make us swerve from it ... We will strive with you to make the kingdom happy, and we hope that our subjects will be the better for our experience of other countries, and what we have seen and suffered ... We desire no effusion of blood ... None shall be reproached for the past.' Charles concluded with the promise of a free and general pardon and full liberty of conscience.[24]

The answering resolution, already prepared, was then proposed and accepted. The Government of England consisted of King, Lords and Commons. 'And whereas,' it continued, 'all the troubles of this realm ... have been caused by the separation of the Head from the limbs, it is necessary first of all to heal this breach and restore the King to his people.' Fifty thousand pounds was then voted to His Majesty, and a deputation chosen to beg his acceptance of the crown. John Grenvile's brother Bernard was to precede this invitation with a letter announcing the news. On the evening of May 9th he reached Breda. Charles was at supper. When Grenvile's name was sent in the King left the table and came to him in another room. Then he read the letter.[25]

So it had come at last. Without a single dissentient voice he had been proclaimed Charles II by the Grace of God Defender of the Faith, King of England, Scotland, Ireland and France.

Charles raised Bernard Grenvile and kissed him. 'Never was a man more welcome to me!' he said. Then he revealed the fear which had haunted him ever since his coronation in Scotland – that he might be forced to return as the servant of the state, as a symbol of monarchy. 'I can now say I am a king, and not a Doge,' he added. So, in the catch-phrase of the day ('no better than a Doge of Venice'), Charles described his abiding, now his only, principle: that his authority should be infallible and the submission of his people implicit.[26]

NOTES

1 Pepys, vol. I, p. 35.
2 *Cal. S. P. Ven.*, vol. XXXI, pp. 116, 119.
3 Hinton, p. 29.
4 *Cal. D. S. P.*, Dec. 10th, 1659.
5 Halifax, pp. 16–19.
6 *Cal. Clar. S. P.*, vol. IV, p. 636.
7 Pepys, vol. I, p. 70.
8 Op. cit., p. 88.
9 Ibid.
10 Op. cit., p. 86.
11 Clarendon, p. 890.
12 Ibid.
13 *Cal. Clar. S. P.*, vol. IV, p. 523.
14 Clarendon, pp. 890–902.

15 J. Price, *Mystery and Method of His Majesty's Restoration*, pp. 142–62.
16 Ibid.
17 Ibid.
18 *Cal. Clar. S. P.*, vol. III, p. 735.
19 Op. cit., vol. IV, p. 652.
20 *Thurloe, S. P.*, vol. VII, p. 872.
21 *Cal. Clar. S. P.*, vol. IV, p. 655.
22 Op. cit., vol. III, p. 739.
23 *Thurloe S. P.*, vol. VII, pp. 858, 897.
24 Cartwright, p. 55.
25 *Cal. D. S. P.*, May 11th, 1660.
26 Baron Lansdowne, *Works*, p. 482.

CHAPTER TEN

THE END OF THE JOURNEY

I

As Bernard Grenvile knelt before the King, the English people, also on their knees, were drinking his health in the streets, while the bonfires crackled and roared and the church bells called to one another. So to prostrate oneself was 'a little too much', Pepys considered.[1] This cool-headed observer had not yet felt (it submerged him a week later) the wave of passionate love and loyalty which was now breaking over England; nor could he believe, as did many less sophisticated persons, that no one, ever again, would be ill treated – except, of course, those evil men whom His Majesty must punish for his blessed father's martyrdom.

While his subjects wept and cheered and danced, the inscrutable, old-young man who had become the idolized symbol of all earthly greatness, justice, virtue and prosperity, remained perfectly self-possessed. When one of his courtiers spoke of the welcome waiting for him, he replied, 'What a world of love we shall have there!'[2] but in such a manner as to create a certain uneasiness – and yet, why? Had His Majesty any reason to doubt his people's devotion?

Charles wrote to Montague, asking for advice about his embarkation. 'I will not stir,' he concluded, 'until I hear from you and General Monk.'[3] During the next few days he was joined by his brothers who, with Mary of Orange and the nine-year-old Prince William, were to travel with him from Breda to the Hague, whence he would embark for Dover. They were followed by his cousin Sophia's husband, the Duke of Brunswick-Lüneburg (ancestor of Queen Elizabeth II), several foreign ambassadors, a party of Stadtholders with the official welcome of the States General, and a number of Royalists. These last did not represent Parliament, or the City, or the Army. They had come on their own, with their axes to grind. Their spokesman dwelt at some length and with deep feeling on their adherence to His Majesty's cause.

Charles, who, with York and Gloucester, had received them in his bedroom, made no reply. Then he called for wine. Having been served on the knee, he drained the glass and said, 'I drink to your health – for I am now even with you, having done as much for you as you have done for me.'⁴ As they backed away, he turned to York, remarking, 'I am out of their debt – ' and retired to compose a further batch of 'very obliging' letters – but not so assiduously as to satisfy Hyde, who pursued him with suggestions and advice that sounded more like orders. It was noted by new arrivals that the Chancellor spoke to His Majesty 'with the air of a governor'. Some of these persons were involved in a plan to prevent Hyde and Ormonde returning to England. When later reports made it clear that Hyde's influence was overrated and Ormonde's almost negligible, this scheme was abandoned. Meanwhile, Monk was writing to the King that 'God hath given to your sceptre the hearts of your people ... to which I take the boldness to add my humble opinion that now Your Majesty's presence and authority is very necessary to preserve that happiness and peace.'⁵

Charles's reply was less fawning than his former letters and entirely practical. 'I must ever acknowledge your extraordinary affection to me,' he wrote, 'and your very discreet conduct of this great work.' He then warned the General about mischief-makers and promised to make good Monk's guarantees to the army. 'I am confident I shall prevent all inconveniences,' he went on; 'I ... tell you again, I will not leave myself bread rather than everything shall not be performed which you promised.' He confirmed his appointment to meet Monk's emissaries at the Hague, dwelt on his 'longing' to see him, and added that he would expect to find Mrs Monk at Dover.⁶

It was impossible to proceed to the Hague till his clothes were ready; and even now, his credit was so bad that until the money voted him by Parliament arrived, he and his courtiers had to remain shabby. When the Commissioners reached Breda they were appalled by His Majesty's 'sad, poor condition ... Their clothes,' said one, 'not being worth 40/- the best of them.'⁷ The presentation of a trunkful of sovereigns solved this problem; the King turned from thanking them to call his brothers and the Princess Mary to look at it. Very soon they were all fitted out – York ordered a suit trimmed with yellow and Gloucester one of grey with red ribbons⁸ – and ready to leave, when an elderly Presbyterian, Mr Case, arrived with a party of ministers in some anxiety about His Majesty's faith. Was it true that he had become a Catholic and intended to persecute the followers of the Word?

Something had to be arranged; and Charles staged a scene in which his freakish humour found satisfaction. One of his courtiers hid Mr Case in the royal closet; there was His Majesty, on his knees, praying aloud. 'O

Lord!' the awestruck minister heard him say, 'since Thou art pleased to restore me to the throne of my ancestors, grant me a heart constant with the exercise and protection of the true Protestant religion. Never may I seek the oppression of those who out of the tenderness of their consciences are not free to conform to outward and indifferent ceremonies.'

'The old gentleman,' Charles's assistant reported, 'was full of joy.' He rejoined his party with a description of the edifying scene and His Majesty's 'serious discourse'. 'God hath sent us a religious King!' they exclaimed, and left Breda sure of his protection.[9] Hyde and Nicholas were not told of this rather heartless trick. They saw their master in his most dignified and gracious mood, as when he received the first deputation from the States General on May 9th. As they entered his presence-chamber he stood up, took off his hat and insisted that they remain covered. In reply to their congratulations, he declared, 'I love this Commonwealth, not only because the Princess Royal my sister and the Prince of Orange – two persons who are extremely dear to me – remain here, but also through interest of estate and for the good of my kingdoms.' Two days later they were again received and the process was repeated, with the same ingenious application of truth and falsehood from the ruler who made war on them four years later.[10]

Before Charles left Breda the Princess Dowager Amalia wrote to offer him the hand of her youngest daughter, Princess Marie, a plain, clever girl of eighteen, and was politely refused. The citizens lent him a magnificent yacht, in which he and his family were to travel to Delft. On May 14th they departed. As soon as they came aboard a great feast was served, at which the Princess Mary did herself so well that when the wind got up she became queasy and retired to her cabin. In the storm which followed she was so ill that Charles, much concerned, approached the captain. 'Is there some means to shelter us, to ease the Princess a little?' he asked. 'No rest to be hoped for,' was the surly reply, 'but at Dort, in one and a half hours.'[11]

Somehow, poor Mary got through the reception at Dort. By the time they reached Rotterdam she was much better, and at Delft was able to share in the festivities. After another banquet they left the Town Hall to be greeted by the coaches, seventy-two in all, each drawn by six thoroughbreds, which were to convey them to the Hague. The royal party was escorted to the most splendid of these; but the four grown-ups were so pressed for room that little William had to sit on his uncle York's knee. James had a great fondness for the child who, twenty-eight years later, was to invade his kingdom and occupy his throne.

The Navy had now declared for Charles, and Montague, in his flagship with her escort of thirty frigates, was standing off Scheveningen. On the quarter-deck the ship's tailor was busy cutting out a cloth on which the royal arms were pasted – there had been no time to embroider them – while Montague was telling Pepys, now his secretary, that His Majesty and the Duke of York had written to him 'as if he were their common friend'. The King and his brothers were expected at any moment, so the Admiral changed into his best suit; then a message came that His Majesty and Their Royal Highnesses would remain at the Hague for a few days. Pepys and his friend Mr Pickering therefore went ashore with the Admiral's little boy on a sight-seeing tour. Near the Binnenhof they met the Reverend Dr Cade, 'a merry, mad parson', who promised to bring them to the King; he dined always in public, and held a reception afterwards, they were told, so it should not be difficult. Meanwhile, the Admiral was in a quandary. The flagship, in which he had sailed before Charles was proclaimed, was still called the *Naseby*. He decided to wait until the King came aboard; then His Majesty himself should re-christen her.[12]

By this time Charles, whose coach had reached the Hague at eleven on the morning of May 16th, was holding receptions all day and every day. The first person to greet him was his aunt Elizabeth, who with the Princess Dowager Amalia stood at the head of the staircase in the Palace of the Mauruitshuis, where he and his brothers received the official delegations from England. The Houses of Parliament presented him with £50,000; York was given £10,000 and appointed Lord High Admiral of England; Gloucester received £5,000. The City of London sent Charles £10,000, and the States General £70,000, which they followed up with a service of gold plate and a huge bed with tapestry hangings embossed in gold and silver, originally made for the Princess Mary's lying-in, but never used because of her husband's death.[13] The Parliamentary representatives, notably their orator, Denzil Holles, one of the five members the King's father had accused of high treason, were a little nervous about their reception. Charles greeted them genially; to the aldermen and sheriffs he was even more reassuring. 'I have always had a particular affection for the City of London, the place of my birth,' he told them, 'and I am very glad you have now so good a part in my Restoration. I am much beholden to every one of you.'[14] He then knighted them all, and with his family proceeded to dinner at the Binnenhof, sitting between Elizabeth of Bohemia and the Princess Mary; little William sat opposite them, silently contemplating his saturnine uncle, who was heard to say, 'I never supped better,' while the orchestra played triumphal airs and the guests became steadily tipsy.[15]

Next day Charles was received by the Assembly of the States General. It was his third appearance there. The first had been in December 1648, when he begged them to intercede for his father's life, the second two years later, when he asked for their help and advice before leaving for Scotland. Whatever his recollections, he was blandly courteous to the rulers who had refused to help him, sided with his enemies and cast him out of their territories. Their uneasiness was concealed by a sycophantic approach and long, flattering speeches. It was then suggested that each state should send delegates to congratulate His Majesty; with agreeable firmness Charles replied that he would take this meeting as representative of all the others, and retired to his sister's private apartments, where he and their aunt sat talking alone, till he was escorted to his state bedchamber: but not to sleep, for the cannon thundered all night, and the fireworks continued to crackle and hiss over the waters of the Vyjver.

Naturally Charles's differences with his brothers and elder sister were healed; it was observed with what attentive warmth he handed the Princess into her coach when she left the Mauruitshuis for the Binnenhof, in the intervals of his receptions for the foreign ambassadors; for now emissaries from all the nations who had either betrayed or dismissed him – France, Spain, Sweden, Denmark, Austria – were begging his favour; and to all he replied with the same dignified yet friendly politeness. It was as if old Newcastle's advice still prompted him. 'You should keep yourself up Prince,' his Governor wrote, 'in all your actions; but I would not have you so seared with Majesty as to think you are not of mankind ... The incommodities to life, and the sustaining of it, and the same things the meanest do, you must do the like, or not live.' For fourteen years incommodities had been Charles's daily bread; and the meanest things had seldom proved too mean for him to turn away from them. Now they seemed forgotten, and he appeared willing to grant any favour – until the Presbyterian delegation arrived.

This meeting recalled those in Scotland. The spokesman for the solemn, black-clad group of ministers began condescendingly, 'We have always wished Your Majesty very well. We are no enemies to moderate episcopacy,' and proceeded, at some length, to ask for toleration. Charles replied, 'I have heard of your good behaviour, and have no purpose to impose hard conditions on you. I have referred all differences to Parliament.' The clergyman, realizing that his group would get short shrift from that quarter, asked the King not to use the Prayer-Book. There was a pause. Then Charles, making no attempt to conceal his displeasure, said, 'While I give you liberty, I will not have my own taken from me. I have always used that form of service, which I think the best in the world, and have never discontinued it in places where it is more disliked than I hope it is by you.'

No one ventured to speak of His Majesty's attendance at Mass or of his Covenanting coronation: but one member suggested that he should forbid the wearing of that popish emblem, the surplice. Charles answered with the same sternness, 'I will not be restrained myself, when I give others so much liberty. It has always been held a decent habit in the Church, and is still retained by me. I will never, in the least degree, discountenance the good old order of the Church in which I have been bred,' and dismissed the assembly. 'I thought he would have been more flexible,' murmured one grieved delegate, as they backed out of the presence-chamber, to make way for a number of afflicted persons, whom Charles touched for the King's Evil.[16]

In the midst of all this splendour the lights flickered and went out, and those of Charles's councillors who were not drunk with triumph saw the writing on the wall; financially, the King had once more been weighed in the balance and found wanting. The vast sums received by himself and his brothers were inadequate for the upkeep of his Court and the payment of his continental debts, as long as the City of Amsterdam refused to honour the London bills of exchange. Hyde, whose gout was so bad that he could not take part in the festivities, had to leave his bed and deal with the problem; somehow, he succeeded, so well indeed that the citizens of Amsterdam gave the King a yacht as a parting present.[17] Yet the shadow of that mistrust remained, as it were a portent of his reign, during the last week of his exile.

Charles seems to have ignored this setback, as he did the attempt of a Portuguese spy to murder him. Yet when Pepys with Dr Cade and Admiral Montague's little son were received at the Binnenhof, the diarist was considerably taken aback by his first sight of the King who, surrounded by a noisy, extravagantly dressed, half tipsy crowd, was strangely grave. Pepys could hardly believe that a man of His Majesty's reputation could appear so withdrawn in the height of his glory. 'The King seems a very sober man,' he noted, as Charles bent to kiss the child.[18] The contrast between the central figure and those about him was enhanced by Charles's choice of clothes. In a kaleidoscopic entourage he was then, and throughout his life, conspicuously sombre, in dress as in colouring; brown, puce, ochre, dark-blue velvet or cloth, with few rings and unbleached laces best suited, as no doubt he knew, his harsh features, sallow skin and the greying hair which was not hidden under a black wig till 1663. On this occasion he was wearing the new 'camions' or buff cloth hose-tops, attached to his breeches, which broadened his tall figure; in the contemporary prints the effect is clumsy and inelegant. He presently discarded these and his loose doublets for the long, closely fitting, richly embroidered coats which he wore till his death; he was never seen in the pastel satins and glittering brocades which adorned his courtiers.

In fact, there was no need for this sartorial isolation. Charles's height and grace, his odd, cool remoteness proclaimed him everywhere, as they had after Worcester; formidably aloof, ironically pleasant, abruptly informal, he now compelled reverence without desiring it, and destroyed hostility with his casual humour, piercing intuition and faultless memory. Deceiving others, he was himself seldom deceived, for he trusted no one, and cared deeply for only two persons in the world: his eldest son and his youngest sister. They had his heart; shrunken and battered though it was, they felt its warmth, while others, bewildered by his amiable indifference, were unable to believe that his unfailing courtesy and indolent kindness masked contempt, cunning and a total disregard of anyone's welfare but his own.

During his last days at the Hague Charles received, among a number of other former enemies, Admiral Montague, whom he kissed 'with a great deal of affection',[19] Monk's brother-in-law Dr Clarges, and George Downing, whom he knighted. Then he and Hyde had a long talk alone in the Chancellor's bedroom. On the morning of May 23rd he and his brothers rode down to Scheveningen, the Princess Mary, the Queen of Bohemia and Prince William following in their coaches. As they approached the shore, now black with people (the crowds were estimated at some 50,000), the guns from the fleet fired two rounds, and Admiral Montague entered the shallop which was to take the King and his family out to the *Naseby*, presently renamed the *Royal Charles*. Glancing back at the shore the King said, 'My own subjects cannot have more tenderness for me than these people,' as if pleasantly surprised. (Some years afterwards he described them as 'Dutch blockheads'.) To the sound of cannon they boarded the great ship – her crew numbered 600 – and sat down by themselves ('a blessed sight' Pepys thought) in the 'coach', or apartment attached to the Admiral's cabin under the poop deck. This chamber, which corresponded to the modern wardroom, was wainscotted, gilded and hung with tapestries. There they feasted off silver plate, and it was arranged that York should sail in the *London* and Gloucester in the *Swiftsure*.[20]

At last the moment came for the brothers to say farewell to their aunt and sister. They all ascended to the poop deck. The Queen of Bohemia, a debonair but plain lady, says Pepys, was moderately calm. Mary cried so bitterly that when she embraced Charles he had to support her. She left him, then came back for another kiss; Charles bent down to bless his nephew and took her in his arms once more.[21] As he leant over the rail to see the last of her, the cannon sounded again, and a great cloud of smoke rose between them. 'Which done,' says Pepys, 'we weighed anchor, and with a fresh gale and most happy weather, we set sail for England.'

II

The story of Charles II's youth achieves its happy ending at this point, partly because his anticipation of triumph turned out to be more satisfactory than his experience of it. As the King watched the coast of Holland fade behind him, he was free to enjoy the prospects of restoration without visualizing his disillusionment or the assaults made on such sensitivity as he still retained. He had endured so much, for so long, that he was usually incapable of deep feeling; and he could not have foretold what effect his memories would have when he returned to places he had neither seen nor thought about since he was a child. Yet already recollections of misery and despair were beginning to sweep over him, with the result that after a week of exhausting public appearances he shrank from rest and solitude. If his brothers had been with him, he might have stayed talking with them in his cabin; but apart from his immediate entourage, he was surrounded by persons he hardly knew, who had submitted to, when they had not worked for, his enemies. They were now at his feet; and it was to them, rather than to those who had shared his bitter fortunes, that he must express himself. Charles and his courtiers knew each other too well; from comparative strangers he was sure of evoking a whole-hearted and reverent response.

Yet though he had to talk, he could not be still. Pepys, who watched him avidly, was amazed at His Majesty's energy; no doubt he had been led to believe that the years of exile had left the King languid and idle. 'Active and stirring', Charles continued to walk 'here and there, up and down'. He was too restless even to steer the ship. As he paced the quarterdeck he began to recount his adventures after Worcester; and so the diarist was provided with the first version of that extraordinary saga, which he recorded in full some twenty years later, at the King's dictation, and which Charles himself corrected and enlarged. The two narratives do not much vary, except in length; for the experiences of those forty-three days were seared on the King's memory. However often he described them, he never freed himself from what became an obsession with him and an ordeal of stifling boredom for those who had to hear them over and over again.

The effect of the King's discourse on the imaginative and warm-hearted Pepys was overwhelming, and he had difficulty in concealing his tears. Afterwards, when it was dusk, and Charles went below to sup alone in the coach, the diarist and his companions could talk of nothing but those days and nights of hunger, terror and pain – though it is noticeable that neither then nor later could the King bring himself to describe (perhaps not even to recall) his collapse, that hideous moment when he had lain sobbing on the ground, begging Captain Careless to let the Roundheads come and take him.

Knowing what was expected of him, Charles dwelt on the comic and pathetic aspects of his story. Pepys's horror-struck attention rose to agony as he heard of His Sacred Majesty's lacerated feet, miserable disguises (nothing but a green coat and a pair of country breeches – think of it!), the bullying abuse of servants and labourers ('What countryman are you that know not how to wind up a jack?') and the cramping discomfort of priests' holes. And then to hear of the King of England being so hungry that he was forced to steal some bread and cheese from the pocket of a poor boy! (Presumably this happened in Rouen, when Charles and Wilmot spent all they had on hiring a room.) Yet it was good to know of those who had risked their lives for him, and of the humble folk who had knelt to kiss his hand, bidding God bless him wherever he went. Pepys went to bed in a rapture of worship, not only for the King but for his entourage, 'very fine gentlemen', with whom he had 'brave discourse' during the next day. The courtier whose company he enjoyed most was Thomas Killigrew. That 'merry droll' was still 'in great esteem' with His Majesty. His treachery was never discovered.

Apart from acquiring a suitable wardrobe for himself and his Court, Charles had had no time to profit by his advantages, even in a minor sense – except in one respect. While Hyde longed to buy books, the King seems to have set his heart on the pet dogs of which the miniature spaniel type is permanently associated with his name. His preference for them may perhaps be connected with the portrait of the Princess Henrietta Anne, which shows her holding one in her arms. The melancholy, brilliant dark eyes of these little creatures have a curious resemblance to those of the man who made them famous and popular in England; and it is not surprising that, just as he liked to bask in his dear, dearest Minette's uncritical adoration, so he sometimes set his dogs' undemanding company above that of persons whose flatteries and requests nauseated and bored him. There were several spaniels on board the *Royal Charles*: none of them was house-trained.[22]

Now the sea was calm, glittering under a full moon. For a little while Charles stood on the poop, looking towards England. Before going below he sent messages to his brothers bidding them join him for breakfast. He slept intermittently, for the cannon continued to sound.

At nine o'clock in the morning of the 24th they sighted land. An elaborate meal had been prepared for the King and the Dukes. While they were waiting for it Charles marked his height at the head of the cabin. Then something was said about the crew's rations of pease, pork and boiled beef. The very thing, said His Majesty – and he and his brothers sat down to share the sailors' favourite dish. As they were nearing Dover much earlier than had been expected, doubts arose as to whether Monk would have arrived, and Charles said that he would not land until the General was there. At one o'clock Monk reached the shore, accompanied by his staff, one of whom ventured to speak of his wonderful achievement. 'It was not I that did this,' the great man solemnly replied. 'You know the jealousies that were had of me, and the oppositions against me. It was God alone who did it. To Him be the glory,' he added, 'whose is the kingdom and the power, over all governments.'[23]

Just before three o'clock the brigantine from which Charles and his brothers were to land approached; he insisted on being rowed ashore with Montague in his barge. While York chatted with Pepys (he called the little secretary by name and promised him his favour), the King's equerries were tipping Montague's servants and Sir Stephen Fox distributed £500 among the officers and men of the *Royal Charles*. Pepys was put in charge of His Majesty's guitar, and, with Captain Mansell and a footman who was carrying the King's favourite spaniel, followed the royal party in another barge. The dog at once 'dirtied the boat, which made us laugh'. A few moments later the diarist reflected that this simple action was in a sense symbolic, as showing that 'a king and all that belong to him are but just as others are'.[24]

As the vast crowds on the cliffs began to shout and sway, Montague handed out the King, himself returning to the barge. Charles, who was wearing one of his dark suits with a scarlet plume in his hat, advanced alone. As his foot touched the shore he knelt and gave thanks to God. Then he walked towards Monk, who was kneeling a few yards away. Behind him stood the Mayor and Aldermen of Dover; and next to them was an unexpected yet familiar figure – His Grace of Buckingham, tall, smiling, completely unabashed, and as ready to welcome his old comrade as if they had never disagreed.[25]

Charles was now standing above the General who had deserted his colours and played cat and mouse with himself for the last five months. He raised Monk and, kissing him on either cheek, said, 'Father!' As the shouts of 'God save the King!' drowned their voices, York kissed the General several times; Gloucester threw up his hat and shouted 'God save General Monk!'[26]

Charles's performance reached its climax when the Mayor approached, offered his white staff and presented him with a magnificent Bible, clasped and stamped in gold. As he took it the King said, 'It is the thing I love above all things in the world.' He and Monk walked on with the Mayor towards a canopy, under which they stood, shouting compliments at one another: for the noise of the cannon was now deafening.

The coach in which Charles, his brothers and the General were to proceed to Canterbury then drew up – and there beside it stood Buckingham, apparently on the assumption that he would be allowed to drive in triumph with the King he had slandered and deserted. Charles accepted the insolence; after all, there was no resisting George, and he was bound to be better company than old Monk. When he saw that the vehicle was full, Buckingham sprang into the boot, one of the small seats covering the hind wheels in which the footmen generally sat. No objection was made, and the equipage proceeded rapidly through the town in an uproar of bells, cannon and hysterically cheering crowds.[27] So the Black Boy came home.

When they reached Barham Down Charles and his brothers left the coach and rode towards Canterbury. It was fifteen years since he had seen this part of his kingdom. Now it spread out before him in the sunshine, starred with spring flowers, freshly green.

III

Just beyond Barham Down a body of troops was lined up for inspection. The officers stood to attention, then kissed the hilts of their swords; they could not restrain the men, who burst out of their ranks when Charles appeared, cheering and blessing him. Among the minority opposed to his restoration was a number of Cromwellian officers, who as he entered Canterbury stood gloomily watching him, then turned away; and a few country gentlemen and parsons showed their disapproval by putting out bonfires and muttering threats which nobody heeded in what a Buckinghamshire clergyman described as 'universal acclamations of wild and sober joy'.[28]

Outside the Archbishop's Palace Charles met the Mayor and Aldermen waiting to present him with a gold tankard and a purse of £250. He spent two nights there, holding a Chapter of the Garter in the half-ruined cathedral, where he invested Monk and then attended morning service. He was alone in his closet when Monk entered and without waiting for permission to speak, said abruptly, 'I cannot do Your Majesty better service than by recommending to you such persons as are most grateful to [popular with] the people, and in respect of their parts and interests are best able to serve you,' and gave him a paper. The King put the paper in his pocket and replied pleasantly, 'I will always be ready to receive your advice, and willing to gratify you in anything you may desire – and which will not be prejudicial to my service.' As soon as Monk left him he read the paper; it was a list of some forty persons whom the General wished to be elected to the Privy Council; only two of them, Hertford and Southampton, had worked for the Royalist cause; the rest were ex-rebels or Presbyterians, or both. 'In more than ordinary confusion,' as he afterwards told Hyde, Charles 'knew not what to think of the General, in whose absolute power he was'.[29] He managed to postpone his rejection of Monk's candidates till he was able to confer with Hyde, to whom fell the awkward task of disappointing the great man.

Meanwhile Charles found time to scribble a note to Minette, which reveals his changing state of mind. 'Monk, with a great number of the nobility,' he wrote, ' ... almost overwhelmed me with kindness and joy for my return. My head is so dreadfully stunned with the acclamations of the people that I know not whether I am writing sense or nonsense.'[30]

'Dreadfully', a word then more literally understood than now, shows the King's mood darkening, partly from exhaustion and partly as a result of Monk's insolence. The process of disillusionment, which was to end in unconcealed bitterness, had already begun, although the accounts of his progress from Canterbury to the capital show no sign of any failure to respond. At Rochester, where he spent the night of the 28th, he watched Morris dancing, inspected more troops, and left early on the morning of the 29th, pausing in Deptford to receive a hundred young girls dressed in white with blue scarves, who threw sweet herbs and flowers at his horse's feet as he passed through the town.

On the afternoon of May 29th – his thirtieth birthday – King Charles rode into London via Blackheath, where he held a last, very brief military

review; for the crowds in the city were so vast that unless he hurried he
would not reach the palace of Whitehall before dark. His first stop was at
St George's Fields. Here the City fathers advanced to meet him; the Lord
Mayor, kneeling, presented him with the sword, and was knighted. The
King was then ushered into a tent hung with tapestry and had a quick
meal. At St Paul's School the headmaster, Dr Reynolds, was waiting to
greet him with a Bible.

The arrangements for the climax of Charles's entry into the capital
entailed his riding between his brothers past Temple Bar, along the Strand
and so to Westminster, where the Houses would receive him with prolonged and elaborate ceremony. The planning of the procession precluded
anyone carrying the large and heavy volume which he now accepted in a
'grave and gracious' manner. 'The greatest part of this day's solemnity,'
he said, 'I must ascribe to God's providence – and I will make this Book
the rule of my life and government.' He then desired Dr Reynolds to
bring it to him at Whitehall.

Most of Charles's first public appearances had culminated in the reception of Bibles; then, his pleasure in such gifts had been simple and sincere.
Now, after fourteen years of religious controversy and intrigue, during
which he had learnt to lie his way out of every awkward situation, his
assurance of piety may have rung hollow in his own ears. He had studied
the Scriptures, and was always ready with a quotation from either Testament; but his promise to Dr Reynolds was, as he himself would have put
it, 'only a grimace'. He knew very well that no rule, from the Bible or any
other book, would avail him in the task he had undertaken; he must make
his own. Now the moment was approaching when his capacity for deception broke down under a shock he could not have foretold and was
unable to withstand.

His enraptured subjects naturally assumed that King Charles was revelling in every moment of his miraculous triumph. That 'the good Angel
of God', as one Royalist put it, had 'brought him honourably and peace-
ably home and set him on his father's throne', eliminated, in their minds,
any doubt of his sharing in their joy; when he said, 'My whole wish is to
make you as happy as I am myself,' they believed him.[31] And so the
Londoners had decked out their city like the King's daughter in the
psalm; she was all glorious within, and her clothing was of wrought gold;
the maidens that bore her company were dressed in white petticoats and
crimson waistcoats. There were, says Evelyn, 'the ways strawed with
flowers, the bells ringing, the streets hung with tapestry, fountains
running with wine; the Mayor, Aldermen and all the City Companies

n their liveries, chains of gold, banners; lords and nobles, cloth of silver, gold and velvet ... the windows and balconies all set with ladies, trumpets, music and people flocking the streets as far as Rochester.'[32] The grey, white and brown of the city had disappeared. Here and there on the roof-tops, grimly contemplating the brilliant scene, stood the dark effigies of Cromwell, waiting to be cast into the bonfires when night fell.

The procession for which everyone had taken their places on the stands and in the streets since the night before was dramatically ordered. First came the gilded coaches, the squadrons of horse in silver doublets, then the old Earl of Cleveland riding ahead of a thousand buff-clad soldiers; then the Sheriffs in gold lace, footmen in red cloaks and green scarves, trumpeters in black velvet and cloth of gold; then the Life-guards, the City Marshal, the heralds, the Lord Mayor bearing the sword; and then a comically incongruous pair – General Monk and the Duke of Buckingham, riding abreast, bare-headed; they were followed by five regiments of horse.

Now the cheering grew wilder and the church spires seemed to sway and rock beneath their silken flags, and the cannon thundered and flashed, and the foot-soldiers, grasping their pikes, braced themselves to keep back mad onrush over the route. There was a space, an unendurable moment of suspense. And suddenly, there he was, riding between his brothers, yet apart in glory – the King from over the water, His Blessed Majesty, adored treasure of his faithful people, deliverer, divinity, hero of a hundred ballads, legends, hopes and prayers ...

In a plain dark suit, with the blue ribbon of the Garter on his breast and a crimson plume in his hat, he rode onwards, slowly, so that everyone saw, and seeing never forgot, his composed grace, his sombre elegance, and felt the mysterious power which set him above other men. 'Raising his eyes to the windows, looking at all, raising his hat to all, and greeting all who with loud shouts and a tremendous noise acclaimed the return of this great Prince, so abounding in virtues and distinguished qualities of every sort', says the Venetian ambassador, he passed, 'with great pomp and triumph, and in the most stately manner ever seen, amid the acclamations and blessings of the people.'[33] 'I stood in the Strand,' wrote Evelyn next day, 'and beheld it, and blessed God. And all this without one drop of blood, and by that very army which rebelled against him ... For such a Restoration was never seen in the mention of any history ... nor so joyful a day and so bright ... in this nation.'

It was late in the afternoon and the shadows were lengthening when he reached Whitehall. As he entered the gateway of the Banqueting House he looked up. There, eleven years ago, had stood the scaffold; there was the window from which his father had stepped forth to speak to his people for the last time. 'It struck such an expression of grief into his sacred heart,' said one who stood near him, 'as had almost burst forth.'[34]

He dismounted and was escorted up the stairs into that pillared and painted chamber of death, where from the ceiling his grandfather looked down in ineffable benignancy. He took his place under the canopy. (Was it true that no efforts had been able to remove the bloodstains from the fourth window-sill?) The Lords came forward, and 'solemnly cast themselves at his feet, with vows of affection and fidelity to the world's end' He signed to their Speaker, Lord Manchester, and they rose. A long address of slavish adulation was poured forth. Then he spoke – and it was almost as if he were pleading for their compassion. 'I am so disordered,' he began, 'by my journey, and the noise still sounding in my ears, that cannot express myself so full as I wish. Nevertheless, I take no greater satisfaction to myself than in this my change. I promise you that, looking first to Heaven, I will have a careful eye towards my three kingdoms.'

This was the preliminary to the speech he had written out, and which was later published in full. He could not go on. The Lords made way for the Commons.

By the time that former pillar of the Long Parliament, Sir Harbottle Grimston, concluded his address, King Charles had collected himself His brief reply must have come as a shock: for it sprang from the depth of a bitter and ruthless determination. 'The laws and liberties of my people,' he said, 'with the Protestant religion – *next to my life and crown –* I will preserve.'[35]

Hyde, Ormonde, Nicholas and the rest of his father's servants who had shared Charles II's misery and degradation have left no comment on this disconcerting answer. The Chancellor, firmly optimistic, concludes his record with a brief recapitulation of the 'horrid circumstances' of the past twenty years, adding, 'Yet did the merciful hand of God bind up all these wounds,' as if determined to ignore his master's unfortunate outspokenness, which is capable of two interpretations. The King's promise to care for his life and crown 'next to' the Protestant faith could have meant that he intended to put them first; in any case, he was reminding his audience that whatever they chose to ignore or forget, his memories would direct his future policy, and so his assurance of a 'careful eye' on his kingdoms holds a hint of menace. In fact, he was warning everyone that his rule and conduct would be based on a negative – that of never going on his travels again. All other duties and obligations were to be subordinated to that single condition.

Having thus relieved his sacred heart, the King sank into the passivity of exhaustion, but for one piece of self-assertion. It had been arranged that, having received the homage of the Houses, he should proceed to Westminster Abbey for a service of thanksgiving. He refused. A message was sent to the Dean, and Charles left the Banqueting Hall. As the chapel was still dismantled, he knelt to pray in the crowded Presence Chamber.[36] Meanwhile the uproariousness of his subjects had so increased as to alarm the authorities, who composed, in His Majesty's name, a declaration against drunkenness and swearing, to be issued the next morning. It had no effect of any kind.

It was now past eight o'clock. Charles had been on show without a moment's rest for some fourteen hours, and had finally been subjected to an ordeal which momentarily destroyed his poise and his self-control. The result was that when he took his place under the canopy of state he seemed dazed. The Earl of Leicester, one of the first to kiss his hand, attributed this indifference to the noise and lack of organization. In the general excitement, while the courtiers were pushing and shoving about the dais, protocol and precedence were forgotten. 'There was so great disorder and confusion,' says Leicester, 'that the King scarce knew or took notice of anybody.[37]

This rather squalid scene did not produce the final irony. When the pressure diminished Charles found himself standing in a circle of privileged persons. As they waited for him to speak, he smiled, looking from one to another – and none knew better than he which were the sheep and which the wolves. Then he said, in that agreeable yet faintly satirical tone which made reply so difficult, 'I doubt it has been my own fault I have been absent so long – for I see nobody that does not protest he has ever wished for my return.'[38]

There was some sycophantic laughter. Then he added, 'Where are all my enemies?'[39]

To this harsh rhetoric there could be no answer but the truth; and that must remain unspoken. In this manner the gulf between Charles II and his so-called intimates was defined, once and for always. For the next twenty-five years, no one crossed it; no one knew what he was thinking or planning; no one could be sure whether or not his genial, robust philosophy, so concisely and wittily expressed, was a mask. He stood apart.

And then at last he put his cards – the cards he had played with such consummate coolness and skill – on the table and left the game. His hastily collected winnings included the right to enter, after an appropriate interval, the Courts of Heaven. In those of history he remains what he desired to be: an enigma.

NOTES

1 Pepys, vol. I, pp. 96–7.
2 L. Eachard, *History of England*, p. 551.
3 Price, pp. 142–62.
4 E. Ludlow, *Memoirs*, vol. III, p. 2.
5 *Cal. Clar. S. P.*, vol. III, p. 747.
6 Op. cit., pp. 745, 749.
7 Pepys, vol. I, pp. 133–5.
8 Op. cit., pp. 133–5, 141.
9 *Secret History of Charles II* (anon.), pp. 20, 21.
10 W. Lower, *A Relation in the form of a Journal*, pp. 5–108.
11 Ibid.
12 Pepys, ibid.
13 Heath, p. 763.
14 Clarendon, pp. 908–10.
15 Sir Stephen Fox, *Memoirs*, p. 80.
16 Lower, ibid.
17 Clarendon, ibid.
18 Pepys, ibid.
19 Op. cit., p. 114.
20 Op. cit., p. 144.
21 Sir Stephen Fox, p. 90.
22 Pepys, vol. I, pp. 145–6.
23 Price, p. 162.
24 Pepys, vol. I, p. 149.
25 Whitelocke, vol. IV, pp. 415–16.
26 Sir Richard Baker, *A Chronicle of the Kings of England*, p. 480.
27 Whitelocke, ibid.
28 Bryant, *King Charles II*, p. 77.
29 Clarendon, p. 995.
30 J. Ady, *Madame*, p. 77.
31 *Cal. S. P. Ven.*, vol. XXXI, p. 155.
32 Evelyn, p. 406.
33 *Cal. S. P. Ven.*, ibid.
34 C. Walker, p. 107.
35 Ibid.; Baker, p. 712.
36 J. McGrath, *Flemings in Oxford*, vol. I, p. 129.
37 *Sidney Papers* (ed. R. W. Blencowe), p. 158.
38 Clarendon, p. 910.
39 L. Hutchinson, *Memoirs of the Life of Colonel Hutchinson*, p. 319.

EPILOGUE

GIOVANNI. What do the dead do, uncle? Do they eat,
    Hear music, go a-hunting, and be merry,
    As we that live?
FRANCISCO DE' MEDICI. No, coz; they sleep.
GIOVANNI. Lord, Lord, that I were dead!
    I have not slept these six nights. – When do they wake?
FRANCISCO DE' MEDICI. When God shall please . . .

The White Devil

BETWEEN seven and eight in the evening of February 5th, 1685, Father Huddleston, who had been living at the Palace of Whitehall for some sixteen years, was called to the private entrance of Queen Catherine's apartments, and told to bring with him 'all things necessary for a dying person'.

Father Huddleston may have hoped for, though he could not have been counting on, the summons which preceded the greatest moment of his life. Early in the morning of the 1st King Charles had had a stroke, and the doctors announced that he could not live for more than a few hours. He then rallied, and the bells were rung to celebrate his recovery. Now he was sinking into unconsciousness. During those four days there had been no question of his sending for, or even expressing a wish to see, a priest of the old faith. He was surrounded by Anglican clergy imploring him to receive the Sacraments of the Church whose Head he was. He had either replied, 'Time enough', or seemed not to take in what was being said. He was far gone; and as Father Huddleston hurried through passages and galleries he began to fear that His Majesty would not be in a state to confess his sins or to receive absolution.

When Huddleston was admitted to the Queen's apartments he was told 'not to stir from thence till further notice'. Then he realized that in his flurry he had forgotten the Host – what was to be done? One of Queen Catherine's Portuguese priests was summoned and went to get it. Father Huddleston was shrouded in an Anglican cassock; a black wig completed his disguise. Still empty-handed, he was taken up the privy stair to the King's bedchamber.

Doctors, bishops and courtiers had been dismissed and were waiting in the ante-rooms beyond. The Earls of Bath and Feversham, young Lord

Bruce and the Duke of York were standing round the bed. The ticking of some thirty clocks and the heavy breathing of the dying man were the only sounds. The Duke bent down and said, 'Sire, here is a man that saved your life, and is now come to save your soul.' The answer came in a whisper. 'He is very welcome.' Huddleston approached and knelt by the bed. The watchers withdrew; he and the King were alone.

Huddleston said, 'What service can I perform for God's honour and the happiness of Your Majesty's soul at this last moment, on which eternity depends?' There was a pause; then Charles, summoning all his strength, replied as if he had been long prepared, in the accepted terms. 'I desire to die in the faith and communion of the Holy Roman Catholic Church. I am most heartily sorry for all the sins of my life past, and particularly for that I have deferred my reconciliation so long. I hope for salvation through the merits of Christ's Passion. I am in charity with all the world. With all my heart I pardon my enemies, and desire pardon from all those whom I have in any wise offended. If it please God to spare me longer life, I will amend it, detesting all sin.'

Huddleston spoke of the Sacrament of penance. Charles made his confession, repeated the Act of contrition, and was absolved. Huddleston asked him if he would receive the Host. 'By all means,' replied the King. 'If I am worthy, pray fail not to let me have it.' Still the Portuguese father had not arrived – had he been denied entrance? Huddleston said, 'It will be brought to Your Majesty very speedily,' and asked leave to administer Extreme Unction. Just as he finished anointing Charles he was called to the door to take the Host. Returning to the bed, he found the King trying to raise himself and gasping out, 'Let me meet my heavenly Lord in a better posture than in my bed.'

Now that he was fully equipped, Huddleston took charge. He said, 'I humbly beg Your Majesty to repose yourself. God Almighty, who sees your heart, will accept of your intention.' He then administered the Sacrament, which Charles received 'with all the symptoms of devotion imaginable'. Huddleston said, 'Your Majesty hath now received the comfort and benefit of all the Sacraments that a good Christian, ready to depart out of this world, can have or desire.' As the King sank into speechless exhaustion he began, 'Now it only remains that you think upon the death and Passion of our dear Saviour Jesus Christ.' Holding up the crucifix which had been hidden beneath his cassock, he went on, 'Lift up therefore the eyes of your soul to your sweet Saviour here crucified, bowing down His head to kiss you; His arms stretched out to embrace you; His Body and members all bloody and pale with death to redeem you. And as you see

Him dead and fixed upon the Cross for your redemption, beseech Him
with all humility to pardon and forgive you all your offences and finally to
receive your soul into His blessed hands, to grant you a joyful resurrection
and an eternal crown of glory in the next – in the name of the Father, of
the Son, and of the Holy Ghost.'

There was no answer; no sound but the ticking of the clocks. The tears
streaming down his face, Huddleston kissed the King's hand and left the
bedchamber. Courtiers, clergymen and physicians crowded in to watch
the end. York knelt by the bedside; Lord Bruce held his master in his
arms. Then the King rallied once more, and gave his brother directions
about his children – all but Monmouth, whom he did not name – and
his mistresses. He sent messages to the Queen, and asked James to tell the
Duchess of Portsmouth how much he loved her. He became drowsy; the
doctors roused him so that he might be bled. He spoke of his longing for
death, and of his sufferings. So the night passed. As dawn broke he opened
his eyes and said, 'Lift me up, that I may once more see the day.'

It was done; and he seemed to be listening to the sounds from the river.
Then he said, 'That clock must be wound tomorrow' (it was an eight-day
clock), and sank back. Two, three, four hours went by. Once more he
was bled; he seemed unaware of what was happening. Now it was noon,
and the tide had come to the full. A few seconds later, without a struggle
or a sigh, King Charles II ceased to breathe.

As night fell the watchers began their vigil in the bedchamber. Among
them were some whose memories extended over the last quarter of a
century; they had witnessed what might be described as the betrothal
of a nation passionately in love with a bridegroom of extraordinary fascination, great talents, and a genial frankness of manner that made him,
as he himself said, the man of his people: the brilliant, easy-going husband
of a temperamental wife.

So the marriage took place in an ecstasy of devotion – what a king!
Was there anything he did not understand and could not do? Science,
mathematics, sport, gunnery, theology, politics, anatomy, astronomy,
ship-building – he not only discussed them with experts, but practised
them himself. Everything he said and did became him; even his vices were
endearing – for who could seriously object to the spectacle of that troupe
of lovely women and elegant, accomplished Cavaliers, wild and extravagant though they were? King Charles's subjects shared in his pleasures, or
at least were made to feel that they did, as they crowded into the Matted
Gallery and the Presence Chamber, or watched him at dinner, in the park,

on the race-course, beating time to the anthem in chapel, pulling off his hat to all who greeted him, laughing at some, teasing others, complimenting one statesman, standing up to another, tolerating, with his inimitable, indolent grace, bores, fanatics, spongers, sycophants and critics. Surely there never had been such a man as His Blessed Majesty, 'debonair, easy of access, not bloody nor cruel', their 'great and gracious master'. He had brought in the millennium – to say nothing of new fashions, new entertainments, and 'a politer way of living'. He and his people settled down to live happily ever after ...

Then came a vague uneasiness: doubt: inquiries; then a torturing jealousy, growing with the years till it reached monstrous proportions. For there was still that same rival in the English Eden, half seen, sometimes quiescent and forgotten, then suddenly horribly active and menacing – the enchantress of Rome, feared, detested and flouted; she whom King Hal had set down (though he died in her arms), who had defeated Henry II and John Lackland, and debauched Queen Mary. Not even Queen Bess had been able to destroy her, when she beheaded her handmaid of Scotland and banished her satellite, that other Mary, She of Heaven, from her kingdoms.

Could it be – was it really possible – that their adored and glorious King Charles was in touch, perhaps beginning an intimacy with, that deadly creature, eternal in her evil? Might he, one day, yield to her spells? Had he perhaps already done so? Some said he had; and indeed, as the years went by, he was seen to be surrounded by her minions. Clifford of the Cabal was suspected of being one; Henry Bennet, now Earl of Arlington, became another. He had a Catholic Queen (poor barren woman, dull, plain and dowdy, one could not but pity her), two Catholic mistresses, a Catholic heir-presumptive, and, most dreaded and loathed of all, a Catholic patron and ally, Louis of France. What did it mean? Had His Majesty been unfaithful to his marriage vows – broken his coronation oath?

Charles's reassurances were nicely calculated; he knew better than to protest too much. He continued to attend Anglican services – not always decorously, for he joined in his courtiers' smothered laughter when his chaplain preached on chastity – and to repeat his promise that 'nothing shall ever alter my affection to the Protestant religion'. Shortly after his Restoration, he approached Clement IX with suggestions for what might be described as a doctored form of Catholicism, which would pave the way towards reconciliation with the Holy See, and which he abandoned almost at once; for all his perspicacity, he had not then quite grasped the frenzied violence of the Anglicans, whose horror of toleration was expressed by their rejection of his Declaration of Indulgence for Dissenters and Papists. In fact, Charles's indifference to all forms of religion helped to soothe the national suspicions; and very soon he perceived that his subjects' loathing of Popery had little or no spiritual inspiration. 'Beyond sea,' he said, 'it seemed as if people worshipped God in earnest – but here, in jest.' His verdict on the English clergy was similarly contemptuous. 'They will do nothing and have me do everything – and most of them do worse than if they did nothing.' Of a nonconformist parson to whom he gave a benefice he remarked that he was 'a very silly fellow. But,' he added, 'his nonsense suits their nonsense, for he has brought them all to church.' Presently his resentment against this section was more bitterly expressed. Such persons merely pretended to be holier than others, and were therefore the greatest knaves; later he announced, 'I will have the laws put into execution against all Dissenters, for I have given them liberty so long that they have now almost taken mine.'

It was partly through finance that Charles's liberty – what he called his prerogative – was curtailed. After the Dutch war of 1665 it became clear that it was impossible to run the country on the sum originally voted him, and that he must borrow from abroad; so the pattern of the exile was repeated. In the autumn of 1669 it was agreed between himself and Louis XIV that, in return for £300,000, he would restore the old faith and publicly declare his own reconciliation with Rome. Next year, through the secret Treaty of Dover, he accepted Louis's offer of £154,000 and 6,000 French troops to crush the rebellion of 'unquiet spirits', while the announcement of his own beliefs was left to his discretion. The French ambassador begged His Majesty not to act precipitately, and to begin his Catholic campaign by betraying his alliance with Holland and Sweden; with convincing reluctance Charles agreed to restrain his pious zeal; then he momentarily quenched his people's fear by banishing all Catholic priests and enforcing the laws against recusants. He never announced his own Catholicism; and he began to reconstruct the Navy with Louis's money.

By 1667 Charles had got rid of Hyde – whose fall and exile were partly due to his signing the ignominious Peace of Breda and his refusal to call Parliament when the Dutch sailed up the Medway – and had made it clear to Queen Catherine that their relationship must include her reception of his mistresses. This was easy enough: for that unfortunate lady had fallen hopelessly in love with him, and was prepared to do anything he wanted. He became quite fond of her, and was nearly always kind. 'I thought,' he told one of his gentlemen soon after the marriage, 'that they had brought me a bat instead of a woman – but it is too late to find fault, and I must make the best of a bad matter.' So he did; he teased her affectionately, gave her one or two nice presents, rose in the middle of the night to clear up the mess when she was sick all over the bed-clothes, wept and cared for her during a dangerous illness, and assured her, 'It is a very pretty boy,' when she deliriously announced that she had been delivered of a Prince of Wales. He only left her to sup with Lady Castlemaine and to dance their children in his arms.

For he was still, and always would be, a family man, although by the autumn of 1670 he had had to re-create the atmosphere such a phrase implies. Gloucester, the Princess Mary, Henrietta Maria, Elizabeth of Bohemia and Minette were dead; he would have been very lonely without Monmouth (now in his twenty-second year and himself a husband and father) and his other bastards. His childhood hero, Prince Rupert, was still at Court; but, sport and chemistry apart, they had little in common, for the Prince took no interest in politics or finance; also, Rupert was on bad terms with York (who, as a declared Catholic, lost his popularity and his place of Lord High Admiral in 1673) and had no knowledge of the precipices over which Charles had stretched a tight-rope of his own especial brand. Nor had anyone else.

In his seven years of office Hyde's conscientiousness and his unpopularity with all classes had enabled Charles to perfect a technique which deceived everyone about him and which he practised for the rest of his life; it was that of appearing, even to his intimates, as a lazy, good-tempered, rather vague person who left difficult tasks to his ministers, and who could be influenced by anyone subscribing to his pleasures. The King established this façade of frivolity so unobtrusively and yet so effectively that long after his death his reputation remained what he intended it to be: in fact, more than two hundred and fifty years went by before some of his biographers began to see through it, to grasp the whole extent of his personal triumph and to perceive the convolutions of his peculiar policy. And this was odd, because Charles made no secret of his views; indeed it is difficult, even now, to understand how it was that for twenty-five years anyone, of whatever ingenuity, could tell so many obvious lies to so many people and escape ruin, let alone denunciation. He got out of awkward situations by saying, 'Send me a memorial', or by referring the applicant to one of his advisers, while he disappeared to race or to hunt or to take his ease in the apartments of 'the buffoons and ladies of pleasure'.

Thus, when Charles prorogued his disobliging and rebellious Parliaments, the assumption was that he would not work against them during the intervals; for was he not seen doing everything *but* work – on the tennis-court, in his yacht, fishing, swimming or discussing some invention (new beehives for the Whitehall gardens, or the prevention of London smog) with his protégés? The series of manoeuvres through which he ensured his brother's succession and enhanced his own power was accompanied by startlingly frank asides; some of these must have been repeated to his enemies in both Houses. And at one point, those enemies not only seemed individually abler than himself, but were allied against him. After such bouts, when he had assured them, on the word of a king, that he loved Parliaments and intended to call them at frequent intervals, he would remark to one of his gentlemen, 'I will have no more Parliaments, for my affairs are in so good a posture that I have no occasion to ask for supplies,' or 'A King of England that is not slave to five hundred kings is great enough.' He would then return to tell the Houses, 'You shall never repent any trust reposed in me,' and that same night say to the same confidant, 'Oddsfish! they have put a set of men about me, but they shall know nothing – give them but enough rope, and they will hang themselves.' That particular set did not oblige by committing suicide; but Charles's use of the rope was so skilful that one Parliament followed another, either through prorogation or dissolution, to the scaffold, while the people they represented continued to applaud the smiling hangman, who modestly remarked, 'I do not pretend to be without infirmities, but I have never broken my word,' shortly after sacrificing the 'tender consciences' of his Presbyterian subjects and throwing the Catholics to the lions.

This combination of frankness and deceit became so habitual as to make Charles believe some of his own lies; otherwise he could not have told his cherished Minette that he would not buy Louis XIV's friendship on 'dishonourable terms' and then cheat that benefactor out of an extra £50,000 by pretending to misunderstand the rate of exchange. His bewildered distress – what should he know of foreign currency? – drowned the protests of the French ambassador. 'For God's sake,' exclaimed His Majesty, 'do not speak to me of this affair! Go to the Treasurer, and do as you and he shall understand the matter – as to myself, I am driven to despair whenever it is mentioned to me,' took the defeated emissary by the arm and himself opened the door for him.

Charles had need of a more subtle ingenuity when the semi-republican Country Party, headed by Shaftesbury and Buckingham, began to suspect that the Dover Treaty had placed him – and England – in Louis's power.

Knowing that they also were in his cousin's pay, he continued plaintively to ask for 'cheerful aid' against France and to strengthen his naval defences, while every now and then assuming a majestic yet benevolent tone. 'I will maintain my prerogative; on the other hand, I will not have my subjects give me the law,' he told the Houses, adding, 'Peace and war are matters with which you ought not to meddle' – and his asides became graciously soothing. 'I would have everyone live under his own vine and fig-tree. Give me my just prerogative, and I will never ask more.' His defence of the ministers on whom he depended was another triumph. 'The House of Commons intend to impeach my Lord Danby, which will be very prejudicial to my affairs,' he told a Whig peer, who replied, 'The only expedient is to impeach somebody else, which will spend their fury and waste their time.' 'That is right, but who shall it be?' asked Charles. 'Duke Lauderdale is very odious, would there be any harm in falling upon him?' suggested the other. 'That will do,' said the King, and when both Lauderdale and Danby were impeached he managed to save them from execution, although Danby was imprisoned for five years.

Still he sustained the illusion of carefree idleness (although his ministers complained that he was up and about by five in the morning, they drew no conclusions from this inconvenient habit) combined with an unmoved acceptance of the most insolent censures. 'Matters are in a very ill state,' one of his more privileged associates told him, 'but there is a good, able man that if Your Majesty would employ, all would soon be mended.' As the King raised his eyebrows, he went on, 'This is one Charles Stuart, who now spends his time f—ing about the Court – but if you were to give him this employment, he would be the fittest man.' When publicly rebuked, Charles said to one of his equerries, 'Tell Dr Frampton that I am not angry for to be told of my faults – but I would have it done in a gentlemanlike manner,' and burst out laughing when another chaplain interrupted his sermon to say to Lauderdale, 'My lord, my lord! You snore so loud you will wake the King!'

Such stories went the rounds, and so endeared him to the people that they became far more royalist than the King who rejected reverence, and mocked at the pomposity of his fellow-monarchs. 'He will not piss but another must hold the chamber-pot,' was his verdict on one; and his brutally humorous moods reflected the current attitude towards moral issues. When a still-born child was 'dropped' during a Court ball, he made no tactless inquiries, but had it conveyed to his private laboratory, where he proceeded to dissect it, remarking, 'It being a boy, I have lost a subject by the business.' And his consideration was as all-embracing as his informality. 'You have but thin shoes, get a stronger pair to prevent getting cold,' he called out to one gentleman – and to Judge Jeffreys, 'It is a hot summer, and you are going the circuit, therefore I desire you will not drink too much,' while he merely smiled when the gayest of his mistresses greeted him at Newmarket with 'Charles! I hope I shall have your company to-night, shall I not?'

So the national devotion became impregnable: a suit of chain mail, which gave him freedom of movement (the speed of his movements was sometimes very disconcerting) and which was not pierced, even by Shaftesbury. This period, the most dramatic of his reign, which extended from the first stage of the Popish Plot in 1678 to his surprise dissolution of the Oxford Parliament in 1681, is aptly illustrated by the nicknames of the principals, some of them invented by Charles himself. Alderman George, Little Sincerity, Prince Perkin, the Protestant Whore, Old Rowley, Squire James, Fubbs, Lisbon Kate, the Salamanca Doctor – such were the protagonists.*

By the time the curtain rose on the penultimate act of the reign, the most unruly people in Europe, part terrorized audience, part hysterical chorus, were convinced that the Catholics had been responsible for the Fire of London and the Dutch invasion. All they needed was the instigator of a Catholic St Bartholomew, and a leader who would represent the hounding down, torture and massacre of all papists as a patriotic and religious duty. They found the first in Titus Oates and the second in Shaftesbury. And in the still unsolved murder of Sir Edmund Berry Godfrey, Oates and Shaftesbury found a seemingly inexhaustible store of ammunition against their enemies, of whom Charles, from Shaftesbury's point of view, was the principal; for the great Achitophel had decided to establish an oligarchy, guided by himself, with Monmouth as puppet king.

With his front of brass, his tongue of silver and his genius for the exploitation of mass hysteria, Shaftesbury, an ageing invalid, nearly succeeded in destroying not only the Catholic community, but the monarchy itself. Charles's few supporters were so inept, or so treacherous, that he stood alone. The dearest of his children had deserted him; his brother's Catholicism was an appalling liability; he was, as ever, in financial straits. There remained his people's frenzied possessiveness (they firmly believed that the Jesuits had tried to murder him), his long experience of human degradation, and the knife-like intelligence which now achieved a

* Buckingham, Shaftesbury, Monmouth, Nell Gwyn, Charles II, the Duke of York, the Duchess of Portsmouth, Queen Catherine, Titus Oates.

supremacy generated by such cool ruthlessness as Henry VIII might have envied and Machiavelli recorded with respect.

Through a combination of tireless patience, complicated double-crossing and apparent conciliation, Charles kept control of all the developments within the Plot, and so brought off his greatest victory single-handed, aided by a few hundred thousands from France. He savoured it to the full when he confronted the frail, hollow-eyed figure in the huge golden wig and said, 'My lord, let there be no self-delusion. I am none of those that grow more timorous with age – rather, I grow more resolute, the nearer I am to my grave. I intend to take a greater care of my own preservation – and that of my people – ' he added hastily – 'than any of you all that pretend to so much concern.' His subjects, wearying now of Shaftesbury's over-dramatized machinations, and fearful of another Civil War, were still behind him. 'Remember your royal father,' someone called, as he drove out of Oxford, 'and keep the staff in your own hands.' 'Aye, by God, I will!' Charles shouted back, 'and the sword too!' He kept this promise. Some thirty-nine innocent Catholics had been executed. 'God knows,' said the King, when the death-warrants were presented, 'I sign with tears in my eyes.' That ready fount was soon dried, and his aside was characteristically apt. Watching the protean Mr Hart as Macbeth, Charles waited till the entrance of the Murderers and then, turning to his gentlemen, said loudly, 'Pray, what is the reason that we never see a rogue in a play, but Oddsfish! they always clap on him a black periwig, when it is well known the greatest rogue in England wears a fair one?'

So he maintained his brother's rights and protected his wife against an arranged divorce. 'She is a weak woman and has some disagreeable humours,' he said (poor Catherine's habits seem to have made her unacceptable to the fastidious), 'but, considering my faultiness towards her, I think it a horrid thing to abandon her.' And he serenely added, 'I look on falsehood and cruelty as the greatest crimes in the sight of God. I know I have led a bad life – but I will never do a base or a wicked thing.' Of his duel with Shaftesbury he spoke more tersely. 'At Doomsday,' he remarked, 'we shall see whose arse is blackest.' And when the Little Lord was dead, Charles found in the Rye House Plot the means of destroying the rest of his party. 'If I do not have his life, he will soon have mine,' he said of one, and of another, 'I cannot pardon him because I dare not.' His basic motive was casually revealed to the indignant York, who was urging revenge and precautions. 'Brother, you may travel if you will – I am resolved to make myself easy for the rest of my life. I am sure no man in England will take away my life to make you king.'

So he went about unguarded, as always. His walks were shorter now; but he still played tennis, rode his own horse at Newmarket and was outwardly cheerful, though considerably aged, dozing off after dinner and inclined to theoretical speculation. 'What account will you give at the Day of Judgement,' he asked one of his courtiers, who was looking at a book of his own plays, 'of all the idle words in that book?' 'Why, truly,' was the answer, 'I shall give a better account than Your Majesty shall of all your idle promises, which have undone many,' and the King received the impertinence with a shrug and a smile, just as he accepted Bishop Burnet's letter of reproof without protest. He went through it twice before he threw it in the fire, mildly remarking, 'I am no atheist, but I cannot think God would damn a man for taking a little pleasure out of the way.'

The defeat of the Country Party was followed by Charles's final establishment of his power. During the last four years of his life – described by one of his younger courtiers as 'a golden age' – he received £340,000 from Louis XIV; this sum and the improved administration of the Treasury enabled him to reign without the 'five hundred kings' he had so often cajoled and exploited. He then did what no Tudor would have dared to attempt. He controlled the boroughs by calling in their charters. The composition of the new ones ensured the election of Tory administrators. When the City of London refused, judgment was entered against them and they were forced to submit. Thus he achieved his only ideal, that exemplified by the system of Mazarin and Louis XIV, for which his father had striven in vain. But Charles wore his absolutism with a difference: a silken robe hid his armour; still he seemed to be strolling, in casual ease, from one diversion to another. When a deputation from Berkshire begged him to release this strangle-hold by calling a Parliament, he replied amiably, 'I marvel that my neighbours should meddle with my business – but we shall agree better when we meet over a cup of ale at Windsor,' and they left Whitehall flattered, puzzled but loyal, while an observer reflected that His blessed Majesty was 'so gracious and great in his expressions that he could send away a person better pleased at receiving nothing than those in the good King his father's time that had requests granted them'. So what Archbishop Laud had once described as 'the barking of discontented persons' was stifled. Similarly, Charles had evaded a lesser imbroglio by replying, 'I never meddle with the *souls* of ladies,' when urged to prevent one of his mistresses changing her faith, and greatly endeared himself to the Lords when Lady Mohun brought an action against Mrs Browne on the grounds that the latter had thrown a candle-stick at her knee. 'May I be judge,' came the King's voice from the fireplace, 'as to whether the candle-stick hurt my Lady Mohun's knee?'

In fact, it was impossible for all but those he had deprived of everything they possessed to think of him as a tyrant. His behaviour to the meanest combined intimacy, courtliness and an enchanting humour – as when he received William Penn, whose Quakerism enforced his keeping his hat on in the royal presence. Charles at once removed his, upon which Penn inquired, 'Friend Charles, why dost thou not put on thy hat?' 'In this place,' the King replied, 'it is the custom for only one person at a time to remain covered.' So no one realized that Whitehall had become a shoddy imitation of Versailles. The contrasting personalities of the strutting little Sun King and his lounging, saturnine pensioner made the comparison impossible.

In an age when monarchy passed for semi-divine – even the sophisticated Pepys, seeing a storm break over the royal barge, felt his esteem lessen for a King 'that he should not be able to command the rain' – such unconventionality was irresistible, especially when allied to a confiding friendliness, which made his listeners feel that they alone knew his real nature. 'If I were a poet – and I think I am poor enough to be one – ' he began, when suggesting a theme to the Laureate; he would lean over a composer's shoulder to hum the air; he would show his pictures, his books and his lacquered cabinets to stray visitors, and then escort them to Portsmouth's bedchamber where, surrounded by his courtiers, she stood with her hair about her neck. At night he would retire to talk with the intimate few – that was the time to ask for a place or a pension – in the privy, and then climb into the great bed where he slept without stirring, while the spaniels snored and fidgeted and the Scotch coal crashed in the grate and the clocks chimed the quarters against one another.

As the hours ticked away, his rare fits of spite or anger ('I hope one day to see you ugly and willing,' he told the only woman who refused him) yielded to a detached and far-seeing resignation. 'I am weary of travelling, I am resolved to go abroad no more,' he said to an old friend a few weeks before he died. 'But when I am dead and gone, I know not what my brother will do; I am much afraid that when he comes to the crown he will be obliged to travel again – and yet I will take care to leave my kingdoms to him in peace, wishing he may long keep them so. But this hath all of my fears, little of my hopes and less of my reason.' Now his religious policy became more defined; the Dissenters were worse treated, and the Catholics more leniently. Having consolidated his position through his support of the Church of England, he jotted down his contempt for its inconsistencies. 'I do not desire to be the Head of nothing ... Every man thinks himself as competent a judge of the Scriptures as the Apostles themselves, hence a world of heresies ... It is not left to every fantastical man's head to believe as he pleases.'

He continued to eat heartily, to drink 'only for his thirst', to deplore, while tolerating, '*la sottise de mon frère*', to experiment in his laboratory, to struggle with financial problems, to sail and hawk and saunter as in the gay days of the Restoration, when he had declared 'I will not deny myself an hour's divertisement for the sake of any man,' and called for the country dances he had practised in the meadows of Germany and the taverns of the Low Countries. 'Cuckolds All Awry – the old dance of England!'

As King Charles led his people into the final movement he was still setting the pace. When the last note had died away and the echo of the last footstep faded and the spaniels sniffed and whined unheeded and the watchers stood weeping outside the palace, the secrets of that great master of king-craft, who 'knew men to a hair', remained inviolate. After the embalmers had done their work and the long, gaunt, 'black and slender-faced' figure had been decently composed, Grinling Gibbons came to immortalize those lined, harsh features. At midnight on February 24th he was buried in Westminster Abbey, privately and without ceremony. No inscription, no monument was ordered for the King whose farewell gesture had been that of an affably cynical illusionist.

There was no need of any. His image was not diminished; nor is his power lessened. Still his people find it pleasanter to believe in his half-truths and to be charmed by his jests than to remember how often, and how agreeably, they were deceived.

BIBLIOGRAPHY

Acton, Lord	*Historical Essays and Studies*
Adams, William H. D.	*The White King*
Ady, J.	*Madame*
Aikin, Lucy	*Memoirs of the Court of King Charles the First*
Ailesbury, Lord	*Memoirs*
Airy, Osmund	*Charles II*
Amiguet, Philippe	*La Grande Mademoiselle et son Siècle*
Ancaster MSS (H.M.C.)	*Diet of Charles I*
Anon.	*Secret History of Charles II*
	The King's and Queen's Entertainment
Arber, E.	*Stuart Tracts*
Ashley, Maurice P.	*Oliver Cromwell*
	England in the Seventeenth Century
Aubrey, John	*Brief Lives*
Aylmer, Gerald E.	*The King's Servants: The Civil Service of Charles I, 1625–42*
Baillie, Robert	*Letters and Journals (1637–1662)*
Baker, Sir Richard	*A Chronicle of the Kings of England (–1643)*
Balleine, George R.	*A History of the Island of Jersey*
Barwick, Peter	*The Life of the Reverend Dr John Barwick, D.D.*
Bath MSS (H.M.C.)	
Beaufort MSS (H.M.C.)	
Blair, Robert	*Life and Letters*
Blencowe, Robert W. (editor)	*Sidney Papers*
Bryant, Sir Arthur	*King Charles II*
	Samuel Pepys: The man in the making
Buckingham and Normanby, John Sheffield, Duke of	*Character of Charles II*
Bulstrode, Sir Richard	*Memoirs and Reflections*
Burnet, Gilbert, Bishop of Salisbury	*History of My Own Time*
	The Dukes of Hamilton
Burton, R.	*History of Charles and James II*

Calendar of Domestic
   State Papers
Calendar of State Papers
   Venetian
Calendar of Clarendon
   State Papers
Clarendon MSS
Cameron, Sir Ewen   *Memoirs of Sir Ewen Cameron of Lochiel*
Carte, T.   *A Collection of Original Letters and Papers (of*
                          Ormonde's, 1641–60)
                 A History of the Life of James, Duke of Ormonde
                 A General History of England (–1654)
Cartwright, J.   *Madame*
Cary, H.   *Memoirs*
Charles I   *The Letters, Speeches and Proclamations (edited*
                 by Sir Charles Petrie)
Chéruel, A.   *Histoire de France pendant la Minorité de Louis*
                 XIV
Clarendon, Edward   *History of the Rebellion, Life and Continuation*
   Hyde, 1st Earl of
Clarke, James S.   *Life of James II*
Cobbett, William   *Cobbett's Complete Collection of State Trials etc.*
Coke, R. A.   *Detection*
Cook, Aurelian   *Titus Britannicus*
Cottrell MSS (H.M.C.)
Cowper MSS (H.M.C.)
Cunningham, P.   *The Story of Nell Gwyn; and the Sayings of*
                 Charles II
Dampier, W.   *The Restoration of Charles II*
Davies, Godfrey   *Restoration of Charles II, 1658–1660*
                 The Early Stuarts, 1603–1660
D'Ewes, G.   *Journal*
D'Oyley, Elizabeth   *James, Duke of Monmouth*
Eachard, Laurence   *The History of England (–1688)*
Eglesfield, Francis   *Monarchy Revived*
Ellis, H.   *Original Letters illustrative of English History*
Evelyn, John   *Diary*
'Eyewitness'   *The Royal Pilgrimage (1660)*
Exeter MSS (H.M.C.)
Fanshawe, Lady Anne   *Memoirs*

Fea, Allan   *King Monmouth*
                               After Worcester Fight
                               The Flight of the King
Firth, Sir Charles (editor)   *Scotland and the Protectorate. Letters and Papers*
Fox, Charles James   *A History of the early part of the Reign of*
                                  James II
Fox, Sir Stephen   *Memoirs*
Gardiner, Samuel   *History of England*
                               Civil War
                               Commonwealth and Protectorate
                               Letters and Papers illustrating the relations be-
                                  tween Charles II and Scotland in 1650
Goodman, Bishop G.   *The Court of King James the First*
Gotch, J.   *Catalogue of the Drawings attributed to Inigo*
                                  Jones
Green, Mary A. Everett   *Lives of the Princesses of England (vol. VI)*
Halifax, Marquess of   *The Character of a Trimmer*
                               A Character of King Charles the Second
Hamilton Papers
   (H.M.C.)
Harris, William   *Charles II*
Harleian Miscellany
Hartmann, Cyril H.   *The King my Brother*
Hastings MSS (H.M.C.)
Hearsey, John E. N.   *Bridge, Church and Palace*
Heath, James   *A Brief Chronicle of the late intestine wars in the*
                                  Three Kingdoms . . . 1637–1663
Henrietta Maria   *Letters, 1623–1673 (edited by Mary A. Everett*
                                  Green)
Herbert, Sir Henry   *Dramatic Records*
Herbert, Sir Thomas   *Memoirs of the two last years of the Reign of . .*
                                  Charles I
Hinton, Sir John   *Memoirs*
Historical Manuscripts Commission (H.M.C.), Reports 3, 9, 10, 11
Historical Monuments (Royal Commission)
Hoskins, Samuel E.   *Charles II in the Channel Islands*
Huddleston, Father   *A Brief Account, &c.*
Hughes, John   *The Boscobel Tracts*
Hutchinson, L.   *Memoirs of the Life of Colonel Hutchinson*
Jaffray, Alexander   *Diary*

Jesse, John H.	*Memoirs of the Court of England*
Johnson, George W. (editor)	*The Fairfax Correspondence. Memoirs of the Reign of Charles the First*
Kenyon, John P.	*The Stuarts. A Study in English Kingship*
Knowler, W.	*The Earl of Strafford's Letters and Dispatches*
Laing MSS (H.M.C.)	
La Mothe, Marie C., Comtesse d'Aulnoy	*Memoirs of the Court of England in 1675 (translated by George D. Gilbert)*
Lansdowne, Baron	*Works*
Lauderdale MSS (H.M.C.)	
Law, Ernest	*A Short History of Hampton Court*
Lilly, William	*Several Observations upon the Life and Death of Charles I*
Lower, William	*A Relation in the form of a Journal*
Ludlow, Edmund	*Memoirs*
Lyon, Charles J.	*Personal History of Charles II*
Mackay, Janet	*Little Madam*
Macpherson, James	*Original Papers*
Magdalen MSS (H.M.C.)	
McGrath, J.	*Flemings in Oxford*
Mainwaring, Sir Henry	*Life and Works*
Mathew, David	*The Age of Charles I*
Mayor, J.	*Two Lives of Nicholas Ferrar*
	MSS in Various Collections (H.M.C.)
Milne-Hume MSS (H.M.C.)	
Miscellanea Aulica	
Montagu-Douglas-Scott, G.	*Lucy Walter – Wife or Mistress?*
Montpensier, Mlle de	*Mémoires*
Morrah, Patrick	*1660, the Year of Restoration*
Motteville, Mme de	*Mémoires*
Muddiman, Joseph G. (ed.)	*Trial of Charles I*
Murray, A.	*Autobiography*
Nash, Joseph	*The Mansions of England in the Olden Time*
Newcastle, M.	*The Duke and Duchess of Newcastle*
Newton, Evelyn Legh, Baroness	*The House of Lyme*
Nicholas, Sir E.	*The Nicholas Papers (edited by G. F. Warner)*

Nicoll, Allardyce	*Stuart Masques, and the Renaissance Stage*
Nicoll, John	*A Diary of Public Transactions &c.*
North, Roger	*Examen &c.*
Nyevelt, Baroness van	*Court Life in the Dutch Republic, 1633–1689*
Ogg, David	*England in the Reign of Charles II*
Oldmixon, John	*The History of England, during the reigns of the Royal House of Stuart*
Oman, Carola M. A.	*Henrietta Maria*
Orléans, Pierre Joseph d'	*Histoire des Révolutions d'Angleterre*
Ormonde MSS (H.M.C.)	
Pease, Theodore C.	*The Leveller Movement*
Peck, Francis	*Desiderata Curiosa*
Pepys, Samuel	*Diary*
Pickel, Margaret B.	*Charles I as Patron of Poetry and Drama*
Phillips, John Roland	*Memoirs of the Civil War in Wales and in the Marches, 1642–1649*
Price, J.	*Mystery and Method of His Majesty's Restoration*
Ranke, Leopold von	*A History of England (vol. III)*
Reresby, Sir John	*Memoirs*
Retz, Cardinal de	*Mémoires*
Robb, Nesca A.	*William of Orange*
Rugge, W.	*Diurnal*
Rutland MSS (H.M.C.)	
Scott, Eva	*Rupert Prince Palatine*
	The King in Exile
	The Travels of the King
Scottish History Society	*Scotland and the Commonwealth*
Somers, J.	*Tracts*
Sophia, Electress of Hanover	*Memoirs 1630–1680*
Spence, Joseph	*Anecdotes*
Steinmann, G.	*Althorp Memoirs*
Strickland, Agnes	*Lives of the Queens of England (vol. IV)*
	Lives of the Tudor and Stuart Princesses
Terry, Sir Henry M. Imbert	*A Misjudged Monarch*
Thurloe State Papers	
Tipping, Henry Avray	*English Homes (vol. I)*
Townshend, Dorothea	*George Digby, Earl of Bristol*

Trevelyan, G. M.	*England under the Stuarts*
Tuke, Sir Samuel	*A Character of Charles II*
Turner, Francis C.	*James II*
Turner, Sir James	*Memoirs of his own Life and Times 1632–70*
Venetian State Papers	
Walker, Clement	*The History of Independency*
Walker, E.	*Works*
Warburton, B. E. G.	*Memoirs of Prince Rupert and the Cavaliers*
Warwick, Sir Philip	*Memoirs*
Wedgwood, C. V.	*Montrose*
	The King's Peace
	The King's War
	Thomas Wentworth, First Earl of Strafford
	Truth and Opinion
Welwood, James	*Memoirs*
Whitelocke, B.	*Memorials of English Affairs*
Willcock, John	*The Great Marquess*
Wodrow Society	*Selections*
Wormald, B.	*Clarendon: Politics, History and Religion 1640–1660*
Wraxall, Sir Nathaniel	*Historical Memoirs*
Wright, George R.	*Archeologia and Historical Fragments*
Zumthor, Paul	*Daily Life in Rembrandt's Holland*

INDEX

INDEX

INDEX

INDEX